KAPLAN PUBLISHING

AF854814

THIS EXAM KIT COMES WITH FREE ONLINE ACCESS TO EXTRA RESOURCES AIMED AT HELPING YOU PASS YOUR EXAMS

IN ADDITION TO THE OFFICIAL QUESTIONS AND ANSWERS IN THIS BOOK, GO ONLINE AND EN-gage WITH:

- An iPaper version of the Exam Kit
- Articles including Key Examinable Areas
- Material updates
- Latest Official ACCA exam questions
- Extra question assistance using the Signpost icon
- Timed Questions with an online tutor debrief using the Clock icon

And you can access all of these extra resources anytime, anywhere using your EN-gage account.

How to access your online resources

If you are a Kaplan Financial tuition, full-time or distance learning student	You will already have an EN-gage account and these extra resources will be available to you online. You do not need to register again, as this process was completed when you enrolled. If having problems accessing online materials, please ask your course administrator.
If you purchased through Kaplan Flexible Learning or via the Kaplan Publishing website	You will automatically receive an e-mail invitation to EN-gage online. Please register your details using this e-mail to gain access to your content. If you do not receive the e-mail or book content, please contact our Technical Support team at engage@twinsystems.com.
If you are already a registered EN-gage user	Go to www.EN-gage.co.uk and log in. Select the 'add a book' feature and enter the ISBN number of this book and the unique pass key at the bottom of this card. Then click 'finished' or 'add another book'. You may add as many books as you have purchased from this screen.
If you are a new EN-gage user	Register at www.EN-gage.co.uk and click on the link contained in the e-mail we sent you to activate your account. Then select the 'add a book' feature, enter the ISBN number of this book and the unique pass key at the bottom of this card. Then click 'finished' or 'add another book'.
Your Code and Information	**This code can only be used once** for the registration of one book online. This registration will expire when the final sittings for the examinations covered by this book have taken place. Please allow one hour from the time you submitted your book details for us to process your request.

EN-gage

Please scratch the film to access your Engage code

Please be aware that this code is case-sensitive and you will need to include the dashes within the passcode, but not when entering the ISBN. For further technical support, please visit www.EN-gage.co.uk

Professional Examinations

Paper F6

Taxation
(Finance Act 2011)

EXAM KIT

KAPLAN PUBLISHING

British Library Cataloguing-in-Publication Data

A catalogue record for this book is available from the British Library.

Published by:

Kaplan Publishing UK

Unit 2 The Business Centre

Molly Millar's Lane

Wokingham

Berkshire

RG41 2QZ

ISBN: 978 0 85732 313 2

Printed and bound by CPI Group (UK) Ltd, Croydon, CR0 4YY

Acknowledgements

The past ACCA examination questions are the copyright of the Association of Chartered Certified Accountants. The original answers to the questions from June 1994 onwards were produced by the examiners themselves and have been adapted by Kaplan Publishing.

We are grateful to the Chartered Institute of Management Accountants and the Institute of Chartered Accountants in England and Wales for permission to reproduce past examination questions. The answers have been prepared by Kaplan Publishing.

CONTENTS

Key features in this edition

In addition to providing a wide ranging bank of real past exam questions, we have also included in this edition:

- An analysis of all of the recent examination papers.
- Paper specific information and advice on exam technique.
- Our recommended approach to make your revision for this particular subject as effective as possible.

  This includes step by step guidance on how best to use our Kaplan material (Complete text, pocket notes and exam kit) at this stage in your studies.
- An increased number of enhanced tutorial answers packed with specific key answer tips, technical tutorial notes and exam technique tips from our experienced tutors.
- Complementary online resources including full tutor debriefs and question assistance to point you in the right direction when you get stuck.

December 2010, June and December 2011 – Real examination questions with enhanced tutorial answers

The real December 2010, June 2011, and December 2011 exam questions with enhanced "walk through answers" and full "tutor debriefs", updated in line with legislation relevant to your exam sitting, is available on Kaplan EN-gage at:

www.EN-gage.co.uk

You will find a wealth of other resources to help you with your studies on the following sites:

www.EN-gage.co.uk

www.accaglobal.com/students/

INDEX TO QUESTIONS AND ANSWERS

INTRODUCTION

The new syllabus was first introduced in June 2011 and brought in a new tax, Inheritance tax, and a few small additional topics to other taxes. The format of the exam changed slightly, but not significantly, and the style of some questions changed.

Accordingly, we have included some new questions on Inheritance tax in this version of the exam kit in line with recent exams, and adapted many of the old ACCA questions within this kit. The adaptations have been made to reflect the new style of paper, the new legislative changes in recent Finance Acts, Tax law rewrites and IAS terminology. We have included the new topics brought into the syllabus in some questions.

Finally, we have integrated the 2007 Pilot Paper into the main body of questions in the kit. Whilst the questions (as adapted) are still representative of questions that could appear in the new syllabus exam, the pilot paper itself no longer represents the correct format of an entire exam for the new syllabus.

The questions within the kit are past ACCA exam questions, the more recent questions (from 2005) are labelled as such in the index. Note that if a question within this kit has been changed in any way from the original version, this is indicated in the end column of the index below with the mark *(A).*

KEY TO THE INDEX

PAPER ENHANCEMENTS

We have added the following enhancements to the answers in this exam kit:

Key answer tips

All answers include key answer tips to help your understanding of each question.

Tutorial note

All answers include more tutorial notes to explain some of the technical points in more detail.

Top tutor tips

For selected questions, we "walk through the answer" giving guidance on how to approach the questions with helpful 'tips from a top tutor', together with technical tutor notes.

These answers are indicated with the "footsteps" icon in the index.

ONLINE ENHANCEMENTS

Timed question with Online tutor debrief

For selected questions, we recommend that they are to be completed in full exam conditions (i.e. properly timed in a closed book environment).

In addition to the examiner's technical answer, enhanced with key answer tips and tutorial notes in this exam kit, online you can find an answer debrief by a top tutor that:

- works through the question in full
- points out how to approach the question
- how to ensure that the easy marks are obtained as quickly as possible, and
- emphasises how to tackle exam questions and exam technique.

These questions are indicated with the "clock" icon in the index.

Online question assistance

Have you ever looked at a question and not know where to start, or got stuck part way through?

For selected questions, we have produced "Online question assistance" offering different levels of guidance, such as:

- ensuring that you understand the question requirements fully, highlighting key terms and the meaning of the verbs used
- how to read the question proactively, with knowledge of the requirements, to identify the topic areas covered
- assessing the detail content of the question body, pointing out key information and explaining why it is important
- help in devising a plan of attack

With this assistance, you should then be able to attempt your answer confident that you know what is expected of you.

These questions are indicated with the "signpost" icon in the index.

Online question enhancements and answer debriefs will be available from Spring 2011 on Kaplan EN-gage at:

www.EN-gage.co.uk

INCOME TAX AND NATIONAL INSURANCE

		Page number		
		Question	*Answer*	*Past exam (Adapted)*
Income tax basics and employment income				
1	Sally and Sandra Burton	1	87	*(A)*
2	Vigorous plc	2	91	*(A)*
3	Ali Patel	4	94	*(A)*
4	Edmund Brick	4	97	*Dec 07 (A)*
5	Peter Chic	5	101	*Dec 08 (A)*
Income tax basics and income from self employment				
6	Carol Courier	7	107	
7	Chatru	8	109	*(A)*
8	Olive Green	9	114	*(A)*
9	Foo Dee	10	118	*Dec 06 (A)*
10	Mark Kett	12	122	*Pilot 07 (A)*
11	Li Fung	13	127	*Pilot 07*
12	Sam and Kim White	13	129	*Jun 08 (A)*
13	Gomez brothers	15	136	*Jun 09 (A)*
14	Andrew Zoom	17	142	*Jun 09*
15	Na Style	17	145	*Dec 09*
16	Simon House	19	151	*Dec 09*
Trading losses				
17	Norma	20	154	*(A)*
18	Leonardo	20	158	
19	Dee Zyne	20	160	*Jun 05*
20	Samantha Fabrique	22	164	*Dec 07 (A)*

CHARGEABLE GAINS

INHERITANCE TAX

CORPORATION TAX

ANALYSIS OF PAST PAPERS

The table below summarises the key topics that have been tested in the new syllabus examinations to date.

Note that the references are to the number of the question in this edition of the exam kit, but the Pilot Paper is produced in its original form at the end of the kit and therefore these questions have retained their original numbering in the paper itself.

	Pilot 2007	Dec 2007	Jun 2008	Dec 2008	Jun 2009	Dec 2009	Jun 2010
Ethics							
Tax avoidance vs tax evasion							Q28
Ethics of non-disclosure							Q28
Money laundering							Q28
Income tax							
Exempt income	Q10	Q25		Q5	Q13	Q15	
Basic income tax computation	Q10	Q25	Q12	Q5	Q13	Q15	Q65
					Q14	Q16	
Pension contributions		Q25			Q13		
Gift Aid	Q10			Q5	Q13		
Husband and wife			Q12				
Age allowance					Q13		
Property income	Q10	Q4		Q5			
Furnished holiday lettings		Q4					
Rent-a-room relief		Q4					
ISAs			Q12			Q15	
Residence							Q23
Employed individual							
Factors indicating employment					Q14		
Car and fuel benefit		Q25		Q5			
Living accommodation				Q5			
Beneficial loan	Q10		Q12				
Use of assets				Q5			
Mileage allowance	Q10		Q12		Q13		
Self employed individual							
Adjustment to profits			Q12			Q15	Q23
						Q16	
Capital allowances	Q10	Q25	Q12	Q22	Q13		Q23
Basis of assessment rules	Q11			Q22		Q15	Q23
Change of accounting date	Q11			Q22			
Partnerships				Q22			Q23
Pensions							
Basic relief				Q26			
Excess contributions charge				Q26			
No relevant earnings				Q26			

	Pilot 2007	Dec 2007	Jun 2008	Dec 2008	Jun 2009	Dec 2009	Jun 2010
Income tax losses							
Factors influencing choice of loss relief		Q20					
Ongoing losses		Q20					
Relief against gains		Q20					
National insurance contributions							
Class 1		Q25		Q5	Q14		Q65
Class 1A				Q5			
Class 2		Q25			Q14	Q15	
Class 4		Q25			Q14	Q15	Q23
Capital gains tax							
Basic CGT computation	Q32	Q33	Q34	Q38	Q35	Q16	Q39
Residence / ordinary residence			Q34				
Exempt assets	Q32	Q33					
Chattels	Q32	Q33			Q35		
Part disposal	Q32		Q34	Q38			Q39
Shares	Q32	Q33	Q34	Q38	Q35	Q36	Q39
Takeover				Q38			
Wasting asset					Q35		
Insurance for damaged assets			Q34				Q39
Husband and wife	Q32	Q33					
Capital losses		Q20			Q35		
Reliefs							
Entrepreneurs' relief	Q32		Q34		Q35		
Principal private residence relief	Q32	Q33			Q35	Q36	
Gift relief			Q34			Q36	
Rollover relief			Q34				Q39
Incorporation relief			Q34			Q36	
Self assessment – individual							
Pay dates		Q25	Q27			Q15	
Payments on account		Q25	Q27			Q15	
Filing dates			Q27		Q13		
HMRC enquiry			Q27				Q28
Retention of records	Q10				Q13		
Discovery assessment							Q28
Interest							Q28
Penalties							Q28
Corporation tax							
Definition of accounting periods			Q55				
Adjustment to profits	Q54	Q58		Q59	Q49	Q52	
Capital allowances – P & M	Q54	Q58	Q47 Q54	Q59	Q49	Q52	Q65

	Pilot 2007	Dec 2007	Jun 2008	Dec 2008	Jun 2009	Dec 2009	Jun 2010
Corporation tax							
Lease premiums	Q54				Q49		Q65
Basic TTP computation	Q54		Q55	Q38 Q59		Q52	Q65 Q50
Property income	Q54			Q59	Q49		Q65
Overseas income			Q55			Q52	Q65
Chargeable gains				Q38			Q39
Long period of account			Q48				
Straddling 31 March liability comp			Q48				
Corporation tax losses							
Choice of loss relief – factors	Q57					Q60	
Trading losses	Q57	Q58		Q59		Q60	Q65
Capital losses				Q38			
Groups							
Associated companies				Q59	Q49	Q52	Q65 Q50
Group relief		Q58					Q65
Capital gains group					Q49		
Self assessment – companies							
Due dates and interest					Q49		Q50
Penalties				Q59			
Value added tax							
Registration			Q55			Q52	
Pre-registration input VAT			Q55			Q52	
Deregistration					Q73		
VAT return computation		Q25			Q73		Q23
Tax point							Q23
Valid invoice			Q55				
Default surcharge	Q54			Q59			
Errors in a VAT return	Q54					Q52	
Transfer of going concern					Q73		
Annual accounting scheme				Q59			
Cash accounting scheme					Q73		
Flat rate scheme		Q25					Q23

ANALYSIS OF MOST RECENT EXAMS

The table below summarises the key topics that have been tested in the most recent exams.

Note that the references are to the number of the question in the original exam. These exams can be found, with enhanced "walk through answers", updated in line with legislation relevant to your exam sitting, on Kaplan EN-gage at:

www.EN-gage.co.uk

	Dec 10	Jun 11
Income tax		
Exempt income		Q1
Basic income tax computation	Q1	Q1
Pension contributions	Q1	
Reduction of personal allowance	Q1	Q1
Employed individual		
Exempt benefits	Q1	
Salary and bonus	Q1	Q1
Car and fuel benefit	Q3	
Beneficial loan	Q1	
Use of assets	Q1	
Childcare vouchers	Q1	
Comparison re-provision of car	Q4	
Net after tax cost calculations	Q4	
Self employed individual		
Adjustment to profits		Q1
Basis of assessment rules		Q1
Partnerships – allocation		Q1
Pensions		
Basic relief	Q1	Q3
Income tax losses		
Ongoing losses	Q5	
Relief against gains	Q5	
Tax savings	Q5	
National insurance contributions		
Class 1	Q4	Q1
Class 1A	Q4	
Class 2		Q1
Class 4		Q1

	Dec 10	Jun 11
Capital gains tax		
Basic CGT computation	Q3	
Enhancement	Q3	
Chattels	Q3	
Part disposal	Q3	
Shares	Q3	Q3
Takeovers	Q3	Q3
Reliefs		
Entrepreneurs' relief	Q3	Q3
Self assessment – individual		
Payments on account		Q1
Interest and penalties		Q1
PAYE forms	Q1	
Corporation tax		
Adjustment to profits	Q2	Q2
Capital allowances	Q2	Q2
Lease premiums	Q2	Q2
Basic TTP computation	Q2,Q3	Q2
Property income		Q2
Overseas income	Q2	
Interest income		Q2
Chargeable gains		Q2
Groups		
Associated companies	Q2	
Self assessment – companies		
Quarterly instalments		Q2
Value added tax		
Registration		Q4
Output VAT payable	Q2	
Invoices	Q2	Q4
Default surcharge	Q2	
Errors in a VAT return		Q4
Overseas supplies		Q4
Annual accounting scheme		Q4
Pay dates		Q4
Inheritance tax		
PETs		Q5
CLTs		Q5
Estate computation		Q5
Due dates		Q5

EXAM TECHNIQUE

- Use the allocated **15 minutes reading and planning time** at the beginning of the exam:
  - read the questions and examination requirements carefully, and
  - begin planning your answers.

  See the Paper Specific Information for advice on how to use this time for this paper.
- **Divide the time** you spend on questions in proportion to the marks on offer:
  - there are 1.8 minutes available per mark in the examination
  - within that, try to allow time at the end of each question to review your answer and address any obvious issues

  Whatever happens, always keep your eye on the clock and **do not over run on any part of any question!**
- Spend the last **five minutes** of the examination:
  - reading through your answers, and
  - **making any additions or corrections**.
- If you **get completely stuck** with a question:
  - leave space in your answer book, and
  - **return to it later.**
- Stick to the question and **tailor your answer** to what you are asked.
  - pay particular attention to the verbs in the question.
- If you do not understand what a question is asking, **state your assumptions**.

  Even if you do not answer in precisely the way the examiner hoped, you should be given some credit, if your assumptions are reasonable.
- You should do everything you can to make things easy for the marker.

  The marker will find it easier to identify the points you have made if your **answers are legible**.
- **Written questions**:

  Your answer should have:
  - a clear structure
  - a brief introduction, a main section and a conclusion.

  Be concise.

  It is better to write a little about a lot of different points than a great deal about one or two points.
- **Computations**:

  It is essential to include all your workings in your answers.

  Many computational questions require the use of a standard format:

  e.g. income tax computations, corporation tax computations and capital gains.

  Be sure you know these formats thoroughly before the exam and use the layouts that you see in the answers given in this book and in model answers.
- **Reports, memos and other documents**:

  Some questions ask you to present your answer in the form of a report, a memo, a letter or other document.

  Make sure that you use the correct format – there could be easy marks to gain here.

PAPER SPECIFIC INFORMATION

THE EXAM

FORMAT OF THE EXAM

		Number of marks
5 compulsory questions which will be **predominantly computational**:		
Question 1:	Income tax	25 or 30
Question 2:	Corporation tax	25 or 30
Question 3:	Chargeable gains (personal or corporate)	15
Question 4:	Any area of the syllabus	15
Question 5:	Any area of the syllabus	15
		100

Total time allowed: 3 hours plus 15 minutes reading and planning time.

Note that:

- Question 1 will focus on income tax and question 2 will focus on corporation tax. The two questions will be for a total of 55 marks, with one of the questions being for 30 marks and the other being for 25 marks.
- There will always be a minimum of 10 marks on VAT. These marks will normally be included within question 1 or 2, although there could be a separate question on value added tax.
- National Insurance Contributions will not be examined as a separate question, but may be examined in any question involving income tax or corporation tax.
- Groups and overseas aspects of corporation tax may be examined within question 2 or 5.
- Questions 1 and 2 may include a small element of chargeable gains.
- Any of the five questions might include the consideration of issues relating to the minimisation or deferral of tax liabilities.

PASS MARK

The pass mark for all ACCA Qualification examination papers is 50%.

READING AND PLANNING TIME

Remember that all three hour paper based examinations have an additional 15 minutes reading and planning time.

ACCA GUIDANCE

ACCA guidance on the use of this time is as follows:

This additional time is allowed at the beginning of the examination to allow candidates to read the questions and to begin planning their answers before they start to write in their answer books.

This time should be used to ensure that all the information and, in particular, the exam requirements are properly read and understood.

During this time, candidates may only annotate their question paper. They may not write anything in their answer booklets until told to do so by the invigilator.

KAPLAN GUIDANCE

As all questions are compulsory, there are no decisions to be made about choice of questions, other than in which order you would like to tackle them.

Therefore, in relation to F6, we recommend that you take the following approach with your reading and planning time:

- **Skim through the whole paper**, assessing the level of difficulty of each question.
- **Write down** on the question paper next to the mark allocation **the amount of time you should spend on each part.** Do this for each part of every question.
- **Decide the order** in which you think you will attempt each question:

  This is a personal choice and you have time on the revision phase to try out different approaches, for example, if you sit mock exams.

  A common approach is to tackle the question you think is the easiest and you are most comfortable with first.

  Others may prefer to tackle the longest questions first, or conversely leave them to the last.

  Psychologists believe that you usually perform at your best on the second and third question you attempt, once you have settled into the exam, so not tackling the bigger Section A questions first may be advisable.

  It is usual however that student tackle their least favourite topic and/or the most difficult question in their opinion last.

  Whatever you approach, you must make sure that you leave enough time to attempt all questions fully and be very strict with yourself in timing each question.

- **For each question** in turn, read the requirements and then the detail of the question carefully.

  Always read the requirement first as this enables you to **focus on the detail of the question with the specific task in mind**.

  For computational questions:

  Highlight key numbers / information and key words in the question, scribble notes to yourself on the question paper to remember key points in your answer.

  Jot down proformas required if applicable.

  For written questions:

  Take notice of the format required (e.g. letter, memo, notes) and identify the recipient of the answer . You need to do this to judge the level of financial sophistication required in your answer and whether the use of a formal reply or informal bullet points would be satisfactory.

  Plan your beginning, middle and end and the key areas to be addressed and your use of titles and sub-titles to enhance your answer.

  For all questions:

  Spot the easy marks to be gained in a question and parts which can be performed independently of the rest of the question. For example, writing down due dates of payment of tax, due dates for making elections, laying out basic proformas correctly.

  Make sure that you do these parts first when you tackle the question.

  Don't go overboard in terms of planning time on any one question – you need a good measure of the whole paper and a plan for all of the questions at the end of the 15 minutes.

  By covering all questions you can often help yourself as you may find that facts in one question may remind you of things you should put into your answer relating to a different question.

- With your plan of attack in mind, **start answering your chosen question** with your plan to hand, as soon as you are allowed to start.

Always keep your eye on the clock and do not over run on any part of any question!

DETAILED SYLLABUS

The detailed syllabus and study guide written by the ACCA can be found at:

www.accaglobal.com/students/

KAPLAN'S RECOMMENDED REVISION APPROACH

QUESTION PRACTICE IS THE KEY TO SUCCESS

Success in professional examinations relies upon you acquiring a firm grasp of the required knowledge at the tuition phase. In order to be able to do the questions, knowledge is essential.

However, the difference between success and failure often hinges on your exam technique on the day and making the most of the revision phase of your studies.

The **Kaplan complete text** is the starting point, designed to provide the underpinning knowledge to tackle all questions. However, in the revision phase, pouring over text books is not the answer.

Kaplan Online fixed tests help you consolidate your knowledge and understanding and are a useful tool to check whether you can remember key topic areas.

Kaplan pocket notes are designed to help you quickly revise a topic area, however you then need to practice questions. There is a need to progress to full exam standard questions as soon as possible, and to tie your exam technique and technical knowledge together.

The importance of question practice cannot be over-emphasised.

The recommended approach below is designed by expert tutors in the field, in conjunction with their knowledge of the examiner and their recent real exams.

The approach taken for the fundamental papers is to revise by topic area. However, with the professional stage papers, a multi topic approach is required to answer the scenario based questions.

You need to practice as many questions as possible in the time you have left.

OUR AIM

Our aim is to get you to the stage where you can attempt exam standard questions confidently, to time, in a closed book environment, with no supplementary help (i.e. to simulate the real examination experience).

Practising your exam technique on real past examination questions, in timed conditions, is also vitally important for you to assess your progress and identify areas of weakness that may need more attention in the final run up to the examination.

In order to achieve this we recognise that initially you may feel the need to practice some questions with open book help and exceed the required time.

The approach below shows you which questions you should use to build up to coping with exam standard question practice, and references to the sources of information available should you need to revisit a topic area in more detail.

Remember that in the real examination, all you have to do is:

- attempt all questions required by the exam
- only spend the allotted time on each question, and
- get them at least 50% right!

Try and practice this approach on every question you attempt from now to the real exam.

EXAMINER COMMENTS

We have included the examiners comments to the specific new syllabus examination questions in this kit for you to see the main pitfalls that students fall into with regard to technical content.

However, too many times in the general section of the report, the examiner comments that students had failed due to:

- "misallocation of time"
- "running out of time" and
- showing signs of "spending too much time on an earlier questions and clearly rushing the answer to a subsequent question".

Good exam technique is vital.

THE KAPLAN PAPER F6 REVISION PLAN

Stage 1: Assess areas of strengths and weaknesses

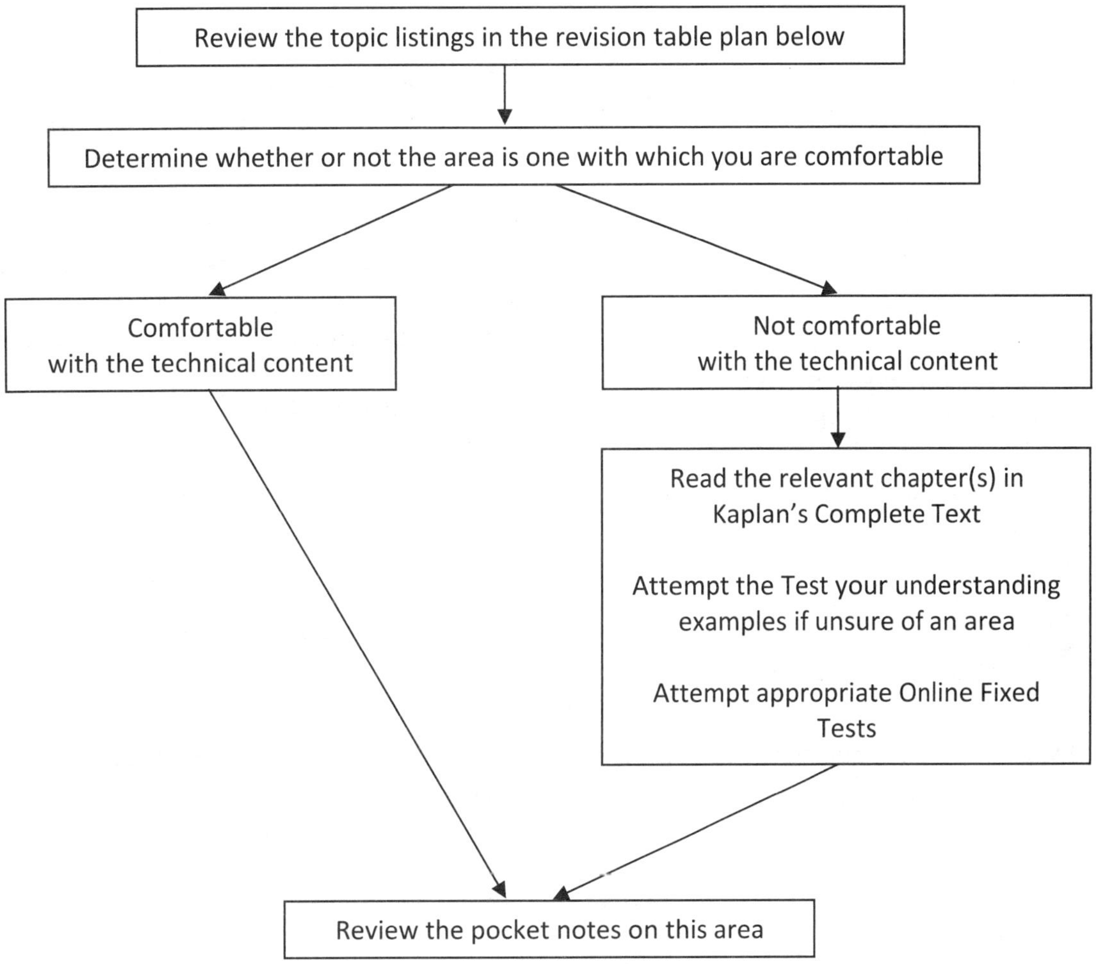

Stage 2: Practice questions

Follow the order of revision of topics as recommended in the revision table plan below and attempt the questions in the order suggested. Note that although the plan is organised into different subject areas, the real exam questions will cover more than one topic, and therefore some parts of the exam questions set below will be on topics covered later in the revision plan.

Try to avoid referring to text books and notes and the model answer until you have completed your attempt.

Try to answer the question in the allotted time.

Review your attempt with the model answer and assess how much of the answer you achieved in the allocated exam time.

Fill in the self-assessment box below and decide on your best course of action.

Comfortable with question attempt

→ Only revisit when comfortable with questions on all topic areas

Not comfortable with question attempts

→ Focus on these areas by:

- Reworking test your understanding examples in Kaplan's Complete Text
- Revisiting the technical content from Kaplan's pocket notes
- Working any remaining questions on that area in the exam kit
- Reattempting an exam standard question in that area, on a timed, closed book basis

Note that :

The "footsteps questions" give guidance on exam techniques and how you should have approached the question.

The "clock questions" have an online debrief where a tutor talks you through the exam technique and approach to that question and works the question in full.

Stage 3: Final pre-exam revision

We recommend that you **attempt at least one three hour mock examination** containing a set of previously unseen exam standard questions.

It is important that you get a feel for the breadth of coverage of a real exam without advanced knowledge of the topic areas covered – just as you will expect to see on the real exam day.

Ideally this mock should be sat in timed, closed book, real exam conditions and could be:

- a mock examination offered by your tuition provider, and/or
- the last real examination paper (available shortly afterwards on Kaplan EN-gage with "enhanced walk through answers" and a full "tutor debrief").

THE DETAILED REVISION PLAN

Topic	*Complete Text Chapter*	*Pocket note Chapter*	*Questions to attempt*	*Tutor guidance*	*Date attempted*	*Self assessment*
Personal income tax computation	2	1	–	Review the layout of an income tax computation and rates of tax. Question 1 in the exam will include at least one income tax computation, and it is crucial that you are comfortable with the proforma.		
– Employment income and assessable benefits	4	2	2 5 14	A popular exam topic, almost guaranteed to form part of the exam. There are many questions on this area. Start with Q2 which is a basic warm up question covering a number of employment benefits. Build up to Q5 which is a more demanding past exam questions on this area. Q14 tests the rules for determining whether an individual is employed or self employed and the consequences of this decision.		
– Property income	3	1	4	This is a detailed question solely on property income which is an excellent test of your retention of these rules. However, be aware that this topic often appears as part of a big income tax computation, where property is just one of a few sources of income for an individual.		
– Badges of trade	5	3	16	Revise the badges of trade rules from the pocket notes, before attempting this question. Note that although you are not required to apply the rules to a particular scenario in this question, you may be asked to do so in the exam.		

Topic	*Complete Text Chapter*	*Pocket note Chapter*	*Questions to attempt*	*Tutor guidance*	*Date attempted*	*Self assessment*
				The consequences of the decision are however covered and this question demonstrates the importance of the badges of trade and how an individual is taxed as a consequence.		
– Adjusted trading profit, including capital allowances	5 & 6	3 & 4	8 12 18	An adjustment of profits calculation is almost certain to be tested in the exam, although it may form part of question 1 for a sole trader/partnership or question 2 for a company. Q8 tests many of the typical adjustments you may see, and having practiced this question you can then attempt Q12 to time. Q18 tests the rules for determining whether an individual is employed or self employed.		
– Basis of assessment	7	5	7 10 11	You may benefit from practicing the test your understandings from the complete text before attempting these questions. The opening year rules are commonly tested and Q10 provides good practice. Q11 tests the change of accounting date rules, which are not regularly examined, but many students find these difficult, and would benefit from practice here.		
– National insurance	11	8	25(a)	National insurance regularly forms part of a longer question, and can provide easy marks to a well-prepared student. This question covers NICs for both an employee and a self-employed individual.		

Topic	*Complete Text Chapter*	*Pocket note Chapter*	*Questions to attempt*	*Tutor guidance*	*Date attempted*	*Self assessment*
– Trading losses for individuals	9	7	20 19 17	These questions cover the range of ways losses can be tested – in an ongoing business, losses in the opening years and losses on cessation. In the current climate, losses are topical and it is important to be familiar with each of the reliefs.		
– Partnerships	8	6	23(a)	The allocation of profits between partners is a relatively straightforward computation, but does require practice.		
– Pensions	10	8	24 26	Like National Insurance, pensions is a topic which is likely to form a small part of a longer question, however the two questions listed here provided excellent practice of the various ways this topic could be tested.		
– Tax admin for individuals	12	9	27 28	Administration rarely appears as a standalone question (although this was the case in June 2010); however, it is regularly tested at the end of a longer income tax question. It is very important to learn the dates for submission and payment as well as the potential penalties and interest.		
Consolidation of personal tax			15 22	Having revised all of the above topics, attempt Q15 and Q22 which are recent questions incorporating many aspects of the taxation of individuals.		
Inheritance tax	17	13	40 to 44	A new tax to the syllabus and highly likely to be examined in 2012 examinations. Use your pocket notes to revise the key facts and techniques. Warm up with Q40 and build up to Q44.		

Topic	***Complete Text Chapter***	***Pocket note Chapter***	***Questions to attempt***	***Tutor guidance***	***Date attempted***	***Self assessment***
Corporation tax computation	18	14	–	Review the layout of a corporation tax computation and the rates of tax. Question 2 will include a corporation tax computation, and it is crucial that you are comfortable with the proforma. You should also ensure you know how to calculate the tax liability for an accounting period which straddles 31 March 2011 as this is highly examinable.		
– Adjustment of profits and capital allowances	19	14	46 54(a)	It is important to be comfortable with the differences between sole traders and companies for adjustments to profits and capital allowances. Use Q46 to check that you are clear about these differences, then attempt Q54, which is a more recent question on this topic.		
– Property income	19	14	65	There are minor but important differences between taxing property income for individuals and companies. This question covers property income for a company, and also covers group relief, which you could leave until you revise that area, or have a go and see what you remember!		
– Long periods of account	19	14	48 53	In order to deal with a long period of account, you need to learn the rules regarding apportioning different types of income between the two periods. Having revised these rules from the pocket notes, practice them using these questions.		

Topic	***Complete Text Chapter***	***Pocket note Chapter***	***Questions to attempt***	***Tutor guidance***	***Date attempted***	***Self assessment***
– Corporation tax losses	21	16	60	Many students are daunted by loss questions, however a systematic approach is all that is required and practice is key. Remind yourself of the layout required using the pocket notes, and practice the test your understandings from the complete text if you are not confident, before attempting Q60.		
– Groups	22	17	58 63	Groups and overseas aspects will only be tested in question 2 for no more than a third of the marks. The questions listed therefore only contain a small element in relation to groups. Q58 tests group relief, and Q63 covers both group relief and the capital gains aspects of groups		
– Overseas	23	18	51 52(a)	As above, Q51 and Q52 only contain a small element in relation to overseas issues. These questions show the ways the topic may appear in the real exam.		
– Tax admin for a company	24	19	50	It is rare to see a standalone question on administration in the exam (although this was the case in June 2010), however there are often easy marks available as part of other questions. It is therefore very important to learn the submission and payment dates as well as the penalty and interest rules.		
Chargeable gains for individuals	13	10	–	Chargeable gains will be tested in question 3 in the exam, and these questions will usually test a wide variety of the topics below. Revise the basic computation using the pocket notes before looking at the detailed areas.		

Topic	***Complete Text Chapter***	***Pocket note Chapter***	***Questions to attempt***	***Tutor guidance***	***Date attempted***	***Self assessment***
– Chattels, shares, PPR, Entrepreneurs relief	14 & 16	11 & 12	33 32 30	These questions demonstrate how various aspects of capital gains will be tested in one question. Few of these areas are technically challenging, however, it is important that you can tackle them all.		
– Deferral reliefs	16	12	34 36	Recognising which deferral reliefs apply and whether they are available in full is an important aspect of capital gains. These questions cover all of the deferral reliefs and provide excellent practice.		
Chargeable gains for companies	20	15	38	Remind yourself of the different gains rules for companies, and test your understanding using Q38.		
– Quoted shares	15 & 20	11 & 15	39	A brief revision of the share pool and matching rules from the pocket notes may be useful before attempting this question. Q38 tests the capital gains rules for companies, including share pooling and also asks for calculations of the indexed base costs of assets retained, which had not previously been required.		
Value added tax	25 & 26	20	73 23(b) 25(b) 52(b) 55(b) 59(b)	Start by reviewing the examiner's VAT article. VAT usually appears as part of question 1 or question 2 (for up to 10 marks); however Q70 is a standalone VAT question from the June 2009 exam. The remainder of the questions listed here contain VAT but are not included in the VAT section of the kit; however any of Qs 66-72 also provide further practice.		

Note that not all of the questions are referred to in the programme above.
We have recommended an approach to build up from the basic to exam standard questions.
The remaining questions are available in the kit for extra practice for those who require more questions on some areas.

TAX RATES AND ALLOWANCES

Throughout this exam kit:

1. **Calculations and workings need only to be made to the nearest £.**
2. **All apportionments should be made to the nearest month.**
3. **All workings should be shown.**

The tax rates and allowances below will be reproduced in the examination paper for Paper F6 in the 2012 examination sittings. In addition, other specific information necessary for candidates to answer individual questions will be given as part of the question.

INCOME TAX

		Normal rates	Dividend rates
		%	%
Basic rate	£1 – £35,000	20	10
Higher rate	£35,001 to £150,000	40	32.5
Additional rate	£150,001 and over	50	42.5

A starting rate of 10% applies to savings income where it falls within the first £2,560 of taxable income.

Personal allowances

Personal allowance	Standard	£7,475
Personal allowance	65 – 74	£9,940
Personal allowance	75 and over	£10,090
Income limit for age related allowances		£24,000
Income limit for standard personal allowance		£100,000

Car benefit percentage

The base level of CO_2 emissions is 125 grams per kilometre.

	%
Petrol cars with CO_2 emissions of 75 grams per kilometre or less	5
Petrol cars with CO_2 emissions between 76 and 120 grams per kilometre	10

Car fuel benefit

The base figure for calculating the car fuel benefit is £18,800.

Pension scheme limits

The maximum contribution that can qualify for tax relief without any earnings is £3,600.

Authorised mileage allowance: cars

Up to 10,000 miles	45p
Over 10,000 miles	25p

Capital allowances

	Rate of allowance
Plant and machinery	%
Main pool	20
Special rate pool	10
Motor cars (purchases since 6 April 2009 (1 April 2009 for limited companies))	
CO_2 emissions up to 110 grams per kilometre	100
CO_2 emissions between 111 and 160 grams per kilometre	20
CO_2 emissions above 160 grams per kilometre	10
Annual investment allowance	
First £100,000 of expenditure	100

Individual Savings Accounts (ISAs)

Cash investment limit	£5,340
Stocks and shares investment limit	£10,680
Overall investment limit	£10,680

CORPORATION TAX

Financial year	*2009*	*2010*	*2011*
Small profits rate	21%	21%	20%
Main rate	28%	28%	26%
Lower limit	£300,000	£300,000	£300,000
Upper limit	£1,500,000	£1,500,000	£1,500,000
Standard fraction	7/400	7/400	3/200

Marginal relief

Standard fraction × (U – A) × N/A

VALUE ADDED TAX

Standard rate of VAT	20%
Registration limit	£73,000
Deregistration limit	£71,000

INHERITANCE TAX

Tax rates

	%
£1 – £325,000	Nil
Excess – Death rate	40
– Lifetime rate	20

INHERITANCE TAX
Taper relief

Years before death:	% reduction
Over 3 but less than 4 years	20
Over 4 but less than 5 years	40
Over 5 but less than 6 years	60
Over 6 but less than 7 years	80

CAPITAL GAINS TAX

Rates of tax	– Lower rate	18%
	– Higher rate	28%
Annual exemption		£10,600
Entrepreneurs' relief	– Lifetime limit	£10,000,000
	– Rate of tax on gain	10%

NATIONAL INSURANCE CONTRIBUTIONS
(Not contracted out rates)

		%
Class 1 Employee	£1 – £7,225 per year	Nil
	£7,226 – £42,475 per year	12.0
	£42,476 and above per year	2.0
Class 1 Employer	£1 – £7,072 per year	Nil
	£7,073 and above per year	13.8
Class 1A		13.8
Class 2	£2.50 per week	
Class 4	£1 – £7,225 per year	Nil
	£7,226 – £42,475 per year	9.0
	£42,476 and above per year	2.0

RATES OF INTEREST

Official rate of interest:	4.0%
Rate of interest on underpaid tax:	3.0%
Rate of interest on overpaid tax:	0.5%

TIME LIMITS AND ELECTION DATES

Income tax

Election / claim	**Time limit**	**For 2011/12**
Agree the amount of trading losses to carry forward	4 years from the end of the tax year in which the loss arose	5 April 2016
Current and prior year set-off of trading losses against total income (and chargeable gains)	12 months from 31 January following the end of the tax year in which the loss arose	31 January 2014
Three year carry back of trading losses in the opening years	12 months from 31 January following the end of the tax year in which the loss arose	31 January 2014
Three year carry back of terminal trading losses in the closing years	4 years from the end of the last tax year of trading	5 April 2016

National Insurance Contributions

Class 1 primary and secondary – pay days	14 days after the end of each tax month under PAYE system	19th of each month
Class 1 A NIC – pay day	19 July following end of tax year	19 July 2012
Class 2 NICs – pay days	Monthly direct debit or six monthly invoicing	31 January 2012 & 31 July 2012
Class 4 NICs – pay days	Paid under self assessment with income tax	

Capital gains tax

Replacement of business asset relief for individuals (Rollover relief)	4 years from the end of the tax year in which the disposal occurred	5 April 2016
Holdover relief of gain on the gift of a business asset (Gift relief)	4 years from the end of the tax year in which the disposal occurred	5 April 2016
Entrepreneurs' relief	12 months from 31 January following the end of the tax year in which the disposal occurred	31 January 2014
Determination of principal private residence	2 years from the acquisition of the second property	

Self assessment – individuals

Election / claim	**Time limit**	**For 2011/12**
Pay days for income tax and Class 4 NIC	1st instalment: 31 January in the tax year 2nd instalment: 31 July following the end of tax year Balancing payment: 31 January following the end of tax year	 31 January 2012 31 July 2012 31 January 2013
Pay day for CGT	31 January following the end of tax year	31 January 2013
Filing dates If return issued by 31 October in the tax year If return issued after 31 October in the tax year	 Paper return: 31 October following end of tax year Electronic return: 31 January following end of tax year 3 months from the date of issue of the return	 31 October 2012 31 January 2013
Retention of records Business records Personal records	 5 years from 31 January following end of the tax year 12 months from 31 January following end of the tax year	 31 January 2018 31 January 2014
HMRC right of repair	9 months from date the return was filed	
Taxpayers right to amend a return	12 months from 31 January following end of the tax year	31 January 2014
Taxpayers claim for overpayment relief	4 years from the end of the tax year	5 April 2016
HMRC can open an enquiry	12 months from submission of the return	
HMRC can raise a discovery assessment – No careless or deliberate behaviour – Tax lost due to careless behaviour – Tax lost due to deliberate behaviour	 4 years from the end of the tax year 6 years from the end of the tax year 20 years from the end of the tax year	 5 April 2016 5 April 2018 5 April 2032
Taxpayers right of appeal against an assessment	30 days from the assessment – appeal in writing	

Corporation tax

Election / claim	Time limit
Replacement of business asset relief for companies (Rollover relief)	4 years from the end of the chargeable accounting period in which the disposal occurred
Agree the amount of trading losses to carry forward	4 years from the end of the chargeable accounting period in which the loss arose
Current year set-off of trading losses against total profits (income and gains), and 12 month carry back of trading losses against total profits (income and gains)	2 years from the end of the chargeable accounting period in which the loss arose
Surrender of current period trading losses to other group companies (Group relief)	2 years after the claimant company's chargeable accounting period
Election for transfer of capital gain or loss to another company within the gains group	2 years from the end of the chargeable accounting period in which the disposal occurred by the company actually making the disposal

Self assessment – companies

Election / claim	Time limit
Pay day for small and medium companies	9 months and one day after the end of the chargeable accounting period
Pay day for large companies	Instalments due on 14th day of: – Seventh, Tenth, Thirteenth, and Sixteenth month **after the start** of the chargeable accounting period
Filing dates	Later of: – 12 months from the end of the chargeable accounting period – 3 months form the issue of a notice to deliver a corporation tax return
Companies claim for overpayment relief	4 years from the end of the chargeable accounting period
HMRC can open an enquiry	12 months from the actual submission of the return
Retention of records	6 years from the end of the chargeable accounting period

Value added tax

Election / claim	**Time limit**
Compulsory registration Historic test: – Notify HMRC – Charge VAT Future test: – Notify HMRC – Charge VAT	 30 days from end of the month in which the threshold was exceeded Beginning of the month, one month after the month in which the threshold was exceeded 30 days from the date it is anticipated that the threshold will be exceeded the date it is anticipated that the threshold will be exceeded (i.e. the beginning of the 30 day period)
Compulsory deregistration	30 days from cessation
Filing of VAT return and payment of VAT	End of month following the return period

Section 1

PRACTICE QUESTIONS

INCOME TAX AND NATIONAL INSURANCE

INCOME TAX BASICS AND EMPLOYMENT INCOME

1 SALLY AND SANDRA BURTON (ADAPTED) ***Online question assistance***

Sally and Sandra Burton, aged 66 and 76 respectively, are sisters.

The following information is available for 2011/12:

Sally Burton

(1) Sally is employed by Burton plc as a part time manager working 3 days a week in one of the company's nationwide chain of retail clothing shops. She is paid a gross annual salary of £17,000 from which PAYE of £2,400 was deducted by her employer.

(2) Sally was provided with a petrol powered motor car which has a list price of £17,118 on 6 June 2011. Sally made a capital contribution of £2,000 towards the cost of the motor car when it was first provided. The official CO_2 emission rate for the motor car is 187 grams per kilometre. Burton plc paid for all of the motor car's maintenance costs of £2,400 during 2011/12 as well as car parking costing £1,200. Her employer did not provide any fuel for private journeys.

(3) Burton plc has provided Sally with living accommodation since 2010. The property was purchased in 2003 for £105,000, and was valued at £120,000 when first provided to Sally. It has an annual value of £1,632. Sally was not required by her job to live in the accommodation provided by her employer. Sally was required to reimburse her employer £75 each month for the use of the accommodation.

(4) In addition to her employment income, Sally received interest of £1,000 on the maturity of a savings certificate from the National Savings & Investments bank during the tax year 2011/12. This was the actual cash amount received.

(5) During 2011/12 Sally received building society interest of £1,800. This was the actual cash amount received.

Sandra Burton

(1) Sandra is self-employed running a retail grocery shop. Her income statement for the year ended 5 April 2012 is as follows:

	£	£
Gross profit		60,105
Depreciation	2,425	
Motor expenses (Note 2)	5,400	
Property expenses (Note 3)	9,600	
Other expenses (all allowable)	24,680	
		(42,105)
Net profit		18,000

(2) The motor expenses all relate to Sandra's motor car. During the year ended 5 April 2012 Sandra drove a total of 12,000 miles, of which 4,000 were for private journeys. The car originally cost £18,000 in March 2009, and at 6 April 2011 had a tax written down value of £9,600. She does not own any other assets that qualify for capital allowances.

(3) Sandra purchased her grocery shop in 2003 for £105,000. She lives in a flat that is situated above the shop, and one-third of the total property expenses of £9,600 relate to this flat.

(4) In addition to her self employed income, Sandra received £895 from an investment account at the National Savings & Investment bank during 2011/12. This was the actual cash amount received.

(5) During 2011/12 Sandra received dividends of £900. This was the actual cash amount received.

Required:

(a) Calculate Sally's income tax payable for 2011/12. (13 marks)

(b) Calculate Sandra's income tax payable for 2011/12. (12 marks)

(Total 25 marks)

Online question assistance

2 VIGOROUS PLC (ADAPTED)

Vigorous plc runs a health club. The company has three employees who received benefits during 2011/12, and it therefore needs to prepare forms P11D for them. Each of the three employees is paid an annual salary of £45,000.

The following information is relevant:

Andrea Lean

(1) Andrea was employed by Vigorous plc throughout 2011/12.

(2) Throughout 2011/12 Vigorous plc provided Andrea with a 2200 cc petrol powered company motor car with a list price of £19,400. The official CO_2 emission rate for the motor car is 265 grams per kilometre. Vigorous plc paid for all of the motor car's running costs of £6,200 during 2011/12, including petrol used for private journeys. Andrea pays £150 per month to Vigorous plc for the use of the motor car.

(3) Vigorous plc has provided Andrea with living accommodation since 1 November 2009. The property was purchased on 1 January 2007 for £130,000. The company spent £14,000 improving the property during March 2008, and a further £8,000 was spent on improvements during May 2011.

The value of the property on 1 November 2009 was £170,000, and it has a rateable value of £7,000. The furniture in the property cost £6,000 during November 2009. Andrea personally pays for the annual running costs of the property amounting to £4,000.

(4) Throughout 2011/12 Vigorous plc provided Andrea with a mobile telephone costing £500. The company paid for all business and private telephone calls.

Ben Slim

(1) Ben commenced employment with Vigorous plc on 1 July 2011.

(2) On 1 July 2011 Vigorous plc provided Ben with an interest free loan of £120,000 so that he could purchase a new main residence. He repaid £20,000 of the loan on 1 October 2011.

(3) During 2011/12 Vigorous plc paid £9,300 towards the cost of Ben's relocation. His previous main residence was 125 miles from his place of employment with the company. The £9,300 covered the cost of disposing of Ben's old property and of acquiring his new property.

(4) From 1 July 2011 Vigorous plc provided Ben with a petrol powered second hand motor car which has a list price of £9,200. The official CO_2 emission rate for the motor car is 112 g/km. No fuel was provided by the company; Ben just claimed fuel for his business mileage. Ben had the use of the car until 30 September 2011 when his new company car arrived.

(5) During the period from 1 October 2011 until 5 April 2012 Vigorous plc provided Ben with a new diesel powered company motor car which has a list price of £11,200. The official CO_2 emission rate for the motor car is 129 g/km. Ben reimburses Vigorous plc for the fuel used for private journeys.

(6) On 1 July 2011 Ben joined the company's childcare scheme which provides employees with childcare vouchers of £60 per week to buy care from an approved child carer. Ben received vouchers to provide care for 36 weeks in 2011/12.

Chai Trim

(1) Chai was employed by Vigorous plc throughout 2011/12.

(2) During 2011/12 Vigorous plc provided Chai with a two-year old company van, which was available for private use. The van was unavailable during the period 1 August to 30 September 2011. Chai was also provided with private fuel for the van.

(3) Vigorous plc has provided Chai with a television for her personal use since 6 April 2009. The television cost Vigorous plc £800 in April 2009. On 6 April 2011 the company sold the television to Chai for £150, although its market value on that date was £250.

(4) Throughout 2011/12 Vigorous plc provided Chai with free membership of its health club. The normal annual cost of membership is £800. This figure is made up of direct costs of £150, fixed overhead costs of £400 and profit of £250. The budgeted membership for the year has been exceeded, but the health club has surplus capacity.

(5) On 1 January 2012 Vigorous plc provided Chai with a new computer costing £1,900. She uses the computer at home for personal study purposes.

Required:

(a) Explain what is meant by the term 'P11D employee'. (3 marks)

(b) Calculate the benefit figures that Vigorous plc will have to include on the forms P11D for Andrea, Ben, and Chai for 2011/12. (19 marks)

(c) Explain how the income tax liability in respect of benefits is collected by HM Revenue & Customs. (3 marks)

(Total: 25 marks)

3 ALI PATEL (ADAPTED) *Walk in the footsteps of a top tutor*

You should assume that today's date is 15 March 2011.

Ali Patel has been employed by Box plc since 1 January 2008, and is currently paid an annual salary of £29,000. On 6 April 2011 Ali is to be temporarily relocated for a period of 12 months from Box plc's head office to one of its branch offices. He has been offered two alternative remuneration packages:

First remuneration package

(1) Ali will continue to live near Box plc's head office, and will commute on a daily basis to the branch office using his private motor car.

(2) He will be paid additional salary of £500 per month.

(3) Box plc will pay Ali an allowance of 38 pence per mile for the 1,600 miles that Ali will drive each month commuting to the branch office.

Ali's additional cost of commuting for 2011/12 will be £1,800.

Second remuneration package

(1) Box plc will provide Ali with rent-free living accommodation near the branch office.

(2) The property will be rented by Box plc at a cost of £800 per month. The annual value of the property is £4,600.

(3) Ali will rent out his main residence near Box plc's head office, and this will result in property business income of £6,000 for 2011/12.

Required:

(a) Calculate Ali's income tax liability and Class 1 national insurance contributions for 2011/12, if he:

(i) accepts the first remuneration package offered by Box plc; (6 marks)

(ii) accepts the second remuneration package offered by Box plc. (5 marks)

(b) Advise Ali as to which remuneration package is the most beneficial from a financial perspective.

Your answer should be supported by a calculation of the amount of income, net of all costs including income tax and Class 1 national insurance contributions, which he would receive for 2011/12 under each alternative. (4 marks)

(Total: 15 marks)

4 EDMOND BRICK (ADAPTED) *Walk in the footsteps of a top tutor*

Edmond Brick owns four properties which are let out.

The following information relates to the tax year 2011/12:

Property one

This is a freehold house that qualifies as a trade under the furnished holiday letting rules. The property was purchased on 6 April 2011. During the tax year 2011/12 the property was let for eighteen weeks at £370 per week. Edmond spent £5,700 on furniture and kitchen equipment during April 2011. Due to a serious flood £7,400 was spent on repairs during November 2011. The damage was not covered by insurance. The other expenditure on this property for the tax year 2011/12 amounted to £2,710, and this is all allowable.

Property two

This is a freehold house that is let out furnished. The property was let throughout the tax year 2011/12 at a monthly rent of £575, payable in advance. During the tax year 2011/12 Edmond paid council tax of £1,200 and insurance of £340 in respect of this property. He claims the wear and tear allowance for this property.

Property three

This is a freehold house that is let out unfurnished. The property was purchased on 6 April 2011, and it was empty until 30 June 2011. It was then let from 1 July 2011 to 31 January 2012 at a monthly rent of £710, payable in advance. On 31 January 2012 the tenant left owing three months rent which Edmond was unable to recover. The property was not re-let before 5 April 2012. During the tax year 2011/12 Edmond paid insurance of £290 for this property and spent £670 on advertising for tenants. He also paid loan interest of £6,700 in respect of a loan that was taken out to purchase this property.

Property four

This is a leasehold office building that is let out unfurnished. Edmond pays an annual rent of £6,800 for this property, but did not pay a premium when he acquired it. On 6 April 2011 the property was sub-let to a tenant, with Edmond receiving a premium of £15,000 for the grant of a five-year lease. He also received the annual rent of £4,600 which was payable in advance. During the tax year 2011/12 Edmond paid insurance of £360 in respect of this property.

Furnished room

During the tax year 2011/12 Edmond rented out one furnished room of his main residence. During the year he received rent of £5,040, and incurred allowable expenditure of £1,140 in respect of the room. Edmond always computes the taxable income for the furnished room on the most favourable basis.

Required:

(a) State the income tax advantages of property one being treated as a trade under the furnished holiday letting rules. (2 marks)

(b) Calculate Edmond's furnished holiday letting loss in respect of property one for the tax year 2011/12. (3 marks)

(c) Calculate Edmond's property business profit in respect of the other three properties and the furnished room for the tax year 2011/12. (10 marks)

(Total: 15 marks)

5 PETER CHIC (ADAPTED) *Walk in the footsteps of a top tutor*

Peter Chic is employed by Haute-Couture Ltd as a fashion designer. The following information is available for the tax year 2011/12:

Employment

(1) During the tax year 2011/12 Peter was paid a gross annual salary of £75,600 by Haute-Couture Ltd. Income tax of £42,000 was deducted from this figure under PAYE.

(2) In addition to his salary, Peter received two bonus payments from Haute-Couture Ltd during the tax year 2011/12. The first bonus of £14,300 was paid on 30 April 2011 and was in respect of the year ended 31 December 2010. Peter became entitled to this first bonus on 10 April 2011. The second bonus of £13,700 was paid on 31 March 2012 and was in respect of the year ended 31 December 2011. Peter became entitled to this second bonus on 25 March 2012.

(3) Throughout the tax year 2011/12 Haute-Couture Ltd provided Peter with a diesel powered motor car which has a list price of £22,500. The motor car cost Haute-Couture Ltd £21,200, and it has an official CO_2 emission rate of 222 g/km.

Peter made a capital contribution of £2,000 towards the cost of the motor car when it was first provided to him. Haute-Couture Ltd also provided Peter with fuel for private journeys.

(4) Haute-Couture Ltd has provided Peter with living accommodation since 1 January 2009. The company had purchased the property in 2008 for £160,000, and it was valued at £185,000 on 1 January 2009. Improvements costing £13,000 were made to the property during June 2010. The annual value of the property is £9,450.

(5) Throughout the tax year 2011/12 Haute-Couture Ltd provided Peter with two mobile telephones. The telephones had each cost £250 when purchased by the company in January 2011 and are both used for both private and business calls.

(6) On 5 January 2012 Haute-Couture Ltd paid a health club membership fee of £510 for the benefit of Peter.

(7) During February 2012 Peter spent five nights overseas on company business. Haute-Couture Ltd paid Peter a daily allowance of £10 to cover the cost of personal expenses such as telephone calls to his family.

Property income

(1) Peter owns two properties, which are let out. Both properties are freehold houses, with the first property being let out furnished and the second property being let out unfurnished.

(2) The first property was let from 6 April 2011 to 31 August 2011 at a monthly rent of £500, payable in advance. On 31 August 2011 the tenant left owing two months' rent which Peter was unable to recover. The property was not re-let before 5 April 2012. During March 2012 Peter spent £600 repairing the roof of this property.

(3) The second property was purchased on 1 July 2011, and was then let from 1 August 2011 to 5 April 2012 at a monthly rent of £2,820, payable in advance. During July 2011 Peter spent £875 on advertising for tenants. For the period 1 July 2011 to 5 April 2012 he paid loan interest of £7,800 in respect of a loan that was taken out to purchase this property.

(4) Peter insured both of his rental properties at a total cost of £660 for the year ended 30 June 2011, and £1,080 for the year ended 30 June 2012. The insurance is payable annually in advance.

(5) Where possible, Peter claims the wear and tear allowance.

Other information

(1) During the tax year 2011/12 Peter received building society interest of £4,760 and dividends of £2,700. These were the actual cash amounts received.

(2) On 4 August 2011 Peter received a premium bond prize of £100.

(3) During the tax year 2011/12 Peter made Gift Aid donations totalling £2,340 (net) to national charities.

Required:

(a) Calculate the income tax payable by Peter Chic for the tax year 2011/12. (21 marks)

(b) Calculate the total amount of national insurance contributions that will have been paid by Peter Chic and Haute-Couture Ltd in respect of Peter's earnings and benefits for the tax year 2011/12. (4 marks)

(Total: 25 marks)

INCOME TAX BASICS AND INCOME FROM SELF-EMPLOYMENT

6 CAROL COURIER

For the purposes of this question you should assume that today's date is 15 March 2011.

Carol Courier is employed by Quick-Speed plc as a delivery driver, and is paid a salary of £37,500 p.a. She contributes 5% of her gross salary into Quick-Speed plc's HM Revenue & Customs registered occupational pension scheme.

As an alternative to being employed, Quick-Speed plc have offered Carol the opportunity to work for the company on a self-employed basis.

The details of the proposed arrangement for the year ended 5 April 2012 are as follows:

(1) Carol will commence being self-employed on 6 April 2011.

(2) Her income from Quick-Speed plc is expected to be £43,500.

(3) When not working for Quick-Speed plc, Carol will be allowed to work for other clients. Her income from this work is expected to be £8,000.

(4) Carol will lease a delivery van from Quick-Speed plc, and 100% of the mileage will be for business purposes. The cost of leasing and running the van will be £4,400.

(5) When she is unavailable Carol will have to provide a replacement driver to deliver for Quick-Speed plc. This will cost her £2,800.

(6) Carol will contribute £2,000 (gross) into a personal pension scheme during 2011/12. This will provide her with the same benefits as the occupational pension scheme provided by Quick-Speed plc.

Required:

(a) Assuming that Carol does not accept the offer from Quick-Speed plc and continues to be employed by the company, calculate her income tax and Class 1 NIC liability for 2011/12. (5 marks)

(b) Assuming that Carol accepts the offer to work for Quick-Speed plc on a self-employed basis from 6 April 2011 onwards, calculate her income tax, Class 2 NIC and Class 4 NIC liability for 2011/12. (6 marks)

(c) Advise Carol as to whether it will be beneficial to accept the offer to work for Quick-Speed plc on a self-employed basis.

Your answer should be supported by a calculation of the amount by which Carol's income for 2011/12 (net of outgoings, income tax and NIC) will increase or decrease if she accepts the offer. (4 marks)

(Total: 15 marks)

7 CHATRU (ADAPTED) *Walk in the footsteps of a top tutor*

(1) Chatru started trading on 1 November 2007. His first accounts were prepared to 30 April 2009 and thereafter to 30 April annually. He ceased trading on 31 March 2012.

His trading results, adjusted for income tax purposes were:

	£
1.11.07 – 30.4.09	40,500
Year ended 30.4.10	12,000
Year ended 30.4.11	24,000
Period to 31.3.12	50,000

Required:

(a) Calculate the assessable income for all years in question. (8 marks)

(b) Calculate whether there would have been any income tax benefit in Chatru continuing to trade one extra month and preparing final accounts to his normal accounting date, on the assumption that his tax-adjusted profit for April 2012 was £4,200. (3 marks)

(2) Chatru, who is aged 63, had the following additional income and expenditure in 2011/12:

Investment income

(i) He received dividends of £33,500, bank interest of £2,500 and interest from an Individual Savings Account of £1,500.

Property income

(i) He rented out a room in his house to a student and charged rent of £150 per month.

(ii) From 6 April 2011 he rented out a furnished property on which he received rent of £11,100. During the year he made payments on a loan which he had taken out to acquire the property of which £500 related to interest charges. He incurred allowable expenses of £1,600 which included £800 council tax and £300 water rates. He also spent £400 on a cooker for the property.

(iii) Chatru and his wife, Sandra, jointly owned a piece of land in the ratio 25:75. They received rent of £4,000 per annum from renting the land to a local farmer.

Other information

(i) On 1 March 2012 Chatru made a payment of £5,000 to a national charity under the Gift Aid scheme.

(ii) Sandra works part-time earning £8,000 per annum and has no other income other than mentioned above.

(iii) Chatru and Sandra have not made any elections in respect of their income.

For the purposes of this part assume that Chatru ceased to trade on 31 March 2012.

Required:

(a) Compute the income tax payable by Chatru for the tax year 2011/12. (15 marks)

(b) Advise Chatru and Sandra of two ways in which they may have reduced their joint income tax liability in 2011/12. (4 marks)

(Total: 30 marks)

8 OLIVE GREEN (ADAPTED) *Walk in the footsteps of a top tutor*

Olive Green is self-employed running a health food shop. Her income statement for the year ended 31 March 2012 is as follows:

	£	£
Gross profit		130,750
Expenses:		
Depreciation	2,350	
Light and heat (Note 1)	1,980	
Motor expenses (Note 2)	9,700	
Rent and rates (Note 1)	5,920	
Sundry expenses (Note 3)	2,230	
Wages and salaries (Note 4)	78,520	
	———	(100,700)
		———
Net profit		30,050
		———

Note 1 – Private accommodation

Olive lives in a flat that is situated above the health food shop. 30% of the expenditure included in the income statement for light, heat, rent and rates relates to the flat.

Note 2 – Motor expenses

Motor expenses include £4,700 for the running of Olive's car. During the year ended 31 March 2012 Olive drove a total of 20,000 miles, of which 8,000 were for business purposes.

The motor expenses also include £3,000 leasing costs. This relates to the lease of a car with CO_2 emissions of 175 grams per kilometre which is used by the shop manager.

Note 3 – Sundry expenses

The figure of £2,230 for sundry expenses includes £220 for a fine in respect of health and safety regulations, £180 for the theft of cash by an employee, £100 for a donation to a political party, and £140 for a trade subscription to the Health and Organic Association.

Note 4 – Wages and salaries

The figure of £78,520 for wages and salaries includes an annual salary of £14,000 paid to Olive's daughter. She works in the health food shop as a sales assistant. The other sales assistants doing the same job are paid an annual salary of £10,500.

Note 5 – Goods for own use

Each week Olive takes health food from the shop for her personal use without paying for it. The weekly cost of this food is £30, and it has a selling price of £45.

Note 6 – Plant and machinery

The only item of plant and machinery is Olive's motor car which was purchased in October 2008. The tax written down value of this vehicle at 1 April 2011 was £15,800.

Note 7 – Patent royalties

Olive pays a patent royalty of £150 (gross) every quarter for the use of equipment that allows her to make her own organic breakfast cereal. This has not been accounted for in arriving at the net profit of £30,050.

Other income

(1) Olive has a part-time employment for which she was paid a gross salary of £6,000 during 2011/12. Income tax of £1,200 has been deducted from this figure under PAYE.

(2) During 2011/12 Olive received building society interest of £1,440 and dividends of £1,080. These were the actual cash amounts received.

(3) On 30 November 2011 Olive sold some investments, and this resulted in a chargeable gain of £12,800.

Other information

(1) During 2011/12 Olive paid interest of £220 (gross) on a loan taken out on 1 January 2010 to purchase equipment for use in her part-time employment.

(2) Olive contributed £2,600 (gross) into a personal pension scheme during 2011/12.

(3) Olive's payments on account of income tax in respect of 2011/12 totalled £4,900.

Required:

(a) Calculate Olive's tax adjusted trading profit for the year ended 31 March 2012.

Your computation should commence with the net profit figure of £30,050, and should list all of the items referred to in Notes (1) to (7), indicating by the use of zero (0) any items that do not require adjustment. (8 marks)

(b) (i) Calculate the income tax and capital gains tax payable by Olive for 2011/12; (11 marks)

(ii) Calculate Olive's balancing payment for 2011/12 and her payments on account for 2012/13, stating the relevant due dates.

You should ignore National Insurance contributions. (3 marks)

(c) Advise Olive of the consequences of not making the balancing payment for 2011/12 until 30 April 2013. (3 marks)

(Total: 25 marks)

9 FOO DEE (ADAPTED)

On 31 December 2011 Foo Dee resigned as an employee of Gastronomic-Food plc. The company had employed her as a chef since 2000. On 1 January 2012 Foo commenced self-employment running her own restaurant, preparing accounts to 30 September.

The following information is available for 2011/12:

Employment

(1) During the period 6 April 2011 to 31 December 2011 Foo's total gross salary from her employment with Gastronomic-Food plc was £38,000. Income tax of £5,600 was deducted from this figure under PAYE.

(2) Foo used her private motor car for both business and private purposes during the period from 6 April 2011 to 31 December 2011. She received no reimbursement from Gastronomic-Food plc for any of the expenditure incurred.

Foo's total mileage during this period was 15,000 miles, made up as follows:

	miles
Normal daily travel between home and permanent workplace	4,650
Travel between home and permanent workplace in order to turn off a fire alarm	120
Travel between permanent workplace and Gastronomic-Food plc's suppliers	750
Travel between home and a temporary workplace for two months	3,800
Private travel	5,680
	15,000

(3) On 1 October 2011 Gastronomic-Food plc paid £12,900 towards Foo's removal expenses when she was permanently relocated to a different restaurant owned by the company. The £12,900 covered the cost of disposing of Foo's old property and of acquiring her new property.

(4) Foo contributed 6% of her gross salary of £38,000 into Gastronomic-Food plc's HM Revenue & Customs' registered occupational pension scheme.

Self-employment

(1) Foo's income statement for her restaurant business for the nine-month period ended 30 September 2012 is as follows:

	£	£
Gross profit		196,930
Depreciation	3,500	
Motor expenses (Note 2)	4,200	
Property expenses (Note 3)	12,800	
Other expenses (all allowable)	50,700	
		71,200
Net profit		125,730

(2) During the period 1 January 2012 to 30 September 2012 Foo drove a total of 6,000 miles, of which 2,000 were for private journeys.

(3) Foo purchased her restaurant on 1 January 2012. She lives in a flat that is situated above the restaurant, and one-quarter of the total property expenses of £12,800 relate to this flat.

(4) On 1 January 2012 Foo purchased a motor car with CO_2 emissions of 145 grams per kilometre for £14,600 (see note 2 above) and equipment for £81,200.

Other income

(1) During the tax year 2011/12 Foo received building society interest of £640 and dividends of £360. These were the actual cash amounts received.

(2) On 10 July 2011 Foo sold some investments, and this resulted in a capital gain of £17,600.

Other information

(1) Foo contributed £1,600 (net) into a personal pension scheme during the period 1 January 2012 to 5 April 2012.

(2) She did not make any payments on account of income tax in respect of the tax year 2011/12.

Required:

(a) Calculate Foo's tax adjusted trading profit for the nine-month period ended 30 September 2012.

Assume that the current tax rates and allowances apply throughout. (6 marks)

(b) (i) Calculate the income tax and capital gains tax payable by Foo for the tax year 2011/12. (13 marks)

(ii) Calculate Foo's balancing payment for the tax year 2011/12 and her payments on account for the tax year 2012/13, stating the relevant due dates. Ignore National Insurance contributions. (3 marks)

(c) Advise Foo of the consequences of not making the balancing payment for the tax year 2011/12 until 31 May 2013. (3 marks)

(Total: 25 marks)

10 MARK KETT (ADAPTED) *Walk in the footsteps of a top tutor*

On 31 December 2011 Mark Kett ceased trading as a marketing consultant. He had been self-employed since 6 April 2005, and had always prepared his accounts to 5 April. On 1 January 2012 Mark commenced employment as the marketing manager of Sleep-Easy plc. The company runs a hotel.

The following information is available for the tax year 2011/12.

Self-employment

(1) Mark's tax adjusted trading profit for the nine-month period ended 31 December 2011 is £21,700. This figure is before taking account of capital allowances.

(2) The tax written down values for capital allowances purposes at 6 April 2011 were:

	£
General pool	13,800
Expensive motor car	14,600

The expensive motor car was used by Mark, and 40% of the mileage was for private purposes.

(3) On 15 June 2011 Mark had purchased office furniture for £1,900. All of the items included in the general pool were sold for £18,800 on 31 December 2011. On the cessation of trading, Mark personally retained the expensive motor car. Its value on 31 December 2011 was £11,800.

Employment

(1) Mark is paid a salary of £3,250 (gross) per month by Sleep-Easy plc, from which income tax of £620 per month has been deducted under PAYE.

(2) During the period from 1 January 2012 to 5 April 2012 Mark used his private motor car for business purposes. He drove 2,500 miles in the performance of his duties for Sleep-Easy plc, for which the company paid an allowance of 21 pence per mile.

(3) On 1 January 2012 Sleep-Easy plc provided Mark with an interest free loan of £95,000 so that he could purchase a new main residence.

(4) During the period from 1 January 2012 to 5 April 2012 Mark was provided with free meals in Sleep-Easy plc's staff canteen. The total cost of these meals to the company was £400.

Property income

(1) Mark let out a furnished property throughout the tax year 2011/12. He received gross rents of £8,600, 5% of which was paid to a letting agency. During December 2011 Mark spent £540 on replacing dilapidated furniture and furnishings.

(2) From 6 April 2011 to 31 December 2011 Mark let out a spare room in his main residence, receiving rent of £350 per month.

(3) Mark claims the wear and tear allowance where available.

Investment income

(1) During the tax year 2011/12 Mark received dividends of £2,880, interest from government stocks (gilts) of £2,900, and interest of £430 from an individual savings account (ISA). These were the actual cash amounts received.

(2) On 3 May 2011 Mark received a premium bond prize of £100.

Other information

(1) On 15 December 2011 Mark made a gift aid donation of £800 (net) to a national charity.

(2) Mark's payments on account of income tax in respect of the tax year 2011/12 totalled £11,380.

Required:

(a) Compute the income tax payable by Mark for the tax year 2011/12, and the balancing payment or repayment that will be due for the year. (22 marks)

(b) Advise Mark as to how long he must retain the records used in preparing his tax return for the tax year 2011/12, and the potential consequences of not retaining the records for the required period. (3 marks)

(Total: 25 marks)

11 LI FUNG

Li Fung commenced in self-employment on 1 October 2007. She initially prepared accounts to 30 June, but changed her accounting date to 31 March by preparing accounts for the nine-month period to 31 March 2011.

Li's trading profits since she commenced self-employment have been as follows:

	£
Nine-month period ended 30 June 2008	18,600
Year ended 30 June 2009	24,900
Year ended 30 June 2010	22,200
Nine-month period ended 31 March 2011	16,800
Year ended 31 March 2012	26,400

Required:

(a) State the qualifying conditions that must be met for a change of accounting date to be valid. (3 marks)

(b) Compute Li's trading income assessments for each of the five tax years 2007/08, 2008/09, 2009/10, 2010/11 and 2011/12. (9 marks)

(c) Advise Li of the advantages and disadvantages for tax purposes of changing her accounting date from 30 June to 31 March. (3 marks)

(Total: 15 marks)

12 SAM AND KIM WHITE (ADAPTED) *Walk in the footsteps of a top tutor*

Timed question with Online tutor debrief

Sam and Kim White are a married couple. Sam is aged 46 and Kim is aged 51. The following information is available for the tax year 2011/12:

Sam White

(1) Sam is self-employed running a retail clothing shop. His income statement for the year ended 5 April 2012 is as follows:

	Note	£	£
Gross profit			190,300
Depreciation		7,600	
Motor expenses	2	8,800	
Patent royalties	3	700	
Professional fees	4	1,860	
Other expenses	5	71,340	
			(90,300)
Net profit			100,000

(2) During the year ended 5 April 2012 Sam drove a total of 25,000 miles, of which 5,000 miles were driven when he visited his suppliers in Europe. The balance of the mileage is 25% for private journeys and 75% for business journeys in the United Kingdom.

(3) During the year ended 5 April 2012 Sam paid patent royalties of £700 (gross) in respect of specialised technology that he uses when altering clothes for customers.

(4) The figure for professional fees consists of £1,050 for legal fees in connection with an action brought against a supplier for breach of contract and £810 for accountancy. Included in the figure for accountancy is £320 in respect of personal capital gains tax advice for the tax year 2010/11.

(5) The figure for other expenses of £71,340 includes £560 for gifts to customers of food hampers costing £35 each and £420 for gifts to customers of pens carrying an advertisement for the clothing shop costing £60 each.

(6) Sam uses one of the eight rooms in the couple's house as an office for when he works at home. The total running costs of the house for the year ended 5 April 2012 were £5,120. This cost is not included in the income statement expenses of £90,300.

(7) Sam uses his private telephone to make business telephone calls. The total cost of the private telephone for the year ended 5 April 2012 was £1,600, and 25% of this related to business telephone calls. The cost of the private telephone is not included in the income statement expenses of £90,300.

(8) During the year ended 5 April 2012 Sam took goods out of the clothing shop for his personal use without paying for them and no entry has been made in the accounts to record this. The goods cost £820, and had a selling price of £1,480.

(9) The tax written down values for capital allowance purposes at 6 April 2011 were:

General pool	£14,800
Expensive motor car bought January 2008	£20,200

The expensive motor car is used by Sam.

Kim White

(1) Kim is employed as a sales person by Sharp-Suit plc, a clothing manufacturing company. During the tax year 2011/12 she was paid a gross annual salary of £21,600.

(2) On 1 June 2011 Sharp-Suit plc provided Kim with an interest free loan of £14,250 so that she could purchase a new motor car.

(3) During the period from 1 June 2011 to 5 April 2012 Kim used her private motor car for business and private purposes. She received no reimbursement from Sharp-Suit plc for any of the expenditure incurred.

Kim's mileage during this period included the following:

	Miles
Normal daily travel between home and permanent workplace	3,400
Travel between permanent workplace and Sharp-Suit plc's customers	11,200
Travel between home and a temporary workplace for one month	1,300

(4) During the tax year 2011/12 Kim paid interest of £140 (gross) on a personal loan taken out on 1 January 2010 to purchase a laptop computer for use in her employment with Sharp-Suit plc. She also made a charitable contribution of £800, which she does every year.

Joint income – Building society deposit account

The couple have savings of £25,000 in a building society deposit account which is in their joint names.

During the tax year 2011/12 Sam and Kim received building society interest totalling £1,200 from this joint account. This was the actual cash amount received.

Required:

(a) Calculate Sam's tax adjusted trading profit for the year ended 5 April 2012.

Your computation should start with the net profit of £100,000 and should list all the items referred to in Notes (1) to (8), indicating with a zero (0) any items that do not require adjustment. (11 marks)

(b) Calculate Sam and Kim's respective income tax liabilities for the tax year 2011/12.

You should ignore any capital allowances that Kim might be entitled to. (10 marks)

(c) Explain to Sam and Kim how their overall income tax liability could be reduced if they were to either:

(i) transfer their joint building society deposit account into individual savings accounts (ISAs); or (2 marks)

(ii) transfer their joint building society deposit account into Kim's sole name. (2 marks)

Assume that 2011/12 rates and allowances continue to apply.

(Total: 25 marks)

> ***Calculate your allowed time, allocate the time to the separate parts....................***

13 GOMEZ BROTHERS (ADAPTED) *Walk in the footsteps of a top tutor*

Domingo, Erigo and Fargo Gomez are three brothers. The following information is available for the tax year 2011/12:

Domingo Gomez

(1) Domingo is aged 67.

(2) During the tax year 2011/12 he received the state pension of £4,500 and a private pension of £2,300.

(3) In addition to his pension income Domingo received building society interest of £15,200 and interest of £600 on the maturity of a savings certificate from the National Savings and Investments Bank during the tax year 2011/12. These were the actual cash amounts received.

(4) During the tax year 2011/12 Domingo made donations of £300 (gross) to local charities. These were not made under the Gift Aid scheme.

Erigo Gomez

(1) Erigo is aged 56.

(2) He is employed as a business journalist by Economical plc, a magazine publishing company. During the tax year 2011/12 Erigo was paid a gross annual salary of £36,000.

(3) During the tax year 2011/12 Erigo used his private motor car for business purposes. He drove 18,000 miles in the performance of his duties for Economical plc, for which the company paid an allowance of 20 pence per mile.

(4) During June 2011 Economical plc paid £11,400 towards the cost of Erigo's relocation when he was required to move his place of employment. Erigo's previous main residence was 140 miles from his new place of employment with the company. The £11,400 covered the cost of disposing of Erigo's old property and of acquiring a new property.

(5) Erigo contributed 6% of his gross salary of £36,000 into Economical plc's HM Revenue and Customs' registered occupational pension scheme.

(6) During the tax year 2011/12 Erigo donated £100 (gross) per month to charity under the payroll deduction scheme.

Fargo Gomez

(1) Fargo is aged 53.

(2) He commenced self-employment as a business consultant on 6 July 2011. Fargo's tax adjusted trading profit based on his draft accounts for the nine-month period ended 5 April 2012 is £112,800. This figure is before making any adjustments required for:

   (i) Advertising expenditure of £2,600 incurred during May 2011. This expenditure has not been deducted in calculating the profit of £112,800.

   (ii) Capital allowances.

(3) The only item of plant and machinery owned by Fargo is his motor car. This cost £11,000 on 6 July 2011 and has CO_2 emissions of 152 g/km. During the nine-month period ended 5 April 2012 Fargo drove a total of 24,000 miles, of which 8,000 were for private journeys.

(4) During the tax year 2011/12 Fargo contributed £5,200 (gross) into a personal pension scheme, and made Gift Aid donations totalling £2,400 (net) to national charities.

Tax returns

For the tax year 2011/12 Domingo wants to file a paper self-assessment tax return and have HM Revenue and Customs prepare a self-assessment on his behalf. Erigo also wants to file a paper tax return but will prepare his own self-assessment. Fargo wants to file his tax return online.

Required:

(a) Calculate the respective income tax liabilities for the tax year 2011/12 of:

   (i) Domingo Gomez; **(6 marks)**

   (ii) Erigo Gomez; **(6 marks)**

   (iii) Fargo Gomez. **(7 marks)**

(b) Advise Domingo, Erigo and Fargo Gomez of the latest dates by which their respective self-assessment tax returns for the tax year 2011/12 will have to be submitted given their stated filing preferences. **(3 marks)**

(c) Advise Domingo, Erigo and Fargo Gomez as to how long they must retain the records used in preparing their respective tax returns for the tax year 2011/12, and the potential consequences of not retaining the records for the required period.

(3 marks)

(Total: 25 marks)

14 ANDREW ZOOM *Walk in the footsteps of a top tutor*

Andrew Zoom is a cameraman who started working for Slick-Productions Ltd on 6 April 2011. The following information is available in respect of the year ended 5 April 2012:

(1) Andrew received gross income of £50,000 from Slick-Productions Ltd.

He works a set number of hours each week and is paid an hourly rate for the work that he does.

When Andrew works more than the set number of hours he is paid overtime.

(2) Andrew is under an obligation to accept the work offered to him by Slick-Productions Ltd, and the work is carried out under the control of the company's production manager.

He is obliged to do the work personally, and this is all performed at Slick-Productions Ltd's premises.

(3) All of the equipment that Andrew uses is provided by Slick-Productions Ltd.

Andrew has several friends who are cameramen, and they are all treated as self-employed. He therefore considers that he should be treated as self-employed as well in relation to his work for Slick-Productions Ltd.

Required:

(a) List those factors that indicate that Andrew Zoom should be treated as an employee in relation to his work for Slick-Productions Ltd rather than as self-employed.

You should confine your answer to the information given in the question. (4 marks)

(b) Calculate Andrew Zoom's income tax liability and national insurance contributions for the tax year 2011/12 if he is treated:

(i) As an employee in respect of his work for Slick-Productions Ltd;

You are not required to calculate the employers' National Insurance contributions. (3 marks)

(ii) As self-employed in respect of his work for Slick-Productions Ltd. (3 marks)

(10 marks)

15 NA STYLE *Walk in the footsteps of a top tutor*

Na Style commenced self-employment as a hairdresser on 1 January 2009. She had tax adjusted trading profits of £25,200 for the six-month period ended 30 June 2009, and £21,600 for the year ended 30 June 2010.

The following information is available for the tax year 2011/12:

Trading profit for the year ended 30 June 2011

(1) Na's income statement for the year ended 30 June 2011 is as follows:

	Note	£	£
Income			61,300
Expenses			
Depreciation		1,300	
Motor expenses	2	2,200	
Professional fees	3	1,650	
Property expenses	4	12,900	
Purchases	5	4,700	
Other expenses	6	16,550	
			(39,300)
Net profit			22,000

(2) Na charges all the running expenses for her motor car to the business. During the year ended 30 June 2011 Na drove a total of 8,000 miles, of which 7,000 were for private journeys.

(3) The figure for professional fees consists of £390 for accountancy and £1,260 for legal fees in connection with the grant of a new five-year lease of parking spaces for customers' motor cars.

(4) Na lives in a flat that is situated above her hairdressing studio, and one-third of the total property expenses of £12,900 relate to this flat.

(5) During the year ended 30 June 2011 Na took goods out of the hairdressing business for her personal use without paying for them, and no entry has been made in the accounts to record this. The goods cost £250, and had a selling price of £450.

(6) The figure for other expenses of £16,550 includes £400 for a fine in respect of health and safety regulations, £80 for a donation to a political party, and £160 for a trade subscription to the Guild of Small Hairdressers.

(7) Na uses her private telephone to make business telephone calls. The total cost of the private telephone for the year ended 30 June 2011 was £1,200, and 20% of this related to business telephone calls. The cost of the private telephone is not included in the income statement expenses of £39,300.

(8) Capital allowances for the year ended 30 June 2011 are £810.

Other information

(1) During the tax year 2011/12 Na received dividends of £1,080, building society interest of £560, interest of £310 from an individual savings account (ISA), interest of £1,100 on the maturity of a savings certificate from the National Savings & Investments Bank, and interest of £370 from government stocks (gilts). These were the actual cash amounts received in each case.

(2) Na's payments on account of income tax in respect of the tax year 2011/12 totalled £3,200.

Required:

(a) Calculate the amount of trading profits that will have been assessed on Na Style for the tax years 2008/09, 2009/10 and 2010/11 respectively, clearly identifying the amount of any overlap profits. (5 marks)

(b) Calculate Na Style's tax adjusted trading profit for the year ended 30 June 2011.

Your computation should commence with the net profit figure of £22,000, and should list all of the items referred to in Notes (1) to (8) indicating by the use of zero (0) any items that do not require adjustment. (8 marks)

(c) (i) Calculate the income tax payable by Na Style for the tax year 2011/12.
(6 marks)

(ii) Calculate Na Style's balancing payment for the tax year 2011/12 and her payments on account for the tax year 2012/13, stating the relevant due dates.

You should ignore national insurance contributions. (3 marks)

(d) Advise Na Style of the consequences of not making the balancing payment for the tax year 2011/12 until 31 May 2013.

Your answer should include calculations as appropriate. (3 marks)

(Total: 25 marks)

16 SIMON HOUSE *Walk in the footsteps of a top tutor*

On 1 May 2011 Simon House purchased a derelict freehold house for £127,000. Legal fees of £1,800 were paid in respect of the purchase.

Simon then renovated the house at a cost of £50,600, with the renovation being completed on 10 August 2011. He immediately put the house up for sale, and it was sold on 31 August 2011 for £260,000. Legal fees of £2,600 were paid in respect of the sale.

Simon financed the transaction by a bank loan of £150,000 that was taken out on 1 May 2011 at an annual interest rate of 6%. The bank loan was repaid on 31 August 2011.

Simon had no other income or capital gains for the tax year 2011/12 except as indicated above.

Simon has been advised that whether or not he is treated as carrying on a trade will be determined according to the six following 'badges of trade':

(1) Subject matter of the transaction.

(2) Length of ownership.

(3) Frequency of similar transactions.

(4) Work done on the property.

(5) Circumstances responsible for the realisation.

(6) Motive.

Required:

(a) Briefly explain the meaning of each of the six 'badges of trade' listed in the question.

You are not expected to quote from decided cases. (3 marks)

(b) Calculate Simon House's income tax liability and his Class 2 and Class 4 national insurance contributions for the tax year 2011/12, if he is treated as carrying on a trade in respect of the disposal of the freehold house. (8 marks)

(c) Calculate Simon House's capital gains tax liability for the tax year 2011/12, if he is not treated as carrying on a trade in respect of the disposal of the freehold house.
(4 marks)

(Total 15 marks)

TRADING LOSSES

17 NORMA (ADAPTED)

Norma, who had been in business as a confectioner since 1 May 2007, disposed of the business and retired on 31 May 2011. She does not intend to start any other business, but will be employed part-time from 1 June 2011 on an annual salary of £9,000.

Her trading profits/(losses), as adjusted for taxation were:

	£	
Period ended 31.12.07	21,000	Profit
Year ended 31.12.08	17,000	Profit
Year ended 31.12.09	15,500	Profit
Year ended 31.12.10	6,000	Profit
Period ended 31.5.11	(11,000)	Loss

Norma has received bank interest of £2,000 (gross) each year since April 2007. In addition she realised a taxable gain (i.e. after the annual exemption), of £40,000 in June 2010.

Required:

(a) Calculate Norma's taxable income and gains for each tax year that she was in business before any relief for the loss arising in the period ended 31 May 2011.

(b) Explain the options available to Norma to utilise the loss and explain the effect on her tax liability of the loss relief claims identified.

Assume that rates and allowances for 2011/12 apply throughout. (15 marks)

18 LEONARDO

Leonardo, an art dealer commenced to trade on 1 September 2008. His trading results, adjusted for income tax, are:

	£	
1.9.08 to 31.5.09	40,500	Profit
1.6.09 to 31.5.10	(54,000)	Loss
1.6.10 to 31.5.11	(27,000)	Loss
1.6.11 to 31.5.12	11,000	Profit

Leonardo does not foresee making any significant profits in the next 2 or 3 years.

Leonardo has not had any other income in any of the years in question, or earlier.

Required:

(a) Show how his trading loss can be utilised most effectively, giving your reasons. (8 marks)

(b) State by what date(s) the claims you are proposing in part (a) should be submitted to HM Revenue & Customs. (2 marks)

(Total: 10 marks)

19 DEE ZYNE *Walk in the footsteps of a top tutor*

On 5 July 2011 Dee Zyne resigned as an employee of Trendy-Wear plc. The company had employed her as a fashion designer since 2002. On 6 July 2011 Dee commenced self-employment running her own clothing business, preparing accounts to 5 April.

The following information is available for 2011/12.

Employment

(1) During the period 6 April 2011 to 5 July 2011 Dee's total gross salary from her employment with Trendy-Wear plc was £26,000. Income tax of £5,400 was deducted from this figure under PAYE.

(2) During the period 6 April 2011 to 5 July 2011 Trendy-Wear plc provided Dee with a petrol-powered company motor car with a list price of £17,500. The official CO_2 emission rate for the motor car was 208 grams per kilometre. Trendy-Wear plc also provided Dee with fuel for private journeys. Dee paid £100 per month to Trendy-Wear plc for the use of the motor car, and she also made a capital contribution of £1,500 towards the cost of the motor car when it was first provided to her. The motor car was not available to Dee after 5 July 2011.

(3) On 1 January 2010 Trendy-Wear plc had provided Dee with an interest-free loan of £60,000 so that she could purchase a yacht. Dee repaid £45,000 of the loan on 5 May 2011, and repaid the balance of the loan of £15,000 on 6 July 2011.

(4) During the period from 6 April 2011 to 5 July 2011 Dee was provided with free meals in Trendy-Wear plc's staff canteen. The total cost of these meals to the company was £350.

Self-employment

(1) Dee's tax adjusted trading loss for the period 6 July 2011 to 5 April 2012 was £11,440. This figure is before taking account of the information in Note (2) and capital allowances.

(2) During the period 6 July 2011 to 5 April 2012 Dee paid patent royalties of £500 (gross) in respect of specialised technology that she uses in her clothing business.

(3) Dee purchased the following assets during the period ended 5 April 2012:

		£
10 July 2011	Computer	1,257
16 August 2011	Office furniture	2,175
13 November 2011	Motor car (1)	10,400
21 January 2012	Motor car (2)	17,800

Motor car (1) purchased on 13 November 2011 has CO_2 emissions of 135 grams per kilometre, is used by an employee, and 15% of the mileage is for private purposes.

Motor car (2) purchased on 21 January 2012 has CO_2 emissions of 165 grams per kilometre, is used by Dee, and 20% of the mileage is for private purposes.

Other information

(1) During the period 6 April 2011 to 5 July 2011 Dee paid interest of £110 (gross) on a personal loan taken out on 1 August 2010 to purchase a computer for use in her employment with Trendy-Wear plc.

(2) Dee's total income for each of the years 2005/06 to 2010/11 was £80,000.

Required:

(a) Calculate Dee's tax adjusted trading loss for 2011/12. (6 marks)

(b) Assuming that Dee claims loss relief against her total income for 2011/12, calculate the income tax repayable to her for 2011/12. (15 marks)

(c) Describe the alternative ways in which Dee could have relieved her trading loss for 2011/12 against total income, and explain why these claims would have been more beneficial than the actual claim made in (b) above.

You should assume that the tax rates for 2011/12 apply throughout. (4 marks)

(Total: 25 marks)

20 SAMANTHA FABRIQUE (ADAPTED)

Samantha Fabrique has been a self-employed manufacturer of clothing since 2001. She has the following gross income and chargeable gains for the tax years 2010/11 to 2012/13:

	2010/11	*2011/12*	*2012/13*
	£	£	£
Trading profit/(loss)	21,600	(34,000)	10,500
Building society interest	2,100	3,800	1,500
Chargeable gains/(loss)	23,300	(3,400)	11,000

The chargeable gains do not qualify for Entrepreneurs' relief.

Required:

(a) State the factors that will influence an individual's choice of loss relief claims.
(3 marks)

(b) Calculate Samantha's taxable income and taxable gains for each of the tax years 2010/11, 2011/12 and 2012/13 on the assumption that she relieves the trading loss of £34,000 for the tax year 2011/12 on the most favourable basis.

Explain your reasoning behind relieving the loss on the most favourable basis.

You should assume that the tax allowances for the tax year 2011/12 apply throughout. **(12 marks)**

(Total: 15 marks)

PARTNERSHIPS

21 PETER, QUINTON AND ROGER (ADAPTED)

(1) Peter and Quinton commenced in partnership on 1 January 2009. Roger joined as a partner on 1 January 2010, and Peter resigned as a partner on 31 December 2011. Profits and losses have always been shared equally.

The partnership's tax adjusted profits and losses are as follows:

	£	
Year ended 31 December 2009	40,000	Profit
Year ended 31 December 2010	90,000	Profit
Year ended 31 December 2011	(30,000)	Loss

All of the partners were in employment prior to becoming partners, and each of them has investment income. None of the partners has any capital gains.

Required:

(a) Briefly explain the basis by which trading profits are assessed on partners when they join a partnership. **(2 marks)**

(b) Calculate the trading income assessments of Peter, Quinton and Roger for 2008/09, 2009/10 and 2010/11. **(6 marks)**

(c) State the possible ways in which Peter, Quinton and Roger can relieve their share of the trading loss for 2011/12.

Your answer should include a calculation of the amount of loss available for relief to each partner. **(7 marks)**

(2) Following Peter's retirement from the partnership Quinton has recently taken over responsibility for the partnership's Value Added Tax (VAT) affairs. He has contacted you with some queries regarding VAT interest charges and penalties.

Required:

(a) State when a VAT 'default surcharge' arises and for how long a 'default surcharge period' lasts (3 marks)

(b) State under what circumstances HM Revenue & Customs may raise assessments for VAT 'default interest' and the period for which interest is charged. (3 marks)

(c) Explain the consequences of Quentin finding an error on an earlier VAT return submitted by the partnership. (4 marks)

(Total: 25 marks)

22 AE, BEE, CAE, DEE AND EUE (ADAPTED) *Walk in the footsteps of a top tutor*

Timed question with Online tutor debrief

(a) Ae and Bee commenced in partnership on 1 July 2009 preparing accounts to 30 June. Cae joined as a partner on 1 July 2011. Profits have always been shared equally.

The partnership's trading profits since the commencement of trading have been:

	£
Year ended 30 June 2010	54,000
Year ended 30 June 2011	66,000
Year ended 30 June 2012	87,000

Required:

Calculate the trading income assessments of Ae, Bee and Cae for each of the tax years 2009/10, 2010/11 and 2011/12. (5 marks)

(b) Dee commenced in self-employment on 6 April 2008. She initially prepared accounts to 5 April, but changed her accounting date to 31 July by preparing accounts for the four-month period to 31 July 2010.

Dee's trading profits since she commenced trading have been as follows:

	£
Year ended 5 April 2009	35,160
Year ended 5 April 2010	32,880
Four-month period ended 31 July 2010	16,240
Year ended 31 July 2011	54,120

Required:

(i) Calculate the amount of trading profits that will have been assessed on Dee for each of the tax years 2009/10, 2010/11 and 2011/12; (4 marks)

(ii) State the amount of Dee's unrelieved overlap profits as at 5 April 2012. (1 mark)

(c) Eue ceased trading on 30 September 2012, having been self-employed since 1 July 2003.

(1) Eue's trading profits for the final two periods of trading were as follows:

	£
Year ended 30 June 2011	61,200
Fifteen-month period ended 30 September 2012	72,000

Both these figures are before taking account of capital allowances.

(2) The capital allowances for the year ended 30 June 2011 were £2,100.

The tax written-down value of the capital allowances general pool at 1 July 2011 was £6,300. On 15 November 2011 Eue purchased a motor car with CO_2 emissions of 142 grams per kilometre for £2,400. All of the items included in the general pool were sold for £4,300 on 30 September 2012.

(3) Until the final period of trading Eue had always prepared accounts to 30 June. Her overlap profits for the period 1 July 2003 to 5 April 2004 were £19,800.

Required:

Calculate the amount of trading profits that will have been assessed on Eue for each of the tax years 2011/12 and 2012/13. (5 marks)

(Total: 15 marks)

Calculate your allowed time, allocate the time to the separate parts....................

23 AUY MAN AND BIM MEN (ADAPTED) *Walk in the footsteps of a top tutor*

Timed question with Online tutor debrief

Auy Man and Bim Men have been in partnership since 6 April 2002 as management consultants. The following information is available for the tax year 2011/12:

Personal information

Auy is aged 32. During the tax year 2011/12 she spent 190 days in the United Kingdom (UK).

Bim is aged 56. During the tax year 2011/12 she spent 100 days in the UK. Bim has spent the same amount of time in the UK for each of the previous five tax years.

Income statement for the year ended 5 April 2012

The partnership's summarised income statement for the year ended 5 April 2012 is:

	Notes	£	£
Sales	1		142,200
Expenses:	2		
Depreciation		3,400	
Motor expenses	3	4,100	
Other expenses	4	1,800	
Wages and salaries	5	50,900	
			(60,200)
Net profit			82,000

Notes

(1) The sales figure of £142,200 is exclusive of output value added tax (VAT) of £28,440.

(2) The expenses figures are exclusive of recoverable input VAT of:

Motor expenses	£180
Other expenses	£140

(3) The figure of £4,100 for motor expenses includes £2,600 in respect of the partners' motor cars, with 30% of this amount being in respect of private journeys.

(4) The figure of £1,800 for other expenses includes £720 for entertaining employees. The remaining expenses are all allowable.

(5) The figure of £50,900 for wages and salaries includes the annual salary of £4,000 paid to Bim (see the profit sharing note below), and the annual salary of £15,000 paid to Auy's husband, who works part-time for the partnership. Another part-time employee doing the same job is paid a salary of £10,000 per annum.

Plant and machinery

On 6 April 2011 the tax written down values of the partnership's plant and machinery were:

	£
Main pool	3,100
Motor car (1)	18,000
Motor car (2)	14,000

The following transactions took place during the year ended 5 April 2012:

		Cost/(Proceeds)
		£
8 May 2011	Sold motor car (2)	(13,100)
8 May 2011	Purchased motor car (3)	11,600
21 November 2011	Purchased motor car (4)	14,200
14 January 2012	Purchased motor car (5)	8,700

Motor car (1) was purchased in March 2009 and has a CO_2 emission rate of 185 grams per kilometre. It is used by Auy, and 70% of the mileage is for business journeys.

Motor car (2) was purchased in December 2008 and had a CO_2 emission rate of 145 grams per kilometre. It was used by Bim, and 70% of the mileage was for business journeys.

Motor car (3) is a new car purchased on 8 May 2011 has a CO_2 emission rate of 105 grams per kilometre. It is used by Bim, and 70% of the mileage is for business journeys.

Motor car (4) purchased on 21 November 2011 has a CO_2 emission rate of 135 grams per kilometre. Motor car (5) purchased on 14 January 2012 has a CO_2 emission rate of 200 grams per kilometre. These two motor cars are used by employees of the business.

Profit sharing

Profits are shared 80% to Auy and 20% to Bim. This is after paying an annual salary of £4,000 to Bim, and interest at the rate of 5% on the partners' capital account balances.

The capital account balances are:

	£
Auy Man	56,000
Bim Men	34,000

VAT

The partnership has been registered for VAT since 6 April 2002. However, the partnership has recently started invoicing for its services on new payment terms, and the partners are concerned about output VAT being accounted for at the appropriate time.

Required:

(a) Explain why both Auy Man and Bim Men will each be treated for tax purposes as resident in the United Kingdom for the tax year 2011/12. (2 marks)

(b) Calculate the partnership's tax adjusted trading profit for the year ended 5 April 2012, and the trading income assessments of Auy Man and Bim Men for the tax year 2011/12.

Your computation should commence with the net profit figure of £82,000, and should also list all of the items referred to in Notes (2) to (5) indicating by the use of zero (0) any items that do not require adjustment. (15 marks)

(c) Calculate the Class 4 National Insurance contributions payable by Auy Man and Bim Men for the tax year 2011/12. (3 marks)

(d) (i) Advise the partnership of the VAT rules that determine the tax point in respect of a supply of services; (3 marks)

(ii) Calculate the amount of VAT paid by the partnership to HM Revenue & Customs throughout the year ended 5 April 2012;

You should ignore the output VAT scale charges due in respect of fuel for private journeys. (2 marks)

(iii) Advise the partnership of the conditions that it must satisfy in order to join and continue to use the VAT flat rate scheme, and calculate the tax saving if the partnership had used the flat rate scheme to calculate the amount of VAT payable throughout the year ended 5 April 2012.

You should assume that the relevant flat rate scheme percentage for the partnership's trade was 14% throughout the whole of the year ended 5 April 2012. (5 marks)

(Total: 30 marks)

Calculate your allowed time, allocate the time to the separate parts....................

PENSIONS AND NATIONAL INSURANCE

24 DUKE AND EARL UPPER-CRUST (ADAPTED)

Duke and Earl Upper-Crust, aged 44, are twin brothers.

Duke is employed by the High-Brow Bank plc as a financial adviser. During the tax year 2011/12 Duke was paid a gross salary of £115,000. He also received a bonus of £40,000 on 15 March 2012. On 31 March 2012 Duke made a contribution of £45,000 (gross) into a personal pension scheme. He is not a member of High-Brow Bank plc's occupational pension scheme.

Earl is self-employed as a financial consultant. His trading profit for the year ended 5 April 2012 was £34,000. On 31 March 2012 Earl made a contribution of £40,000 (gross) into a personal pension scheme.

Neither Duke nor Earl has any other income.

In previous years Duke and Earl Upper-Crust had the same level of income. Duke paid £45,000 (gross) into his pension scheme and Earl paid £10,000 (gross).

Required:

(a) Calculate Duke and Earl's income tax liabilities for the tax year 2011/12, together with the actual net of tax amounts that Duke and Earl will have paid to their personal pension companies. (9 marks)

(b) Explain the effect of the pension scheme annual allowance limit, and the tax implications if contributions are made in excess of this limit. (2 marks)

(b) Advise Duke and Earl of the maximum additional amounts that they could have contributed into personal pension schemes for the tax year 2011/12 without incurring an annual allowance charge, and the date by which any qualifying contributions would have had to have been paid. (4 marks)

(Total: 15 marks)

25 VANESSA AND SERENE (ADAPTED) *Walk in the footsteps of a top tutor*

(a) Vanessa Serve and Serene Volley, aged 32 and 35 years respectively, are sisters. The following information is available for the tax year 2011/12:

Vanessa Serve

(1) Vanessa is self-employed as a tennis coach. Her tax adjusted trading profit for the year ended 31 March 2012 is £52,400. However, this figure is before taking account of capital allowances.

(2) The only item of plant and machinery owned by Vanessa is her motor car. This was bought in January 2009 for £19,000, and at 1 April 2011 had a tax written down value of £10,400.

During the year ended 31 March 2012 Vanessa drove a total of 20,000 miles, of which 6,000 were for private journeys.

(3) Vanessa contributed £6,400 (gross) into a personal pension scheme during the tax year 2011/12.

(4) In addition to her self-employed income, Vanessa received interest of £1,100 from an investment account at the National Savings & Investments Bank during the tax year 2011/12. This was the actual cash amount received.

(5) Vanessa's payments on account in respect of the tax year 2011/12 totalled £8,705.

Serene Volley

(1) Serene is employed as a sports journalist by Backhand plc, a newspaper publishing company.

During the tax year 2011/12 she was paid a gross annual salary of £26,400. Income tax of £3,985 was deducted from this figure under PAYE.

(2) Throughout the tax year 2011/12 Backhand plc provided Serene with a diesel powered motor car which has a list price of £26,600. The official CO_2 emission rate for the motor car is 87 grams per kilometre.

The company did not provide Serene with any fuel for private journeys.

(3) Serene contributed 5% of her gross salary of £26,400 into Backhand plc's HM Revenue and Customs' registered occupational pension scheme.

(4) In addition to her employment income, Serene received interest of £1,200 on the maturity of a savings certificate from the National Savings & Investments Bank during the tax year 2011/12. This was the actual cash amount received.

(5) Serene did not make any payments on account in respect of the tax year 2011/12.

Required:

(i) Calculate the income tax payable by Vanessa and Serene respectively for the tax year 2011/12. (11 marks)

(ii) Calculate the national insurance contributions payable by Vanessa and Serene respectively for the tax year 2011/12. (4 marks)

(iii) Calculate Vanessa and Serene's respective balancing payments for the tax year 2011/12 and their payments on account, if any, for the tax year 2012/13.

You should state the relevant due dates. (5 marks)

(b) Note that in answering this part of the question you are not expected to take account of any of the information provided in part (a) above.

Unless stated otherwise all of the figures below are exclusive of VAT.

Vanessa Serve is registered for value added tax (VAT), and is in the process of completing her VAT return for the quarter ended 30 June 2012.

The following information is available:

(1) Sales invoices totalling £18,000 were issued in respect of standard rated sales. All of Vanessa's customers are members of the general public.

(2) During the quarter ended 30 June 2012 Vanessa spent £600 on mobile telephone calls, of which 40% related to private calls.

(3) On 3 April 2012 Vanessa purchased a motor car for £12,000. On 18 June 2012 £882 was spent on repairs to the motor car.

The motor car is used by Vanessa in her business, although approximately 10% of the mileage is for private journeys. Both figures are inclusive of VAT at the standard rate.

(4) On 29 June 2012 coaching equipment was purchased for £1,760. Vanessa paid for the equipment on this date, but did not take delivery of the equipment or receive an invoice until 3 July 2012. This purchase was standard rated.

(5) In addition to the above, Vanessa also had other standard rated expenses amounting to £2,200 in the quarter ended 30 June 2012.

This figure includes £400 for entertaining UK suppliers and £200 for entertaining overseas customers.

Required:

(i) Calculate the amount of VAT payable by Vanessa for the quarter ended 30 June 2012. (5 marks)

(ii) Advise Vanessa of the conditions that she must satisfy before being permitted to use the VAT flat rate scheme, and the advantages of joining the scheme.

The relevant flat rate scheme percentage for Vanessa's trade as notified by HM Revenue and Customs for the period is 8.5%.

Your answer should be supported by appropriate calculations of the amount of tax saving if Vanessa had used the flat rate scheme to calculate the amount of VAT payable for the quarter ended 30 June 2012. (5 marks)

(Total: 30 marks)

26 ANN, BASIL AND CHLOE (ADAPTED) *Walk in the footsteps of a top tutor*

You are a trainee accountant and your manager has asked for your help regarding three taxpayers who have all made personal pension contributions during the tax year 2011/12.

Ann Peach

Ann, aged 30, is self-employed as an estate agent. Her trading profit for the year ended 5 April 2012 was £48,000. Ann made contributions of £52,000 (gross) into a personal pension scheme during the tax year 2011/12.

Basil Plum

Basil, aged 42, is employed by the Banana Bank plc as a fund manager. During the tax year 2011/12 Basil was paid a gross salary of £120,000. Basil has made monthly contributions into a personal pension plan totalling £40,000 (gross) each year for the last four years. In 2011/12 he makes total gross contributions of £50,000.

He is not a member of Banana Bank plc's occupational pension scheme but the bank contributed to Basil's personal pension in 2011/12.

Chloe Pear

Chloe, aged 54, lets out unfurnished property. For the tax year 2010/11 her property business profit was £23,900. Chloe made contributions of £8,200 (gross) into a personal pension scheme during the tax year 2011/12.

Neither Ann nor Basil nor Chloe has any other income.

Required:

(a) **For each of the three taxpayers Ann Peach, Basil Plum and Chloe Pear, state, giving reasons the amount of personal pension contributions that will have qualified for tax relief for the tax year 2011/12, and calculate their income tax liabilities for that year.**

Marks are allocated as follows:

Ann Peach 3 marks; Basil Plum 5 marks; and Chloe Pear 2 marks. **(10 marks)**

(b) **Explain the tax consequences of Banana Bank plc contributing £100,000 into Basil's personal pension in 2011/12 and the purpose of the annual allowance.** **(5 marks)**

(15 marks)

SELF ASSESSMENT

27 PI CASSO

Pi Casso has been a self-employed artist since 2001, preparing her accounts to 30 June.

Pi's tax liabilities for the tax years 2009/10, 2010/11 and 2011/12 are as follows:

	2009/10	2010/11	2011/12
	£	£	£
Income tax liability	3,240	4,100	2,730
Class 2 National Insurance contributions	120	125	130
Class 4 National Insurance contributions	1,240	1,480	990
Capital gains tax liability	–	4,880	–

No income tax has been deducted at source.

Required:

(a) **Prepare a schedule showing the payments on account and balancing payments that Pi will have made or will have to make during the period from 1 July 2011 to 31 March 2013, assuming that Pi makes any appropriate claims to reduce her payments on account.**

Your answer should clearly identify the relevant due date of each payment.

(7 marks)

(b) **State the implications if Pi had made a claim to reduce her payments on account for the tax year 2011/12 to £Nil.** **(2 marks)**

(c) **Advise Pi of the latest date by which her self-assessment tax return for the tax year 2011/12 should be submitted if she wants HM Revenue and Customs (HMRC) to prepare the self-assessment tax computation on her behalf.** **(3 marks)**

(d) **State the date by which HMRC will have to notify Pi if they intend to enquire into her self-assessment tax return for the tax year 2011/12 and the possible reasons why such an enquiry would be made.** **(3 marks)**

(Total: 15 marks)

28 ERNEST VADER *Walk in the footsteps of a top tutor*

You should assume that today's date is 30 June 2013.

You are a trainee Chartered Certified Accountant and are dealing with the tax affairs of Ernest Vader.

Ernest's self-assessment tax return for the tax year 2011/12 was submitted to HM Revenue & Customs (HMRC) on 15 May 2012, and Ernest paid the resulting income tax liability by the due date of 31 January 2013. However, you have just discovered that during the tax year 2011/12 Ernest disposed of a freehold property, the details of which were omitted from his self-assessment tax return. The capital gains tax liability in respect of this disposal is £18,000, and this amount has not been paid.

Ernest has suggested that since HMRC's right to raise an enquiry into his self-assessment tax return for the tax year 2011/12 expired on 15 May 2013, no disclosure should be made to HMRC of the capital gain.

Required:

(a) **Briefly explain the difference between tax evasion and tax avoidance, and how HMRC would view the situation if Ernest Vader does not disclose his capital gain.**

(3 marks)

(b) **Briefly explain from an ethical viewpoint how you, as a trainee Chartered Certified Accountant, should deal with the suggestion from Ernest Vader that no disclosure is made to HMRC of his capital gain.** **(3 marks)**

(c) **State the action HMRC will take should they wish to obtain information from Ernest Vader regarding his capital gain.** **(1 mark)**

(d) **Explain why, even though the right to raise an enquiry has expired, HMRC will still be entitled to raise an assessment should they discover that Ernest Vader has not disclosed his capital gain.** **(2 marks)**

(e) Assuming that HMRC discover the capital gain and raise an assessment in respect of Ernest Vader's capital gains tax liability of £18,000 for the tax year 2011/12, and that this amount is then paid on 31 July 2013:

(i) Calculate the amount of interest that will be payable;

You should assume that the rates for the tax year 2011/12 continue to apply.

(2 marks)

(ii) Advise Ernest Vader as to the amount of penalty that is likely to be charged as a result of the failure to notify HMRC, and how this could have been reduced if the capital gain had been disclosed. (4 marks)

(Total: 15 marks)

CHARGEABLE GAINS

Tutorial note:

In the new syllabus, Question 3 will be the question on capital gains and will be allocated 15 marks. Past exam questions in the old syllabus however were 20 marks.

Some of the old questions have become easier than when they were originally set with the simplification of the capital gains tax rules. These questions would now be worth 15 marks but they are still comparable to the sort of question you will see in the new syllabus.

However, more recent questions cannot be easily reduced and so they are reproduced here as they were originally set (but updated to FA2011 and are worth 20 marks).

In the new syllabus, the questions on capital gains will be very similar to these questions but they will not be as long, with possibly less disposals to deal with.

INDIVIDUALS – CAPITAL GAINS TAX

29 ALICE LIM (ADAPTED)

Alice Lim disposed of the following assets during 2011/12:

(a) On 24 June 2011 Alice sold a freehold office building for £152,000. The office building had been purchased on 2 March 2010 for £134,000.

Prior to this on 15 April 2010 Alice had sold a freehold warehouse for £149,000 making a gain of £56,000. Alice made a claim to roll over the gain arising on the disposal of the warehouse against the cost of the office building.

Both the office building and the warehouse were used entirely for business purposes in a manufacturing business run by Alice as a sole trader.

(b) On 9 January 2012 Alice sold 150,000 £1 ordinary shares in Alilim Ltd, an unquoted trading company, for £275,000.

Alilim Ltd had been formed on 17 October 2011 in order to incorporate a retail business that Alice had run as a sole trader since 18 May 2001. She became a director shareholder of the company and continued to run the business as a company.

All of the business assets were transferred to Alilim Ltd. The market value of the retail business on 17 October 2011 was £300,000. The consideration consisted of 200,000 £1 ordinary shares valued at £200,000, and £100,000 in cash.

The transfer of the business assets resulted in total chargeable gains of £120,000. This figure is before taking account of any rollover relief that was available upon incorporation.

(c) On 27 February 2012 Alice sold 40,000 £1 ordinary shares (a 40% shareholding) in Family Ltd, an unquoted trading company, for £230,000. Alice had acquired the shares on 21 May 2011 when she purchased them from her mother for £120,000.

Alice's mother had originally purchased the shares on 19 December 2002 for £128,000. Alice and her mother elected to hold over the gain arising on 21 May 2011 as a gift of a business asset. The market value of the shares on that date was £168,000.

(d) On 1 March 2012 Alice sold a house for £180,000. The property had originally been purchased on 1 April 2003 for £50,000 by Alice's husband. He transferred the property to Alice on 1 April 2007 when it was valued at £80,000. The house has always been rented out to tenants.

Required:

Calculate the chargeable gains arising from Alice's disposals during 2011/12, ignoring Entrepreneurs' relief and the annual exemption.

For part (b), also state the advice you would give to Alice to reduce her taxable gains. Calculations are not required, however you should consider Entrepreneurs' relief in your advice.

Alice is a higher rate taxpayer.

Marks for this question will be allocated on the basis of:

3 marks to (a), 7 marks to (b), 3 marks to (c) and 2 marks to part (d). **(15 marks)**

30 CHANDRA KHAN (ADAPTED)

Chandra Khan disposed of the following assets during 2011/12:

(a) On 15 June 2011 Chandra sold 10,000 £1 ordinary shares (a 30% shareholding) in Universal Ltd, an unquoted trading company, to her daughter for £75,000. The market value of the shares on this date was £110,000.

The shareholding was purchased on 10 July 1999 for £38,000. Chandra and her daughter have elected to hold over the gain as a gift of a business asset. Chandra is not employed by Universal Ltd.

(b) On 8 November 2011 Chandra sold a freehold factory for £146,000. The factory was purchased on 3 January 1999 for £72,000.

75% of the factory has been used in a manufacturing business run by Chandra as a sole trader. However, the remaining 25% of the factory has never been used for business purposes.

Chandra has claimed to rollover the gain on the factory against the replacement cost of a new freehold factory that was purchased on 10 November 2011 for £156,000. The new factory is used 100% for business purposes by Chandra.

(c) On 8 March 2012 Chandra incorporated a wholesale business that she has run as a sole trader since 1 May 2010. The market value of the business on 8 March 2012 was £250,000.

All of the business assets were transferred to a new limited company, with the consideration consisting of 200,000 £1 ordinary shares valued at £200,000 and £50,000 in cash. The only chargeable asset of the business was goodwill, and this was valued at £100,000 on 8 March 2012. The goodwill has a nil cost.

(d) On 1 April 2012 Chandra sold a house for £350,000. She had purchased the house, as her main residence, for £75,000 on 1 April 2004.

Chandra occupied the house until 1 April 2008 when she went to live with a friend. She rented out the house until it was sold on 1 April 2012.

Required:

Calculate the chargeable gains, if any, arising from Chandra's disposals during 2011/12.

Each of the four sections of this question carries equal marks (5 marks each). (20 marks)

31 MICHAEL CHIN (ADAPTED) *Online question assistance*

Michael Chin made the following gifts of assets to his daughter, Mika, during 2011/12:

(1) On 30 June 2011 Michael gave Mika a business that he had run as a sole trader since 1 January 2007. The market value of the business on 30 June 2011 was £250,000, made up as follows:

	£
Goodwill	60,000
Freehold property	150,000
Net current assets	40,000
	250,000

The goodwill has been built up since 1 January 2007, and had a nil cost. The freehold property had cost £86,000 on 20 May 2009. Michael used 75% of this property for business purposes, but the other 25% has never been used for business purposes.

(2) On 8 December 2011 Michael gave Mika his entire holding of 50,000 50p ordinary shares (a 60% holding) in Minnow Ltd, an unquoted trading company. The market value of the shares on that date was £180,000.

Michael had originally purchased the shares on 5 January 2011 for £87,500. On 8 December 2011 the market value of Minnow Ltd's chargeable assets was £250,000, of which £200,000 was in respect of chargeable business assets. Michael has never been employed by Minnow Ltd.

(3) On 15 February 2012 Michael gave Mika 18,000 £1 ordinary shares in Whale plc, a quoted trading company. On that date the shares were quoted at £6.36 – £6.52.

Michael had originally purchased 15,000 shares in Whale plc on 7 December 2010 for £63,000, and he purchased a further 12,000 shares on 21 August 2011 for £26,400. The total shareholding was less than 1% of Whale plc's issued share capital.

(4) On 28 February 2012 Michael gave Mika a painting. On that date the painting was valued at £7,500. He had originally acquired the painting on 1 June 2010 for £4,000.

(5) On 2 March 2012 Michael gave Mika five acres of land attached to an investment property. He had acquired the property, together with the land for £500,000 in May 2011. The value of the land given to Mika on 2 March 2012 was £50,000 and the value of the investment property which Michael retained was £600,000.

(6) On 15 March 2012 Michael gave Mika an antique necklace. On that date the necklace was valued at £4,000. Michael had acquired the necklace for £2,000 on 1 April 2010.

Where possible, Michael and Mika have elected to hold over any gains arising.

Michael incurred a capital loss of £16,800 during 2009/10, and made a capital gain of £11,800 during 2010/11. Michael's taxable income is £41,250.

Required:

Calculate Michael's capital gains tax liability for 2011/12, clearly showing the amount of any gains that can be held over. Ignore Entrepreneurs' relief.

You should assume that the rate of annual exemption for 2011/12 applies throughout.

(15 marks)

Online question assistance

32 PAUL OPUS (ADAPTED)

Paul Opus disposed of the following assets during the tax year 2011/12:

(1) On 10 July 2011 Paul sold 5,000 £1 ordinary shares in Symphony Ltd, an unquoted trading company, for £23,600. He had originally purchased 40,000 shares on 23 June 2008 for £110,400. Paul has never been employed by Symphony Ltd.

(2) On 15 July 2011 Paul made a gift of his entire shareholding of 10,000 £1 ordinary shares in Concerto plc to his daughter. On that date the shares were quoted on the Stock Exchange at £5.10 – £5.18, with recorded bargains of £5.00, £5.15 and £5.22. Paul's shareholding had been purchased on 29 April 1995 for £14,000. The shareholding is less than 1% of Concerto plc's issued share capital, and Paul has never been employed by Concerto plc.

(3) On 9 August 2011 Paul sold a motor car for £16,400. The motor car had been purchased on 21 January 2008 for £12,800.

(4) On 4 October 2011 Paul sold an antique vase for £8,400. The antique vase had been purchased on 19 January 2010 for £4,150.

(5) On 31 December 2011 Paul sold a house for £220,000. The house had been purchased on 1 April 2005 for £114,700. Paul occupied the house as his main residence from the date of purchase until 30 June 2008. The house was then unoccupied until it was sold on 31 December 2011.

(6) On 16 February 2012 Paul sold three acres of land for £285,000. He had originally purchased four acres of land on 17 July 2009 for £220,000. The market value of the unsold acre of land as at 16 February 2012 was £90,000.

(7) On 5 March 2012 Paul sold a freehold holiday cottage for £125,000. The cottage had originally been purchased on 28 July 2009 for £101,600 by Paul's wife. She transferred the cottage to Paul on 16 November 2010 when it was valued at £114,800.

(8) Paul has taxable income of £64,000.

Required:

(a) Compute Paul's capital gains tax liability for the tax year 2011/12, and advise him by when this should be paid. (11 marks)

(b) State the conditions necessary to obtain Entrepreneurs' relief on the disposal of shares. (3 marks)

(c) Calculate the capital gains tax reduction for Paul assuming that he did qualify for Entrepreneurs' relief on the disposal of shares in Symphony Ltd. (1 mark)

(Total: 15 marks)

33 DAVID AND ANGELA BROOK (ADAPTED) *Walk in the footsteps of a top tutor*

David and Angela Brook are a married couple. They disposed of the following assets during the tax year 2011/12:

Jointly owned property

(1) On 29 July 2011 David and Angela sold a classic Ferrari motor car for £34,400. The motor car had been purchased on 17 January 2001 for £27,200.

(2) On 30 September 2011 David and Angela sold a house for £381,900. The house had been purchased on 1 October 1991 for £86,000.

David and Angela occupied the house as their main residence from the date of purchase until 31 March 1995. The house was then unoccupied between 1 April 1995 and 31 December 1998 due to Angela being required by her employer to work elsewhere in the United Kingdom.

From 1 January 1999 until 31 December 2005 David and Angela again occupied the house as their main residence. The house was then unoccupied until it was sold on 30 September 2011.

Throughout the period 1 October 1991 to 30 September 2011 David and Angela did not have any other main residence.

David Brook

(1) On 18 April 2011 David sold an antique table for £5,600. The antique table had been purchased on 27 May 2008 for £3,200.

(2) On 5 May 2011 David transferred his entire shareholding of 20,000 £1 ordinary shares in Bend Ltd, an unquoted trading company, to Angela. On that date the shares were valued at £64,000. David's shareholding had been purchased on 21 June 2009 for £48,000.

(3) On 14 February 2012 David made a gift of 15,000 £1 ordinary shares in Galatico plc to his son. On that date the shares were quoted on the Stock Exchange at £2.90 – £3.10. David had originally purchased 8,000 shares in Galatico plc on 15 June 2010 for £17,600, and he purchased a further 12,000 shares on 24 August 2010 for £21,600. David's total shareholding was less than 1% of Galatico plc's issued share capital.

Angela Brook

(1) On 5 May 2011 Angela sold an antique clock for £7,200. The antique clock had been purchased on 14 June 2009 for £3,700.

(2) On 7 July 2011 Angela sold 15,000 of the 20,000 £1 ordinary shares in Bend Ltd that had been transferred to her from David. The sale proceeds were £62,400.

Angela has taxable income of £34,300 for the tax year 2011/12. David does not have any taxable income.

Required:

Compute David and Angela's respective capital gains tax liabilities for the tax year 2011/12. **(20 marks)**

34 WILSON BIAZMA (ADAPTED)

Wilson Biazma is resident and ordinarily resident in the United Kingdom for tax purposes. He is a higher rate taxpayer.

He disposed of the following assets during the tax year 2011/12:

(1) On 21 July 2011 Wilson sold a freehold office building for £246,000. The office building had been purchased on 3 January 1993 for £104,000. Wilson has made a claim to rollover the gain on the office building against the replacement cost of a new freehold office building that was purchased on 14 January 2011 for £136,000. Both office buildings have always been used entirely for business purposes in a wholesale business run by Wilson as a sole trader.

(2) On 26 July 2011 Wilson incorporated a retail business that he had run as a sole trader since 1 June 2007. The market value of the business on 26 July 2011 was £200,000. All of the business assets were transferred to a new limited company, with the consideration consisting of 140,000 £1 ordinary shares valued at £140,000 and £60,000 in cash.

The only chargeable asset of the business was goodwill and this was valued at £120,000 on 26 July 2011. The goodwill has a nil cost. Wilson claimed Entrepreneurs' relief, but elected to disapply incorporation relief.

(3) On 17 August 2011 Wilson made a gift of his entire holding of 10,000 £1 ordinary shares (a 100% holding) in Gandua Ltd, an unquoted trading company, to his daughter. The market value of the shares on that date was £160,000. The shares had been purchased on 8 January 2011 for £112,000. On 17 August 2011 the market value of Gandua Ltd's chargeable assets was £180,000, of which £150,000 was in respect of chargeable business assets. Wilson and his daughter have elected to hold over the gain on this gift of a business asset. Wilson has never worked for Gandua Ltd.

(4) On 3 October 2011 an antique vase owned by Wilson was destroyed in a fire. The antique vase had been purchased on 7 November 2008 for £49,000. Wilson received insurance proceeds of £68,000 on 20 December 2011 and on 22 December 2011 he paid £69,500 for a replacement antique vase. Wilson has made a claim to defer the gain arising from the receipt of the insurance proceeds.

(5) On 9 March 2012 Wilson sold ten acres of land for £85,000. He had originally purchased twenty acres of land on 29 June 2003 for £120,000. The market value of the unsold ten acres of land as at 9 March 2012 was £65,000. The land has never been used for business purposes.

Required:

(a) Briefly explain when a person will be treated as resident or ordinarily resident in the United Kingdom for a particular tax year and state how a person's residence status establishes whether or not they are liable to capital gains tax.

You are not expected to explain the rules concerning people leaving or coming to the United Kingdom. (4 marks)

(b) Calculate Wilson's capital gains tax liability for 2011/12, clearly identifying the effects of the reliefs claimed in respect of disposals (1) to (4). (16 marks)

(Total: 20 marks)

35 NIM AND MAE LOM (ADAPTED) *Walk in the footsteps of a top tutor*

Nim and Mae Lom are a married couple. They disposed of the following assets during the tax year 2011/12:

Nim Lom

(1) On 20 July 2011 Nim made a gift of 10,000 £1 ordinary shares in Kapook plc to his daughter. On that date the shares were quoted on the Stock Exchange at £3·70 – £3·90, with recorded bargains of £3·60, £3·75 and £3·80. Nim has made the following purchases of shares in Kapook plc:

19 February 2003	8,000 shares for £16,200
6 June 2008	6,000 shares for £14,600
24 July 2011	2,000 shares for £5,800

Nim's total shareholding was less than 5% of Kapook plc, and so holdover relief is not available.

(2) On 13 August 2011 Nim transferred his entire shareholding of 5,000 £1 ordinary shares in Jooba Ltd, an unquoted company, to his wife, Mae. On that date the shares were valued at £28,200. Nim's shareholding had been purchased on 11 January 2009 for £16,000.

(3) On 26 November 2011 Nim sold an antique table for £8,700. The antique table had been purchased on 16 May 2007 for £5,200.

(4) On 2 April 2012 Nim sold UK Government securities (Gilts) for £12,400. The securities had been purchased on 18 August 2009 for £10,100.

Mae Lom

(1) On 28 August 2011 Mae sold 2,000 of the 5,000 £1 ordinary shares in Jooba Ltd that had been transferred to her from Nim (see (2) above). The sale proceeds were £30,400. Entrepreneurs' relief is not available in respect of this disposal.

(2) On 30 September 2011 Mae sold a house for £186,000. The house had been purchased on 1 October 2001 for £122,000.

Throughout the period of ownership the house was occupied by Nim and Mae as their main residence, but one of the house's eight rooms was always used exclusively for business purposes by Mae.

Entrepreneurs' relief is not available in respect of this disposal.

(3) On 30 November 2011 Mae sold a business that she had run as a sole trader since 1 December 2003. The sale resulted in the following capital gains:

	£
Goodwill	80,000
Freehold office building	136,000
Investment property	34,000

The assets were all owned for more than one year prior to the date of disposal. The investment property has always been rented out.

Mae claimed Entrepreneurs' relief in respect of this disposal.

(4) On 31 March 2012 Mae sold a copyright for £9,600. The copyright had been purchased on 1 April 2007 for £10,000 when it had an unexpired life of 20 years.

Other information

Nim does not have any taxable income for the tax year 2011/12. He has unused capital losses of £16,700 brought forward from the tax year 2010/11.

Mae has taxable income of £30,000 for the tax year 2011/12. She has unused capital losses of £8,500 brought forward from the tax year 2010/11.

Required:

Compute Nim and Mae Lom's respective capital gains tax liabilities, if any, for the tax year 2011/12.

In each case, the amount of unused capital losses carried forward to future tax years, if any, should be clearly identified. **(Total: 20 marks)**

36 AMANDA, BO AND CHARLES *Walk in the footsteps of a top tutor*

You are a trainee accountant and your manager has asked for your help regarding three taxpayers who have all disposed of assets during the tax year 2011/12.

(a) **Amanda Moon**

On 30 June 2011 Amanda incorporated a business. She had run the business as a sole trader since 1 July 2005. The market value of the business assets on 30 June 2011 was £300,000.

This figure, along with the respective cost of each asset, is made up as follows:

	Market value	*Cost*
	£	£
Goodwill	90,000	Nil
Freehold shop	165,000	120,000
Net current assets	45,000	45,000
	300,000	

The freehold shop has always been used by Amanda for business purposes. All of the business assets were transferred to a new limited company, Ammoon Ltd, with the consideration consisting of 300,000 £1 ordinary shares valued at £300,000. Amanda took full advantage of the available incorporation relief.

Required:

(i) Calculate Amanda Moon's chargeable gains, if any, for the tax year 2011/12, and the base cost of her 300,000 £1 ordinary shares in Ammoon Ltd. **(4 marks)**

(ii) Explain how your answer to (i) above would have differed if the consideration for the transfer of Amanda Moon's business had instead consisted of 200,000 £1 ordinary shares and £100,000 in cash. **(3 marks)**

You should ignore Entrepreneurs' relief.

(b) **Bo Neptune**

On 31 July 2011 Bo made a gift of his entire holding of 50,000 £1 ordinary shares (a 100% holding) in Botune Ltd, an unquoted trading company, to his son. The market value of the shares on that date was £210,000. The shares had been purchased by Bo on 22 January 2005 for £94,000. Bo and his son have elected to hold over the gain as a gift of a business asset.

Required:

(i) Calculate Bo Neptune's chargeable gain, if any, for the tax year 2011/12, and the base cost of his son's 50,000 £1 ordinary shares in Botune Ltd. (3 marks)

(ii) Explain how your answer to (i) above would have differed if the shares in Botune Ltd had instead been sold to Bo Neptune's son for £160,000. (2 marks)

You should ignore Entrepreneurs' relief.

(c) **Charles Orion**

On 30 September 2011 Charles sold a house for £282,000. The house had been purchased on 1 October 1999 for £110,000.

He occupied the house as his main residence from the date of purchase until 31 March 2001. The house was unoccupied between 1 April 2001 and 31 December 2009 when Charles went to live with his parents due to his father's illness. From 1 January 2010 until 30 September 2011 Charles again occupied the house as his main residence.

Throughout the period 1 October 1999 to 30 September 2011 Charles did not have any other main residence.

Required:

(i) Calculate Charles Orion's chargeable gain, if any, for the tax year 2011/12. (5 marks)

(ii) Explain how your answer to (i) above would have differed if Charles Orion had rented out his house during the period 1 April 2001 to 31 December 2009. (3 marks)

(Total: 20 marks)

COMPANIES – CHARGEABLE GAINS

37 FORWARD LTD (ADAPTED)

(i) Forward Ltd sold the following assets during the year ended 31 March 2012:

(1) On 31 May 2011 Forward Ltd sold a freehold office building for £290,000. The office building had been purchased on 15 July 1992 for £148,000. The retail price index (RPI) for July 1992 was 138.8, and for May 2011 it was 234.8.

Forward Ltd purchased a replacement freehold office building on 1 June 2011 for £260,000.

(2) On 30 November 2011 Forward Ltd sold 5,000 £1 ordinary shares in Backward plc for £62,500. Forward Ltd had originally purchased 9,000 shares in Backward plc on 20 April 1986 for £18,000, and purchased a further 500 shares on 1 November 2011 for £6,500. Assume the retail price index for April 1986 was 97.7, and for November 2011 it was 238.2.

Forward Ltd purchased 10,000 £1 ordinary shares in Sideways plc on 1 December 2011 for £65,000.

(ii) On 1 May 1997 Forward Ltd had purchased a painting for the conference room for £15,000. On 1 December 2011, when it was worth £45,000, the painting was damaged. After the damage the painting was worth £20,000. Insurance proceeds of £22,000 were received on 1 February 2012. The proceeds were not used to repair the painting. Assume the retail price index for May 1997 was 156.9, for December 2011 was 239.8 and for February 2012 was 242.9.

Where possible, Forward Ltd has claimed to roll over any gains arising.

Forward Ltd's only other income for the year ended 31 March 2012 is its tax adjusted trading profit of £78,000. There are no associated companies.

Required:

(a) **Calculate Forward Ltd's corporation tax liability for the year ended 31 March 2012, and state by when this should be paid.**

Your answer should clearly identify the amount of any gains that have been rolled over. Capital allowances should be ignored. **(12 marks)**

(b) **Explain how Forward Ltd's rollover relief claim would have altered if on 1 June 2011 it had acquired a leasehold office building on a 15-year lease for £300,000, rather than purchasing the freehold office building for £260,000.** **(3 marks)**

(Total: 15 marks)

38 HAWK LTD *Walk in the footsteps of a top tutor*

Hawk Ltd sold the following assets during the year ended 31 March 2012:

(1) On 30 April 2011 a freehold office building was sold for £260,000. The office building had been purchased on 2 July 1991 for £81,000, and had been extended at a cost of £43,000 during May 2003.

Hawk Ltd incurred legal fees of £3,200 in connection with the purchase of the office building, and legal fees of £3,840 in connection with the disposal. The office building has always been used by Hawk Ltd for business purposes.

The relevant retail prices indexes (RPIs) are as follows:

July 1991	133.8
May 2003	181.5
April 2011	233.9

(2) On 29 August 2011 5,000 £1 ordinary shares in Albatross plc were sold for £42,500. Hawk Ltd had purchased 6,000 shares in Albatross plc on 1 August 2011 for £18,600, and purchased a further 2,000 shares on 17 August 2011 for £9,400.

(3) On 27 October 2011 10,000 £1 preference shares in Cuckoo plc were sold for £32,000. Hawk Ltd had originally purchased 5,000 £1 ordinary shares in Cuckoo plc on 2 October 2011 for £60,000. On 18 October 2011 Cuckoo plc had a reorganisation whereby each £1 ordinary share was exchanged for three new £1 ordinary shares and two £1 preference shares. Immediately after the reorganisation each new £1 ordinary share was quoted at £4.50 and each £1 preference share was quoted at £2.25.

(4) On 28 March 2012 two acres of land were sold for £120,000. Hawk Ltd had originally purchased three acres of land on 1 March 2012 for £203,500. The market value of the unsold acre of land as at 28 March 2012 was £65,000.

Hawk Ltd's only other income for the year ended 31 March 2012 was a trading profit of £125,000.

Hawk Ltd does not have any associated companies.

Required:

(a) **Calculate Hawk Ltd's corporation tax liability for the year ended 31 March 2012.** **(16 marks)**

(b) Advise Hawk Ltd of:

(i) The minimum amount that will have to be reinvested in qualifying replacement business assets in order for the company to claim the maximum possible amount of rollover relief in respect of its chargeable gains for the year ended 31 March 2012. (2 marks)

(ii) The period during which the reinvestment must take place. (1 mark)

(iii) The amount of corporation tax that will be deferred if the maximum possible amount of rollover relief is claimed for the year ended 31 March 2012. (1 mark)

(Total: 20 marks)

39 PROBLEMATIC LTD *Walk in the footsteps of a top tutor*

Timed question with Online tutor debrief

Problematic Ltd sold the following assets during the year ended 31 March 2012:

(1) On 14 June 2011 16,000 £1 ordinary shares in Easy plc were sold for £54,400. Problematic Ltd had originally purchased 15,000 shares in Easy plc on 26 June 1994 for £12,600. On 28 September 2006 Easy plc made a 1 for 3 rights issue.

Problematic Ltd took up its allocation under the rights issue in full, paying £2.20 for each new share issued.

The relevant retail prices indexes (RPIs) are as follows:

June 1994	144.7
September 2006	200.1
June 2011	235.3

(2) On 1 October 2011 an office building owned by Problematic Ltd was damaged by a fire. The indexed cost of the office building on that date was £169,000. The company received insurance proceeds of £36,000 on 10 October 2011, and spent a total of £41,000 during October 2011 on restoring the office building. Problematic Ltd has made a claim to defer the gain arising from the receipt of the insurance proceeds. The office building has never been used for business purposes.

(3) On 28 January 2012 a freehold factory was sold for £171,000. The indexed cost of the factory on that date was £127,000. Problematic Ltd has made a claim to holdover the gain on the factory against the cost of a replacement leasehold factory under the rollover relief (replacement of business assets) rules. The leasehold factory has a lease period of 20 years, and was purchased on 10 December 2011 for £154,800. The two factory buildings have always been used entirely for business purposes.

(4) On 20 February 2012 an acre of land was sold for £130,000. Problematic Ltd had originally purchased four acres of land, and the indexed cost of the four acres on 20 February 2012 was £300,000. The market value of the unsold three acres of land as at 20 February 2012 was £350,000. Problematic Ltd incurred legal fees of £3,200 in connection with the disposal. The land has never been used for business purposes.

Problematic Ltd's only other income for the year ended 31 March 2012 is a tax adjusted trading profit of £108,056.

Required:

(a) Calculate Problematic Ltd's taxable total profits for the year ended 31 March 2012. **(16 marks)**

(b) Advise Problematic Ltd of the carried forward indexed base costs for capital gains purposes of any assets included in (1) to (4) above that are still retained at 31 March 2012. **(4 marks)**

(Total: 20 marks)

Calculate your allowed time, allocate the time to the separate parts....................

INHERITANCE TAX

40 BRUCE VINCENT

Bruce Vincent died in August 2011 owning the following assets and owing the following liabilities:

	£
Assets:	
House	450,000
Holiday cottage	280,000
Quoted shares	145,000
Bank and cash	10,000
Personal chattels	50,000
Liabilities:	
Mortgage (interest only)	100,000
Credit card debt	12,000
Outstanding income tax	8,000

The executors paid £7,500 in funeral expenses and £4,500 in executor's fees.

Bruce left £10,000 to his wife, who is independently wealthy, and the remainder of the estate to his son.

During his lifetime he made the following gifts:

1. January 2007: Gift to a trust for £350,000
2. May 2008: Gift to nephew for £100,000.

Bruce paid any IHT arising on the gift to the trust.

Required:

Calculate the inheritance tax payable during Bruce's lifetime and as a result of his death. State the due dates of payment and who will pay the tax in each case.

The nil rate bands for earlier years are as follows:

2006/07	**£285,000**
2008/09	**£312,000**

(15 marks)

41 PETER DAY

Peter died on 3 November 2011. He had made the following lifetime gifts:

(1) On 1 May 2007 he gave a cash gift of £500 to his granddaughter.

(2) On 1 June 2008 he gave his nephew a gift of £7,500 on the occasion of his marriage.

(3) On 1 July 2008 he gave cash of £337,000 to a trust. Peter agreed to pay any tax liabilities arising from this transfer.

At the date of his death Peter owned the following assets:

(1) A house that he has always lived in worth £210,000. This has an outstanding interest only mortgage of £40,000

(2) Ordinary shares in Beach plc worth £50,000

(3) Funds held in cash ISA cash bank accounts of £45,000.

(4) Car worth £10,000.

He had taken out a loan to acquire the car. The balance outstanding on the loan at 3 November 2011 was £2,000.

Funeral expenses amounted to £6,000.

Peter left £150,000 to his wife and the balance of his estate to his son.

Required:

(a) Calculate the inheritance tax payable during Peter's lifetime and as a result of his death. (13 marks)

(b) State the due dates of payment and who will pay the tax in each case. (2 marks)

The nil rate bands for earlier years are as follows:

2007/08 £300,000

2008/09 £312,000

(15 marks)

42 PAUL MASTERS

Paul Masters, due to ill health, is expected to die in the near future. You should assume that today's date is 31 December 2011.

The current value of his estate, and forecast value for 12 months time, is as follows:

	Present value	Forecast value
	£	£
20,000 shares (1% holding) in Banjo plc, a quoted company	50,000	45,000
8,000 shares (2% holding) in Guitar plc, a quoted company	70,000	85,000
Main residence	330,000	350,000
Holiday cottage	130,000	110,000
	580,000	590,000

Under the terms of the will, Paul left all of his assets to his son. His son has two children.

Paul's wife is also ill, and it not expected to live for more than three months. She does not have any assets of her own, but Paul is confident that his son will look after her upon his death.

Paul has made the following transfers of value during his lifetime:

1. On 1 November 2003, he made a gift of £203,000 into a trust. The trust paid any IHT arising on the gift.
2. On 1 October 2008, he gave his son £150,000 as a wedding gift.
3. On 1 July 2009, he gave £200 to a niece.

Required:

(a) Calculate the IHT liabilities that would arise if Paul were to die on 31 December 2011 and state the relevant due dates of payment.

The nil rate bands for earlier years are as follows:

2003/04	**£255,000**
2008/09	**£312,000**
2009/10	**£325,000**

(10 marks)

(b) Explain:

(i) The main advantages in lifetime giving for IHT purposes.

(ii) The main factors that need to be considered in deciding which assets to gift.

(5 marks)

(15 marks)

43 HENRY HIGGINS *Walk in the footsteps of a top tutor*

Timed question with Online tutor debrief

Henry Higgins, aged 70, died on 5 October 2011. He was survived by his wife, Sally, also aged 70, and two children, Cecil and Ida.

Sally is herself in a frail condition and not expected to live for much longer. Both Cecil and Ida have children of their own and are relatively wealthy in their own right.

Henry owned the following assets:

1. 100,000 £1 ordinary shares in Petal plc, a quoted company, with an issued share capital of 10,000,000 £1 ordinary shares.

   On 5 October 2011, the value of these shares was 202 p per share.
2. £20,000 20% Government Stock valued at £20,100.
3. The following capital deposits both of which have been held for several years:
   - £25,000 deposited with a building society
   - £18,000 invested in an ISA account.
4. A house valued on 5 October 2011 at £450,000. This property was his and Sally's family home but was owned outright by Henry.

Under the terms of his will, Henry has left £20,000 to Cecil, £675,000 to his wife and the remainder of his estate to Ida. Sally's will currently leaves her estate equally to their two children.

The only gifts made by Henry during his lifetime were cash gifts of £181,000 on 1 January 2004 and £164,000 on 1 January 2007 respectively. Both gifts were made to a trust. Henry had agreed to pay any inheritance tax arising on these lifetime gifts.

Henry was due an income tax repayment for 2011/12 of £821.

Required:

(a) Calculate the inheritance tax liabilities arising:

(i) From the lifetime gifts of cash into the trust; (5 marks), and

(ii) Arising as a consequence of Henry's death on 5 October 2011. (7 marks)

(b) Explain the tax implications of the executors of Sally's estate claiming to transfer Harry's unused nil rate band to Sally on her death.

State the date by which such an election must be made. (3 marks)

The nil rate bands for earlier years are as follows:

2003/04	**£255,000**
2006/07	**£285,000**

(15 marks)

Calculate your allowed time, allocate the time to the separate parts....................

44 HELGA EVANS *Walk in the footsteps of a top tutor*

Assume today's date is 30 June 2012.

Helga is aged 78 years. She is married to Gordon, who is independently wealthy in his own right. They have one child, Louise.

Helga has unfortunately recently become terminally ill and is expected to live for only another four years.

She owns the following assets:

1. 10,000 ordinary £1 shares in Starling plc, a quoted UK resident trading company with an issued share capital of 1 million ordinary shares. The shares are currently valued at £14.62 p per share.
2. A 25% interest in £100,000 10% loan stock in Wren plc, currently valued at £25,750.
3. Main residence valued at £500,000.
4. Cash deposits amount to £151,333.
5. Sundry personal chattels collectively worth £20,000.

Under the terms of Helga's will, all of her assets are to be left to Louise with the exception of the house and her sundry personal chattels which are bequeathed to Gordon.

Due to her failing health, Helga and her family are considering whether she should either:

(i) Gift all of her assets, with the exception of the house and her sundry personal chattels, to Louise upon her death in four years time, or

(ii) Make these gifts to Louise now.

In four years time her assets are expected to be valued at the following amounts for inheritance tax purposes:

	£
Starling plc shares	200,000
25% of the Wren loan stock	25,000
Residence	600,000
Antique plates	10,000
Cash deposits	170,000
Sundry personal chattels	20,000
	1,025,000

The only previous gift made by Helga was a cash gift, net of annual exemptions, of £360,000 made to Louise in September 2010.

Required:

Advise Helga whether she should:

(i) Make the transfers of the selected assets to Louise upon her death in four years time, or

(ii) Make the transfers on 6 July 2012.

Your answer should consider the likely IHT implications and should include a calculation of any tax likely to arise under each option.

You should assume that the rates and allowances for 2011/12 continue to apply.

The nil rate band for 2010/11 was £325,000. (15 marks)

CORPORATION TAX

CORPORATION TAX BASICS AND ADMINISTRATION

45 ARABLE LTD (ADAPTED)

Arable Ltd commenced trading on 1 February 2011 as a manufacturer of farm equipment, preparing its first accounts for the nine-month period ended 31 October 2011. The following information is available:

Trading profit

The tax adjusted trading profit is £301,189. This figure is before taking account of capital allowances and any deduction arising from the premiums paid in respect of leasehold property.

Plant and machinery

Arable Ltd purchased the following assets in respect of the nine-month period ended 31 October 2011.

		£
5 January 2011	Machinery	31,000
18 January 2011	Building alterations necessary for the installation of the machinery	3,700
20 April 2011	Lorry	22,000
12 June 2011	Motor car (1)	11,200
14 June 2011	Motor car (2)	14,600
17 June 2011	Motor car (3)	13,000
29 October 2011	Computer	5,400

Motor car (1) purchased on 12 June 2011 for £11,200 has a CO_2 emission rate of 136 grams per kilometre. Motor car (2) purchased on 14 June 2011 for £14,600 has a CO_2 emission rate of 168 grams per kilometre. Motor car (3), purchased on 17 June 2011 for £13,000, has CO_2 emissions of 109 grams per kilometre.

The company will not make any short life asset elections.

Leasehold property

On 1 February 2011 Arable Ltd acquired two leasehold office buildings. In each case a premium of £75,000 was paid for the grant of a 15-year lease.

The first office building was used for business purposes by Arable Ltd throughout the period ended 31 October 2011.

The second office building was empty until 31 July 2011, and was then sub-let to a tenant. On that date Arable Ltd received a premium of £50,000 for the grant of a five-year lease, and annual rent of £14,800 which was payable in advance.

Loan interest received

Loan interest of £6,000 was received on 31 July 2011, and £3,000 was accrued at 31 October 2011. The loan was made for non-trading purposes.

Dividends received

During the period ended 31 October 2011 Arable Ltd received dividends of £18,000 from Ranch plc, an unconnected UK company. This figure was the actual cash amount received.

Profit on disposal of shares

On 5 October 2011 Arable Ltd sold 10,000 £1 ordinary shares in Ranch plc for £37,576. Arable Ltd had originally purchased 15,000 shares in Ranch plc on 10 May 2011 for £12,000. A further 5,000 shares were purchased on 20 August 2011 for £11,250. Arable Ltd's shareholding never represented more than a 1% interest in Ranch plc.

Assume that the relevant indexation factors are as follows:

May 2011	234.8
August 2011	235.8
October 2011	237.1

Other information

Arable Ltd has two associated companies.

Required:

(a) Calculate Arable Ltd's corporation tax liability for the nine-month period ended 31 October 2011. (27 marks)

(b) State the date by which Arable Ltd's self-assessment corporation tax return for the period ended 31 October 2011 should be submitted, and explain how the company can correct the return if it is subsequently found to contain an error or mistake.

(3 marks)

(Total: 30 marks)

46 ZOOM PLC (ADAPTED) *Online question assistance*

Zoom plc is a manufacturer of photographic equipment. The company had taxable total profits of £820,840 for the year ended 31 March 2012.

The income statement of Zoom plc for the year ended 31 March 2012 shows:

	£	£
Operating profit (Note 1)		812,500
Other operating income (Note 3)		16,400
Income from investments		
Bank interest (Note 4)	10,420	
Loan interest (Note 5)	22,500	
Income from property (Note 6)	44,680	
Dividends (Note 7)	49,500	
		127,100
		956,000
Interest payable (Note 8)		(46,000)
Profit before taxation		910,000

Note 1 – Operating profit

Depreciation of £59,160 has been deducted in arriving at the operating profit of £812,500.

Note 2 – Plant and machinery

On 1 April 2011 the tax written down values of plant and machinery were as follows:

	£
General pool	19,600
Expensive motor car	20,200

The following transactions took place during the year ended 31 March 2012:

		Cost/Proceeds £
15 April 2011	Purchased equipment	54,600
19 July 2011	Purchased computer	12,300
29 July 2011	Sold expensive motor car	(23,200)
30 July 2011	Purchased motor car (1)	16,600
3 August 2011	Sold a lorry	(9,800)
22 December 2011	Purchased motor car (2)	11,850
1 February 2012	Purchased motor car (3)	14,200
28 February 2012	Sold equipment (original cost £1,900)	(1,000)

Motor car (1) purchased on 30 July 2011 for £16,600 has a CO_2 emission rate of 170 grams per kilometre. Motor car (2) purchased on 22 December 2011 for £11,850 has a CO_2 emission rate of 156 grams per kilometre. Motor car (3), purchased on 1 February 2012 for £14,200, has CO_2 emissions of 106 grams per kilometre.

The expensive motor car sold on 29 July 2011 for £23,200 originally cost £29,200. The lorry sold on 3 August 2011 for £9,800 originally cost £17,200.

Note 3 – Other operating income

The other operating income consists of trade-related patent royalties that were received during the year ended 31 March 2012.

Note 4 – Bank interest received

The bank interest was received on 31 March 2012. The bank deposits are held for non-trading purposes.

Note 5 – Loan interest receivable

The loan was made for non-trading purposes on 1 July 2011. Loan interest of £15,000 was received on 30 December 2011, and interest of £7,500 was accrued at 31 March 2012.

Note 6 – Income from property

Zoom plc lets out two unfurnished office buildings that are surplus to requirements.

The first office building was let from 1 April 2011 until 31 January 2012 at a rent of £3,200 per month. On 31 January 2012 the tenant left owing two months' rent which Zoom plc was unable to recover. This office building was not re-let until May 2012.

The second office building was not let from 1 April 2011 to 31 July 2011. During this period Zoom plc spent £4,800 on advertising for new tenants, and £5,200 on decorating the office building. On 1 August 2011 the office building was let at an annual rent of £26,400, payable in advance.

Zoom plc insured its two office buildings at a total cost of £3,360 for the year ended 31 December 2011, and £3,720 for the year ended 31 December 2012. The insurance is payable annually in advance.

Note 7 – Dividends received

The dividends were all received from unconnected UK companies. The figure of £49,500 is the actual cash amount received.

Note 8 – Interest payable

The interest is in respect of a loan note that has been used for trading purposes. Interest of £23,000 was paid on 30 September 2011 and again on 31 March 2012.

Note 9 – Other information

Zoom plc made quarterly instalment payments in respect of its corporation tax liability for the year ended 31 March 2011.

Zoom plc has three associated companies.

For the year ended 31 March 2011 Zoom plc had taxable total profits of £780,000.

Required:

(a) (i) Calculate the amount of capital allowances that Zoom plc can claim for the year ended 31 March 2012. (12 marks)

(ii) Prepare a computation for the year ended 31 March 2012 reconciling Zoom plc's profit before taxation with its taxable total profits.

Your reconciliation should commence with the profit before taxation figure of £910,000, clearly identify the tax adjusted trading profit and the amount of property business profit, and end with the figure of £820,840 for taxable total profits.

You should list all of the items referred to in Notes (1) and (3) to (8) that are relevant, indicating by use of zero (0) any items that do not require adjustment. (8 marks)

(b) Explain why Zoom plc was required to make quarterly instalment payments in respect of its corporation tax liability for the year ended 31 March 2012. (3 marks)

(c) Calculate Zoom plc's corporation tax liability for the year ended 31 March 2012 and explain how and when this will have been paid.

You should assume that the company's taxable total profits of £820,840 accrued evenly throughout the year. (3 marks)

(d) **Explain how your answer to part (c) above would differ if Zoom plc had no associated companies.**

Your answer should include a calculation of the revised corporation tax liability for the year ended 31 March 2012. **(4 marks)**

(Total: 30 marks)

Online question assistance

47 BALLPOINT LTD (ADAPTED) *Walk in the footsteps of a top tutor*

Ballpoint Ltd is a manufacturer of pens and other writing implements in the UK. The company is incorporated overseas, although its directors are based in the UK and hold their board meetings in the UK.

Ballpoint Ltd's summarised income statement for the year ended 31 March 2012 is:

	£	£
Gross profit		968,388
Operating expenses:		
Depreciation	71,488	
Gifts and donations (Note 1)	4,100	
Repairs and renewals (Note 2)	40,800	
Professional fees (Note 3)	8,800	
Car lease costs (Note 4)	4,000	
Other expenses (Note 5)	330,000	
		(459,188)
Operating profit		509,200
Income from investments: Dividends (Note 6)		45,000
Profit from sale of fixed assets: Disposal of factory (Note 7)		60,000
		614,200
Interest payable (Note 8)		(94,200)
Profit before taxation		520,000

Note 1 – Gifts and donations

	£
Gifts to customers (pens costing £20 each displaying Ballpoint Ltd's name)	2,040
Gifts to customers (food hampers costing £35 each)	770
Gifts to employees	270
Donation to a national charity (made under the Gift Aid scheme)	600
Donation to a local charity (Ballpoint Ltd received free advertising in the charity's magazine)	120
Donation to a political party	300
	4,100

Note 2 – Repairs and renewals

The figure of £40,800 for repairs and renewals includes £14,800 for replacing the roof of a warehouse, which was in a bad state of repair, and £13,900 for initial repairs to an office building that was acquired on 20 March 2011.

The office building was not usable until the repairs were carried out, and this fact was reflected by a reduced purchase price.

Note 3 – Professional fees

	£
Accountancy and audit fee	2,300
Legal fees in connection with the issue of share capital	3,100
Legal fees in connection with the issue of a loan note to purchase machinery that was subsequently cancelled	1,800
Legal fees in connection with the defence of the company's internet domain name	1,600
	8,800

Note 4 – Car lease costs

Ballpoint Ltd leases a car for its production manager at a cost of £4,000 p.a. The car has a CO_2 emission rate of 159 grams per kilometre.

Note 5 – Other expenses

The figure of £330,000 for other expenses includes £3,700 for entertaining overseas customers, £1,700 for entertaining employees, £400 for counselling services provided to an employee who was made redundant, and a fine of £2,600 for publishing a misleading advertisement. The remaining expenses are all allowable.

Note 6 – Dividends received

During the year ended 31 March 2012 Ballpoint Ltd received dividends of £27,000 from Paper Ltd, an unconnected UK company, and dividends of £18,000 from Pencil Ltd, its 100% UK subsidiary company. Both figures are the actual cash amounts received.

Note 7 – Disposal of factory

The profit of £60,000 is in respect of a factory that was sold on 30 June 2011 for £300,000.

The factory had been purchased on 1 April 2007 for £240,000. The indexation allowance from April 2007 to June 2011 is £35,040.

Note 8 – Interest payable

The interest payable is in respect of the company's loan note that was issued in the year 2006. The proceeds of the issue were used to finance the company's trading activities. Interest of £47,100 was paid on 30 September 2011 and again on 31 March 2012.

Note 9 – Plant and machinery

On 1 April 2011 the tax written down values of plant and machinery were as follows:

	£
General pool	8,200
Expensive motor car	9,800

The following transactions took place during the year ended 31 March 2012:

		Cost/ (Proceeds)
		£
2 May 2011	Purchased equipment	61,260
4 June 2011	Purchased motor car (1)	18,200
4 June 2011	Purchased motor car (2)	11,400
4 June 2010	Purchased motor car (3)	9,200
18 August 2011	Purchased equipment	4,300
12 November 2011	Sold equipment	(2,700)
20 December 2011	Sold motor car (2)	(10,110)

Motor car (1) purchased for £18,200 has a CO_2 emission rate of 164 grams per kilometre. Motor car (2) purchased for £11,400 has a CO_2 emission rate of 149 grams per kilometre. Motor car (3) purchased for £9,200 has CO_2 emissions of 102 grams per kilometre.

The equipment sold on 12 November 2011 for £2,700 was originally purchased for £13,800 on 10 July 2007.

Note 10 – Group relief

For the year ended 31 March 2012 Ballpoint Ltd has claimed group relief of £42,000 from its 100% subsidiary company, Pencil Ltd.

Note 11 – Other information

Ballpoint Ltd has only one associated company, Pencil Ltd.

Required:

(a) **Explain why Ballpoint Ltd is treated as being resident in the United Kingdom, and state what difference it would make if the directors were based overseas and were to hold their board meetings overseas.** **(3 marks)**

(b) **Calculate Ballpoint Ltd's tax adjusted trading profit for the year ended 31 March 2012.**

Your computation should commence with the profit before taxation figure of £520,000, and should list all of the items referred to in Notes (1) to (8) indicating by the use of zero (0) any items that do not require adjustment. **(20 marks)**

(c) **Calculate Ballpoint Ltd's corporation tax liability for the year ended 31 March 2012.** **(7 marks)**

(Total: 30 marks)

48 DO-NOT-PANIC LTD (ADAPTED)

Do-Not-Panic Ltd is a United Kingdom resident company that installs burglar alarms.

The company commenced trading on 1 January 2011 and its results for the fifteen-month period ended 31 March 2012 are summarised as follows:

(1) The trading profit as adjusted for tax purposes is £315,000. This figure is before taking account of capital allowances.

(2) Do-Not-Panic Ltd purchased equipment for £24,000 on 20 February 2011.

(3) On 21 December 2011 Do-Not-Panic Ltd disposed of some investments and this resulted in a capital loss of £4,250. On 28 March 2012 the company made a further disposal and this resulted in a chargeable gain of £42,000.

(4) Franked investment income of £25,000 was received on 22 February 2012.

Do-Not-Panic Ltd has no associated companies.

Required:

(a) **Calculate Do-Not-Panic Ltd's corporation tax liabilities in respect of the fifteen-month period ended 31 March 2012 and advise the company by when these should be paid.** **(10 marks)**

(b) **Calculate Do-Not-Panic Ltd's corporation tax liabilities and advise the company by when these should be paid, assuming that instead of producing a fifteen-month period of account, they decided to produce:**

- **a three month set of accounts to 31 March 2011, and then**
- **a twelve month set of accounts to 31 March 2012.**

Assume that trading profits accrue evenly over the fifteen month period. **(9 marks)**

(c) **State which approach will give the lower total tax bill.** **(1 mark)**

(20 marks)

49 GASTRON LTD *Walk in the footsteps of a top tutor*

Gastron Ltd, a United Kingdom resident company, is a luxury food manufacturer.

Its summarised income statement for the year ended 31 March 2012 is as follows:

	Note	£	£
Gross profit			876,500
Operating expenses			
Depreciation		85,660	
Amortisation of leasehold property	1	6,000	
Gift and donations	2	2,700	
Professional fees	3	18,800	
Other expenses	4	230,240	
			(343,400)
Operating profit			533,100
Income from investments			
Income from property	5	20,600	
Bank interest	6	12,400	
Dividends	7	54,000	
			87,000
Profit from sale of fixed assets			
Disposal of shares	8		80,700
			700,800
Interest payable	9		(60,800)
Profit before taxation			640,000

Note 1 – Leasehold property

On 1 April 2011 Gastron Ltd acquired a leasehold office building, paying a premium of £60,000 for the grant of a new ten-year lease. The office building was used for business purposes by Gastron Ltd throughout the year ended 31 March 2012. No legal costs were incurred by Gastron Ltd in respect of this lease.

Note 2 – Gifts and donations

Gifts and donations are as follows:

	£
Gifts to customers (pens costing £60 each and displaying Gastron Ltd's name)	1,200
Gifts to customers (hampers of food costing £25 each)	1,100
Donation to local charity	
(Gastron Ltd received free advertising in the charity's magazine)	400
	2,700

Note 3 – Professional fees

Professional fees are as follows:

	£
Legal fees in connection with the renewal of a 45-year property	
lease in respect of a warehouse	3,600
Legal fees in connection with the issue of a loan note (see Note 9)	15,200
	18,800

Note 4 – Other expenses

The figure of £230,240 for other expenses includes £1,300 for entertaining suppliers and £900 for entertaining employees.

Note 5 – Income from property

Gastron Ltd lets out the whole of an unfurnished freehold office building that is surplus to requirements. The office building was let from 1 April 2011 to 31 December 2011 at a monthly rent of £1,800, payable in advance. On 31 December 2011 the tenant left owing two months' rent which Gastron Ltd was unable to recover. During January 2012 the company spent £3,700 decorating the property. The office building was then re-let from 1 February 2012 at a monthly rent of £1,950, on which date the new tenant paid six months' rent in advance.

Note 6 – Bank interest received

The bank interest was received on 31 March 2012. The bank deposits are held for non-trading purposes.

Note 7 – Dividends received

During the year ended 31 March 2012 Gastron Ltd received dividends of £36,000 from Tasteless plc, an unconnected UK company, and dividends of £18,000 from Culinary Ltd, a 100% UK subsidiary company (see Note 11). Both figures are the actual cash amounts received.

Note 8 – Profit on disposal of shares

The profit on disposal of shares is in respect of a 1% shareholding that was sold on 14 October 2011. The disposal resulted in a chargeable gain of £74,800. This figure is after taking account of indexation.

Note 9 – Interest payable

The interest payable is in respect of the company's loan note that was issued on 1 April 2011. The proceeds of the issue were used to finance the company's trading activities. Interest of £30,400 was paid on 30 September 2011 and again on 31 March 2012.

Note 10 – Plant and machinery

On 1 April 2011 the tax written down values of plant and machinery were as follows:

	£
General pool	16,700
Expensive motor car	18,400

The following transactions took place during the year ended 31 March 2012:

		Cost/ (Proceeds) £
19 May 2011	Purchased equipment	21,600
12 July 2011	Purchased motor car (1)	9,800
11 August 2011	Purchased motor car (2)	16,200
5 October 2011	Purchased a lorry	17,200
5 March 2012	Sold equipment	(3,300)

Motor car (1) purchased on 12 July 2011 for £9,800 has a CO_2 emission rate of 147 grams per kilometre. Motor car (2), purchased on 11 August 2011 for £16,200, has a CO_2 emission rate of 109 grams per kilometre. The equipment sold on 5 March 2012 for £3,300 was originally purchased in 2006 for £8,900.

Note 11 – Subsidiary company

Gastron Ltd owns 100% of the ordinary share capital of Culinary Ltd. On 13 February 2012 Culinary Ltd sold a freehold factory and this resulted in a capital loss of £66,000. For the year ended 31 March 2012 Culinary Ltd made no other disposals and paid corporation tax at the small profits rate of 20%.

Required:

(a) **Calculate Gastron Ltd's tax adjusted trading profit for the year ended 31 March 2012, after deducting capital allowances.**

Your computation should commence with the profit before taxation figure of £640,000, and should list all of the items referred to in Notes (1) to (9) indicating by the use of zero (0) any items that do not require adjustment. **(15 marks)**

(b) **Calculate Gastron Ltd's corporation tax liability for the year ended 31 March 2012, on the basis that no election is made between Gastron Ltd and Culinary Ltd in respect of capital gains.** **(7 marks)**

(c) **State the date by which Gastron Ltd's corporation tax liability for the year ended 31 March 2012 should be paid, and advise the company of the interest that will be due if the liability is not paid until 31 August 2013.** **(3 marks)**

(d) **Explain the group relationship that must exist in order for two or more companies to form a group for capital gains purposes.** **(2 marks)**

(e) **State the time limit for Gastron Ltd and Culinary Ltd to make a joint election such that Culinary Ltd is treated as making the chargeable gain on the disposal of shares (see Note 8), and explain why such an election will be beneficial.** **(3 marks)**

(Total: 30 marks)

50 QUAGMIRE LTD *Walk in the footsteps of a top tutor*

For the year ended 31 January 2012 Quagmire plc had taxable total profits of £1,200,000 and franked investment income of £200,000.

For the year ended 31 January 2011 the company had taxable total profits of £1,600,000 and franked investment income of £120,000.

Quagmire plc's profits accrue evenly throughout the year. Quagmire plc has one associated company.

Required:

(a) **Explain why Quagmire plc will have been required to make quarterly instalment payments in respect of its corporation tax liability for the year ended 31 January 2012. (3 marks)**

(b) **Calculate Quagmire plc's corporation tax liability for the year ended 31 January 2012, and explain how and when this will have been paid. (3 marks)**

(c) **Explain how your answer to part (b) above would differ if Quagmire plc did not have an associated company.**

Your answer should include a calculation of the revised corporation tax liability for the year ended 31 January 2012. (4 marks)

(Total: 10 marks)

WITH OVERSEAS ASPECTS

51 ALBERT LTD (ADAPTED)

(a) **Year ended 31 March 2012**

Albert Ltd is a UK resident trading company with no associated companies.

For the year ended 31 March 2012 it had an operating profit of £873,429. The following expenses have been deducted in calculating this figure:

	£
Depreciation	82,000
Donation under Gift Aid scheme	15,500
Donation to political party	48,000
Legal fees for collection of trade debts	3,500

Capital allowances

On 1 April 2011 the tax written down values of plant and machinery were:

	£
General pool	45,200
Expensive motor car	22,400
Special rate pool	150,000

The following transactions took place during the year ended 31 March 2012:

		Cost/(Proceeds)
		£
3 June 2011	Purchased machine	63,000
1 July 2011	Sold the expensive car	(18,200)
15 July 2011	Purchased a motor car	25,000

The motor car purchased on 15 July 2011 for £25,000 has a CO_2 emission rate of 107 grams per kilometre. The expensive motor car sold on 1 July 2011 was used by the finance director, and 60% of his mileage was for private journeys.

Other information

In the year to 31 March 2012 Albert Ltd had interest income of £12,000 and realised a capital gain on the sale of an office building of £120,000. As at 1 April 2011 the company had trading losses brought forward of £25,000.

Required:

Calculate Albert Ltd's corporation tax liability for the year ended 31 March 2012.

In your adjustment of profits computation you should commence with operating profit of £873,429, and you should list all of the expenses deducted from operating profit referred to, indicating by the use of zero (0) any items that do not require adjustment. (20 marks)

(b) Year ended 31 March 2013

In the year ended 31 March 2013 Albert Ltd is forecasting to have a tax adjusted trading profit of £1,200,000. It will have no other income or gains.

Albert Ltd is planning to set up an overseas operation which is expected to make a trading profit of £180,000 in the year to 31 March 2013.

Albert Ltd is undecided as to whether the overseas operations should be set up as a branch of Albert Ltd or as a separate wholly owned overseas resident company. In either case the expected overseas profits would remain the same and the overseas tax payable on these profits would be £45,000.

If the operation is set up as an overseas subsidiary then gross dividends of £60,000 would be remitted to Albert Ltd in the year ending 31 March 2013. The overseas country withholds 10% withholding tax on dividends paid to overseas companies.

Required:

Calculate Albert Ltd's corporation tax liability for the year ended 31 March 2013 if the overseas operation is set up as:

(i) a branch (3 marks)

(ii) a wholly owned overseas resident company. (2 marks)

Assume that tax rates and allowances for FY2011 continue into the future

(Total: 25 marks)

52 CRASH BASH LTD (ADAPTED) *Walk in the footsteps of a top tutor*

(a) Crash-Bash Ltd commenced trading on 1 July 2011 as a manufacturer of motor cycle crash helmets in the United Kingdom. The company is incorporated overseas, although its directors are based in the United Kingdom and hold their board meetings in the United Kingdom.

Crash-Bash Ltd prepared its first accounts for the nine-month period ended 31 March 2012. The following information is available:

Trading profit

The tax adjusted trading profit based on the draft accounts for the nine-month period ended 31 March 2012 is £442,400.

This figure is before making any adjustments required for:

(1) Capital allowances.

(2) Advertising expenditure of £12,840 incurred during June 2011. This expenditure has not been deducted in arriving at the tax adjusted trading profit for the period ended 31 March 2012 of £442,400.

Plant and machinery

The accounts for the nine-month period ended 31 March 2012 showed the following additions and disposals of plant and machinery:

		Cost
		£
2 October 2011	Purchased machinery	90,000
28 November 2011	Purchased a motor car (1)	13,200
1 February 2012	Sold machinery	10,000
12 February 2012	Purchased motor car (2)	14,000

Motor car (1) purchased on 28 November 2011 for £13,200 has a CO_2 emission rate of 109 grams per kilometre. Motor car (2) purchased on 12 February 2012 has a CO_2 emission rate of 140 grams per kilometre. The machinery sold on 1 February 2012 was acquired on 2 October 2011 for £11,000.

Overseas dividend

On 31 March 2012 Crash-Bash Ltd received a dividend of £14,250 (net) from a 100% owned subsidiary company, Safety Inc, that is resident overseas. Withholding tax was withheld from the dividend at the rate of 5%.

Dividends received

During the period ended 31 March 2012 Crash-Bash Ltd received dividends of £36,000 from Flat-Out plc, an unconnected United Kingdom company. This figure was the actual cash amount received.

Export of crash helmets to Safety Inc

Safety Inc, Crash-Bash Ltd's 100% owned overseas subsidiary company, sells crash helmets that have been manufactured by Crash-Bash Ltd. Crash-Bash Ltd is a large company for the purposes of transfer pricing legislation.

Other information

With the exception of Safety Inc, Crash-Bash Ltd does not have any associated companies.

Required:

(i) Explain why Crash-Bash Ltd is treated as being resident in the United Kingdom. (2 marks)

(ii) Calculate Crash-Bash Ltd's corporation tax liability for the nine-month period ended 31 March 2012. (14 marks)

(iii) Explain the corporation tax implications if Crash-Bash Ltd were to invoice Safety Inc for the exported crash helmets at a price that was less than the market price. (4 marks)

(b) *Note that in answering this part of the question you are not expected to take account of any of the information provided in part (a) above.*

Crash-Bash Ltd's outputs and inputs for the first two months of trading from 1 July 2011 to 31 August 2011 were as follows:

	July	*August*
	£	£
Outputs		
Sales	13,200	18,800
Inputs		
Goods purchased	94,600	193,100
Services incurred	22,300	32,700

The above figures are stated exclusive of value added tax (VAT).

On 1 September 2011 Crash-Bash Ltd realised that its sales for September 2011 were going to exceed £100,000, and therefore immediately registered for VAT. On that date the company had a stock of goods that had cost £108,600 (exclusive of VAT).

During February 2012 Crash-Bash Ltd discovered that a number of errors had been made when completing its VAT return for the quarter ended 30 November 2011. As a result of these errors the company will have to make an additional payment of VAT to HM Revenue and Customs (HMRC).

Required:

(i) Explain why Crash-Bash Ltd was required to compulsorily register for VAT from 1 September 2011, and state what action the company then had to take as regards notifying HM Revenue and Customs of the registration. (3 marks)

(ii) Calculate the amount of input VAT that Crash-Bash Ltd was able to recover in respect of inputs incurred prior to registering for VAT on 1 September 2011.

Your answer should include an explanation as to why the input VAT is recoverable. (4 marks)

(iii) Explain how Crash-Bash Ltd could have voluntarily disclosed the errors relating to the VAT return for the quarter ended 30 November 2011, and state the circumstances in which default interest would have been due.

(3 marks)

(Total: 30 marks)

WITH VAT ASPECTS

53 STRETCHED LTD (ADAPTED)

(1) Stretched Ltd has always prepared its accounts to 31 December, but has decided to change its accounting date to 31 March. The company's results for the 15-month period ended 31 March 2012 are as follows:

(i) The tax adjusted trading profit is £330,000. This figure is before taking account of capital allowances.

(ii) Until January 2012 the company has never been entitled to capital allowances as all assets were leased. However, on 15 January 2012 the company bought a machine for £27,000.

(iii) There is a property business profit of £45,000 for the 15-month period ended 31 March 2012.

(iv) On 15 April 2011 the company disposed of some investments, and this resulted in a chargeable gain of £44,000. On 8 February 2012 the company made a further disposal, and this resulted in a capital loss of £6,700.

(v) Franked investment income of £30,000 was received on 10 September 2011.

(vi) A Gift Aid donation of £5,000 was made on 31 March 2012.

As at 1 January 2011 Stretched Ltd had unused trading losses of £23,000, and unused capital losses of £3,000.

Stretched Ltd has no associated companies.

Required:

(a) Calculate Stretched Ltd's corporation tax liabilities in respect of the 15-month period ended 31 March 2012, and advise the company by when these should be paid. (13 marks)

(b) State the advantages for tax purposes of a company having an accounting date of 31 March instead of 31 December. (2 marks)

(2) Stretched Ltd is registered for VAT. The following information is available in respect of its VAT return for the quarter ended 30 June 2012.

(i) On 10 June 2012 Stretched Ltd received an order for goods, together with a deposit of £5,000. It despatched the goods to the customer on 20 June 2012 and raised an invoice for the balance due of £25,000 on 1 July 2012. The invoice was paid on 30 July 2012.

(ii) On 1 June 2012 Stretched Ltd received an invoice for £12,500 in respect of a new car for the sales director. On 1 June 2012 the director's old car was taken to auction and the company received a cheque for £7,000 in respect of the sale of the car. The private use of both cars by the sales director was 20%. In the quarter to 30 June 2012 the company paid fuel bills of £600 in respect of the sales director's cars.

(iii) During the quarter ended 30 June 2012 the company incurred standard-rated costs of £1,000, in respect of the company's annual dinner dance for staff, and £500 on entertaining potential UK customers.

All figures are inclusive of VAT.

In the quarter to 30 September 2011 the company had submitted and paid its VAT liability late. The returns and payment for the quarters to 31 December 2011 and 31 March 2012 were submitted on time.

Required:

(a) Advise Stretched Ltd how the transactions in (i) to (iii) above should be dealt with in the VAT return for the quarter to 30 June 2012. (7 marks)

(b) Explain the implications if Stretched Ltd is two months late in submitting its VAT return and in paying the related VAT liability for the quarter ended 30 June 2012. (3 marks)

(Total: 25 marks)

54 SCUBA LTD (ADAPTED) *Walk in the footsteps of a top tutor*

(a) Scuba Ltd is a manufacturer of diving equipment. The following information is relevant for the year ended 31 March 2012:

Operating profit

The operating profit is £198,400.

The expenses that have been deducted in calculating this figure include:

	£
Depreciation and amortisation of lease	45,200
Entertaining customers	7,050
Entertaining employees	2,470
Gifts to customers (diaries costing £25 each displaying Scuba Ltd's name)	1,350
Gifts to customers (food hampers costing £80 each)	1,600

Leasehold property

On 1 July 2011 Scuba Ltd acquired a leasehold office building that is used for business purposes. The company paid a premium of £80,000 for the grant of a twenty-year lease.

Plant and machinery

On 1 April 2011 the tax written down values of plant and machinery were as follows:

	£
General pool	47,200
Expensive motor car	22,400

The following transactions took place during the year ended 31 March 2012:

		Cost/(Proceeds)
		£
3 April 2011	Purchased machinery	22,800
29 May 2011	Purchased a computer	1,100
4 August 2011	Purchased a motor car	10,400
1 September 2011	Purchased a motor car	15,400
18 November 2011	Purchased machinery	7,300
1 February 2012	Purchased a motor car	20,000
15 February 2012	Sold a lorry	(12,400)

The motor car purchased on 4 August 2011 for £10,400 has CO_2 emissions of 140 grams per kilometre and is used by the factory manager, and 40% of the mileage is for private journeys.

The motor car purchased on 1 September 2011 for £15,400 has CO_2 emissions of 170 grams per kilometre and has no private use.

The motor car purchased on 1 February 2012 for £20,000 has CO_2 emissions of 105 grams per kilometre and has no private use.

The lorry sold on 15 February 2012 for £12,400 originally cost £19,800.

Property income

Scuba Ltd lets a retail shop that is surplus to requirements. The shop was let until 31 March 2011 but was then empty from 1 April 2011 to 31 July 2011. During this period Scuba Ltd spent £6,200 on decorating the shop, and £1,430 on advertising for new tenants. The shop was let from 1 August 2011 to 31 March 2012 at a quarterly rent of £7,200, payable in advance.

Interest received

Interest of £430 was received from HM Revenue & Customs on 31 October 2011 in respect of the overpayment of corporation tax for the year ended 31 March 2010.

Other information

Scuba Ltd has no associated companies, and the company has always had an accounting date of 31 March.

Required:

(i) **Compute Scuba Ltd's tax adjusted trading profit for the year ended 31 March 2012.**

Your computation should commence with the operating profit of £198,400, and should list all of the items referred to that are relevant to the adjustment of profits, indicating by the use of zero (0) any items that do not require adjustment.

You should ignore value added tax (VAT). **(15 marks)**

(ii) **Compute Scuba Ltd's corporation tax liability for the year ended 31 March 2012. (4 marks)**

(b) Scuba Ltd registered for value added tax (VAT) on 1 April 2009.

The company's VAT returns have been submitted as follows:

Quarter ended	*VAT paid/ (refunded)* £	*Submitted*
30 June 2009	18,600	One month late
30 September 2009	32,200	One month late
31 December 2009	8,800	On time
31 March 2010	3,400	Two months late
30 June 2010	(6,500)	One month late
30 September 2010	42,100	On time
31 December 2010	(2,900)	On time
31 March 2011	3,900	On time
30 June 2011	18,800	On time
30 September 2011	57,300	Two months late
31 December 2011	9,600	On time

Scuba Ltd always pays any VAT that is due at the same time that the related return is submitted.

During February 2012 Scuba Ltd discovered that a number of errors had been made when completing its VAT return for the quarter ended 31 December 2011.

As a result of these errors the company will have to make an additional payment of VAT to HM Revenue & Customs.

Required:

(i) **State, giving appropriate reasons, the default surcharge consequences arising from Scuba Ltd's submission of its VAT returns for the quarter ended 30 June 2009 to the quarter ended 30 September 2011 inclusive. (8 marks)**

(ii) **Explain how Scuba Ltd can voluntarily disclose the errors relating to the VAT return for the quarter ended 31 December 2011, and state whether default interest will be due. (3 marks)**

(Total: 30 marks)

55 WIRELESS LTD (ADAPTED) *Walk in the footsteps of a top tutor*

(a) Wireless Ltd, a United Kingdom resident company, commenced trading on 1 October 2011 as a manufacturer of computer routers. The company prepared its first accounts for the six-month period ended 31 March 2012.

The following information is available:

Trading profit

The tax adjusted trading profit based on the draft accounts for the six-month period ended 31 March 2012 is £95,626.

This figure is before making any adjustments required for:

(1) Capital allowances.

(2) Director's remuneration of £23,000 paid to the managing director of Wireless Ltd, together with the related employer's Class 1 national insurance contributions.

The remuneration is in respect of the period ended 31 March 2012 but was not paid until 5 April 2012. No accrual has been made for this remuneration in the draft accounts.

The managing director received no other remuneration from Wireless Ltd during the tax year 2011/12.

Plant and machinery

Wireless Ltd purchased the following assets in respect of the six-month period ended 31 March 2012:

		£
20 September 2011	Office equipment	10,400
5 October 2011	Machinery	10,200
6 October 2011	Van	15,000
10 October 2011	Computer (including software of £8,000)	40,000
11 October 2011	Building alterations necessary for the installation of the machinery	4,700
18 February 2012	Motor car	10,600

The van purchased on 6 October 2011 has a CO_2 emission rate of 165 grams per kilometre. The motor car purchased on 18 February 2012 for £10,600 has a CO_2 emission rate of 136 grams per kilometre. It is used by the sales manager, and 15% of the mileage is for private journeys.

Loan interest received

Loan interest of £1,110 was received on 31 March 2012. The loan was made for non-trading purposes.

Overseas dividend

On 31 March 2012 Wireless Ltd received a dividend of £14,680 (net) from a 100% owned subsidiary company that is resident overseas. Withholding tax was withheld from the dividend at the rate of 25%.

Overseas branch profits

For the six-month period ended 31 March 2012, Wireless Ltd operated abroad through an overseas branch which made trading profits of £6,750 (net) after the deduction of withholding tax of 10%.

Donation

A donation to charity of £1,800 was paid on 20 March 2012. The donation was made under the Gift Aid scheme.

Required:

(i) **Explain when an accounting period starts for corporation tax purposes; (2 marks)**

(ii) **Calculate Wireless Ltd's taxable total profits for the six-month period ended 31 March 2012.**

In your adjustment of profits computation you should commence with £95,626, and you should adjust for capital allowances and costs relating to the employment of the director. (14 marks)

(b) *Note that in answering this part of the question you are not expected to take account of any of the information provided in part (a) above.*

Wireless Ltd's sales since the commencement of trading on 1 October 2011 have been:

		£
2011	October	9,700
	November	18,200
	December	21,100
2012	January	14,800
	February	23,300
	March	24,600

The above figures are stated exclusive of value added tax (VAT).

The company's sales are all standard rated and are made to VAT registered businesses.

Wireless Ltd only sells goods and since registering for VAT has been issuing sales invoices to customers that show:

(1) the invoice date and the tax point

(2) Wireless Ltd's name and address

(3) the VAT-exclusive amount for each supply

(4) the total VAT-exclusive amount, and

(5) the amount of VAT payable.

The company does not offer any discount for prompt payment.

Required:

(i) Explain from what date Wireless Ltd was required to compulsorily register for VAT and state what action the company then had to take as regards notifying HM Revenue and Customs (HMRC) of the registration. (4 marks)

(ii) Explain the circumstances in which Wireless Ltd would have been allowed to recover input VAT incurred on goods purchased and services incurred prior to the date of VAT registration. (4 marks)

(iii) Explain why it would have been beneficial for Wireless Ltd to have voluntarily registered for VAT from 1 October 2011. (3 marks)

(iv) State the additional information that Wireless Ltd must show on its sales invoices in order for them to be valid for VAT purposes. (3 marks)

(Total: 30 marks)

RELIEF FOR TRADING LOSSES

56 HALF-LIFE LTD (ADAPTED)

Half-Life Ltd commenced trading on 1 April 2008 and ceased trading on 30 June 2012.

The company's results for all its periods of trading are as follows:

	y/e 31.3.09	y/e 31.3.10	y/e 31.3.11	p/e 30.6.11	y/e 30.6.12
	£	£	£	£	£
Tax adjusted profit/(loss)	224,000	67,400	38,200	(61,700)	(308,800)
Property business profit	8,200	12,200	6,500	4,400	–
Capital gains	–	–	5,600	–	23,700
Gift Aid	(1,200)	(1,000)	–	–	(700)

Half-Life Ltd does not have any associated companies.

Required:

(a) **Assuming that Half-Life Ltd claims the maximum possible relief for its trading losses, calculate the company's taxable total profits for the years ended 31 March 2009, 2010 and 2011, the period ended 30 June 2011, and the year ended 30 June 2012.**

Your answer should clearly identify the amounts of any losses and Gift Aid payments that are unrelieved. **(9 marks)**

(b) **State the dates by which Half-Life Ltd must make the loss relief claims in part (a).** **(2 marks)**

(c) **Calculate the amount of corporation tax that will be repaid to Half-Life Ltd as a result of making the loss relief claims in part (a).**

Assume that the corporation tax rates for FY 2008 are the same as in FY 2009. **(4 marks)**

(Total: 15 marks)

57 LOSER LTD (ADAPTED)

Loser Ltd 's results for the year ended 30 June 2009, the nine month period ended 31 March 2010, the year ended 31 March 2011 and the year ended 31 March 2012 are:

	y/e 30.6.09	p/e 31.3.10	y/e 31.3.11	y/e 31.3.12
	£	£	£	£
Trading profit/(loss)	86,600	(25,700)	27,300	(78,300)
Property business profit	–	4,500	8,100	5,600
Gift Aid payments	(1,400)	(800)	(1,200)	(1,100)

Loser Ltd does not have any associated companies.

Required:

(a) **State the factors that will influence a company's choice of loss relief claims.** **(3 marks)**

(b) **Assuming that Loser Ltd claims relief for its losses as early as possible, compute the company's taxable total profits for the year ended 30 June 2009, the period ended 31 March 2010, the year ended 31 March 2011 and the year ended 31 March 2012.**

Your answer should clearly identify the amount of any losses that are unrelieved. **(5 marks)**

(c) **Explain how your answer to (b) above would have differed if Loser Ltd had ceased trading on 31 March 2012.** **(2 marks)**

(Total: 10 marks)

58 SOFA LTD (ADAPTED) *Online question assistance*

(a) Sofa Ltd is a manufacturer of furniture.

The company's summarised income statement for the year ended 31 March 2012 is as follows:

	Note	£	£
Gross profit			276,020
Operating expenses			
Depreciation		150,820	
Professional fees	1	19,900	
Repairs and renewals	2	22,800	
Other expenses	3	304,000	
			(497,520)
Operating loss			(221,500)
Profit from sale of fixed assets			
Disposal of shares	4		4,300
Income from investments			
Bank interest	5		8,400
			(208,800)
Interest payable	6		(31,200)
Loss before taxation			(240,000)

Note 1 – Professional fees

Professional fees are as follows:

	£
Accountancy and audit fee	3,400
Legal fees in connection with the issue of share capital	7,800
Legal fees in connection with the renewal of a ten year property lease	2,900
Legal fees in connection with the issue of a loan note (see Note 6)	5,800
	19,900

Note 2 – Repairs and renewals

The figure of £22,800 for repairs and renewals includes £9,700 for constructing a new wall around the company's premises and £3,900 for repairing the wall of an office building after it was damaged by a lorry. The remaining expenses are all fully allowable.

Note 3 – Other expenses

The figure of £304,000 for other expenses includes £1,360 for entertaining suppliers; £700 for entertaining employees; £370 for counselling services provided to an employee who was made redundant; and a fine of £420 for infringing health and safety regulations. The remaining expenses are all fully allowable.

Note 4 – Profit on disposal of shares

The profit on the disposal of shares of £4,300 is in respect of a shareholding that was sold on 29 October 2011.

Note 5 – Bank interest received

The bank interest was received on 31 March 2012. The bank deposits are held for non-trading purposes.

Note 6 – Interest payable

Sofa Ltd issued a loan note on 1 July 2011, and this was used for trading purposes. Interest of £20,800 was paid on 31 December 2011, and £10,400 was accrued at 31 March 2012.

Note 7 – Plant and machinery

On 1 April 2011 the tax written down values of plant and machinery were as follows:

	£
General pool	16,700
Expensive motor car	16,400

The following transactions took place during the year ended 31 March 2012:

		Cost/ (Proceeds)
		£
12 May 2011	Purchased equipment	61,400
8 June 2011	Sold the expensive motor car	(17,800)
8 June 2011	Purchased motor car (1)	22,200
2 August 2011	Purchased motor car (2)	10,900
19 October 2011	Purchased motor car (3)	13,800
8 January 2012	Sold a lorry	(7,600)
18 January 2012	Sold motor car (2)	(8,800)
10 February 2012	Purchased a second-hand office building	280,000

Motor car (1) purchased on 8 June 2011 for £22,200 has a CO_2 emission rate of 162 grams per kilometre. Motor car (2) purchased on 2 August 2011 for £10,900, has CO_2 emissions of 157 grams per kilometre. Motor car (3) purchased on 19 October 2011 for £13,800 has CO_2 emissions of 108 grams per kilometre.

The expensive motor car sold on 8 June 2011 for £17,800 originally cost £26,800. The lorry sold on 8 January 2012 for £7,600 originally cost £24,400.

The cost of the second-hand office building purchased on 10 February 2012 for £280,000 includes fixtures qualifying as plant and machinery. £44,800 of the purchase price of the office relates to these fixtures.

Required:

Calculate Sofa Ltd's tax adjusted trading loss for the year ended 31 March 2012.

Your answer should commence with the loss before taxation figure of £240,000, and should list all of the items referred to in Notes (1) to (6) indicating by the use of zero (0) any items that do not require adjustment.

You should assume that the company claims the maximum available capital allowances. **(20 marks)**

(b) Sofa Ltd has three subsidiary companies:

Settee Ltd

Sofa Ltd owns 100% of the ordinary share capital of Settee Ltd. For the year ended 30 June 2011 Settee Ltd had taxable total profits of £240,000, and for the year ended 30 June 2012 will have taxable total profits of £90,000.

Couch Ltd

Sofa Ltd owns 60% of the ordinary share capital of Couch Ltd. For the year ended 31 March 2012 Couch Ltd had taxable total profits of £64,000.

Futon Ltd

Sofa Ltd owns 80% of the ordinary share capital of Futon Ltd. Futon Ltd commenced trading on 1 January 2012, and for the three-month period ended 31 March 2012 had taxable total profits of £60,000.

Required:

Advise Sofa Ltd as to the maximum amount of group relief that can potentially be claimed by each of its three subsidiary companies in respect of its trading loss for the year ended 31 March 2012.

For the purposes of answering this part of the question, you should assume that Sofa Ltd's tax adjusted trading loss for the year ended 31 March 2012 is £200,000.

(5 marks)

(Total: 25 marks)

Online question assistance

59 JOGGER LTD (ADAPTED) *Walk in the footsteps of a top tutor*

(a) Jogger Ltd is a manufacturer of running shoes. The company's summarised income statement for the year ended 31 March 2012 is as follows:

	Note	£	£
Operating loss	1		(56,400)
Income from investments			
Bank interest	4	8,460	
Loan interest	5	24,600	
Income from property	6	144,000	
Dividends	7	45,000	
			222,060
Profit from sale of fixed assets	8		
Disposal of shares			102,340
Profit before taxation			268,000

Note 1 – Operating profit

Depreciation of £12,340 has been deducted in arriving at the operating loss of £56,400.

Note 2 – Plant and machinery

On 1 April 2011 the tax written down values of plant and machinery were as follows:

	£
General pool	21,600
Expensive motor car	8,800

The following transactions took place during the year ended 31 March 2012:

		Cost/(proceeds)
		£
20 July 2011	Sold the expensive motor car	(11,700)
31 July 2011	Purchased motor car	11,800
31 July 2011	Purchased office furniture	30,000
1 August 2011	Purchased new air-conditioning system	120,000
14 March 2012	Sold a lorry	(8,600)

The motor car purchased on 31 July 2011 for £11,800 has a CO_2 emission rate of 153 grams per kilometre. The expensive motor car sold on 20 July 2011 for £11,700 originally cost £18,400. The air-conditioning system acquired on 1 August 2011 is expected to last 25 years. The lorry sold on 14 March 2012 for £8,600 originally cost £16,600.

Note 3 – Bank interest received

The bank interest was received on 31 March 2012. The bank deposits are held for non-trading purposes.

Note 4 – Loan interest receivable

The loan was made for non-trading purposes on 1 July 2011. Loan interest of £16,400 was received on 31 December 2011, and interest of £8,200 was accrued at 31 March 2012.

Note 5 – Income from property

Jogger Ltd lets out an unfurnished freehold office building that is surplus to requirements. The office building was let throughout the year ended 31 March 2012. On 1 April 2011 Jogger Ltd received a premium of £100,000 for the grant of a ten-year lease, and the annual rent of £44,000 which is payable in advance.

Note 6 – Dividends received

During the year ended 31 March 2012 Jogger Ltd received dividends of £45,000 from Sprinter plc, an unconnected UK company. This figure was the actual cash amount received.

Note 7 – Profit on disposal of shares

The profit on disposal of shares is in respect of a shareholding that was sold on 5 December 2011. The disposal resulted in a chargeable gain of £98,300. This figure is after taking account of indexation allowance.

Note 8 – Other information

Jogger Ltd has two associated companies.

Required:

(i) **Calculate Jogger Ltd's tax adjusted trading loss for the year ended 31 March 2012.**

Your computation should commence with the operating loss of £56,400, and should list all of the items referred to in Notes (1) and (3) to (7), indicating by the use of zero (0) any items that do not require adjustment.

You should assume that the company claims the maximum available capital allowances. (7 marks)

(ii) **Assuming that Jogger Ltd claims relief for its trading loss against total profits, calculate the company's corporation tax liability for the year ended 31 March 2012. (8 marks)**

(iii) **State the date by which Jogger Ltd's self-assessment corporation tax return for the year ended 31 March 2012 should be submitted, and advise the company of the penalties that will be due if the return is submitted eight months late.**

You should assume that the company pays its corporation tax liability at the same time that the self-assessment tax return is submitted. (4 marks)

(b) *In answering this part of the question you are not expected to take account of any of the information provided in part (a) above.*

Jogger Ltd has been registered for value added tax (VAT) since 1 April 2003.

From that date until 30 June 2010 the company's VAT returns were all submitted on time. Since 1 July 2010 the company's VAT returns have been submitted as follows:

Quarter ended	*VAT paid*	*Submitted*
	£	
30 September 2010	42,700	One month late
31 December 2010	41,200	On time
31 March 2011	38,900	One month late
30 June 2011	28,300	On time
30 September 2011	49,100	On time
31 December 2011	63,800	On time
31 March 2012	89,100	Two months late

Jogger Ltd always pays any VAT that is due at the same time as the related return is submitted.

Required:

(i) **State, giving appropriate reasons, the default surcharge consequences arising from Jogger Ltd's submission of its VAT returns for the quarter ended 30 September 2010 to the quarter ended 31 March 2012 inclusive, at the times stated.** **(6 marks)**

(ii) **Advise Jogger Ltd why it might be beneficial to use the VAT annual accounting scheme, and state the conditions that it will have to satisfy before being permitted to do so.** **(5 marks)**

(Total: 30 marks)

60 VOLATILE LTD (ADAPTED) *Walk in the footsteps of a top tutor*

Timed question with Online tutor debrief

Volatile Ltd commenced trading on 1 January 2007. The company's recent results are:

	y/e 31 Dec 2009	p/e 30 Sept 2010	y/e 30 Sept 2011
	£	£	£
Trading profit/(loss)	15,200	78,700	(101,800)
Property business profit	6,500	–	–
Chargeable gains	–	–	9,700
Gift Aid donations	(1,200)	(1,000)	(800)

Required:

(a) **State the factors that will influence a company's choice of loss relief claims. You are not expected to consider group relief.** **(3 marks)**

(b) **Assuming that Volatile Ltd claims relief for its trading losses as early as possible, calculate the company's taxable total profits for the year ended 31 December 2009, nine month period ended 30 September 2010, and year ended 30 September 2011.**

Your answer should also clearly identify the amount of any unrelieved trading losses as at 30 September 2011. **(7 marks)**

(Total: 10 marks)

Calculate your allowed time, allocate the time to the separate parts..................

WITH GROUP ASPECTS

61 STRAIGHT PLC (ADAPTED)

Straight plc is the holding company for a group of companies as follows.

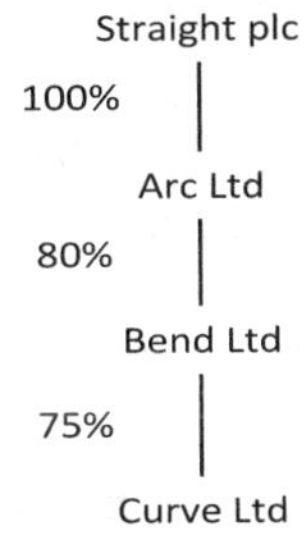

All of the companies in the group have an accounting date of 31 March.

(a) **Straight plc**

For the year ended 31 March 2012 the following information is relevant:

Operating profit

The operating profit is £173,915.

The expenses that have been deducted in calculating this figure include:

	£
Depreciation	21,200
Car lease cost (Note 1)	8,500
Entertaining (Note 2)	12,000
Fine for breach of Health and Safety regulations	1,250

Notes

(1) On 1 April 2011 Straight plc entered into an agreement for the lease of a car for one of the company's salesmen. The car has CO_2 emissions of 162 grams per kilometre.

(2) Entertaining costs consist of £10,000 for entertaining potential overseas customers and £2,000 for a Christmas party for the company's ten staff.

(3) **Plant and machinery**

On 1 April 2011 the tax written down values of plant and machinery were:

	£
General pool	35,200
Expensive motor car	18,400

The following transactions took place during the year ended 31 March 2012:

		Cost/(Proceeds)
		£
3 April 2011	Purchased machinery	12,400
1 May 2011	Sold the expensive car	(15,200)

The expensive motor car sold on 1 May 2011 was used by a salesman, and 40% of his mileage was for private journeys.

Required:

Calculate Straight plc's tax adjusted trading profit for the year ended 31 March 2012.

Your computation should commence with the operating profit of £173,915, and should list all of the relevant items referred to in part (a), indicating by the use of zero (0) any items that do not require adjustment. **(10 marks)**

(b) As at 31 March 2011 Straight plc had unused trading losses of £15,000 and unused capital losses of £10,000.

Straight plc sold a freehold office building on 20 June 2011 for £350,000, and this resulted in a capital gain of £140,000. The company has made a rollover relief claim in respect of a replacement building purchased for £270,000.

During the year ended 31 March 2012 Straight plc received dividends of £18,000 from Arc Ltd, and dividends of £9,000 from Triangle plc, an unconnected company. These figures are the actual amounts received.

Arc Ltd sold a freehold warehouse on 10 March 2012, and this resulted in a capital loss of £40,000.

Required:

(i) **Explain why Straight plc, Arc Ltd, Bend Ltd and Curve Ltd form a group for capital gains purposes, and why Curve Ltd would be excluded from the group if Straight plc's holding in Arc Ltd were only 80% instead of 100%.** **(4 marks)**

(ii) **Before taking into account any transfer of capital gains or losses, calculate the corporation tax payable by Straight plc for the year ended 31 March 2012.** **(8 marks)**

(iii) **State the time limit for Straight plc and Arc Ltd to make a joint election to transfer the capital gain arising on the disposal of Arc Ltd's freehold warehouse, and explain why such an election will be beneficial.**

You are not expected to consider any alternative joint elections. **(3 marks)**

(Total: 25 marks)

62 ANIMAL LTD (ADAPTED)

Animal Ltd is the holding company for a group of companies. The results of each group company for the year ended 31 March 2012 are as follows:

	Tax adjusted trading profit/(loss)	*Property business income*	*Franked Investment Income*
	£	£	£
Animal Ltd	450,000	5,000	20,000
Bat Ltd	65,000	15,000	–
Cat Ltd	85,000	–	–
Dog Ltd	100,000	–	–
Elk Ltd	–	–	–
Fox Ltd	60,000	–	5,000
Gnu Ltd	(200,000)	–	–

Animal Ltd owned 100% of each subsidiary company's ordinary share capital throughout the year ended 31 March 2012 with the following exceptions:

(1) Animal Ltd only owned 90% of Bat Ltd's ordinary share capital.

(2) Animal Ltd's shareholding in Cat Ltd was disposed of on 31 December 2011. The tax adjusted trading profit of £85,000 is for the year ended 31 March 2012.

(3) Animal Ltd's shareholding in Dog Ltd was acquired on 1 January 2012. The tax adjusted trading profit of £100,000 is for the year ended 31 March 2012.

Elk Ltd was a dormant company throughout the year ended 31 March 2012.

Required:

(a) Explain the group relationship that must exist in order that group relief can be claimed. (3 marks)

(b) Explain why there are six associated companies in the Animal Ltd group of companies. Your answer should identify the six associated companies. (3 marks)

(c) Assuming that relief is claimed for Gnu Ltd's trading loss of £200,000 in the most beneficial manner; calculate the taxable total profits of Animal Ltd, Bat Ltd, Cat Ltd, Dog Ltd and Fox Ltd for the year ended 31 March 2012.

Explain your strategy for claiming group relief in the most beneficial manner. (9 marks)

(Total: 15 marks)

63 TOCK-TICK LTD (ADAPTED)

Tock-Tick Ltd is a clock manufacturer. The company's summarised income statement for the year ended 31 March 2012 is as follows:

	£	£
Gross profit		825,020
Operating expenses		
Impaired debts (Note 1)	9,390	
Depreciation	99,890	
Gifts and donations (Note 2)	9,290	
Professional fees (Note 3)	12,400	
Repairs and renewals (Note 4)	128,200	
Other expenses (Note 5)	420,720	
		679,890
Operating profit		145,130
Profit from sale of fixed assets		
Disposal of office building (Note 6)		78,100
Income from investments		
Loan interest (Note 7)		12,330
		235,560
Interest payable (Note 8)		(48,600)
Profit before taxation		186,960

Note 1 – Impaired debts

Impaired debts are as follows:

	£
Trade debts recovered from previous years	(1,680)
Trade debts written off	7,970
Increase in allowance for trade debtors	3,100
	9,390

Note 2 – Gifts and donations

Gifts and donations are as follows:

	£
Gifts to customers (pens costing £45 each displaying Tock-Tick Ltd's name)	1,080
Gifts to customers (food hampers costing £30 each)	720
Donation to a recognised political party	6,450
Long service award to an employee	360
Donation to a national charity (made under the Gift Aid scheme)	600
Donation to a local charity (Tick-Tock Ltd received free advertising in the charity's magazine)	80
	9,290

Note 3 – Professional fees

Professional fees are as follows:

	£
Accountancy and audit fee	5,400
Legal fees in connection with the issue of share capital	2,900
The cost of registering the company's trademark	800
Legal fees in connection with the renewal of a 35-year property lease	1,300
Debt collection	1,100
Legal fees in connection with a court action for not complying with health and safety legislation	900
	12,400

Note 4 – Repairs and renewals

The figure of £128,200 for repairs and renewals includes £41,800 for replacing the roof of an office building, which was in a bad state of repair, and £53,300 for extending the office building.

Note 5 – Other expenses

Other expenses include £2,160 for entertaining suppliers; £880 for counselling services provided to two employees who were made redundant; and the cost of seconding an employee to a charity of £6,400. The remaining expenses are all fully allowable.

Note 6 – Disposal of office building

The profit of £78,100 is in respect of a freehold office building that was sold on 20 February 2012 for £300,000. The office building was purchased on 18 November 1999 for £197,900. Assume the indexation allowance from November 1999 to February 2012 is £90,440.

The building has always been used by Tock-Tick Ltd for trading purposes.

Note 7 – Loan interest received

The loan interest is in respect of a loan that was made on 1 July 2011. Interest of £8,280 was received on 31 December 2011, and interest of £4,050 was accrued at 31 March 2012. The loan was made for non-trading purposes.

Note 8 – Interest payable

The interest payable is in respect of a loan note that is used for trading purposes. Interest of £24,300 was paid on 30 September 2011 and again on 31 March 2012.

Note 9 – Plant and machinery

On 1 April 2011 the tax written down values of plant and machinery were:

	£
General pool	12,200
Expensive motor car	21,600
Short-life asset	2,300

The following transactions took place during the year ended 31 March 2012:

		Cost/(Proceeds)
		£
28 May 2011	Sold the expensive motor car	(34,800)
7 June 2011	Purchased a motor car	14,400
1 August 2011	Sold the short-life asset	(460)
15 August 2011	Purchased equipment	6,700

The motor car purchased on 7 June 2011 has a CO_2 emission rate of 109 g/km.

The expensive motor car sold on 28 May 2011 for £34,800 originally cost £33,600.

Required:

(a) **Calculate Tock-Tick Ltd's tax adjusted trading profit for the year ended 31 March 2012.**

Your computation should commence with the profit before taxation figure of £186,960, and should list all of the items referred to in Note (1) and (8), indicating by the use of zero (0) any items that do not require adjustment.

(19 marks)

(b) **Calculate Tock-Tick Ltd's taxable total profits for the year ended 31 March 2012.**

(5 marks)

(c) It has now been discovered that Tock-Tick Ltd had acquired a 100% shareholding in Clock Ltd on 31 March 2011.

Clock Ltd made a tax adjusted trading loss of £62,400 for the year ended 31 December 2011 but was profitable in the following year.

On 15 March 2012 Clock Ltd purchased a new freehold office building for £294,000, that is to be used 100% for trading purposes.

(i) **State the effect on Tock-Tick Ltd's taxable total profits for the year ended 31 March 2012 of the acquisition of Clock Ltd, assuming all beneficial elections and claims are made in respect of Clock Ltd's trading loss and its acquisition of the office building.** **(4 marks)**

(ii) **Compute the corporation tax liability of Tock-Tick Ltd for the year ended 31 March 2012 assuming the beneficial claims and elections identified in (c)(i) above are made.** **(2 marks)**

(Total: 30 marks)

64 MUSIC PLC (ADAPTED)

Music plc is the holding company for a group of companies. The group structure is as follows:

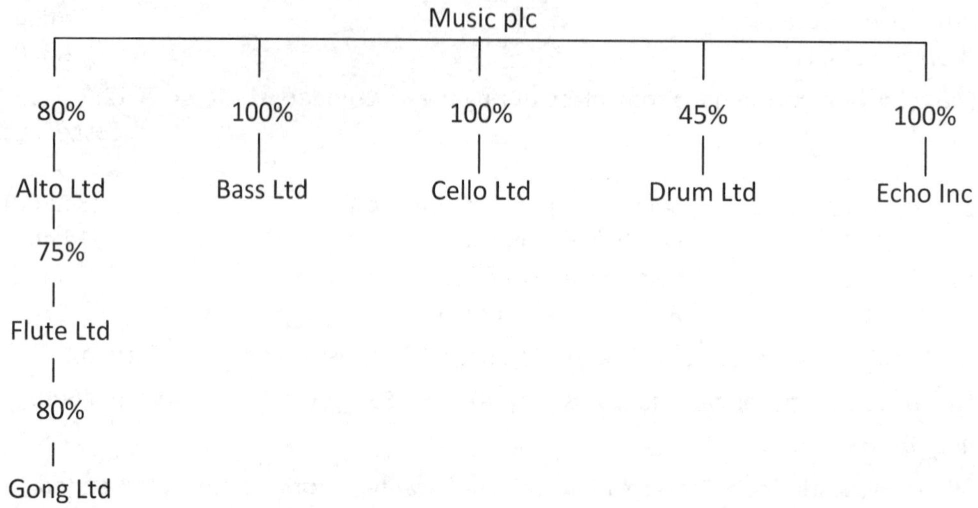

Music plc's shareholding in Bass Ltd was disposed of on 31 December 2011, and the shareholding in Cello Ltd was acquired on 1 January 2012. The other shareholdings were all held throughout the year ended 31 March 2012.

Echo Inc is resident overseas. The other companies are all resident in the United Kingdom.

For the year ended 31 March 2012 Music plc had a tax adjusted trading profit of £92,000. During the year Music plc received franked investment income of £15,000 from an unconnected company, bank interest of £12,000 and a dividend of £5,400 from Bass Ltd.

As at 31 March 2011 Music plc had unused capital losses of £32,000. On 5 January 2012 the company sold a freehold office building, and this resulted in a further capital loss of £65,000.

Alto Ltd sold a freehold warehouse on 10 March 2012, and this resulted in a capital gain of £120,000. An election has been made so that the gain is treated as Music plc's gain.

Music plc also owns a number of properties which it lets out. The following information relates to the properties let out during the year ended 31 March 2012. Music plc claims the wear and tear allowance on its properties, where appropriate.

Property one

Property one is a freehold house which is let out furnished. It was let out from 1 September 2011 at a quarterly rent of £2,500, payable in advance. In April 2011 Music plc incurred £2,500 on redecorating the house and £400 on a new dishwasher. During the year the company also incurred £1,500 on advertising for new tenants and agents fees, council tax of £1,200 and water rates of £600.

Property two

This is a freehold house which is let out unfurnished. It was let until 1 January 2012 at a monthly rent of £650, payable in advance. The tenants left owing the last month's rent, which the company never recovered.

New tenants occupied the house from 1 March 2012 at a rent of £700 per month. The tenants were unable to supply appropriate references and Music plc therefore required the tenants to pay the first six months rent up front.

On 10 April 2012 Music plc paid £500 in connection with repairs to the central heating system which had been carried out in March 2012.

Property three

This is a leasehold retail shop. On 1 June 2011 Music plc paid a premium of £60,000 for the grant of a 30 year lease. The property was sub-let to a tenant on 1 July 2011 in return for the payment of a premium of £45,000 for a 10 year lease and annual rent of £2,000 payable quarterly in advance.

Property four

Property four is a freehold apartment. It was acquired on 1 April 2011 in an uninhabitable condition. Music plc had to incur £4,000 on repairs to the roof and £2,000 on new decoration prior to renting the property. It incurred £250 on letting agency fees and rented the apartment from 1 July 2011 at a monthly rent of £500 payable in advance.

Year ending 31 March 2013

Music plc is considering either acquiring another property which it will rent out or investing in new plant and machinery in the year ending 31 March 2013. In either case it will take out a new bank loan of £100,000 at a 10% interest rate to partly fund the acquisition. Bank arrangement fees will be £300.

Required:

(a) **State, giving appropriate reasons, which companies in the Music plc group of companies form a group for capital gains purposes.** **(5 marks)**

(b) **Explain why Music plc has six associated companies.**

Your answer should identify the six associated companies. **(4 marks)**

(c) **Calculate Music plc's property business profit for the year ended 31 March 2012.** **(8 marks)**

(d) **Calculate Music plc's corporation tax liability for the year ended 31 March 2012.** **(6 marks)**

(e) **Explain how the bank fees and interest costs will be treated for tax purposes if the company acquires another property or it acquires new plant and machinery in the year ended 31 March 2013.** **(2 marks)**

(Total: 30 marks)

65 MICE LTD *Walk in the footsteps of a top tutor*

Timed question with Online tutor debrief

(a) You should assume that today's date is 28 March 2012.

Mice Ltd commenced trading on 1 July 2008 as a manufacturer of computer peripherals.

The company prepares accounts to 31 March, and its results for the first three periods of trading were as follows:

	Period ended 31 March 2009	Year ended 31 March 2010	Year ended 31 March 2011
	£	£	£
Trading profit	83,200	24,700	51,200
Property business profit	2,800	7,100	12,200
Gift Aid donations	(1,000)	(1,500)	–

The following information is available in respect of the year ended 31 March 2012:

Trading loss

Mice Ltd expects to make a trading loss of £180,000.

Business property income

Mice Ltd lets out three office buildings that are surplus to requirements.

The first office building is owned freehold. The property was let throughout the year ended 31 March 2012 at a quarterly rent of £3,200, payable in advance. Mice Ltd paid business rates of £2,200 and insurance of £460 in respect of this property for the year ended 31 March 2012. During June 2011 Mice Ltd repaired the existing car park for this property at a cost of £1,060, and then subsequently enlarged the car park at a cost of £2,640.

The second office building is owned leasehold. Mice Ltd pays an annual rent of £7,800 for this property, but did not pay a premium when the lease was acquired. On 1 April 2011 the property was sub-let to a tenant, with Mice Ltd receiving a premium of £18,000 for the grant of an eight-year lease. The company also received the annual rent of £6,000 which was payable in advance. Mice Ltd paid insurance of £310 in respect of this property for the year ended 31 March 2012.

The third office building is also owned freehold. Mice Ltd purchased the freehold of this building on 1 January 2012, and it will be empty until 31 March 2012. The building is to be let from 1 April 2012 at a monthly rent of £640, and on 15 March 2012 Mice Ltd received three months rent in advance.

On 1 January 2012 Mice Ltd paid insurance of £480 in respect of this property for the year ended 31 December 2012, and during February 2012 spent £680 on advertising for tenants. Mice Ltd paid loan interest of £1,800 in respect of the period 1 January 2012 to 31 March 2012 on a loan that was taken out to purchase this property.

Loan interest received

On 1 July 2011 Mice Ltd made a loan for non-trading purposes. Loan interest of £6,400 was received on 31 December 2011, and £3,200 will be accrued at 31 March 2012.

Overseas dividend

On 15 October 2011 Mice Ltd received a dividend of £7,400 (net) from a 3% shareholding in USB Inc, a company that is resident overseas. Withholding tax was withheld from this dividend at the rate of 7.5%.

Chargeable gain

On 20 December 2011 Mice Ltd sold its 3% shareholding in USB Inc. The disposal resulted in a chargeable gain of £10,550, after taking account of indexation.

Required:

(i) **Calculate Mice Ltd's property business profit for the year ended 31 March 2012;** **(8 marks)**

(ii) **Assuming that Mice Ltd claims relief for its trading loss as early as possible, calculate the company's taxable total profits for the nine-month period ended 31 March 2009, and each of the years ended 31 March 2010, 2011 and 2012.** **(7 marks)**

(b) Mice Ltd has owned 100% of the ordinary share capital of Web-Cam Ltd since it began trading on 1 April 2011. For the three-month period ended 30 June 2011 Web-Cam Ltd made a trading profit of £28,000, and is expected to make a trading profit of £224,000 for the year ended 30 June 2012. Web-Cam Ltd has no other taxable profits or allowable losses.

Required:

Assuming that Mice Ltd does not make any loss relief claim against its own profits, advise Web-Cam Ltd as to the maximum amount of group relief that can be claimed from Mice Ltd in respect of the trading loss of £180,000 for the year ended 31 March 2012. **(3 marks)**

(c) Mice Ltd has surplus funds of £125,000 which it is planning to spend before 31 March 2012. The company will either purchase new equipment for £125,000, or alternatively it will purchase a new ventilation system for £125,000, which will be installed as part of its factory.

Mice Ltd has not made any other purchases of assets during the year ended 31 March 2012, and neither has its subsidiary company Web-Cam Ltd.

Required:

Explain the maximum amount of capital allowances that Mice Ltd will be able to claim for the year ended 31 March 2012 in respect of each of the two alternative purchases of assets.

You are not expected to recalculate Mice Ltd's trading loss for the year ended 31 March 2012, or redo any of the calculations made in parts (a) and (b) above.

(4 marks)

(d) Mice Ltd is planning to pay its managing director a bonus of £40,000 on 31 March 2012. The managing director has already been paid gross director's remuneration of £60,000 during the tax year 2011/12, and the bonus of £40,000 will be paid as additional director's remuneration.

Required:

Advise the managing director as to the additional amount of income tax and National Insurance contributions (both employee's and employer's) that will be payable as a result of the payment of the additional director's remuneration of £40,000.

You are not expected to recalculate Mice Ltd's trading loss for the year ended 31 March 2012, or redo any of the calculations made in parts (a) and (b) above.

(3 marks)

(Total: 25 marks)

Calculate your allowed time, allocate the time to the separate parts....................

VALUE ADDED TAX

The examiner has stated that there will be a minimum of 10 marks on VAT in the exam.

These marks will often be in question one or two, and past exam questions where this has been the case are included in the kit under the heading of the primary tax being examined.

However, the examiner sometimes sets a separate question on VAT, which could be worth up to 15 marks.

66 CONFUSED LTD

(a) Confused Ltd will commence trading in the near future. The company operates a small aeroplane, and is considering three alternative types of business. These are

(1) training, in which case all sales will be standard rated for VAT,

(2) transport, in which case all sales will be zero-rated for VAT, and

(3) an air ambulance service, in which case all sales will be exempt from VAT.

For each alternative Confused Ltd's sales will be £75,000 per month (exclusive of VAT), and standard rated expenses will be £10,000 per month (inclusive of VAT).

Required:

For each of the three alternative types of business

(i) State whether Confused Ltd will be required or permitted to register for VAT when trading commences, and

(ii) Calculate the monthly amount of output VAT due and input VAT recoverable.
(6 marks)

(b) Puzzled Ltd has discovered that a number of errors have been made when preparing its VAT returns for the previous four quarters. As a result of the errors the company will have to make an additional payment of VAT to HM Revenue & Customs.

Required:

Explain how Puzzled Ltd can voluntarily disclose the errors that have been discovered, and when default interest will be due. **(3 marks)**

(c) Perplexed Ltd has been registered for VAT since 1994, but intends to cease trading on 31 December 2012. On the cessation of trading Perplexed Ltd can either sell its fixed assets on a piecemeal basis to individual purchasers, or it can sell its entire business as a going concern to a single purchaser.

Required:

Advise Perplexed Ltd as to what will happen to its VAT registration, and whether output VAT will be due, if the company ceases trading on 31 December 2012 and:

(i) sells its fixed assets on a piecemeal basis, or

(ii) sells its entire business as a going concern. **(6 marks)**

(Total: 15 marks)

67 ASTUTE LTD (ADAPTED)

(a) Astute Ltd registered for VAT on 1 July 2011. The company has annual standard rated sales of £350,000. This figure is inclusive of VAT. As a result of bookkeeping problems Astute Ltd has been late in submitting its VAT returns to date.

Required:

Advise Astute Ltd of the conditions that it must satisfy before being permitted to use the VAT annual accounting scheme, and the advantages of joining the scheme.
(4 marks)

(b) Bright Ltd registered for VAT on 1 January 2012. The company has annual standard rated sales of £75,000, and these are all made to the general public. The company has annual standard rated expenses of £10,000. Both figures are inclusive of VAT. The relevant flat rate scheme percentage for the company's trade for the first twelve months is 11%.

Required:

Advise Bright Ltd of the conditions that it must satisfy before being permitted to use the VAT flat rate scheme, and the advantages of joining the scheme.

Your answer should be supported by appropriate calculations of the potential annual tax saving. **(4 marks)**

(c) Clever Ltd registered for VAT on 1 June 2011. The company has annual standard rated sales of £250,000. This figure is inclusive of VAT. The company pays its expenses on a cash basis, but allows customers three months' credit when paying for sales. Several of Clever Ltd's customers have recently defaulted on the payment of their debts.

Required:

Advise Clever Ltd of the conditions that it must satisfy before being permitted to use the VAT cash accounting scheme, and the advantages of joining the scheme.
(4 marks)

(d) Robert has owned all of the issued share capital of two UK resident companies, Talent Limited and Gifted Limited, for a number of years.

Talent Limited and Gifted Limited trade with each other.

Required:

Advise Robert whether Talented Limited and Gifted Limited can be group registered for VAT purposes and the effect of a VAT group registration. **(3 marks)**

(Total: 15 marks)

68 VICTOR STYLE *Online question assistance*

Victor Style has been a self-employed hairdresser since 1 January 2009. His sales from the date of commencement of the business to 30 September 2011 were £5,600 per month.

On 1 October 2011 Victor increased the prices that he charged customers, and from that date his sales have been £8,810 per month. Victor's sales are all standard rated.

As a result of the price increase, Victor was required to register for value added tax (VAT) and charge VAT on sales from 1 January 2012.

As all of his customers are members of the general public, it was not possible to increase prices any further as a result of registering for VAT.

Victor's standard rated expenses are £400 per month.

Where applicable, the above figures are inclusive of VAT.

Assume that the VAT registration threshold for 2011/12 applied throughout.

Required:

(a) **Explain why Victor was required to compulsorily register for VAT from 1 January 2012, and state what action he then had to take as regards notifying HM Revenue & Customs of the registration.** **(5 marks)**

(b) **Calculate the total amount of VAT payable by Victor during the year ended 31 December 2012.**

You should ignore pre-registration input VAT. **(3 marks)**

(c) **Advise Victor why it would have been beneficial to have used the VAT flat rate scheme from 1 January 2012.**

Your answer should include a calculation of the amount of VAT that Victor would have saved for the year ended 31 December 2012 by joining the scheme.

The flat rate scheme percentage for hairdressing for Victor in the year ended 31 December 2012 is 13%. **(3 marks)**

(d) **Calculate the effect on Victor's net profit for the year ended 31 December 2012 as a consequence of the price increase and subsequent VAT registration.** **(4 marks)**

(Total: 15 marks)

Online question assistance

69 VECTOR LTD (ADAPTED)

Vector Ltd is registered for VAT, and is in the process of completing its VAT return for the quarter ended 31 March 2012. The following information is available.

(1) Sales invoices totalling £128,000 were issued in respect of standard rated sales in the UK. Vector Ltd offers its UK customers a 2.5% discount for prompt payment.

(2) On 15 March 2012 Vector Ltd received an advance deposit of £4,500 in respect of a contract with a UK company that is due to be completed during April 2012. The total value of the contract is £10,000. Both figures are inclusive of VAT.

(3) Vector Ltd also made sales to companies in Ruritania (not in the EU) totalling £35,000, to VAT registered EU companies totalling £48,000 and non-VAT registered EU customers totalling £14,250.

(4) Standard rated expenses amounted to £74,800. This includes £4,200 for entertaining customers.

(5) On 31 March 2012 Vector Ltd wrote off £12,000 due from a customer as a bad debt. The debt was in respect of three invoices, each of £4,000, that were due for payment on 15 August, 15 September and 15 October 2010 respectively.

(6) On 1 January 2012 the company purchased a motor car costing £9,800 for the use of its sales manager. The sales manager is provided with free petrol for private mileage. The car has CO_2 emissions of 205 g/km and the relevant quarterly scale charge is £488. Both figures are inclusive of VAT.

Unless stated otherwise all of the above figures are exclusive of VAT.

Required:

(a) **Calculate the amount of VAT payable by Vector Ltd for the quarter ended 31 March 2012.** **(8 marks)**

(b) State the conditions that Vector Ltd must satisfy before it will be permitted to use the cash accounting scheme, and advise the company of the implications of using the scheme. (4 marks)

(c) If Vector Ltd were a subsidiary in a UK group of companies, explain the advantages and disadvantages of Vector Ltd joining a group VAT registration rather than being registered separately. (3 marks)

(Total: 15 marks)

70 RAM-ROM LTD

Ram-Rom Ltd commenced trading as a manufacturer of computer equipment on 1 May 2011. The company registered for value added tax (VAT) on 1 January 2012.

Its inputs for each of the months from May 2011 to December 2011 are as follows:

		Goods purchased	*Services incurred*	*Fixed assets*
		£	£	£
2011	May	12,300	1,400	42,000
	June	11,200	5,100	–
	July	12,300	7,400	–
	August	16,400	6,300	14,400
	September	14,500	8,500	–
	October	18,800	9,000	–
	November	18,500	9,200	–
	December	23,400	8,200	66,600

During December 2011 Ram-Rom Ltd sold all of the fixed assets purchased during August 2011 for £12,000.

On 1 January 2012 £92,000 of the goods purchased were still in stock.

The above figures are all exclusive of VAT. Ram-Rom Ltd's sales are all standard rated.

A sample of the new sales invoice that Ram-Rom Ltd is going to issue to its customers is as follows:

SALES INVOICE

Ram-Rom Ltd
123 The High Street
London WC1 2AB
Telephone 0207 100 1234

Customer: XYZ Computers plc
Address: 99 The Low Road
Glasgow G1 2CD

Invoice Date and Tax Point: 1 January 2012

Item Description	**Quantity**	**Price**
		£
Hard Drives	5	220.00
Motherboards	2	100.00
Total Amount Payable (Including VAT)		320.00

Directors: Y Ram & Z Rom
Company Number: 1234567
Registered Office: 123 The High Street, London WC1 2AB

Ram-Rom Ltd pays for all of its inputs one month after receiving the purchase invoice. However, many customers are not paying Ram-Rom Ltd until four months after the date of the sales invoice. In addition, several customers have recently defaulted on the payment of their debts.

In order to encourage more prompt payment, Ram-Rom Ltd is considering offering all of its customers a 5% discount if they pay within one month of the date of the sales invoice. No discount is currently offered.

Required:

(a) **Explain why Ram-Rom Ltd was able to recover input VAT totalling £49,840 in respect of inputs incurred prior to registering for VAT on 1 January 2012. (5 marks)**

(b) **State what alterations Ram-Rom Ltd will have to make to its new sales invoices in order for them to be valid for VAT purposes. (3 marks)**

(c) **Explain the VAT implications of Ram-Rom Ltd offering all of its customers a 5% discount for prompt payment. (2 marks)**

(d) **Advise Ram-Rom Ltd of the conditions that it must satisfy before being permitted to use the VAT cash accounting scheme, and the advantages of joining the scheme. (5 marks)**

(Total: 15 marks)

71 LITHOGRAPH LTD (ADAPTED)

Lithograph Ltd runs a printing business, and is registered for VAT. Because its annual taxable turnover is only £250,000, the company uses the annual accounting scheme so that it only has to prepare one VAT return each year. The annual VAT period is the year ended 31 December.

Year ended 31 December 2011

The total amount of VAT payable by Lithograph Ltd for the year ended 31 December 2011 was £10,200.

Year ended 31 December 2012

The following information is available:

(1) Sales invoices totalling £250,000 were issued to VAT registered customers, of which £160,000 were for standard rated sales and £90,000 were for zero-rated sales.

(2) Purchase invoices totalling £45,000 were received from VAT registered suppliers, of which £38,000 were for standard rated purchases and £7,000 were for zero-rated purchases.

(3) Standard rated expenses amounted to £28,000. This includes £3,600 for entertaining overseas customers.

(4) On 1 January 2012 Lithograph Ltd purchased a motor car costing £18,400 for the use of its managing director. The manager director is provided with free petrol for private mileage, and the cost of this is included in the standard rated expenses in Note (3). The car has CO_2 emissions of 210 g/km and the relevant annual scale charge is £2,020. Both figures are inclusive of VAT.

(5) During the year ended 31 December 2012 Lithograph Ltd purchased machinery for £24,000, and sold office equipment for £8,000. Input VAT had been claimed when the office equipment was originally purchased.

(6) On 31 December 2012 Lithograph Ltd wrote off £4,800 due from a customer as a bad debt. The debt was in respect of an invoice that was due for payment on 31 May 2012.

Unless stated otherwise all of the above figures are exclusive of VAT.

Required:

(a) Calculate the monthly payments on account of VAT that Lithograph Ltd will have made in respect of the year ended 31 December 2012, and state in which months these will have been paid. (2 marks)

(b) (i) Calculate the total amount of VAT payable by Lithograph Ltd for the year ended 31 December 2012.

For this part of the question you should ignore the findings of the HM Revenue & Customs control visit. (6 marks)

(ii) Based on your answer to part (i) above, calculate the balancing payment that would have been paid with the annual VAT return, and state the date by which this return was due for submission. (2 marks)

(10 marks)

72 DENZIL DYER

Denzil Dyer has been a self-employed printer since 2005. He has recently registered for value added tax (VAT).

Denzil's sales consist of printed leaflets, some of which are standard rated and some of which are zero-rated. He sells to both VAT registered customers and to non-VAT registered customers.

For a typical printing contract, Denzil receives a 10% deposit at the time that the customer makes the order. The order normally takes fourteen days to complete, and Denzil issues the sales invoice three to five days after completion. Some customers pay immediately upon receiving the sales invoice, but many do not pay for up to two months.

Customers making an order of more than £500 are given a discount of 5% from the normal selling price. Denzil also offers a discount of 2.5% of the amount payable to those customers that pay within one month of the date of the sales invoice.

All of Denzil's printing supplies are purchased from a VAT registered supplier. He pays by credit card and receives a VAT invoice. However, Denzil also purchases various office supplies by cash without receiving any invoices.

Denzil does not use the annual accounting scheme, the cash accounting scheme or the flat rate scheme.

Required:

(a) Explain why it is important for Denzil to correctly identify whether a sale is standard rated or whether it is zero-rated. (2 marks)

(b) Advise Denzil as to when he should account for the output VAT relating to a typical standard rated printing supply. (4 marks)

(c) Explain the VAT implications of the two types of discount that Denzil gives or offers to his customers. (3 marks)

(d) Advise Denzil of the conditions that will have to be met in order for him to recover input VAT.

You are not expected to list those goods and services for which input VAT is non-recoverable. (3 marks)

(e) State the circumstances in which Denzil is and is not required to issue a VAT invoice, and the period during which such an invoice should be issued. (3 marks)

(Total: 15 marks)

73 ANNE ATTIRE *Walk in the footsteps of a top tutor*

Anne Attire runs a retail clothing shop. She is registered for value added tax (VAT), and is in the process of completing her VAT return for the quarter ended 31 May 2012.

The following information is available (all figures are exclusive of VAT):

(1) Cash sales amounted to £42,000, of which £28,000 was in respect of standard rated sales and £14,000 was in respect of zero-rated sales.

(2) Sales invoices totalling £12,000 were issued in respect of credit sales. These sales were all standard rated. Anne offers all of her credit sale customers a 5% discount for payment within one month of the date of the sales invoice, and 90% of the customers pay within this period. The sales figure of £12,000 is stated before any deduction for the 5% discount.

(3) Purchase and expense invoices totalling £19,200 were received from VAT registered suppliers. This figure is made up as follows:

	£
Standard rated purchases and expenses	11,200
Zero rated purchases	6,000
Exempt expenses	2,000
	19,200

Anne pays all of her purchase and expense invoices two months after receiving the invoice.

(4) On 31 May 2012 Anne wrote off two impairment losses (bad debts) that were in respect of standard rated credit sales. The first impairment loss was for £300, and was in respect of a sales invoice due for payment on 15 April 2012. The second impairment loss was for £800, and was in respect of a sales invoice due for payment on 10 November 2011.

Anne does not use the cash accounting scheme.

Anne will soon be 60 years old and is therefore considering retirement. On the cessation of trading Anne can either sell the fixed assets of her business on a piecemeal basis to individual VAT registered purchasers, or she can sell the entire business as a going concern to a single VAT registered purchaser.

Required:

(a) Calculate the amount of VAT payable by Anne Attire for the quarter ended 31 May 2012, and state the date by which the VAT return for this period was due for submission. **(6 marks)**

(b) State the conditions that Anne Attire must satisfy before she will be permitted to use the cash accounting scheme, and advise her of the implications of using the scheme. **(5 marks)**

(c) Advise Anne Attire as to what will happen to her VAT registration, and whether output VAT will be due in respect of the fixed assets, if she ceases trading and then:

(i) Sells her fixed assets on a piecemeal basis to individual VAT registered purchasers; **(2 marks)**

(ii) Sells her entire business as a going concern to a single VAT registered purchaser. **(2 marks)**

(15 marks)

Section 2

ANSWERS TO PRACTICE QUESTIONS

INCOME TAX AND NATIONAL INSURANCE

INCOME TAX BASICS AND EMPLOYMENT INCOME

1 SALLY AND SANDRA BURTON (ADAPTED) *Online question assistance*

Key answer tips

This question requires two income tax computations for taxpayers entitled to a personal age allowance. However, due to the level of income, abatement of the allowance is necessary.

One sister is employed, the other self-employed, allowing the examiner to test a wide range of the personal tax syllabus.

Always watch out for exempt income and consider whether income is received gross or net.

(a) **Sally Burton**

Income tax computation – 2011/12

	Total	*Other income*	*Savings income*
	£	£	£
Salary	17,000		
Car benefit (W1)	3,402		
Living accommodation (W2)	2,532		
Employment income	22,934	22,934	
NS&I Savings Certificate interest	Exempt		
Building society interest (£1,800 × 100/80)	2,250		2,250
Total income	25,184	22,934	2,250
Less: PAA (W3)	(9,348)	(9,348)	
Taxable income	15,836	13,586	2,250

		£
Income tax		
£		
13,586	x 20% (Other income)	2,717
2,250	x 20% (Savings income)	450
15,836		
Income tax liability		3,167
Less: Tax suffered at source		
PAYE		(2,400)
Building society interest (£2,250 x 20%)		(450)
Income tax payable		317

Tutorial note

NS&I Savings Certificate income is exempt from income tax.

NS&I Investment account interest is taxable and received gross

(b) **Sandra Burton**

Income tax computation – 2011/12

	Total	*Other income*	*Savings income*	*Dividend income*
	£	£	£	£
Trading income (W4)	24,145	24,145		
NS&I Investment account interest (received gross)	895		895	
Dividends (£900 × 100/90)	1,000			1,000
Total income	26,040	24,145	895	1,000
Less: PAA (W3)	(9,070)	(9,070)		
Taxable income	16,970	15,075	895	1,000

		£
Income tax		
£		
15,075	x 20% (Other income)	3,015
895	x 20% (Savings income)	179
1,000	x 10% (Dividend income)	100
16,970		
Income tax liability		3,294
Less: Tax credit		
Dividends (£1,000 x 10%)		(100)
Income tax payable		3,194

Workings

(W1) **Car Benefit**

CO_2 emissions = 187 g/km (rounded down to 185), available all year

	%
Petrol	15
Plus: (185 – 125) × $^1/_5$	12
Appropriate percentage	27
	£
List price of car	17,118
Less: Capital contributions	(2,000)
Appropriate percentage	15,118
Car benefit (£15,118 x 27% x 10/12)	3,402

Tutorial note

The maintenance costs are ignored as they are covered in the car benefit percentage. The car parking cost is an exempt benefit.

(W2) **Living accommodation**

	£
Annual value	1,632
Additional benefit for expensive accommodation (£120,000 (Note) – £75,000) x 4%	1,800
	3,432
Less: Contributions to employer (£75 × 12 months)	(900)
	2,532

Tutorial note

The property was bought in 2003, which is more than 6 years before it was made available to Sally. Therefore in the calculation of the additional benefit, the cost must be replaced with the market value of the accommodation when the property was first made available.

(W3) **Personal age allowance**

Sally	£		£
PAA (aged 66)			9,940
Less: Abatement			
Total income	25,184		
Income limit	(24,000)		
Excess	1,184	× 50%	(592)
Reduced PAA			9,348
Sandra			
PAA (aged 76)			10,090
Less: Abatement			
Total income	26,040		
Income limit	(24,000)		
Excess	2,040	× 50%	(1,020)
Reduced PAA			9,070

(W4) **Computation of tax adjusted trading profit**

	£
Net profit as per accounts	18,000
Add: Depreciation	2,425
Motor expenses (£5,400 × 4,000/12,000)	1,800
Private accommodation (£9,600 × 1/3)	3,200
Adjusted trading profit	25,425
Less: Capital allowances (W5)	(1,280)
Tax adjusted trading profit	24,145

(W5) **Capital allowances**

	Expensive car	*Business use*	*Allowances*
	£		£
TWDV b/f	9,600		
Less: WDA (20%)	(1,920)	x (8,000/12,000)	1,280
TWDV c/f	7,680		

Key answer tips

A full blown capital allowances computation is given in the workings to this answer to show how the allowances are calculated. However, where there are not many transactions it is perfectly acceptable to do one or two lines and just calculate the allowances available on each asset acquired rather than a full computation. If you do this however, be careful and make sure you explain your calculations clearly.

2 VIGOROUS PLC (ADAPTED)

Key answer tips

This question required the calculation of three benefit packages for three P11D (i.e. higher paid) employees. All of the key benefits that you need to be able to deal with in the F6 examination appear in this question!

Easy marks were available in parts (a) and (c) for explaining the term P11D and how benefits are assessed.

However, careful calculation is required for the benefits as there are many places where calculations can go wrong. Remember to time apportion the calculation where the benefit is not available all year, and don't forget to deduct any employee contributions paid.

(a) **P11D employees**

- Employees earning at a rate of £8,500 p.a. a year or more, and most directors (irrespective of earnings), are P11D employees.
- Benefits must be included when calculating the figure of £8,500, and these are calculated as if they were received by a P11D employee.
- Full-time working directors are excluded if they earn less than £8,500 p.a. and do not own more than 5% of their company's ordinary share capital.

(b) **Assessable benefits – 2011/12**

Andrea Lean

	£
Car benefit (W1)	4,990
Fuel benefit (W1)	6,580
Living accommodation	
– Ratcable value	7,000
– Additional benefit (W2)	2,760
– Furniture (£6,000 at 20%)	1,200
Mobile telephone	Nil

Tutorial note

1. *The living accommodation cost in excess of £75,000 so there will be an additional benefit.*

   Since the property was purchased within six years of first being provided, the benefit is based on the cost of the property plus improvements prior to 6 April 2011 (see W2).

2. *The annual running costs are personally borne by Andrea and therefore are not included as a benefit. Had her employer paid the costs, a £4,000 benefit would arise which she would have reduced to £Nil if she reimbursed the company directly.*

3. *The provision of one mobile telephone does not give rise to a taxable benefit, even if there is private use.*

Workings

(W1) **Car and fuel benefits**

CO_2 emissions = 265 g/km, available all year

	%	
Petrol	15	
Plus: (265 – 125) × $^1/_5$	28	
Appropriate percentage	43	Restricted to 35%

	£
Car benefit (£19,400 × 35%)	6,790
Less: Contributions (£150 × 12)	(1,800)
	4,990
Fuel benefit (£18,800 × 35%)	6,580

(W2) **Additional benefit for expensive accommodation**

	£	
Cost of property (January 2007)	130,000	
Improvements before 6 April 2011	14,000	
	144,000	
Less: Limit	(75,000)	
	69,000	
Additional benefit	× 4%	£2,760

Tutorial note

Improvements in May 2011 are not taken into account in calculating the benefit for 2011/12, as only improvements up to the start of the tax year are included.

However, they will be taken into account next year in calculating the benefit for 2012/13.

Ben Slim

	£
Beneficial loan (W1)	3,200
Relocation costs (£9,300 – £8,000) (Note 1)	1,300
Car benefit (W2) – Car 1 (Note 2)	230
Car benefit (W3) – Car 2	1,008
Childcare vouchers ((£60 – £28) × 36) (Note 4)	1,152

Tutorial note

1. *Only £8,000 of relocation costs are exempt.*

2. *A reduced percentage of 10% applies to petrol cars with CO_2 emissions between 76 – 120 g/km. If it had been a diesel car, the percentage would be 13%.*

   If the car had CO_2 emissions of less than 76 g/km, the percentage would have been 5% (8% if diesel).
3. *There is no fuel benefit as Ben reimburses the company for the full cost of private diesel.*
4. *For a higher rate taxpayer who joins an employer childcare scheme after 6 April 2011 the payment of up to £28 per week for approved childcare is an exempt benefit.*

Workings

(W1) **Beneficial loan**

Average method	£	
Loan at start of year	120,000	
Loan at end of year	100,000	
	220,000	
Average loan (£220,000 ÷ 2)	110,000	
Assessable benefit (£110,000 × 4% × 9/12)		£3,300
Precise method		
(£120,000 × 4% × 3/12)	1,200	
(£100,000 × 4% × 6/12)	2,000	
		£3,200

Ben will elect for the precise method and the benefit will therefore be £3,200.

(W2) **Car benefit – Car 1**

CO_2 emissions = 112 g/km, available 3 months

Appropriate rate = 10% (petrol car with CO_2 emissions between 76 – 120 g/km)

Car benefit = (£9,200 × 10% × 3/12) = £230

(W3) **Car benefit – Car 2**

CO_2 emissions = 129 g/km (rounded down to 125 g/km), available 6 months

	%
Diesel	18
Plus: (125 – 125) × 1/5	Nil
Appropriate percentage	18
Car benefit (£11,200 x 18% x 6/12)	£1,008

Chai Trim

	£
Van benefit (£3,000 x 10/12)	2,500
Fuel benefit (£550 x 10/12)	458
Television (W)	330
Health club membership	150
Computer (£1,900 x 20% x 3/12)	95

Tutorial note

1. *The van was only available for ten months of 2011/12 so the fixed annual £3,000 benefit is time apportioned.*
2. *Private fuel for the van was provided for ten months of 2011/12 so the benefit is time apportioned.*
3. *In-house benefits are valued according to the marginal cost. The taxable benefit in relation to the health club membership is therefore the direct costs of £150.*
4. *The computer was only available for 3 months of 2011/12 so the benefit is time apportioned.*

Working: Benefit for the sale of the television

Greater of

		£	£
(i)	MV at date of transfer	250	
	Less: Amount paid	(150)	
			100
(ii)	Original cost	800	
	Less: Annual value for 2009/10 and 2010/11 (20% x £800 x 2 years)	(320)	
		480	
	Less: Amount paid	(150)	
			330

(c) **Income tax liability in respect of assessable benefits**

- The income tax on recurring benefits, such as company motor cars, will normally be collected through the PAYE system by a reduction in the employee's tax coding.
- Tax not collected on this basis will be due under the self-assessment system.
- However, tax of less than £2,000 can be collected by an adjustment to an employee's tax coding for a subsequent tax year, whilst tax on minor benefits may be paid under an employer's PAYE settlement agreement.

3 ALI PATEL (ADAPTED) *Walk in the footsteps of a top tutor*

Key answer tips

A common style question requiring the comparison of two remuneration packages and the impact on the income tax computation and national insurance liabilities.

Part (b) requires a decision to be made based on the net cash flow position after taking account of all costs including income tax and national insurance.

Tutor's top tips

Part (a) of this question involves some fairly straightforward income tax computations.

Don't forget that there will be no car benefit if Ali uses his own car for business purposes!

You also need to calculate Class 1 NICs. Remember that for the employee, only cash earnings are subject to national insurance.

(a) **Income tax and Class 1 NICs**

(i) **First remuneration package**

Ali's income tax liability – 2011/12

	£
Salary (£29,000 + (£500 × 12))	35,000
Mileage allowance (W)	496
Employment income	35,496
Less: Personal allowance	(7,475)
Taxable income	28,021
Income tax liability (£28,021 × 20%)	5,604
Class 1 primary NIC – 2011/12	
(£35,000 – £7,225) × 12%	3,333

Working: Mileage allowance

The relocation is not expected to last for more than 24 months, so the branch office will be treated as a temporary workplace.

Mileage for the year = (1,600 x 12) = 19,200 miles

Ali will therefore be taxed on the mileage allowance paid by Box plc as follows:

	£	£
Mileage allowance received (19,200 at 38p)		7,296
Authorised mileage allowance:		
10,000 miles at 45p	4,500	
9,200 miles at 25p	2,300	
		(6,800)
Taxable benefit		496

Tutorial note

For NIC purposes only the excess mileage allowance above 45p per mile is subject to NIC. As Ali will be paid 38p per mile, none of the mileage allowance is charged to NIC.

(ii) ***Second remuneration package***

Ali's income tax liability – 2011/12

	£
Salary	29,000
Living accommodation (W)	9,600
Property business profit	6,000
Total income	44,600
Less: Personal allowance	(7,475)
Taxable income	37,125
Income tax	
£	
35,000 at 20%	7,000
2,125 at 40%	850
37,125	
Income tax liability	7,850

Class 1 primary NIC – 2011/12

(£29,000 – £7,225) × 12%	2,613

Working: Living accommodation

The benefit of living accommodation will be the greater of:

(i)	Annual value	£4,600
(ii)	Rent paid by the employer (£800 x 12)	£9,600

(b) **Most beneficial remuneration package**

Tutor's top tips

When calculating the net disposable income think just in terms of cash and identify all cash coming in and all cash payments going out. Cash payments out obviously include the tax liabilities calculated in part (a), but also includes other expenses such as commuting costs.

Even if you made some mistakes in part (a), as long as you include your tax figures here in this part you will be awarded full marks.

The question specifically asks you to advise Ali as to which remuneration package is most beneficial, so make sure that you do this. A statement of which package should be accepted is therefore needed.

You will be given full marks here if your advice is consistent with your analysis, even if it is the wrong advice!

	Package (1)	*Package (2)*
	£	£
Salary	35,000	29,000
Property business income	Nil	6,000
Mileage allowance received	7,296	Nil
Commuting costs	(1,800)	Nil
Class 1 NIC	(3,333)	(2,613)
Income tax	(5,604)	(7,850)
Net disposable income	31,559	24,537

If he chooses the first remuneration package, Ali will be £7,022 (£31,559 – £24,537) better off.

4 EDMOND BRICK (ADAPTED) *Walk in the footsteps of a top tutor*

Key answer tips

A tricky question, exclusively on property income, covering virtually the whole syllabus on this area. Detailed working knowledge is required. However, there are still a lot of easy marks to be gained.

Tutor's top tips

Part (a) is a classic written part of a question on furnished holiday lettings and should have provided easy marks.

However, be careful, this question only required the income tax advantages of furnished holiday lettings – not any other tax advantages.

So, ensure that you read the question carefully, and do not waste time giving information that scores no marks.

(a) **Income tax advantages of furnished holiday lettings**

- Capital allowances are available on plant and machinery instead of the 10% wear and tear allowance.
- The income qualifies as relevant earnings for the purposes of tax relief on pension contributions.

Tutorial note

A furnished holiday letting property is also treated as a business property for capital gains tax purposes and consequently has the advantage of being eligible for gift relief, rollover relief and Entrepreneurs' relief.

However, remember that mentioning the other tax advantages was not required and gained no marks.

(b) **Furnished holiday letting loss – 2011/12**

Tutor's top tips

Having read the question requirement first, you will have seen that the question clearly requires you to prepare a property income computation.

Therefore, when reading the body of the question, be sure to identify which properties are let furnished and which are let unfurnished (if any). In addition, which of the furnished properties are likely to satisfy the conditions to be treated as furnished holiday lettings (FHL).

Highlight the information on the question paper as you read it, keeping the FHL information separately from the other properties which are pooled together.

	£	£
Rent receivable (£370 × 18)		6,660
Repairs	7,400	
Other expenses	2,710	
Capital allowances (£5,700 × 100% AIA)	5,700	
		(15,810)
Furnished holiday letting loss		(9,150)

Tutorial note

Remember that furnished holiday lettings are treated as profits of a separate trade and therefore the trading income rules are followed.

In particular, capital allowances are given on plant and machinery, furnishings etc – instead of the wear and tear allowance. The annual investment allowance is therefore available and applies to the first £100,000 of expenditure.

(c) Property business profit – 2011/12

Tutor's top tips

There are several properties to deal with in this question. However, only one computation is required.

There is no need to do separate computations to calculate a profit or loss for each property. Edmond will be assessed on the net property income for the year.

Set up your answer with subheadings "income" and "allowable expenses" and leave space underneath to insert the relevant information. Then go through the information in the question about each property in turn and extract the points to go straight into the answer in a logical order.

Note that on your first reading of the question you should already have highlighted the key information. You should have identified which properties are let unfurnished and furnished, and therefore which are eligible for the wear and tear allowance.

The most common mistake made in exams on questions like this is either to forget the wear and tear allowance completely, or to incorrectly apply it to all properties.

In addition, watch out for the rent-a-room relief if the owner rents out any part of his own property. Often the rent is below the deminimis limit of £4,250 and is therefore exempt. However, this is not always the case.

	£	£
Income		
Rent receivable – Property 2 (£575 × 12)		6,900
– Property 3 (£710 × 7)		4,970
– Property 4		4,600
Furnished room – Own property (W2)		790
		17,260
Premium received for sub-lease – Property 4 (Note 1)		
Premium	15,000	
Less: 2% × £15,000 × (5 – 1)	(1,200)	
		13,800
		31,060
Council tax	1,200	
Wear and tear allowance (W1)	570	
Irrecoverable rent (£710 × 3) (Note 2)	2,130	
Advertising	670	
Loan interest (Note 3)	6,700	
Rent paid	6,800	
Insurance (£340 + £290 + £360)	990	
		(19,060)
Property business profit		12,000

Tutorial note

1. *An alternative method of calculating the assessment on the premium received:*
   = £15,000 × (51 – 5) / 50 = £13,800
2. *All rents accrued in the tax year must be included in the computation. However, where all attempts have been made to collect the rent from the tenant, but it is not recoverable, relief is available by deducting the irrecoverable amount as an allowable deduction.*
3. *For individuals, interest payable on a loan taken out to purchase a property which is let out to tenants, is an allowable deduction against rental income. Note that for companies, such interest is not allowable against rental income. Instead, it is allowable against other interest income.*

Workings

(W1) **Wear and tear allowance – Property 2**

	£
Rent receivable	6,900
Less: Council tax	(1,200)
	5,700
Wear and tear allowance (£5,700 x 10%)	570

(W2) **Rent-a-Room Relief**

Claiming rent-a-room relief in respect of the furnished room is more beneficial than the normal basis of assessment as shown below:

		£	£
(i)	*Normal assessment*		
	Rents	5,040	
	Less: Expenses (Note)	(1,140)	
			3,900
(ii)	*Claiming rent-a-room relief*		
	Rents	5,040	
	Less: Rent-a-room limit	(4,250)	
			790

Tutorial note

In the examiner's answers, it was assumed that the expenses of £1,140 included the wear and tear allowance of £504 (£5,040 × 10%).

Even if you had assumed that the wear and tear allowance needed to be deducted as well as the £1,140, the 'normal' assessment would give a higher assessment than claiming rent-a-room relief and the decision would be the same.

Examiner's report

In part (a) some candidates discussed the qualifying conditions for a furnished holiday letting rather than the advantages of a property being so treated.

Parts (b) and (c) presented few problems.

The only aspects that consistently caused difficulty were the capital allowances for the furnished holiday letting (candidates either claimed a wear and tear allowance or deducted the full cost of the capital expenditure without indicating that the AIA is available) and the furnished room (candidates did not appreciate that rent-a-room relief could be claimed).

ACCA marking scheme

		Marks
(a)	Capital allowances	1.0
	Relevant earnings for pension purposes	1.0
		2.0
(b)	Rent receivable	0.5
	Repairs	1.0
	Other expenses	0.5
	Capital allowances	1.0
		3.0
(c)	Lease premium received	1.5
	Rent receivable	1.5
	Furnished room	1.0
	Council tax	0.5
	Wear and tear allowance	1.5
	Impairment losses	0.5
	Advertising	0.5
	Loan interest	1.0
	Rent paid	0.5
	Insurance	1.5
		10.0
Total		15.0

5 PETER CHIC (ADAPTED) *Walk in the footsteps of a top tutor*

Key answer tips

A classic individual income tax computation, covering several aspects of employment income, together with a small element of other types of income.

Initially, due to the amount of information given in the scenario, this question looks very daunting. However, there was nothing that should have caused significant problems.

Tutor's top tips

Part (a) of this question was straight forward if approached logically. Remember to run down each line of the question in turn and consider the implications of each piece of information. Remember not to get held up on any one calculation.

Always ensure that you read the question carefully. The requirement is to calculate income tax payable. Ensure you do not drop easy marks by only calculating the income tax liability.

Make the marker your friend, if you keep your calculations clear and easy to read you will score much higher marks. Always ensure your workings are clearly labelled.

(a) **Peter**

Income tax computation – 2011/12

	Total income	*Other income*	*Savings income*	*Dividend income*
	£	£	£	£
Employment income (W1)	131,285	131,285		
Property income (W4)	13,660	13,660		
Building Society interest (£4,760 x 100/80)	5,950		5,950	
Dividends (£2,700 × 100/90)	3,000			3,000
Premium bond prize	Exempt			
Total income	153,895	144,945	5,950	3,000
Less: Adjusted PA (W5)	(Nil)	(Nil)		
Taxable income	153,895	144,945	5,950	3,000

Income tax:	£		£
Other income – Basic rate (W6)	37,925	× 20%	7,585
Other income – Higher rate	107,020	× 40%	42,808
	144,945		
Savings income – Higher rate	5,950	× 40%	2,380
Dividends – Higher rate	2,030	× 32.5%	660
	152,925		
Dividends – Additional rate	970	× 42.5%	412
	153,895		
Income tax liability			53,845
Less: Tax deducted at source			
Dividends (£3,000 x 10%)			(300)
Building society interest (£5,950 x 20%)			(1,190)
PAYE			(42,000)
Income tax payable			10,355

Tutorial note

The premium bond prize is exempt from income tax.

Workings

(W1) **Employment income**

	£	£
Salary		75,600
Bonus – Paid 30 April 2011		14,300
Bonus – Paid 31 March 2012		13,700
		103,600
Assessable benefits:		
Car Benefit (W2)	7,175	
Fuel Benefit (W2)	6,580	
Living accommodation		
– Annual value	9,450	
– Additional benefit (W3)	3,920	
Mobile phone (£250 x 20%) (Note 1)	50	
Health Club membership (Note 2)	510	
Overnight allowance (Note 3)	Nil	
		27,685
Employment income		131,285

Tutorial note

1. *Entitlement to, and the payment of, both bonuses occurred in 2011/12, therefore both amounts are assessable in that tax year.*
2. *The exemption for mobile telephones does not apply to the second telephone. The normal 20% use of assets benefit applies.*
3. *The membership of the health club is assessed at the cost to the employer.*
4. *Payments for private incidental expenses are exempt up to £10 per night when spent outside the UK.*

(W2) **Car and fuel benefit**

CO_2 emissions = 222 g/km (rounded down to 220 g/km), available all year

	%	
Diesel	18	
Plus: (220 – 125) × $^1/_5$	19	
Appropriate percentage	37	Restricted to 35%

	£	£
List price	22,500	
Less: Capital contribution	(2,000)	
	20,500	
Car benefit (£20,500 x 35%)		7,175
Fuel benefit (£18,800 x 35%)		6,580

(W3) **Living accommodation – Additional benefit**

The living accommodation cost is in excess of £75,000 so there will be an additional benefit.

Since the property was not purchased more than six years before first being provided to Peter, the benefit is based on the cost of the property plus subsequent improvements.

The additional benefit is therefore:

(£160,000 + £13,000 – £75,000) x 4% = £3,920

(W4) **Property income**

	£	£
Income		
Rent receivable– Property 1 (£500 × 5)		2,500
– Property 2 (£2,820 × 8)		22,560
		25,060
Allowable expenses		
Irrecoverable rent (£500 × 2) (Note 1)	1,000	
Repairs	600	
Advertising	875	
Loan interest	7,800	
Insurance ((£660 x 3/12) + (£1,080 x 9/12))	975	
Wear and tear allowance (Note 2)		
(£2,500 – £1,000) × 10%	150	
		(11,400)
Property business profit		13,660

Tutorial note

1. *All rents accrued must be included in the computation. However, where all attempts have been made to collect the rent from the tenant, but it is not recoverable, relief is available by deducting the irrecoverable amount as an allowable deduction.*

2. *The wear and tear allowance can only be claimed in respect of the first property since the second property is not let out furnished.*

The wear and tear allowance on Property 1 is based on the rents actually received of £1,500 (£2,500 rents receivable – £1,000 irrecoverable debts).

Note that on the subject of the calculation of the wear and tear allowance, HMRC manuals refer to "net rents" as the start position and this has been interpreted to mean "rents receivable ***after*** *irrecoverable debts have been deducted".*

However, credit was also given in the exam if the allowance was calculated based on the rents receivable without a deduction for irrecoverable debts.

(W5) **Adjusted Personal Allowance**

	£
Total income = Net income	153,895
Less: Gross Gift Aid donation (£2,340 x 100/80)	(2,925)
Adjusted net income (ANI)	150,970

As ANI is above £114,950, the personal allowance is reduced to £Nil.

(W6) **Extension of basic and additional rate band**

	Basic rate £	*Additional rate* £
Basic rate band threshold	35,000	150,000
Plus: Gross Gift Aid donation (as above)	2,925	2,925
Extended basic and additional rate bands	37,925	152,925

(b) **National Insurance Contributions**

Tutor's top tips

Part (b) required a little care. As long as you remember that NIC is payable on cash earnings only by the employee, and that the employer pays on both the cash earnings (Class 1 secondary) and assessable benefits (Class 1A), then there should not be too many problems.

Note that it does not matter if you have calculated the employment income incorrectly in part (a) as long as you calculate the NIC correctly on whatever figure you have, you will still score maximum marks on this part.

Payable by Peter

	£
(£42,475 – £7,225) x 12%	4,230
(£103,600 – £42,475) x 2%	1,222
Class 1 Primary NICs	5,452

Payable by Haute-Couture Ltd

	£
Class 1 Secondary NIC	
(£103,600 – £7,072) x 13.8%	13,321
Class 1A NICs	
(£27,685 (part (a) (W1)) x 13.8%)	3,821
	17,142

Examiner's report

This question was very well answered by the majority of candidates.

In part (a) a few candidates did not appreciate that both bonuses were to be treated as earnings, whilst the basis of assessing the second mobile telephone was not always known. Some candidates deducted the Gift Aid donation rather than extending the basic rate tax band.

In part (b) the most common mistake was to include taxable benefits when calculating Class 1 National Insurance contributions.

ACCA marking scheme

		Marks
(a)	Salary	0.5
	Bonus payments	1.0
	Car benefit – Relevant percentage	1.0
	– Capital contribution	0.5
	– Calculation	0.5
	Fuel benefit	1.0
	Living accommodation – Annual value	1.0
	– Additional benefit	2.0
	Mobile telephone	1.0
	Health club membership	0.5
	Overseas allowance	0.5
	Property business profit – Rent receivable	1.0
	– Impairment losses	0.5
	– Repairs	0.5
	– Advertising	0.5
	– Loan interest	1.0
	– Insurance	1.0
	– Wear and tear allowance	1.0
	Building society interest	0.5
	Dividends	0.5
	Premium bond prize	0.5
	Personal allowance	0.5
	Extension of basic rate and additional rate band	1.0
	Income tax	1.5
	Tax suffered at source	1.5
		21.0
(b)	Employee Class 1 NIC	1.5
	Employer Class 1 NIC	1.5
	Employer Class 1A NIC	1.0
		4.0
Total		25.0

INCOME TAX BASICS AND FROM SELF-EMPLOYMENT

6 CAROL COURIER

Key answer tips

A straight forward purely computational question dealing with the income tax and national insurance consequences of being employed and self-employed.

Part (c) requires a comparison of the net disposable income arising from the two options.

(a) **Carol continues to be employed**

Carol's income tax liability – 2011/12

	£
Salary	37,500
Less: Pension contributions (£37,500 × 5%)	(1,875)
Employment income	35,625
Less: PA	(7,475)
Taxable income	28,150
Income tax liability (£28,150 × 20%)	5,630
Class 1 NICs – Primary contributions	
(£37,500 – £7,225) × 12%	3,633

(b) **Carol accepts self-employed contract**

Carol's income tax liability – 2011/12

	£
Income (£43,500 + £8,000)	51,500
Less: Expenses (£4,400 + £2,800)	(7,200)
Trading income	44,300
Less: PA	(7,475)
Taxable income	36,825
Income tax liability (£36,825 × 20%) (Working)	7,365
Class 4 NICs	
(£42,475 – £7,225) × 9%	3,172
(£44,300 – £42,475) × 2%	36
	3,208
Class 2 NICs	
(£2.50 for 52 weeks)	130

Working: Extension of the basic rate band

	£
Basic rate band	35,000
Plus: Gross pension contributions	2,000
Extended basic rate band	37,000

All of Carol's taxable income of £36,825 falls into this extended basic rate band and is therefore taxed at 20%.

(c) **Benefit of accepting self-employed contract**

	Employed	*Self employed*
	£	£
Salary	37,500	Nil
Trading income	Nil	44,300
Pension contributions paid (Note)	(1,875)	(1,600)
NIC – Class 1 and Class 4	(3,633)	(3,208)
NIC – Class 2	Nil	(130)
Income tax	(5,630)	(7,365)
Net disposable income	26,362	31,997

It is therefore beneficial for Carol to accept the offer to work on a self-employed basis as her net income will increase by £5,635 (£31,997 – £26,362).

Tutorial note

Carol will pay personal pension contributions net of basic rate tax. If self-employed she will therefore pay £1,600 (£2,000 × 80%).

Key answer tips

When calculating the net disposable income think just in terms of cash and identify all cash coming in and all cash payments going out.

Cash payments out obviously include the tax liabilities but also includes other expenses such as pension contributions.

7 CHATRU (ADAPTED) *Walk in the footsteps of a top tutor*

Key answer tips

A question in two parts but the parts are not independent.

In part 1 (a) and (b) you have to apply the opening and closing year rules to calculate the trading income assessments.

The 2011/12 assessment is then needed in the income tax computation in part 2 (a), which is a straight forward 'bread and butter' computation that should not have caused problems.

Part 2 (b) requires some thought into tax planning advice for a husband and wife. Typically the solution is to recommend the transfer of some assets generating income from the higher rate taxpayer to the lower rate taxpayer. However, there are other valid points that could have been made.

Tutor's top tips

In part 1 (a), be sure to show each tax year; describe the basis of assessment; apply to the question; give the appropriate dates; and then show the working to calculate the number.

Just calculating the number will not gain full marks for this type of question.

(1) (a) **Assessable income**

Tax year	*Basis of assessment*		£
2007/08	Actual basis (1.11.07 – 5.4.08)		
	£40,500 × 5/18		11,250
2008/09	Actual basis (6.4.08 – 5.4.09)		
	£40,500 × 12/18		27,000
2009/10	12 months ended 30.4.09		
	£40,500 × 12/18		27,000
2010/11	CYB (y/e 30.4.10)		12,000
2011/12	Year of cessation – 1.5.10 to 31.3.12		
	(£24,000 + £50,000)	74,000	
	Less: Overlap profits (1.5.08 – 5.4.09)		
	£40,500 × 11/18	(24,750)	
		———	49,250
			———
Total assessable income			126,500
			———

Tutorial note

Check that total assessments = total tax adjusted profits of the business:

(£40,500 + £12,000 + £24,000 + £50,000) = £126,500

(b) **Assessments (cessation 30.4.12)**

Tutor's top tips

You need to show clearly that the effect of trading another month will be that there is another tax year of assessment, and that therefore only the final assessments will be affected.

Make sure that you explain the effect in words as well as in the numbers.

Tax year	*Basis of assessment*	£	£
2007/08	(as above)		11,250
2008/09	(as above)		27,000
2009/10	(as above)		27,000
2010/11	(as above)		12,000
2011/12	CYB (y/e 30.4.11)		24,000
2012/13	Year of cessation – 1.5.11 to 30.4.12		
	(£50,000 + £4,200)	54,200	
	Less: Overlap profits (as above)	(24,750)	
			29,450
			130,700

Tutorial note

Check that total assessments = total tax adjusted profits of the business:

(£126,500 + £4,200) = £130,700

Assessments under the current year basis ensure that all profits earned are assessed. If Chatru continues to trade for one extra month, earning an additional £4,200 his total assessments will increase by £4,200.

However, by trading for one extra month, the amount assessed in 2011/12 is reduced from £49,250 to £24,000. This may be an income tax benefit if Chatru has little or no other income, as profits are now covered by the basic rate band.

Tutorial note

The taxpayer can choose his date of cessation. The choice of date is important as there is an opportunity to alter the timing of assessments over the final years.

This may change the rate of tax at which the profits are assessed and the due date of payment.

In practice this is an important tax planning consideration in the closing years of a business.

Tutor's top tips

Strictly there is no need, in part 1 (a) and (b), to provide a proof that total profits earned equals total profits assessed but it is good practice and will uncover any arithmetic mistakes for you to go back and correct.

However, only go back and correct an answer if you have time. Normally it is better to move on and finish the question.

(2) (a) **Income tax computation – 2011/12**

Tutor's top tips

A straightforward income tax computation is required in part 2 (a) and the trading income figure in the income tax computation comes from part 1 (a).

Remember that even if you got that part wrong, you can get all of the marks in part 2 (a) for following through your computation in the correct way using your trading income figure – so keep going!

	Total	*Other Income*	*Savings income*	*Dividend income*
	£	£	£	£
Trading income (part 1 (a))	49,250	49,250		
Property business income (W1)	10,000	10,000		
Bank interest (£2,500 × 100/80)	3,125		3,125	
ISA interest (Exempt)	Nil			
Dividends (£33,500 × 100/90)	37,222			37,222
Total income	99,597	59,250	3,125	37,222
Less: PA	(7,475)	(7,475)		
Taxable income	92,122	51,775	3,125	37,222

Income tax		£
£		
41,250	at 20% (W2) (Other income)	8,250
10,525	at 40% (Other income)	4,210
51,775		
3,125	at 40% (Savings)	1,250
37,222	at 32.5% (Dividends)	12,097
92,122		
Income tax liability		25,807
Less: Tax suffered at source		
	Dividends (£37,222 at 10%)	(3,722)
	Bank interest (£3,125 at 20%)	(625)
Income tax payable		21,460

Workings

(W1) **Property business income**

(i) **Rent from the room in house**

The rental income is less than £4,250 per annum and is therefore exempt from income tax under the rent a room scheme.

(ii) **Property business profit**

Furnished property	£
Rent received	11,100
Less: Interest paid	(500)
Allowable expenses	(1,600)
Cooker (Note 1)	Nil
Wear & tear allowance (10% × (£11,100 – £800 – £300))	(1,000)
	8,000
Land (£4,000 × 50%) (Note 2)	2,000
Property business profit	10,000

Tutorial note

1. *The purchase of the cooker is capital expenditure and therefore not allowable.*
2. *Income from assets jointly held by husband and wife is split 50:50 between the spouses unless they have elected to have the income taxed in relation to their actual ownership proportions.*

   The question states that Chatru and Sandra have not made any elections in relation to their income. The rental income will therefore be split equally between them for tax purposes.

(W2) **Extended basic rate band**

	£
Basic rate band	35,000
Plus: Gross Gift Aid donation (£5,000 × 100/80)	6,250
Extended basic rate band	41,250

(b) **Chatru and Sandra – Ways to reduce joint income tax liability**

Tutor's top tips

The question only required two ways in which the couple could have saved tax. The full answer below is produced for tutorial purposes.

Sandra's only taxable income is from her part-time earnings of £8,000 and rental income from the land of £2,000 p.a. She is therefore a basic rate taxpayer.

Chatru was a higher rate taxpayer in 2011/12 and if the level of his dividend income remains the same he is likely to continue to be so in future years.

Chatru has suffered tax on his property income and savings income at 40% and on his dividend income at 32.5%.

Sandra has an unused basic rate band of £32,475 (W). She would therefore only pay tax at 20% on this income up to the level of her remaining basic rate band.

Chatru and Sandra should therefore have considered the following to reduce their income tax liability:

(1) Electing for the rental income from the land to be taxed in accordance with their actual ownership proportions of 25:75. This would have reduced their joint tax liability by £200 (£1,000 × (40% – 20%)).

(2) Transferring income generating assets such as the shares and the bank account into Sandra's name in order to produce income to fully utilise her basic rate band.

(3) Transferring funds from either the bank account or the shareholdings into an Individual Savings Account in Sandra's name in order to generate tax free income.

Working: Remaining basic rate band

Tutorial note

Remember that to calculate the remaining basic rate band you need to compare £35,000 to Sandra's taxable income which is after deducting her personal allowance.

	£	£
Basic rate band		35,000
Earnings	8,000	
Property income	2,000	
	10,000	
Less: PA	(7,475)	
Taxable income		(2,525)
Remaining basic rate band		32,475

8 OLIVE GREEN (ADAPTED) *Walk in the footsteps of a top tutor*

Key answer tips

A classic, straightforward income tax computation for a self-employed individual with some self-assessment points at the end.

The adjustment of profit should not have caused problems but remember to layout your answer in the way the examiner has specifically asked for it. Remember also to read the private use / business use proportion of Olive's car carefully and adjust both the profits figure and the capital allowances.

The income tax computation was not difficult; the only area of concern may have been the relief for interest on the loan taken out to purchase an asset for use in Olive's employment.

Calculating balancing payments, payments on account and interest for late payment of tax are commonly examined and should not have been problematic.

(a) **Tax adjusted trading profit – year ended 31 March 2012**

Tutor's top tips

In the adjustment to profits calculation it is important to list all the major items indicated in the question requirement, showing a zero (0) for expenditure that is allowable. This is because credit will be given for showing no adjustment where none is needed.

If required, also add notes to show why you have not adjusted for an item, or why you have added it back. However, lengthy explanations are not required where the requirement is just to 'calculate' the adjusted profits, rather than to explain them.

Always show your workings if the figure you are adjusting for is not clear from the question.

	£	£
Net profit	30,050	
Depreciation	2,350	
Private accommodation (£1,980 + £5,920) × 30%	2,370	
Motor expenses (£4,700 × 12,000/20,000)	2,820	
Lease costs – high emission car (£3,000 × 15%)	450	
Fine (Note 1)	220	
Theft by employee (Note 2)	0	
Donation to political party	100	
Trade subscription (Note 3)	0	
Excessive salary (Note 4) (£14,000 – £10,500)	3,500	
Own consumption (Note 5) (52 × £45)	2,340	
Patent royalties (£150 × 4) (Note 6)		600
Capital allowances (W)		1,200
	44,200	1,800
	(1,800)	
Tax adjusted trading profit	42,400	

Tutorial note

1. *Fines are not allowable except for parking fines incurred by an employee.*
2. *Theft is allowable provided it is by an employee rather than the business owner.*
3. *Trade subscriptions are allowable as they have been incurred wholly and exclusively for the purposes of the trade.*
4. *A salary to a family member must not be excessive. Since Olive's daughter is paid £3,500 more than the other sales assistants, this amount is not allowable.*
5. *Goods for own consumption are valued at selling price. It is assumed that no adjustment has been made in the accounts for these goods. If the goods taken out had already been correctly accounted for, only the profit element of £15 per week would be adjusted for.*
6. *Patent royalties are allowable deductions from trading profit if they are for the purposes of the trade. As they have not yet been deducted in arriving at the profit, a deduction is required.*

   Read the question carefully as normally they have already been accounted for and therefore no adjustment is required.

Working: Capital allowances

	Expensive car	*Business use*	*Allowances*
	£		£
TWDV b/f	15,800		
WDA – restricted	(3,000)	× (8,000/20,000)	1,200
TWDV c/f	12,800		

Tutor's top tips

A familiar full blown capital allowances computation is given in the workings to this answer to show how the allowances are calculated.

However, where there are not many transactions it is perfectly acceptable to do one or two lines and just calculate the allowances available on each asset acquired rather than a full computation.

If you do this however, be careful and make sure you explain your calculations clearly.

(b) **Income tax computation – 2011/12**

Tutor's top tips

A straightforward income tax computation is required.

Note that you would still get full marks for this part, even if your trading income from part (a) is incorrect.

	Total	*Other*	*Savings*	*Dividends*
	£	£	£	£
Trading income (part (a))	42,400	42,400		
Employment income	6,000	6,000		
Building society interest				
(£1,440 × 100/80)	1,800		1,800	
Dividends (£1,080 × 100/90)	1,200			1,200
Total income	51,400	48,400	1,800	1,200
Less: Reliefs				
Loan interest (Note)	(220)	(220)		
Net income	51,180	48,180	1,800	1,200
Less: PA	(7,475)	(7,475)		
Taxable income	43,705	40,705	1,800	1,200

Tutorial note

The interest on the loan to purchase equipment for employment qualifies as a relief deductible from total income since the loan was used by Olive to finance expenditure for a qualifying purpose. Note that the interest is quoted gross and is paid gross.

Income tax		£
£		
37,600	at 20% (Other income) (W)	7,520
3,105	at 40% (Other income)	1,242
40,705		
1,800	at 40% (Savings)	720
1,200	at 32.5% (Dividends)	390
43,705		
Income tax liability		9,872
Less:	Tax suffered at source	
	Dividends (£1,200 at 10%)	(120)
	PAYE	(1,200)
	Building society interest (£1,800 at 20%)	(360)
Income tax payable		8,192

Capital gains tax liability – 2011/12

	£
Chargeable gain	12,800
Less: AE	(10,600)
Taxable gain	2,200
Capital gains tax (£2,200 x 28%)	616

Tutorial note

Capital gains tax is calculated at 28% because capital gains are taxed as the top slice of taxable income and Olive is a higher rate taxpayer.

Balancing payment for 2011/12 – due on 31 January 2013

	£
Total income tax and CGT (£8,192 + £616)	8,808
Less: Payments on account	(4,900)
Balancing payment	3,908

Payments on account – 2012/13

Payments on account are not required for capital gains tax, so the payments on account for 2012/13 will be £4,096 (£8,192 × 50%).

These will be due on 31 January 2013 and 31 July 2013.

Working: Extension of basic rate band

	£
Basic rate band	35,000
Plus: Gross pension contributions	2,600
Extended basic rate band	37,600

(c) **Consequences of paying balancing payment late**

Tutor's top tips

Interest calculations should be made to the nearest month in the examination, unless the question says otherwise.

- Late payment interest is charged where a balancing payment is paid late.

  This will run from 31 January 2013 to 30 April 2013.
- The interest charge will be: (£3,908 × 3% × 3/12) = £29
- In addition, a late payment penalty of £195 (£3,908 at 5%) will be imposed as the balancing payment is more than one month late (but less than six months late).

9 FOO DEE (ADAPTED)

Key answer tips

Part (a) requires a simple adjustment of profit and capital allowances computation which should not have caused any problems if you remembered that it is a 9 month accounting period and therefore the WDAs are time apportioned.

In part (b) the opening year basis of assessment rules have to be applied to calculate the trading income assessment for 2011/12 for inclusion in the income tax computation.

The employment income computation was complicated in working out the business mileage claim allowance to be deducted. Knowledge of the ordinary commuting rules and temporary workplace rules are tested.

Otherwise the income tax, capital gains tax and self-assessment parts were straightforward.

This style of question is often examined, so you need to make sure you know the approach and techniques required.

(a) **Trading profit – period ended 30 September 2012**

	£	£
Net profit	125,730	
Depreciation	3,500	
Motor expenses (£4,200 × 2,000/6,000)	1,400	
Private accommodation (£12,800 × 1/4)	3,200	
Capital allowances (W)		77,390
	133,830	77,390
	(77,390)	
Trading profit	56,440	

Working: Capital allowances – nine months ended 30 September 2012

	£	*Pool* £	*Private use car* £		*Allowances* £
Additions (no AIA)					
Car (111 – 160 g/km)			14,600		
Additions (with AIA)					
Equipment	81,200				
Less: AIA (Note 1)	(75,000)				75,000
		6,200			
WDA (20% x 9/12)(Note 2)			(2,190)	× 4/6	1,460
WDA (20% x 9/12)		(930)			930
TWDV c/f		5,270	12,410		
Total allowances					77,390

Tutorial note

1. *Both the WDA and the AIA available are time apportioned by 9/12 as the accounting period is only 9 months long. The maximum AIA available is therefore £75,000 (£100,000 x 9/12). The remainder is then subject to the WDA.*

2. *Capital allowances on new car purchases are calculated based on the CO_2 emissions.*

   As the car purchased in this question has CO_2 emissions of between 111 – 160 g/km, it is eligible for a WDA at 20%. The WDA then needs to be adjusted for the short accounting period and for the private use by Foo Dee, as only the business use proportion of the allowance can be claimed.

   The business mileage is 4,000 out of 6,000 miles.

(b) **Income tax computation – 2011/12**

	Total	Other	Savings	Dividends
	£	£	£	£
Salary	38,000			
Less: Pension contributions (6%)	(2,280)			
	35,720			
Relocation costs (W1)	4,900			
Expense claim (W2)	(2,048)			
Employment income	38,572	38,572		
Trading profit (W3)	18,813	18,813		
Building society interest (£640 × 100/80)	800		800	
Dividends (£360 × 100/90)	400			400
Total income	58,585	57,385	800	400
Less: PA	(7,475)	(7,475)		
Taxable income	51,110	49,910	800	400

Income tax

£		£
37,000	at 20% (Other income) (W4)	7,400
12,910	at 40% (Other income)	5,164
49,910		
800	at 40% (Savings income)	320
400	at 32·5% (Dividend income)	130
51,110		

	£
Income tax liability	13,014
Less: Tax suffered at source	
Dividends (£400 at 10%)	(40)
PAYE	(5,600)
Building society interest (£800 at 20%)	(160)
Income tax payable	7,214

Capital gains tax liability – 2011/12

	£
Chargeable gain	17,600
Less: AE	(10,600)
Taxable gain	7,000
Capital gains tax (£7,000 x 28%) (Note)	1,960

Tutorial note

Capital gains tax is calculated at 28% as capital gains are taxed as the top slice of taxable income and Foo Dee is a higher rate taxpayer.

Balancing payment and payments on account

- No payments on account have been made, so the balancing payment for 2011/12 due on 31 January 2013 is £9,174 (£7,214 + £1,960).
- Payments on account are not required for CGT, so the payments on account for 2012/13 will be £3,607 (£7,214 × 50%).
- These will be due on 31 January 2013 and 31 July 2013.

Workings

(W1) **Relocation expenses**

Only £8,000 of relocation costs is exempt, and so the taxable benefit is £4,900 (£12,900 – £8,000).

(W2) **Expense claim**

Ordinary commuting (i.e. travel between home and the permanent workplace, including journeys to turn off the fire alarm) and private travel do not qualify for relief.

The travel to a temporary workplace qualifies as business mileage as it is for a period lasting less than 24 months.

Therefore, business mileage = (750 + 3,800) = 4,550 miles

As the company does not reimburse Foo Dee for any mileage, she is allowed to claim an allowable deduction based on the HMRC authorised mileage allowance payments.

Expenses claim = (4,550 miles x 45p) = £1,820

(W3) **Trading income assessment – 2011/12**

9 months ended 30 September 2012		
Trading profit		£56,440
Tax year	*Basis of assessment*	
2011/12	Opening year rules apply	
	Actual basis (1.1.2012 – 5.4.2012)	
	(£56,440 x 3/9)	£18,813

(W4) **Extension of basic rate band**

	£
Basic rate band threshold	35,000
Plus: Personal pension contribution (£1,600 x 100/80)	2,000
Extended basic rate band	37,000

(c) **Consequences of not paying the balancing payment**

> ***Tutor's top tips***
>
> *Interest calculations should be made to the nearest month in the examination, unless the question says otherwise.*

- Late payment interest is charged where a balancing payment is paid late.

  This will run from 31 January 2013 to 31 May 2013.
- The interest charge will be £92 (£9,174 × 3% × 4/12).
- In addition, a late payment penalty of £459 (£9,174 × 5%) will be imposed as the balancing payment is more than one month late (but less than six months late).

10 MARK KETT (ADAPTED) *Walk in the footsteps of a top tutor*

> **Key answer tips**
>
> Income tax questions often test the rules for both self employment and employment together as in this question. You must be ready to prepare a detailed income tax computation and remember to state when income is exempt rather than just leave it out.
>
> Do not ignore the section on administration requirements. There are some easy marks here for stating the rules for record keeping.

> ***Tutor's top tips***
>
> *A fairly straightforward income tax computation, but several workings are required and you need to be well organised. Do not dwell too long on any one calculation.*
>
> *Watch out for the extension of the basic rate band for the Gift Aid payment.*
>
> *As Mark is in his final year of trading the capital allowances computation merely calculates balancing allowances or charges.*

(a) **Income tax computation – 2011/12**

	Total	*Other income*	*Savings income*	*Dividend income*
	£	£	£	£
Trading income (W1)	23,120	23,120		
Employment income (W3)	10,100	10,100		
Property business profit (W6)	7,310	7,310		
Interest from government stocks (received gross)	2,900		2,900	
Dividends (£2,880 × 100/90)	3,200			3,200
ISA interest (exempt)	Nil			
Premium Bond prize (exempt)	Nil			
Total income	46,630	40,530	2,900	3,200
Less: PA	(7,475)	(7,475)		
Taxable income	39,155	33,055	2,900	3,200

			£
Income tax:			
On Other income	33,055	x 20%	6,611
On Savings income	2,900	x 20%	580
On Dividend income	45	x 10%	4
Basic rate threshold (W7)	36,000		
On Dividend income	3,155	x 32.5%	1,025
	39,155		
Income tax liability			8,220
Less: Tax suffered at source			
Dividends (£3,200 at 10%)			(320)
PAYE (£620 × 3)			(1,860)
Income tax payable for 2011/12			6,040
Less: Payments on account			(11,380)
Balancing repayment			(5,340)

Tutorial note

1. *Interest from Individual Savings Accounts (ISAs) and Premium Bond prizes are exempt from income tax.*
2. *Interest on Government stocks is received gross.*
3. *The basic rate band must be extended for the gross Gift Aid donation.*

Workings

(W1) **Trading income**

	£
Trading profit	21,700
Add: Net balancing charge (W2)	1,420
Trading income for 2011/12 (Note)	23,120

Tutorial note

A net balancing charge (see W2) increases the trading profit assessment for the period.

The final assessment assesses profits for the period 6 April to 31 December 2011. As the business has always had a 5 April year end, there are no overlap profits from opening years to deduct in the year of cessation.

(W2) **Capital allowances**

	Pool	*Motor car*		*Allowances*
	£	£		£
TWDV b/f	13,800	14,600		
Addition	1,900			
	15,700			
Disposals	(18,800)	(11,800)		
Balancing charge	(3,100)			(3,100)
Balancing allowance		2,800	× 60%	1,680
Net balancing charge (Note)				(1,420)

Tutorial note

1. *In the year of cessation, there are no AIA, FYA or WDAs. The market value of disposals is deducted and balancing charges and balancing allowances arise.*
2. *If an overall net balancing allowance arises, it is deducted from trading profits.*

   If an overall net balancing charge arises, the net balancing charge is added to the trading profits in the final year.

(W3) **Employment income**

	£
Salary (£3,250 × 3 months)	9,750
Beneficial loan (W4)	950
Staff canteen (Note 1)	Nil
Less: Expense claim (W5) (Note 2)	(600)
Employment income	10,100

Tutorial note

1. *The provision of meals in a staff canteen does not give rise to a taxable benefit.*
2. *When calculating the employment income, remember that Mark can deduct the difference between the mileage allowance received and the official rate of allowance.*

(W4) **Beneficial loan**

The benefit is calculated as 4% of the average loan outstanding during the period, time apportioned if the loan has not been in existence for the whole period.

(£95,000 × 4% × 3/12) = £950

(W5) **Mileage allowance**

	£
Authorised mileage rate (2,500 miles at 45p)	1,125
Less: Mileage allowance paid by company (2,500 at 21p)	(525)
Expense deduction	600

(W6) **Property income**

(i) **Rent from the room in house**

The rental income is less than £4,250 per annum and is therefore exempt from income tax under the rent a room scheme.

(ii) **Property business profit**

	£
Rent receivable	8,600
Less: Agency fees (£8,600 at 5%)	(430)
Wear and tear allowance (£8,600 at 10%)	(860)
Property business profit	7,310

Tutorial note

1. *There is no deduction available for the replacement of furniture and furnishings (renewals basis) as Mark has chosen to claim the wear and tear allowance instead.*
2. *Mark's property income from the rent of his spare room is £3,150 (£350 x 9) which is less than £4,250, and it is therefore exempt under the rent-a-room scheme.*

(W7) **Extension of basic rate band**

	£
Basic rate band threshold	35,000
Plus: Gift Aid donation (£800 x 100/80)	1,000
Extended basic rate band	36,000

(b) **Retention of records**

> ***Tutor's top tips***
>
> *The length of time records need to be kept is often tested. You need to learn the rules and be prepared to apply them to the dates of the question.*
>
> *Remember that this part of the question is independent of the other parts and so could be answered first to get the easy marks, before getting involved in the numbers part of the question.*

- The business records relating to self-employment and property income for 2011/12 must be retained until 31 January 2018 (i.e. five years after the 31 January following the end of the tax year.)
- As Mark is in business during 2011/12, all of his other records relating to employment and investment income must also be retained until the same date.
- A failure to retain records for 2011/12 can result in a penalty of up to £3,000. However, the maximum penalty will only be charged in serious cases.

ACCA marking scheme

			Marks
(a)	Trading profit		0.5
	Capital allowances	– Pool	2.0
		– Motor car	2.0
	Employment income		1.0
	Beneficial loan		1.0
	Staff canteen		0.5
	Expense claim		1.5
	Property business profit		2.0
	Furniture and furnishings		0.5
	Rent-a-room scheme		1.0
	Interest from government stocks		1.0
	Dividends		1.0
	Individual savings account		0.5
	Premium bond prize		0.5
	Personal allowance		0.5
	Extension of basic rate band		1.0
	Income tax		2.5
	Tax suffered at source	– PAYE	1.0
		– Dividends	1.0
	Balancing repayment		1.0
			22.0
(b)	Business records		1.0
	Other records		1.0
	Penalty		1.0
			3.0
Total			25.0

11 LI FUNG

Key answer tips

This question tests both the rules for opening years and for change of accounting date for a sole trader. It is important not to ignore questions like this.

It is possible to pick up some easy marks for the written parts even if you cannot do all the calculations.

(a) **Conditions for a valid change of accounting date**

- The change of accounting date must be notified to HM Revenue & Customs by the 31 January following the tax year in which the change is made (i.e. for 2010/11 by 31 January 2012).
- The first accounts to the new accounting date must not exceed 18 months.
- There must not have been a change of accounting date within the preceding five tax years, although this does not apply if the present change is made for genuine commercial reasons.

(b) **Trading income assessments**

			£
2007/08	Actual basis (1 October 2007 to 5 April 2008) (£18,600 × 6/9) (Note 1)		12,400
2008/09	First 12 months trading (1 October 2007 to 30 September 2008) £18,600 + (£24,900 × 3/12)		24,825
2009/10	CYB (y/e 30 June 2009)		24,900
2010/11	Change of accounting date (1 July 2009 to 31 March 2011) (Note 2)		
	Year ended 30 June 2010	22,200	
	Period ended 31 March 2011	16,800	
		39,000	
	Relief for overlap profits (W)	(18,625)	
			20,375
2011/12	CYB (y/e 31 March 2012)		26,400

Working: Overlap profits

There are overlap profits of:

- £12,400 in respect of the six-month period 1 October 2007 to 5 April 2008, and
- £6,225 (£24,900 × 3/12) in respect of the three-month period 1 July 2008 to 30 September 2008.

The total overlap profits are therefore £18,625 (£12,400 + £6,225).

The overlap profits arise over a 9 month period (6 months and 3 months).

Tutorial note

1. *The assessment for 2008/09 is the first twelve months of trading as the accounting date falling in that year is less than twelve months from the commencement of trading.*
2. *As the accounting year end is moving to a date later in the tax year (i.e. 31 March rather than 30 June), the basis period for the year of change will be the period ending with the new accounting date.*

   In this case, the period from the end of the 2009/10 assessment to 31 March 2011. Therefore, profits for 21 months (from 1 July 2009 to 31 March 2011) are assessed.

   The normal basis of assessment is 12 months. Accordingly, 9 months (21 months – 12 months) of the overlap profits may be offset.

   Therefore, all nine months of overlap profits arising in the opening years are relieved in the year of change.

(c) **Advantages of changing from 30 June to 31 March**

- If Li changes her accounting date from 30 June to 31 March the application of the basis period rules will be simplified.
- The maximum assessment in the year of cessation will be for twelve months.
- Li's existing overlap profits are fully utilised as a result of the change. Otherwise, these overlap profits would not be relieved until the cessation of trading.

Disadvantages of changing from 30 June to 31 March

- The disadvantage is that the interval between earning profits and paying the related tax liability will be 9 months shorter with an accounting date of 31 March.

ACCA marking scheme

			Marks
(a)	Notification		1.0
	18 month limit		1.0
	Change within five years		1.0
			3.0
(b)	Assessments	– 2007/08	1.0
		– 2008/09	1.5
		– 2009/10	1.0
		– 2010/11	2.0
		– 2011/12	0.5
	Overlap profits		2.0
	Relieved in 2010/11		1.0
			9.0
(c)	Simplification		0.5
	Assessment in year of cessation		0.5
	Overlap profits		1.0
	Disadvantages		1.0
			3.0
Total			15.0

12 SAM AND KIM WHITE (ADAPTED) *Walk in the footsteps of a top tutor*

Key answer tips

A classic husband and wife scenario; one employed, the other self-employed and some joint income.

The adjustment of profits was straightforward, except that some may not have known what to do with the patent royalties. In fact, if you did nothing – that was the right thing to do!

Be careful with the calculation of the private use / business use proportion of the car and remember the impact private use has on both the adjustment of profits computation and capital allowances.

Part (c) requires some thought about tax planning advice for a husband and wife; investing in ISAs and transferring assets generating income from the higher rate taxpayer to the lower rate taxpayer.

The highlighted words in the written sections are key phrases that markers are looking for.

Tutor's top tips

The key to success when you are doing an adjustment of profits is to think about what, if anything, has already been included in the income statement.

If an expense is disallowable and it has been deducted, you need to add it back. If it hasn't been deducted you do nothing.

Conversely, if an expense is allowable and it has been deducted, you include it with a zero adjustment. If it hasn't been deducted, you need to deduct it.

Read the question carefully here!

As the question just asks you to 'calculate', you do not need to explain why you are making adjustments, although you do need to make sure you label your answers so that the marker can see which expenses you are adding back or deducting.

It is also important to include all the major items of expenditure in the question, showing a zero for the adjustment figure where the expenditure is allowable.

Always show your workings if the adjustment figure is not clear from the question.

(a) **Sam White**

Trading profit – year ended 5 April 2012

	£	£
Net profit	100,000	
Depreciation	7,600	
Motor expenses (£8,800 × 20%) (W1)	1,760	
Patent royalties (Note 1)	0	
Breach of contract fees (Note 2)	0	
Accountancy fees (Note 2)	0	
Personal capital gains tax advice	320	
Gifts to customers (£560 + £420) (Note 3)	980	
Use of office (£5,120 × 1/8)		640
Private telephone (£1,600 × 25%)		400
Own consumption (Note 4)	1,480	
Capital allowances (W2)		5,360
	112,140	6,400
	(6,400)	
Trading profit	105,740	

Tutorial note

1. *Patent royalties are allowed as a deduction when calculating the trading profit, because they are for the purposes of the trade. As they have already been deducted in arriving at the profit, no adjustment is required.*
2. *The fees incurred for accountancy and the breach of contract defence are allowable as incurred wholly and exclusively for the purposes of the trade.*
3. *Gifts to customers are an allowable deduction if they cost less than £50 per recipient per year, are not of food, drink, tobacco or vouchers exchangeable for goods and carry a conspicuous advertisement for the company making the gift.*
4. *Goods for own consumption must be treated as a sale at full market value. As no entries have been made in the accounts, the full sale proceeds are adjusted for. Had the goods been accounted for already, only the profit element would need to be adjusted for.*

Workings

(W1) **Private / business mileage**

	Total	*Private*	*Business*
Total miles	25,000		
Visiting suppliers	(5,000)		5,000
Allocate (25:75)	20,000	5,000	15,000
		5,000	20,000
(5,000/25,000)		20%	
(20,000/25,000)			80%

Tutor's top tips

A familiar full blown capital allowances computation is given in the workings to this answer to show clearly how the allowances are calculated.

However, where there are not many transactions it is perfectly acceptable to do one or two lines and just calculate the allowances available on each asset acquired rather than a full computation.

If you do this however, be careful and make sure you explain your calculations clearly.

(W2) **Capital allowances**

	Pool	*Expensive car*		*Allowances*
	£	£		£
TWDV b/f	14,800	20,200		
WDA (20%)	(2,960)			2,960
WDA (Restricted)(W1)		(3,000)	× 80%	2,400
TWDV c/f	11,840	17,200		
Total allowances				5,360

(b) **Sam White**

Income tax computation – 2011/12

Tutor's top tips

As long as your calculation of Sam's income tax is based on your trading profit from part (a), you can still score full marks here in this part.

However, it is very important that you show your workings clearly so that the marker can see that you have applied the correct rates to each type of income.

	Total	*Other income*	*Savings income*
	£	£	£
Trading profit	105,740	105,740	
Interest (£1,200 × 100/80) x 1/2	750		750
Total income	106,490		
Less: Adjusted PA (W)	(4,230)	(4,230)	
Taxable income	102,260	101,510	750

	£		£
Income tax:			
On Other income	35,000	@ 20%	7,000
On Other income	66,510	@ 40%	26,604
	101,510		
On Savings income	750	@ 40%	300
	102,260		
Income tax liability			33,904

Working: Adjusted personal allowance

	£		£
Personal allowance			7,475
Total income = net income = ANI	106,490		
Less: Limit	(100,000)		
	6,490	× 50%	(3,245)
Adjusted PA			4,230

Kim White
Income tax computation – 2011/12

> ***Tutor's top tips***
>
> *Another straightforward income tax computation, but watch the dates very carefully here! Where a benefit has only been available for part of the tax year, it must be time apportioned. However, if you forget to do this, you will only be penalised once and could still score full marks for the calculation of tax, as explained above.*

	Total	*Other income*	*Savings income*
	£	£	£
Salary	21,600		
Beneficial loan (£14,250 x 4% x 10/12)	475		
Less: Expense claim (W)	(5,125)		
Employment income	16,950	16,950	
Interest (£1,200 × 100/80) x 1/2	750		750
Total income	17,700	16,950	750
Less: Relief for interest paid (Note)	(140)	(140)	
Net income	17,560	16,810	750
Less: PA	(7,475)	(7,475)	
Taxable income	10,085	9,335	750

	£		£
Income tax:			
On Other income	9,335	@ 20%	1,867
On Savings income	750	@ 20%	150
	10,085		
Income tax liability			2,017

Tutorial note

The loan interest paid of £140 is eligible for relief since the loan was used by Kim to finance expenditure for a relevant purpose. The interest is quoted gross and is paid gross.

Working: Expense claim

Ordinary commuting (i.e. travel between home and the permanent workplace) does not qualify for relief. The travel to a temporary workplace qualifies as it is for a period lasting less than 24 months.

Business mileage is therefore 12,500 miles (11,200 + 1,300)

Expense claim is therefore:

	£
10,000 miles at 45p	4,500
2,500 miles at 25p	625
	5,125

(c) **Husband and wife tax planning suggestions**

Tutor's top tips

It should be clear from your answer to part (b) that Sam is a higher rate taxpayer and Kim is a basic rate taxpayer.

Make sure you set out the rates of tax that each will be subject to, and have a go at calculating the tax saving that could be achieved here.

Individual savings accounts

- Sam and Kim can both invest up to a maximum of £5,340 each tax year into a cash ISA.
- Interest received from ISAs is exempt from income tax, so Sam will save tax at the rate of 40%. Kim will save tax at the rate of 20%.
- They received a 6% gross interest rate of return on their investment in the building society, calculated as:

  Gross interest = £1,200 x 100/80 = £1,500

  Gross rate of interest = £1,500/£25,000 = 6%

- Sam and Kim will therefore each save tax on gross interest of £320 (£5,340 × 6%) if they invested in ISAs.

  This is assuming that the interest that will be received on the ISA will be the same rate of interest as their existing investment.

Transfer to Kim's sole name

- Sam pays income tax at the rate of 40%, whilst Kim's basic rate tax band is not fully utilised.
- Transferring the building society deposit account into Kim's sole name would therefore save tax of £150 (£750 × (40% – 20%)).

Tutorial note

The original question just asked for consideration of the ISA and transfer of assets to Kim.

However, with FA2010, there is another tax planning opportunity in respect of Kim's Gift Aid donations as follows:

- *Kim is making a regular contribution to charity of £1,000 gross.*
- *If Sam made this payment instead, it would reduce his income for the calculation of the personal allowance restriction.*

  This would save £200 (£1,000 reduction would reduce the restriction by £500, and the income is being taxed at 40%).
- *In addition, Sam's basic rate band would be extended by £1,000, reducing the amount of income taxed at 40% and taxing it at 20% instead.*

  This would save a further £200 (£1,000 × (40% – 20%)).

Examiner's report

This question was very well answered by the majority of candidates.

In part (a) the adjustments for use of office, business use of a private telephone and own consumption caused the most problems, with a number of candidates being unsure as to whether adjustments should be added or subtracted in order to arrive at the tax adjusted trading profit.

Part (b) was also well answered, with only the expense claim for the business mileage causing any difficulty. This was often treated as a benefit rather than as an expense.

Part (c) was answered reasonably well, especially the transfer into the spouse's sole name. Many candidates correctly calculated the amount of income tax saving.

ACCA marking scheme

			Marks
(a)	Net profit		0.5
	Depreciation		0.5
	Motor expenses		1.5
	Patent royalties		1.0
	Professional fees		1.5
	Gifts to customers		1.0
	Use of office		1.0
	Private telephone		1.0
	Own consumption		1.0
	Capital allowances	– Pool	1.0
		– Motor car	1.0
			11.0
(b)	Sam White		
	Trading profit		0.5
	Building society interest		0.5
	Personal allowance		1.5
	Income tax		1.0
	Kim White		
	Salary		0.5
	Beneficial loan		1.0
	Expense claim		1.5
	Building society interest		0.5
	Loan interest		1.0
	Personal allowance		0.5
	Income tax		1.5
			10.0
(c)	Individual savings accounts		
	Limit		1.0
	Tax saving		1.0
			2.0
	Transfer to Kim's sole name		
	Tax rates		1.0
	Tax saving		1.0
			2.0
Total			25.0

13 GOMEZ BROTHERS (ADAPTED) ***Walk in the footsteps of a top tutor***

Key answer tips

This question involved preparing three separate income tax computations which covered a broad spectrum of income tax topics, tested compliance knowledge of self assessment and due dates of payment of tax.

The requirements and mark allocation are very clear.

Although there is a wide coverage of the syllabus, all the topics are covered at a basic level and should therefore have been manageable.

Tutor's top tips

For part (a) a systematic approach is needed, taking one individual at a time, and therefore breaking up the information given into smaller, manageable chunks.

As you read the question it is useful to highlight all the information you will need for the income tax computations, and then as you use this information tick each item, so you can easily check you have included everything.

Remember not to ignore exempt income, as credit is given for stating that it is exempt, even though you do NOT include the figure in your computation. Remember not to get held up on any one calculation.

Always ensure that you read the question carefully. The requirement is to calculate income tax liability. Therefore do not waste time calculating income tax payable as this will not gain you any additional marks.

Make the marker your friend, if you keep your calculations clear and easy to read you will score much higher marks. Always ensure your workings are clearly labelled.

(a) (i) **Domingo Gomez**

Income tax computation – 2011/12

	£
Pensions (£4,500 + £2,300)	6,800
Building society interest (£15,200 x 100/80)	19,000
Interest from savings certificate (exempt)	Nil
Total income	25,800
Less: PAA (W)	(9,140)
Taxable income	16,660

Tutorial note

Interest from savings certificates is always exempt from tax.

This income is not the same as interest from a National Savings and Investment Bank account, which is taxable and would be received gross.

Make sure you read the question carefully and have identified the income correctly.

Income tax:

£		£
2,560	at 10% (Note)	256
14,100	at 20%	2,820
16,660		
Income tax liability		3,076

Tutorial note

1. *The non-savings income is fully covered by the personal allowance, so the first £2,560 of savings income is taxed at the starting rate of 10%.*
2. *No tax relief is available in respect of the donations as they were not made under the Gift Aid scheme.*

   If Domingo had made the donation under the Gift Aid scheme it would have enabled the charity to claim an additional £75 (£300 x 20/80) with no additional cost to Domingo. The amount paid of £300 (i.e. gross £375) would be deemed to have had basic rate tax deducted at source and as a basic rate taxpayer no additional tax relief would be due.

   In addition if the donations had been made under the Gift Aid scheme the gross amount (£375) would have been deducted from Domingo's total income for the purposes of calculating the personal age allowance thus decreasing the restriction and increasing the age allowance by £188 (£375 x 50%).

Working: Personal age allowance

	£		£
PAA (aged 67)			9,940
Less: Abatement			
Total income	25,800		
Income limit	(24,000)		
Excess	1,600	x 50%	(800)
Reduced PAA			9,140

(ii) **Erigo Gomez**

Income tax computation – 2011/12

	£
Salary	36,000
Relocation costs (W1)	3,400
Pension contributions (£36,000 x 6%)	(2,160)
Charitable payroll deductions (£12 x 100)	(1,200)
Mileage allowance (W2)	(2,900)
Employment income	33,140
Less: PA	(7,475)
Taxable income	25,665
Income tax liability (£25,665 at 20%)	5,133

Workings

(W1) **Relocation costs**

Only £8,000 of relocation costs are exempt, and so the taxable benefit is £3,400 (£11,400 – £8,000).

(W2) **Mileage allowance**

The mileage allowance received will be tax-free as it falls below the AMAP, and Erigo can make the following expense claim:

	£
10,000 miles at 45p	4,500
8,000 miles at 25p	2,000
AMAP	6,500
Mileage allowance received (18,000 at 20p)	(3,600)
Allowable deduction	2,900

Tutorial note

Charitable donations via a payroll deduction scheme receive full tax relief at source as they are deducted from employment income before it is taxed.

This is exactly the same treatment as pension contributions into an employer's scheme.

(iii) **Fargo Gomez**

Income tax computation – 2011/12

	£
Trading profit (£112,800 – £2,600)	110,200
Less: Capital allowances (W1)	(1,100)
Total income	109,100
Less: Adjusted PA (W2)	(7,025)
Taxable income	102,075

Income tax

£		£
43,200	at 20% (W2)	8,640
58,875	at 40%	23,550
102,075		
Income tax liability		32,190

Tutorial note

1. *The advertising expenditure incurred during May 2011 is pre-trading, and is treated as incurred on 6 July 2011. An adjustment is therefore required.*
2. *Although Fargo's business had commenced during the year, there is no adjustment required under the opening year rules.*

   This is because Fargo has selected a year end of 5 April, which is the only date that will avoid any overlap profits arising.

Workings:

(W1) **Capital allowances**

Fargo's period of account is nine months' long so the capital allowances in respect of his motor car are:

(£11,000 x 20% x 9/12) = £1,650 before adjustment for private use

Capital allowances = £1,650 x (16,000/24,000) = £1,100

Tutorial note

Capital allowances on new purchases of cars are calculated based on their CO_2 emissions. As Fargo's car has CO_2 emissions of between 111 – 160 g/km the car is eligible for a writing down allowance at 20%. This then needs to be adjusted for the short accounting period and for the private use by Fargo.

(W2) **Adjusted personal allowance**

	£		£
Personal allowance			7,475
Total income = net income	109,100		
Less: Gross PPC	(5,200)		
Gross Gift Aid (£2,400 × 100/80)	(3,000)		
ANI	100,900		
Less: Limit	(100,000)		
	900	× 50%	(450)
Adjusted PA			7,025

Tutorial note

1. *Charitable donations under Gift Aid are grossed up before being used to reduce the personal allowance and extend the basic rate band. This is exactly the same treatment as pension contributions to a personal pension scheme.*
2. *As the adjusted net income exceeds £100,000 the allowance is reduced by £1 for every £2 it exceeds the limit. Net income for these purposes is adjusted (i.e. reduced) for both Gift Aid and personal pension contributions made in the year.*

(W3) **Extension of basic rate band**

	£
Basic rate band threshold	35,000
Plus: Gross PPC	5,200
Gross Gift Aid (£2,400 x 100/80)	3,000
Extended basic rate band	43,200

(b) **Self assessment deadlines**

Tutor's top tips

There are easy marks to be had in part (b), provided you have learnt the filing deadlines.

It is very important that you learn the self assessment rules and key dates for filing and payments of tax, as these are very often examined.

- Unless the return is issued late, the latest date that Domingo and Erigo can file paper self-assessment tax returns for 2011/12 is 31 October 2012.
- If Domingo completes a paper tax return by 31 October 2012 then HM Revenue and Customs will prepare a self-assessment tax computation on his behalf.
- Fargo has until 31 January 2013 to file his self-assessment tax return for 2011/12 online.

(c) Retention of records

Tutor's top tips

Again these are easy marks if you have learnt the rules.

As there are three marks available, it is clear that 3 separate points must be made, which gives you a clue that the filing deadlines are not the same for all three brothers.

- Domingo and Erigo were not in business during 2011/12, so their records must be retained until one year after 31 January following the tax year, which is 31 January 2014.
- Fargo was in business during 2011/12, so all of his records (both business and non-business) must be retained until five years after 31 January following the tax year, which is 31 January 2018.
- A failure to retain records for 2011/12 could result in a penalty of up to £3,000. However, the maximum penalty will only be charged in serious cases.

Examiner's report

This question was very well answered by the majority of candidates.

In part (a) many candidates did not appreciate that donations to charity not made under Gift Aid are simply ignored, and some candidates missed the income limit for the age-related personal allowance. The expense claim in respect of the business mileage driven by the employed brother often caused problems. Either it was incorrectly calculated, or it was treated as a benefit.

Part (b) was well answered.

In part (c) few candidates appreciated that the period of retention differs between taxpayers in business and those not in business. However, virtually all candidates were aware of the £3,000 penalty.

ACCA marking scheme

		Marks
(a)(i)	**Domingo Gomez**	
	Pensions	1.0
	Building society interest	1.0
	Interest from savings certificates	0.5
	Donations	0.5
	Personal allowance	2.0
	Income tax	1.0
		6.0
(ii)	**Erigo Gomez**	
	Salary	0.5
	Pension contributions	1.0
	Charitable payroll deductions	1.0
	Relocation costs	1.0
	Mileage allowance	1.5
	Personal allowance	0.5
	Income tax	0.5
		6.0

		Marks
(iii)	**Fargo Gomez**	
	Trading profit	0.5
	Pre-trading expenditure	1.0
	Capital allowances	1.5
	Personal allowance	2.0
	Extension of basic rate band	1.0
	Income tax	1.0
		7.0
(b)	Paper returns	2.0
	Return filed online	1.0
		3.0
(c)	Domingo and Erigo	1.0
	Fargo	1.0
	Penalty	1.0
		3.0
Total		25.0

14 ANDREW ZOOM *Walk in the footsteps of a top tutor*

Key answer tips

A classic tax exam question on self-employed versus employed which was not difficult, but presented in a scenario requiring the application of knowledge to the particular situation given.

This is a newer style of question for F6 students, but is useful preparation for those planning to move on to P6.

Tutor's top tips

It is important to learn the rules for determining whether an individual is self employed.

However, it is not enough here to simply state those rules, instead they must be applied to the situation given.

The question requirement specifically asks only for those factors that indicate employment rather than self-employment.

The answer must therefore focus on those factors, not any factors you can remember and not those that would clearly suggest self employment rather than employment.

Even without detailed knowledge of the rules here, common sense suggestions should enable students to pick up some marks.

(a) **Factors indicating employment**

- Andrew is under the control of Slick-Productions Ltd.
- Andrew is not taking any financial risk.
- Andrew works a set number of hours, is paid by the hour and is paid for overtime.
- Andrew cannot profit from sound management.
- Andrew is required to do the work personally.
- There is an obligation to accept work that is offered.
- Andrew does not provide his own equipment.

(b) (i) **Treated as an employee**

> ***Tutor's top tips***
>
> *Part (b) involves straightforward income tax and NIC calculations, which you should be able to score well on, regardless of your answer to part (a).*
>
> *Don't miss the opportunity to gain these easy marks by being put off by the first part of the question, or by running out of time.*

Andrew's income tax liability for 2011/12 will be:

	£	£
Employment income		50,000
Less: PA		(7,475)
Taxable income		42,525
Income tax		
£		£
35,000 at 20%		7,000
7,525 at 40%		3,010
42,525		
Income tax liability		10,010
Class 1 NIC for 2011/12 will be:		
(£42,475 – £7,225) x 12%	4,230	
(£50,000 – £42,475) x 2%	150	
		4,380
Total income tax and NICs		14,390

(ii) **Treated as self-employed**

	£	£
Andrew's trading profit for 2011/12 will be £50,000, so his income tax liability will be unchanged (as above)		10,010
Class 2 NIC for 2011/12 (52 weeks x £2.50)		130
Class 4 NIC for 2011/12:		
(£42,475 – £7,225) x 9%	3,172	
(£50,000 – £42,475) x 2%	150	
		3,322
Total income tax and NICs		13,462

Examiner's report

This question was very well answered by the majority of candidates.

However, in part (a) only a few candidates pointed out that the taxpayer did not take any financial risk or profit from sound management.

The only common mistake in part (b) was that candidates often based their NIC calculations on the taxable income figure rather than on employment income or trading profit.

ACCA marking scheme		
		Marks
(a)	Control	0.5
	Financial risk	0.5
	Basis of remuneration	1.0
	Sound management	0.5
	Required to do the work personally	0.5
	Obligation to accept work offered	0.5
	Equipment	0.5
		4.0
(b)(i)	**Treated as an employee**	
	Employment income	0.5
	Personal allowance	0.5
	Income tax liability	0.5
	Class 1 NIC	1.5
		3.0
(ii)	**Treated as self employed**	
	Income tax liability	0.5
	Class 2 NIC	1.0
	Class 4 NIC	1.5
		3.0
Total		10.0

15 NA STYLE *Walk in the footsteps of a top tutor*

Key answer tips

This question is a classic self-employed individual scenario, testing the rules on the adjustment of profits, opening year's basis of assessment and the compilation of an income tax computation. There is also an element of self-assessment at the end.

The first three parts are relatively easy to score highly on.

Part (d) was straightforward provided the self-assessment rules had been learnt and applied to the information given.

Tutor's top tips

Remember to read the requirement carefully.

This question has clear mark allocations, which should be used to allocate the time spent on each section. You need to adopt a logical approach, using the requirements to break down the information and plan your answer.

It is possible to score very well on this sort of question, which is not technically difficult, as long as you do not panic over the quantity of information.

The first part just requires the application of the opening year rules to figures given in the question.

Be sure to explain your answer; clearly showing the tax year, basis of assessment and calculation so that method marks can be given even if the maths goes awry!

Don't forget to highlight the overlap profits as they are specifically asked for and will therefore be mark earning.

(a) **Assessable trading profits – first three tax years**

Tax year	*Basis of assessment*	£
2008/09	Actual basis	
	(1 January 2009 to 5 April 2009)	
	(£25,200 × 3/6)	12,600
2009/10	First 12 months trading	
	(1 January 2009 to 31 December 2009)	
	£25,200 + (£21,600 × 6/12)	36,000
2010/11	Current year basis	
	(Year ended 30 June 2010)	21,600

Overlap profits

Tax year	*Profits taxed for second time*	£
2009/10	(1 January 2009 to 5 April 2009)	
	(£25,200 × 3/6)	12,600
2010/11	(1 July 2009 to 31 December 2009)	
	(£21,600 × 6/12)	10,800
		23,400

Tutorial note

The assessment for 2009/10 is the first 12 months of trading as the accounting date falling in that year is less than 12 months from the commencement of trading.

(b) **Tax adjusted trading profit for the year ended 30 June 2011**

Tutor's top tips

Part (b) gives you clear guidance on the approach that is needed, and you should follow this – starting with the net profit and then making the necessary adjustments.

Work through the notes in order, and ensure you have dealt with every single item, as credit is given for showing nil where an adjustment is not necessary, as stated in the requirement.

If you are not sure of how to deal with an item, make a sensible assumption and move on, but do not ignore it, or waste unnecessary time.

Note that as the question has asked you to 'calculate' the adjusted profits you do not need to explain each adjustment that you make, but you should show any workings.

As you read the question it is useful to highlight all the information you will need for the computation, and then as you use this information tick each item, so you can easily check you have included everything.

	£	£
Net profit	22,000	
Depreciation	1,300	
Motor expenses (£2,200 × 7,000/8,000)	1,925	
Accountancy	0	
Legal fees in connection with the grant of a new lease	1,260	
Property expenses (£12,900 × 1/3)	4,300	
Own consumption	450	
Fine	400	
Donation to political party	80	
Trade subscription	0	
Private telephone (£1,200 × 20%)		240
Capital allowances		810
	31,715	1,050
	(1,050)	
Tax adjusted trading profit	30,665	

Tutorial note

1. *The legal cost relating to the grant of a new lease (short or long) is not allowable. Only the legal costs relating to the renewal of a short lease is specifically allowable.*
2. *Goods for own consumption are treated as if Na Style has sold the goods to herself at full market value.*

   As no entries have been made in the accounts for the withdrawal of the items, the full selling value must be adjusted for.

   If the withdrawal had been correctly accounted for at cost, only the profit element would need to be added in the adjustment of profits computation.
3. *Business expenses paid for out of Na Style's own bank accounts are still allowable deductions in her adjustment of profits computation.*

(c) (i) **Income tax computation – 2011/12**

Tutor's top tips

For part (c) a systematic approach is needed.

Remember not to ignore exempt income, as credit is given for stating that it is exempt, even though you do NOT include the figure in your computation.

Always ensure that you read the question carefully – make sure you understand where the cut off points are in an income tax computation.

The requirement for part (c)(i) is to calculate income tax payable; therefore you need to calculate the liability and deduct the tax credits for tax already suffered at source.

Part (c)(ii) goes on to require the balancing payment after taking account of payments on account (POAs) already paid, and then requires the POAs to be paid in the following year.

	£
Trading profit	30,665
Building society interest (£560 × 100/80)	700
Interest from Individual Savings Account (exempt)	Nil
Interest from National Savings Certificate (exempt)	Nil
Interest from government stocks (received gross)	370
Dividends (£1,080 × 100/90)	1,200
Total income	32,935
Less : PA	(7,475)
Taxable income	25,460

Analysis of income (Note)
Dividends = £1,200;
Savings (£700 + £370) = £1,070;
Other income (£25,460 – £1,200 – £1,070) = £23,190

Income tax

£		£
23,190	× 20% (other income)	4,638
1,070	× 20% (savings income)	214
1,200	× 10% (dividend income)	120
25,460		
Income tax liability		4,972
Less: Tax suffered at source		
	Dividends (£1,200 at 10%)	(120)
	Building society interest (£700 at 20%)	(140)
Income tax payable		4,712

Tutorial note

There is nothing wrong in presenting your computation in columnar form if you prefer to, however there is also no need to do so if you do not want to.

However, you do need to be able to break down the taxable income into the different types of income, namely: dividends, savings and other income, in order to apply the correct rates of tax to each type of income.

(ii) **Tax payments**

- Na's balancing payment for 2011/12 due on 31 January 2013 is £1,512 (£4,712 – £3,200).
- Her payments on account for 2012/13 will be £2,356 (£4,712 × 50%). These will be due on 31 January 2013 and 31 July 2013.

(d) **Late payment of balancing payment**

Tutor's top tips

Part (d) carries only 3 marks, so there are likely to be three clear bullet points to make.

You have either learnt these rules or not, but even if you cannot remember the exact rules, do not ignore this part.

Remember that an educated guess should have enabled you to write something worthy of a mark!

Note that there is usually interest to pay on late tax and a penalty, depending on the timing.

Calculations of interest should be to the nearest month unless the question says otherwise.

- Late payment interest is charged where a balancing payment is paid late.

  This will run from 31 January 2013 to 31 May 2013.
- The interest charge will be £15 (£1,512 × 3% × 4/12).
- In addition, a late payment penalty of £76 (£1,512 at 5%) will be imposed as the balancing payment is made more than one month late (but less than six months late).

Examiner's report

This question was very well answered, and there were many high scoring answers.

In part (a) some candidates lost marks because they did not show the relevant tax years in which profits were assessable.

There were few problems as regards the calculation of the trading profit or the income tax payable, although many candidates did not appreciate that interest from government stocks is received gross and is taxable.

As regards the balancing payment and payments on account, candidates were often not aware of the relevant dates.

In part (d) many candidates did not appreciate that a late payment penalty would be imposed in addition to the interest charge.

ACCA marking scheme

				Marks
(a)	2008/09			1.0
	2009/10	– Assessment		1.5
		– Overlap profits		1.0
	2010/11	– Assessment		0.5
		– Overlap profits		1.0
				5.0
(b)	Net profit			0.5
	Depreciation			0.5
	Motor expenses			1.0
	Accountancy			0.5
	Legal fees			0.5
	Property expenses			1.0
	Own consumption			1.0
	Fine			0.5
	Donation to political party			0.5
	Trade subscription			0.5
	Private telephone			1.0
	Capital allowances			0.5
				8.0
(c)	(i)	Income tax computation		
		Trading profit		0.5
		Building society interest		0.5
		Individual Savings Account		0.5
		Interest from National Savings Certificate		0.5
		Interest from government stocks		1.0
		Dividends		0.5
		Personal allowance		0.5
		Income tax		1.0
		Tax suffered at source		1.0
				6.0
	(ii)	Tax payments		
		Balancing payment		1.5
		Payments on account		1.5
				3.0
(d)	Interest			1.0
	Calculation			1.0
	Penalty			1.0
				3.0
Total				25.0

16 SIMON HOUSE *Walk in the footsteps of a top tutor*

Key answer tips

A very familiar style question covering the Badges of Trade and requiring the calculation of the tax consequences of a transaction being deemed to be a trading transaction or a capital event.

Easy marks should have been picked up in this question.

Tutor's top tips

Usually these questions start with the requirement for you to list and then apply the six Badges of Trade. However, this question is unusual in that it kindly gives you the six Badges of Trade, but then it requires you to explain the ***meaning*** *of each for only 3 marks.*

It is fairly certain that half a mark will be allocated to each explanation and so therefore it is not possible, or necessary, to write huge amounts on any one explanation.

Try to be clear and succinct and to the point and move on!

(a) **Badges of trade**

- Trading is indicated where the property (subject matter) does not yield an ongoing income or give personal enjoyment to its owner.
- The sale of property within a short time of its acquisition is an indication of trading.
- Trading is indicated by repeated transactions in the same subject matter.
- A trading motive is indicated where work is carried out to the property to make it more marketable, or where steps are taken to find purchasers.
- A forced sale to raise cash for an emergency is an indication that the transaction is not of a trading nature.
- If a transaction is undertaken with the motive of realising a profit, this is a strong indication of trading.

(b) **Treated as carrying on a trade**

Tutor's top tips

If the transaction is treated as a trade transaction, a straightforward trading profit computation is required.

Simon is then liable to income tax and Class 4 NICs on the trading profit, and Class 2 NICs as he will be self-employed.

Make sure you show your calculations for each liability clearly.

Income tax – 2011/12

	£	£
Income		260,000
Cost of property	127,000	
Renovation costs	50,600	
Loan interest (£150,000 × 6% × 4/12)(Note)	3,000	
Legal fees (£1,800 + £2,600)	4,400	
		(185,000)
Trading profit		75,000
Less: PA		(7,475)
Taxable income		67,525
£		
35,000 × 20%		7,000
32,525 × 40%		13,010
67,525		
Income tax liability		20,010

Tutorial note

If treated as a trade, all costs incurred wholly and exclusively for the purposes of the trade are allowable deductions – including interest on the loan taken out to finance the transaction.

National Insurance – 2011/12

	£
Class 2 NIC (18 weeks × £2.50)	45
Class 4 NIC	
(£42,475 – £7,225) × 9%	3,172
(£75,000 – £42,475) × 2%	650
	3,822

(c) **Treated as a capital transaction**

Tutor's top tips

You should know that the consequences of applying the Badges of Trade are to determine whether or not the transaction is a trading one, or a capital event.

However, you did not necessarily need to remember that in this question as the examiner has kindly told you to what to do (i.e. calculate the capital gains tax liability).

Capital gains tax liability – 2011/12

	£	£
Proceeds		260,000
Less: Incidental costs – legal fees		(2,600)
		257,400
Less: Cost	127,000	
Enhancement expenditure	50,600	
Loan interest (Note)	Nil	
Incidental costs	1,800	
		(179,400)
Chargeable gain		78,000
Less: AE		(10,600)
Taxable gain		67,400
£		
35,000 × 18%		6,300
32,400 × 28%		9,072
67,400		
Capital gains tax liability		15,372

Tutorial note

If it is treated as a capital transaction, no relief is available for the interest on the loan used to finance the transaction.

PPR and letting relief are not available as the property has never been his principal private residence.

Entrepreneurs' relief is not available as the house is an investment property, not a business, and it has been owned for less than 12 months.

The gain is taxed at 18% to the extent that it falls in the basic rate band, and 28% on the excess. As Simon has no other income or gains, the first £35,000 is taxed at 18%.

Examiner's report

This question was very well answered, and often helped marginal candidates to achieve a pass mark.

In part (a) a number of candidates failed to score any marks because they did not state what did or did not indicate trading. For example, stating that the 'length of ownership' means how long an item has owned did not score any marks. It was necessary to explain that the sale of property within a short time of its acquisition is an indication of trading.

Part (b) presented no problems for most candidates. In this type of question it is always best to produce full computations for each option. This will maximise marks if any mistakes are made.

It was pleasing to see that many candidates correctly restricted the Class 2 NIC to 18 weeks' contributions.

ACCA marking scheme

		Marks
(a)	The subject matter	0.5
	Length of ownership	0.5
	Frequency	0.5
	Work done	0.5
	Circumstances responsible for realisation	0.5
	Motive	0.5
		3.0
(b)	Income	0.5
	Cost of property	0.5
	Renovation costs	0.5
	Loan interest	1.0
	Legal fees	1.0
	Personal allowance	0.5
	Income tax liability	1.0
	Class 2 NIC	1.5
	Class 4 NIC	1.5
		8.0
(c)	Proceeds	0.5
	Cost	0.5
	Enhancement expenditure	0.5
	Incidental costs	0.5
	Loan interest	0.5
	Annual exemption	0.5
	Capital gains tax	1.0
		4.0
Total		15.0

TRADING LOSSES

17 NORMA (ADAPTED)

Key answer tips

The first part required the computation of taxable income for five tax years before considering loss relief.

Easy marks should have been gained here in laying out proforma computations and filling in the easy numbers before applying the opening and closing year rules to establish the trading income assessments.

A loss arises in the final tax year and so the trading income assessment in that year will be £Nil.

The second part involved consideration of the options available for loss relief, including a terminal loss.

It is important to communicate to the examiner that you know the loss relief rules, however you must apply the knowledge to the specific facts of the question.

(a) **Taxable income and gains before loss relief**

	2007/08	*2008/09*	*2009/10*	*2010/11*	*2011/12*
	£	£	£	£	£
Trading income (W)	25,250	17,000	15,500	6,000	Nil
Employment income (£9,000 × 10/12)					7,500
Interest income	2,000	2,000	2,000	2,000	2,000
Total income	27,250	19,000	17,500	8,000	9,500
Less: PA	(7,475)	(7,475)	(7,475)	(7,475)	(7,475)
Taxable income	19,775	11,525	10,025	525	2,025
Taxable gain				40,000	

Working: Trading income

Tax year	*Basis of assessment*	£	£
2007/08	Actual basis (1.5.07 – 5.4.08)		
	Period to 31.12.07	21,000	
	1.1.08 – 5.4.08 (£17,000 × 3/12)	4,250	
			25,250
2008/09	Year ended 31.12.08		17,000
2009/10	Year ended 31.12.09		15,500
2010/11	Year ended 31.12.10		6,000
2011/12	Year of cessation		
	Period to 31 May 2011	(11,000)	
	Less: Overlap profits (1.1.08 – 5.4.08) (£17,000 × 3/12)	(4,250)	
	Trading loss / Trading assessment	(15,250)	Nil

Tutorial note

If the trader does not have a 31 March (or 5 April) year end you should be looking for overlap relief. The overlap relief increases the loss of the final year and is included in the calculation of the terminal loss.

(b) **Options available to utilise loss arising in period ended 31 May 2011**

(1) **Relief against total income**

The loss arising in 2011/12 can be set against total income in 2011/12 and/or 2010/11.

(i) Setting the loss against total income of 2011/12 (i.e. employment income and bank interest) would reduce total income to £Nil, would waste the personal allowance and save tax at 10% on £2,000 and 20% on £25.

The remaining loss of £5,750 (£15,250 – £9,500) could be offset against total income of 2010/11, wasting most of the personal allowance and saving tax at 10% on £525 (see Tutorial Note).

(ii) Setting the loss against total income of 2010/11 would reduce total income to £Nil, would waste the personal allowance and save tax at 10% on £525.

The remaining loss of £7,250 (£15,250 – £8,000) could be offset against total income of 2011/12, which would waste part of the personal allowance and save tax at 10% on £2,000 and 20% on £25.

Tutorial note

The rate of tax saving in 2010/11 on £525 and in 2011/12 on £2,000 is 10% because Norma's taxable income includes savings income which will fall into the first £2,560 of taxable income in those years.

(2) **Relief against chargeable gains**

Alternatively, once a claim has been made to offset trading losses against total income in 2010/11, a claim can be made to offset any remaining losses against chargeable gains in 2010/11 instead of total income in 2011/12.

Accordingly, the £7,250 loss remaining after the offset against total income in 2010/11 could be set against the chargeable gain arising in that year.

Assuming that the current tax rates apply throughout this question, this will save tax at 18% on some of the gain and 28% on the remaining gain (see Tutorial note).

Tutorial note

Currently, before loss relief, there is £34,475 (£35,000 – £525) of gain in the basic rate band and £5,525 (£40,000 – £34,475) in the higher rate band.

So using £7,250 of loss against the gain would save 28% on the top £5,525 of the gain, and 18% on £1,725 (£7,250 – £5,525).

(3) **Terminal loss relief**

The loss arising in the final 12 months of trading can be set against:

- available trading profits
- in the year of cessation, and
- the three preceding tax years
- on a last-in-first-out (LIFO) basis.

Calculation of terminal loss			£
(1) 6 April before cessation to date of cessation (6.4.11 – 31.5.11) (£11,000 loss × 2/5)			4,400
(2) 12 months before cessation to 5 April before cessation	£		
1.6.10 – 31.12.10 (£6,000 profit × 7/12)	3,500	Profit	
1.1.11 – 5.4.11 (£11,000 loss × 3/5)	(6,600)	Loss	
	(3,100)	Net Loss	3,100
(3) Overlap relief 1.1.08 – 5.4.08 (£17,000 × 3/12)			4,250
Terminal loss			11,750

Utilisation of terminal loss

Norma has no trading profits in 2011/12, the year of cessation.

The terminal loss can therefore be carried back against the trading profits arising in the preceding three years, on a LIFO basis, as follows:

	2008/09	*2009/10*	*2010/11*
	£	£	£
Trading income	17,000	15,500	6,000
Less: Terminal loss relief	(Nil)	(5,750)	(6,000)
	17,000	9,750	Nil
Interest income	2,000	2,000	2,000
Net income	19,000	11,750	2,000
Less: PA	(7,475)	(7,475)	(7,475)
Taxable income	11,525	4,275	Nil

The terminal loss reduces taxable income in 2010/11 to £Nil, wasting the personal allowance and saving tax at 10% on £525.

The remaining loss of £5,750 (£11,750 – £6,000) is then offset against the taxable income in 2009/10, saving tax at 10% on £285 and 20% on £3,990.

Tutorial note

Taxable income in 2009/10 of £4,275 comprises non-savings income of £2,275 (£15,500 – £5,750 loss – £7,475 PA) and savings income of £2,000. Tax is therefore saved at 10% on savings income of £285 (£2,560 – £2,275) which falls into the first £2,560 of taxable income and at 20% on the balance.

18 LEONARDO

Key answer tips

An opening year loss relief question, requiring a calculation of the assessments for the first few tax year and consideration of loss claims available.

Part (b) should have provided easy marks in stating due dates for making elections.

(a) **Assessments**

Tax year	*Basis period*		£
2008/09	Actual basis		
	(1.9.08 – 5.4.09)	7/9 × £40,500	31,500
2009/10	First 12 months		
	(1.9.08 – 31.8.09)	£40,500 – (3/12 × £54,000)	27,000
2010/11	CYB (y/e 31.5.10)	Loss	Nil
2011/12	CYB (y/e 31.5.11)	Loss	Nil
2012/13	CYB (y/e 31.5.12)		11,000

Key answer tips

As Leonardo will not be making any significant profits in the foreseeable future there is no point in carrying losses forward, therefore offset the losses as soon as possible.

Note the question does not require any calculation of tax savings, just computations to show how the loss would be utilised.

Loss memoranda

	£
Loss in 2010/11	
Loss in y/e 31.5.2010	54,000
Less: Relief given in 2009/10 when applying the opening year rules (£54,000 x 3/12)	(13,500)
	40,500
Less: Special opening year loss relief – in 2008/09	(31,500)
– in 2009/10	(9,000)
	Nil

	£
Loss in 2011/12	
Loss in y/e 31.5.2011	27,000
Less: Special opening year loss relief in 2009/10	(18,000)
Loss carried forward to 2012/13	9,000

Assessments after loss relief claims

	2008/09	*2009/10*	*2010/11*	*2011/12*	*2012/13*
	£	£	£	£	£
Trading income	31,500	27,000	Nil	Nil	11,000
Less: Loss relief b/f	–	–	–	–	(9,000)
	31,500	27,000	Nil	Nil	2,000
Less: Special opening year loss relief:					
– 2010/11 Loss	(31,500)	(9,000)			
– 2011/12 Loss		(18,000)			
Net income	Nil	Nil	Nil	Nil	2,000

Tutorial note

*Under special opening year loss provisions, losses that arise in the **first four tax years** of a trade may be set off against:*

- *the total income*
- *of the three years preceding the tax year of loss*
- *on a first-in-first-out (FIFO) basis.*

(b) **Loss relief time limits**

(i) **Special opening year loss relief and 'normal' loss relief against total income**

For claims to carry back losses in the first four years of a trade against income of the three preceding years, and claims to set-off losses against income of the year of the loss and income of the preceding year, the claim must be made:

– within 12 months from 31 January next following the year of assessment in which the loss was sustained.

In the case of the loss sustained in the year ended 31 May 2010 (i.e. the loss in 2010/11), the claim must be made:

– by 31 January 2013.

In the case of the loss sustained in the year ended 31 May 2011 (i.e. the loss in 2011/12), the claim must be made:

– by 31 January 2014.

(ii) **Carry forward of losses**

There is no specific statutory time limit on claims to carry forward losses against future trading income.

However, a claim to establish the amount of the loss to be carried forward must be made:

– within four years from the end of the tax year in which the loss was sustained

In the case of the loss sustained in the year ended 31 May 2011 (i.e. the loss in 2011/12)

– by 5 April 2016.

19 DEE ZYNE *Walk in the footsteps of a top tutor*

Key answer tips

An individual that is employed for part of the year, then sets up a business which is initially loss-making, is a common scenario in examination questions.

The calculation of the adjusted loss was straight forward provided you remember to time apportion WDAs in the opening period of account.

The employment income computation tested classic benefit rules and you were instructed to utilise the loss against the employment income.

Part (c) required consideration of alternative claims and it was fairly obvious why they would be more beneficial than a current year claim.

The highlighted words in the written sections are key phrases that markers are looking for.

Tutor's top tips

In this question, Dee has 5 April as her year end, so the capital allowances are calculated for the period ended 5 April 2012.

However, where a sole trader chooses a different year end, remember that the capital allowances are always calculated for the accounting period before matching profits or losses to tax years.

(a) **Tax adjusted trading loss – 2011/12**

	£
Trading loss	(11,440)
Patent royalties (Note)	(500)
Capital allowances (W)	(6,060)
	(18,000)

Tutorial note

The patent royalties were incurred for the purposes of the trade and are therefore deductible in computing the tax adjusted trading loss. As the question says that they have not been accounted for in arriving at the loss of £11,440, they must be adjusted for and will increase the loss.

Working – Capital allowances

		Pool	*Car*	*Allowances*
	£	£	£	£
Additions (no AIA)				
Car (between 111 – 160 g/km)		10,400		
Car (> 160 g/km) (Note 1)			17,800	
Additions (with AIA)				
Computer	1,257			
Office furniture	2,175			
	3,432			
Less: AIA (Note 2)	(3,432)			3,432
		Nil		
Less: WDA (20% × 9/12)		(1,560)		1,560
Less: WDA (10% × 9/12) (Note 3)			(1,335) × 80%	1,068
TWDV c/f		8,840	16,465	
Total allowances				6,060

Tutorial note

1. *Capital allowances on new purchases of cars are calculated based on their CO_2 emissions.*

   The car with CO_2 emissions of between 111 – 160 g/km is put in the main pool and is eligible for a writing down allowance at 20%.

   The car with CO_2 emissions of > 160 g/km is a private use car, has its own column and is eligible for a writing down allowance at 10%.

2. *The maximum AIA and the WDAs are time apportioned because Dee's period of account is only nine months' in length.*

   However, the maximum AIA of £75,000 (£100,000 x 9/12) exceeds the total qualifying expenditure and therefore all of the expenditure is eligible for relief.

3. *Only private use by the owner restricts capital allowances. Private use of the employee's motor car therefore does not affect the capital allowance claim, but will instead result in an assessable employment benefit for that employee.*

(b) **Income tax computation – 2011/12**

Tutor's top tips

Watch the dates carefully here! Where a benefit has only been available for part of the tax year, it must be time apportioned.

If you are leaving out a benefit because it is exempt, it is always a good idea to say so, as there will often be a mark available for this.

Don't worry if your loss calculation in part (a) was not completely right. You could still score full marks in this section if your calculations are correct, based on your figures. Make sure you show your workings, so that the marker can see what rates you have used.

	£
Salary	26,000
Car benefit (W1)	940
Fuel benefit (W1)	1,457
Beneficial loan (W2)	300
Staff canteen (exempt) (Note 1)	Nil
Employment income	28,697
Less: Reliefs	
Loan interest (Note 2)	(110)
Loss relief – current year claim	(18,000)
Net income	10,587
Less: PA	(7,475)
Taxable income	3,112
Income tax liability (£3,112 x 20%)	622
Less: Tax suffered at source – PAYE	(5,400)
Income tax repayable	(4,778)

Tutorial note

1. *The provision of meals in a staff canteen does not give rise to a taxable benefit.*
2. *The loan interest qualifies as a deduction against total income since the loan was used by Dee to finance expenditure for a qualifying purpose.*

   The qualifying interest is deducted from total income in priority to the loss relief.

Workings

(W1) **Car and fuel benefits**

CO_2 emissions = 208 g/km, available 3 months

	%
Petrol	15
Plus: (205 – 125) × $^1/_5$	16
Appropriate percentage	31
	£
List price	17,500
Less: Capital contribution	(1,500)
	16,000
Car benefit (£16,000 x 31% x 3/12)	1,240
Less: Contribution for provision of car (£100 x 3)	(300)
	940
Fuel benefit (£18,800 x 31% x 3/12)	1,457

(W2) **Beneficial loan**

Tutor's top tips

Where the amount of the loan has changed during the year, you should always show both calculations of the benefit; the average and the precise method.

Average method	£	£
Loan at start of year	60,000	
Loan at end of the loan	15,000	
	75,000	
Average loan (£75,000 ÷ 2)	37,500	
Assessable benefit (£37,500 × 4% × 3/12)		375
Precise method		
(£60,000 x 4% x 1/12)	200	
(£15,000 x 4% x 2/12)	100	
		300

Dee will elect for the precise method to apply.
The benefit will be £300.

Tutorial note

Remember that if the average method gives the lower benefit, the taxpayer can use the average method.

However, HMRC can insist that the precise method be used, although they do not usually do so unless the difference between the two methods is material.

(c) **Alternative use of trading loss**

Tutor's top tips

When you are describing use of losses, you must be very specific about exactly what the loss can be set against, and when. For example, don't just say "the loss can be set off in the current year". Specify in which tax year that is, and state that the loss can be set against total income.

The examiner has said that the use of section numbers is not required and is not encouraged at the expense of explaining the relief.

- The loss could have been claimed against total income for 2010/11.
- The loss is incurred within the first four years of trading, so a claim for special opening year loss relief could have been made against total income for the three years 2008/09 to 2010/11, earliest first.
- By claiming loss relief against her total income for 2011/12, Dee has relieved the loss entirely at the basic rate of 20% and reduced her income tax liability by £3,600 (£18,000 at 20%).
- As Dee's total income in the years 2005/06 to 2010/11 was £80,000, either of the alternative loss relief claims would have relieved the loss at the higher rate of 40%, and resulted in an income tax refund of £7,200 (£18,000 at 40%).

20 SAMANTHA FABRIQUE (ADAPTED)

Key answer tips

A losses question requiring you to choose the best use of the loss.

Given the information about gains it should be fairly obvious that you need to consider a claim against capital gains. However, remember that this only saves tax at 18% or 28% (for a higher rate taxpayer) and can only happen after a claim against total income has been made first in that year.

Part (a) should have provided easy marks listing the factors a taxpayer takes into account when deciding what to do with a loss.

(a) **Factors influencing choice of loss relief claims**

- The rate of income tax or capital gains tax at which relief will be obtained, with preference being given to income charged at the higher rate of 40%.
- The timing of the relief obtained, with a claim against total income/chargeable gains of the current year or preceding year resulting in earlier relief than a claim against future trading profits.
- The extent to which personal allowances and the capital gains annual exemption may be wasted.

Key answer tips

As long as you addressed the factors influencing the choice of relief, not what the relief options are, you should have scored well here.

(b) **Taxable income and gains**

	2010/11	*2011/12*	*2012/13*
	£	£	£
Trading income	21,600	Nil	10,500
Interest	2,100	3,800	1,500
	23,700	3,800	12,000
Less: Loss relief	(23,700)	(Nil)	
	Nil	3,800	12,000
Less: PA	(wasted)	(7,475)	(7,475)
Taxable income	Nil	Nil	4,525

	2010/11	*2011/12*	*2012/13*
	£	£	£
Capital gains	23,300	Nil	11,000
Less: Trading loss relief	(10,300)		
	13,000	Nil	11,000
Less: Capital loss b/f	–	–	(400)
	13,000	Nil	10,600
Less: AE	(10,600)	(wasted)	(10,600)
Taxable gains	2,400	Nil	Nil

Loss memorandum

	£
Loss in 2011/12	34,000
Less: Relief against total income	
2011/12 (no claim as income covered by PA)	(Nil)
2010/11	(23,700)
Loss remaining	10,300
Less: Relief against chargeable gains	
2010/11	(10,300)
Loss carried forward	Nil

Utilisation of losses

Trading loss

Loss relief has been claimed:

- against total income for 2010/11,
- then against the chargeable gains of 2010/11.

This gives relief at the earliest date and at the highest rates of tax.

Capital loss

The capital loss for 2011/12 is carried forward and set against the chargeable gains for 2012/13.

The use of brought forward capital losses can be restricted and only needs to reduce gains down to equal the annual exempt amount (£11,000 – £400 = £10,600).

The balance of the loss £3,000 (£3,400 – £400) is carried forward against future gains.

Tutorial note

For 2010/11, if relief is claimed, the personal allowance is wasted in that year and the tax saving will be at 20% for income tax and 18% for capital gains.

Offsetting losses in 2011/12 however would utilise £3,800 of the loss, would waste the personal allowance and would not save any tax.

A claim against total income must be made before relief against chargeable gains can be considered.

Carrying all of the loss forward would use £10,500 of loss, would waste the personal allowance and would only save tax of £905 (20% × £4,525).The remaining loss would not be relieved until subsequent years.

The optimum relief is therefore to claim against total income for 2010/11, then against the chargeable gains of 2010/11, since this gives relief at the earliest date and at the highest rates of tax.

Examiner's report

This question was generally not answered well.

Although it was technically the most demanding question on the paper, requiring a bit more thought than the other four questions, it was quite short and should not have presented too many difficulties for reasonably well prepared candidates.

In part (a) many candidates explained the loss reliefs that were available rather than the factors that must be taken into account when deciding which loss reliefs to actually claim.

In part (b) it was extremely disappointing to see the vast majority of candidates include the capital gains in their computation of taxable income. The capital gains annual exemption was often then deducted against the combined figure of taxable income and taxable gains.

Many candidates claimed loss relief against the total income for the year of the loss despite this income clearly being covered by the personal allowance.

Very few candidates, even if they showed the capital gains separately, claimed loss relief against capital gains.

ACCA marking scheme

		Marks
(a)	Rate of tax	1.0
	Timing of relief	1.0
	Personal allowance and annual exemption	1.0
		3.0
(b)	Trading income	0.5
	Loss relief – carry forward	1.0
	Building society interest	0.5
	Loss relief against total income	2.0
	Personal allowance	0.5
	Capital gains	1.5
	Loss relief against capital gains	1.0
	Explanation of most beneficial route	5.0
		12.0
Total		15.0

PARTNERSHIPS

21 PETER, QUINTON AND ROGER (ADAPTED)

Key answer tips

A loss making partnership presents a tricky problem and it is important to approach the computation in part (b) with care.

Firstly, profits / (losses) need to be allocated to each partner and then the opening year rules applied for each partner according to the date they joined the firm.

There are many loss relief options available. A brief mention of each is all you have time for in the exam. Be careful not to go into too much detail and there is no need to discuss the relative merits of each option in this question.

It is much better to mention all the reliefs available and applicable to the question succinctly than to talk about any one relief in great detail.

Part (2) concentrates on VAT topics. The VAT rules are not hard, they are however extensive and they will be examined. Emphasis in your revision must therefore be put into learning the VAT rules as there is a guaranteed 10% of the exam on VAT each sitting.

(1) (a) **Basis of assessment – Joining partners**

- Each partner is treated as a sole trader running a business.
- The commencement rules therefore apply when a partner joins the partnership, with the first year of assessment being on an actual basis (i.e. date of commencement to the following 5 April).

(b) **Trading income assessments**

	Peter	Quinton	Roger
	£	£	£
2008/09			
Peter and Quinton			
Actual basis (1 January 2009 to 5 April 2009)			
(£40,000 × 1/2 × 3/12)	5,000	5,000	
2009/10			
Peter and Quinton			
CYB (y/e 31 December 2009)			
(£40,000 × 1/2)	20,000	20,000	
Roger			
Actual basis (1 January 2010 to 5 April 2010)			
(£90,000 × 1/3 × 3/12)			7,500
2010/11			
All partners – CYB (y/e 31 December 2010)			
(£90,000 × 1/3)	30,000	30,000	30,000

Tutorial note

The commencement rules apply to:

- *Peter and Quinton from 2008/09, as the partnership started on 1 January 2009.*
- *Roger from 2009/10, since he joined as a partner on 1 January 2010.*

(c) **Possible methods of relieving trading loss for 2011/12**

- Peter, Quinton and Roger each have a tax adjusted trading loss of £10,000 (£30,000 × 1/3) for 2011/12.
- Peter resigned as a partner on 31 December 2011. His unrelieved overlap profits of £5,000 (1 January 2009 to 5 April 2009) will therefore increase his loss to £15,000 (£10,000 + £5,000).

- Carry forward relief:

  Quinton and Roger can carry their share of the loss forward against their first available future trading profits arising in the same trade.

- Relief against total income:

  Peter, Quinton and Roger can claim relief against their total income for 2011/12 and/or 2010/11.

- Special opening year loss relief:

  Peter, Quinton and Roger can carry back their share of the loss against their total income for 2008/09 to 2010/11, earliest year first.

- Terminal loss relief:

  Peter can carry back his share of the loss of the last 12 months trading against his trading profits for 2010/11.

  He has insufficient losses to carry back the loss any further. If he had more losses, he could carry back the loss and make a claim in respect of 2009/10 and 2008/09, in that order.

Key answer tips

The requirement is to "State the possible ways to relieve the losses". Therefore there will be no marks for discussing in detail the relative merits of each claim and which would be the most beneficial.

Remember that it is much better to mention all the reliefs available and applicable to the question succinctly than to talk about any one relief in great detail.

(2) **VAT interest and penalties**

(a) **Default surcharge**

A 'default surcharge' arises when a VAT return is submitted late, or a late payment of VAT due is made.

The 'surcharge default period' will initially be for 12 months and will only come to an end when no further defaults have occurred for a continuous 12-month period.

(b) **Default interest**

HM Revenue & Customs may assess taxpayers to VAT where:

(i) no returns have been submitted;

(ii) evidence to back up the returns is deficient;

(iii) the returns and/or information are considered to be incorrect.

Such assessments bear 'default interest' which runs from the original due date of payment of the VAT until the payment is made.

(c) **Errors on a VAT return**

If Quentin discovers an error on a previous partnership VAT return, he must disclose the error to HM Revenue & Customs.

How he should notify them depends on the amount of the error.

If the error is up to the de minimis limit, it is acceptable to notify by making the necessary correction of the error on the next VAT return.

However, if the error exceeds the de minimis limit, separate notification is required.

The deminimis limit of error is the greater of:

(i) £10,000, and

(ii) 1% of turnover

subject to an upper limit of £50,000.

If the error is not notified, the standard penalty for the submission of an incorrect VAT return may be levied. A penalty can also be levied even if disclosure is made, but it will be a lower amount and is likely to be reduced to Nil for an error below the deminimis limit.

Key answer tips

In each part, particularly part 2 (a) your study text contains more detail on the topic of the question. But these were not asked for.

The examiner has clearly spelt out his requirements and they should be followed to the letter. Avoid answering questions with all you know about a topic and make sure you address the specific requirements of each question.

22 AE, BEE, CAE, DEE & EUE (ADAPTED) *Walk in the footsteps of a top tutor*

Key answer tips

This question tests the basis of assessment rules, but the application of the rules to partnerships, and includes the opening year rules, overlap profits and the cessation rules.

A well prepared student should have been able to secure good marks on this question and each part is independent.

Part (c) of this question has been adapted to take account of the change in rules for capital allowances.

Tutor's top tips

Part (a) deals with both the partnership profit sharing rules together with straightforward opening year rules. This part should not have caused any problems.

(a) **Ae, Bee & Cae**

Tax year	*Basis of assessment*	*Ae*	*Bee*	*Cae*
		£	£	£
2009/10	Actual basis 1 July 2009 to 5 April 2010 £54,000 × 9/12 × ½	20,250	20,250	
2010/11	CYB (y/e 30 June 2010) £54,000 × 1/2	27,000	27,000	
2011/12	CYB (y/e 30 June 2011) £66,000 × 1/2	33,000	33,000	
	Actual basis 1 July 2011 to 5 April 2012 £87,000 × 9/12 × 1/3			21,750

Tutorial note

The commencement rules apply for Ae & Bee in the tax year 2009/10 and for Cae in the tax year 2011/12, as this is the tax year in which each partner started to trade.

In the case of Cae, the fact that the partnership had been trading in the years before is not relevant.

(b) (i) **Dee – Assessable trading profits**

Tutor's top tips

Part (b) deals with a change in accounting date. This was straightforward as long as you remember that 12 months trading profits needs to be taxed in each tax year.

Tax year	*Basis of assessment*	£
2009/10	CYB (y/e 5 April 2010)	32,880
2010/11	Change of accounting date (Note) (1 August 2009 to 31 July 2010) (£32,880 × 8/12) + £16,240	38,160
2011/12	CYB (y/e 31 July 2011)	54,120

Tutorial note

The tax year of change is 2010/11. The tax years before and after are assessed on a normal CYB basis (i.e. assess the 12 months accounts ending in that year).

As the new accounting date falls earlier in the tax year (i.e. 31 July rather than 5 April, which is the last day of the tax year!), the assessment for 2010/11 is the 12 months to the new accounting date of 31 July.

As a result, overlap profits are created.

(ii) **Unrelieved overlap profits**

There are no overlap profits created on the commencement of trade as the business has a 5 April accounting date.

However, in 2010/11 there are overlap profits of £21,920 (£32,880 x 8/12) created in respect of the eight-month period 1 August 2009 to 5 April 2010.

Tutorial note

The complication with this question arises not from the commencement of trade, which due to the date of the year-end does not cause overlap, but from the change in accounting date occurring after April 2010.

In order to tax 12 months of trade, the year to 5 April 2010 is pro-rated to 8 months and added to the short 4 month trading period, thus making a total of 12 months. As this 8 month period has already been taxed in the 2009/10 year, overlap profits arise.

(c) **Eue**

Tutor's top tips

Part (c) deals with the cessation of trade. The key rule to remember for cessation is that all profits not yet assessed need to be taxed, before deducting any overlap profits.

Tax year	*Basis of assessment*	£
2011/12	CYB (y/e 30 June 2011)	61,200
	Capital allowances (given)	(2,100)
		59,100
2012/13	Period ended 30 September 2012	72,000
	Balancing allowance (W)	(4,400)
		67,600
	Less: Overlap profits	(19,800)
		47,800

Working: Capital allowances

	Pool	Allowances
Period ended 30 September 2012	£	£
TWDV b/f	6,300	
Addition – Car (CO_2 between 111 – 160 g/km)	2,400	
	8,700	
Disposal	(4,300)	
Balancing allowance	4,400	4,400

Tutorial note

Note that there is no AIA and no WDA in the final period of trade.

As all of the items in the pool are disposed of for less than the TWDV, there is a balancing allowance arising.

A common error is to give an AIA and calculate a WDA in the final period of trade, then calculate a balancing allowance/charge. The net effect on the total allowances is the same, but the principle is incorrect.

Examiner's report

This question was extremely well answered by the majority of candidates, many of whom scored maximum marks.

One of the main problems in the answers of poorer candidates was not showing the appropriate tax years, thus losing a lot of marks throughout.

The only common mistake was that in part (b) for the year of change, candidates often used an actual basis rather than the 12 months to the new accounting date.

ACCA marking scheme	
	Marks
Ae, Bee & Cae – 2009/10	1.5
– 2010/11	1.0
– 2011/12 Ae & Bee	1.0
– 2011/12 Cae	1.5
	5.0
Dee – 2009/10	1.0
– 2010/11	2.0
– 2011/12	1.0
Overlap profits	1.0
	5.0
Eue – 2011/12 Assessment	1.5
– 2012/13 Assessment	1.0
– 2012/13 Capital allowances	1.5
Relief for overlap profits	1.0
	5.0
Total	15.0

23 AUY MAN AND BIM MEN (ADAPTED) *Walk in the footsteps of a top tutor*

Key answer tips

This question was unusual in that the scenario was a partnership. However, this should not have caused concern as there were many easy marks to be gained.

Part (a) may have caused some problems if the definition of residence status had not been learnt, however it was only worth 2 marks.

Parts (b) and (c), comprising over half of the marks, involved preparing familiar adjustment of profits and capital allowances computations, followed by a straightforward allocation of profits between the partners and Class 4 NIC calculations.

Part (d) was an independent VAT section for 10 marks requiring the statement of some rules and straightforward calculations of VAT payable. Easy to score highly on, provided the rules have been learnt.

Tutor's top tips

Remember to read the requirement carefully.

This question has clear mark allocations, which should be used to allocate the time spent on each section. Don't overrun on parts which carry only a few marks.

The first part required the application of the residence status rules. Note that just stating the rules would not have gained full marks. You must apply the knowledge to the facts of the specific individuals.

(a) **Residence status**

- Auy will be treated as resident in the United Kingdom for 2011/12 as she was present in the United Kingdom for 183 days or more.
- Bim will be treated as resident in the United Kingdom for 2011/12 as she has made substantial visits to the United Kingdom.

  Her visits have averaged 91 days or more over four consecutive years.

Tutorial note

Note that there is no legal definition of residence; however case law has established the following definition: An individual is treated as resident in the UK if he or she:

1. *Is physically present in the UK for a period (or periods) of 6 months or more in any tax year, or*
2. *Has made 'frequent and substantial' visits to the UK.*

Visits of (in aggregate) 3 months a year, on average, for four consecutive years are regarded as 'frequent and substantial'.

(b) **Tax adjusted trading profit – year ended 5 April 2012**

Tutor's top tips

Part (b) gives you clear guidance on the approach that is needed for an adjustment of profits, and you should follow this – starting with the net profit and then making the necessary adjustments.

Work through the notes in order, and ensure you have dealt with every single item, as credit is given for showing nil where an adjustment is not necessary, as stated in the requirement.

If you are not sure of how to deal with an item, make a sensible assumption and move on, but do not ignore it, or waste unnecessary time.

Note that as the question has asked you to 'calculate' the adjusted profits you do not need to explain each adjustment that you make, but you should show any workings.

As you read the question it is useful to highlight all the information you will need for the computation, and then as you use this information tick each item, so you can easily check you have included everything.

Beware of the information in the question Notes 1 and 2 about VAT. This information could have caused problems for some students – but this information is only required for part (d) of the question. It has no impact on the adjustment of profits statement. The notes are just telling you that the VAT has been correctly accounted for and that sales and expenses correctly appear in the income statement net of VAT.

	£	£
Net profit	82,000	
Depreciation	3,400	
Input VAT (Note 1)	0	
Motor expenses (£2,600 × 30%)	780	
Entertaining employees (Note 2)	0	
Appropriation of profit (Note 3)	4,000	
Excessive salary (£15,000 – £10,000) (Note 4)	5,000	
Capital allowances (W1)		15,180
	95,180	15,180
	(15,180)	
Tax adjusted trading profit	80,000	

Tutorial note

1. *No adjustment is required in respect of the input VAT as the expense figures are already exclusive of VAT and therefore the VAT has correctly not been deducted from profit.*
2. *The only exception to the non-deductibility of entertainment expenditure is when it is in respect of employees.*

3. *Salaries paid to a partner are not allowable. They merely represent an agreed form of allocation of the partnership profits in the partnership agreement. Appropriations of profit (i.e. drawings such as partner's salaries) need to be added back to profit.*

4. *Salaries paid to family members are allowable provided the amount is reasonable remuneration for services provided. Where an excessive amount is paid, the excess is not allowable.*

Allocation of profits – 2011/12

Tutor's top tips

Once the net profit of the partnership has been calculated, it must be allocated between the partners in accordance with the partnership agreement in force in the accounting period.

Note that full marks can be obtained for this part in showing clearly how you have allocated the amounts; even if your tax adjusted trading profit figure is incorrect.

	Total	*Auy Man*	*Bim Men*
	£	£	£
Salary	4,000		4,000
Interest (£56,000/£34,000 at 5%)	4,500	2,800	1,700
Balance (80%/20%)	71,500	57,200	14,300
	80,000	60,000	20,000

Trading income assessments – 2011/12

	£
Auy Man	60,000
Bim Man	20,000

Tutorial note

The profit share for each partner must now be assessed in the correct tax year. The basis of assessment rules need to be applied to determine in which tax year the profits are assessed.

However, in this question the partnership has a 5 April year end and therefore the rule is simple: the actual profits for the year ended 5 April 2012 will be assessed in 2011/12.

Working – Capital allowances

Tutor's top tips

A standard capital allowances computation is required; however it is slightly unusual in that the only transactions in the year involve cars. There are no other additions and therefore there is no AIA.

The rules for cars need to be known in detail and applied carefully here.

Also, watch out for the information given.

The examiner gave the CO_2 emissions of Motor Car (1), however this is irrelevant information as it is an 'old expensive car brought forward' and therefore the allowances available follow the 'old rules' for cars.

This could have thrown some students who did not know the rules in detail or did not read the question carefully.

		Main pool	*Motor car (1)*	*Motor car (2)*	*Special rate pool*	*Allow-ances*
	£	£	£	£	£	£
TWDV b/f		3,100	18,000	14,000		
Additions (no AIA)						
Motor car (4)		14,200				
Motor car (5)					8,700	
Disposal – Motor car (2)				(13,100)		
		17,300	18,000	900		
Balancing allowance				(900) × 70%		630
WDA (20%)		(3,460)				3,460
WDA (restricted)			(3,000) × 70%			2,100
WDA (10%)					(870)	870
Addition (with FYA)						
Motor car (3)	11,600					
FYA (100%)	(11,600) × 70%					8,120
		Nil				
TWDV c/f		13,840	15,000		7,830	
Total allowances						15,180

Tutorial notes

1. *Capital allowances on new car purchases are calculated based on the CO_2 emissions of the car as follows:*
   - *CO_2 emissions of ≤ 110 g/km:*
     eligible for a FYA of 100% (i.e. Motor Car (3))
   - *CO_2 emissions of between 111 – 160 g/km:*
     put in main pool and eligible for a WDA at 20% (i.e. Motor Car (4))
   - *CO_2 emissions of > 160 g/km:*
     put in special rate pool and eligible for a WDA at 10% (i.e. Motor Car (5))

   However, cars with an element of private use by a partner (i.e. owner of the business) are given a separate column and only the business use percentage of the allowances can be claimed.

2. *Motor car (1) was owned at 6 April 2009 and as it has a TWDV b/f on 6 April 2011 of £18,000. It must have cost more than £12,000, and is therefore an 'expensive car' under the old rules for cars.*

   It therefore continues to qualify for a WDA at the rate of 20% subject to a maximum of £3,000. This must then be adjusted for private use.

3. *Motor car (2) was owned at 6 April 2009 and as it has a TWDV b/f on 6 April 2011 of £14,000, it is also an old 'expensive car'. However, it is disposed of in the year.*

The sale proceeds are deducted in the pool and a balancing allowance arises.

Note that the lower of cost and sale proceeds is deducted from the pool. As the TWDV b/f is £14,000, the cost must have been more than £14,000 and therefore the cost is greater than the sale proceeds received.

(c) **Class 4 National Insurance Contributions – 2011/12**

Tutor's top tips

Straightforward computations are required for this part.

Remember that full marks can be obtained for this part, even if your allocation of profit to the partners is incorrect, provided that you use the partners' profit allocations which you have calculated in part (b) as the basis of your national insurance calculations. Just make sure that you clearly show the method of calculation.

Auy Man

	£
(£42,475 – £7,225) × 9%	3,172
(£60,000 – £42,475) × 2%	350
	3,522

Bim Men

(£20,000 – £7,225) × 9%	1,150

(d) (i) **Tax point**

Tutor's top tips

Part (d) of this question is an independent part and could be answered before the other parts.

All of the information required for this part is given in question Notes 1 and 2 and the last paragraph of the question.

Remember that VAT will always feature in the exam for between 10 – 15 marks and the requirements are usually straightforward and easy to score highly on provided you put in the time to learn the rules.

However, even if you are a bit vague on some of the areas, you still need to attempt each part and write something – but be mindful of the mark allocation given to each sub-part.

Part (d)(i) should have been straightforward as it required the application of the basic tax point rules. Note that for 3 marks you would be expected to think of three key valid points.

Part (d)(ii) was a straightforward calculation of VAT payable.

For part (d)(iii) you have either learnt the rules for the flat rate scheme, or you haven't.

You would struggle on this part if you haven't. If you have, a few facts followed by a simple calculation would gain easy marks.

- The basic tax point (BTP) is the date when services are completed.
- If an invoice is issued or payment received before the BTP, then this becomes the actual tax point (ATP).
- If an invoice is issued within 14 days of the BTP, the invoice date will usually replace the BTP date and become the ATP.

(ii) **VAT paid for the year ended 5 April 2012**

- The partnership's output VAT is £28,440 and its total input VAT is £320 (£180 + £140).
- Therefore VAT of £28,120 (£28,440 – £320) will have been paid to HM Revenue & Customs in respect of the year ended 5 April 2012.

Tutorial notes

The partnership input and output VAT is given in Notes 1 and 2 in the question, and all that the examiners required is a deduction of the input VAT from output VAT.

(iii) **Flat rate scheme**

- The partnership can join the flat rate scheme if its expected taxable turnover (excluding VAT) for the next 12 months does not exceed £150,000.
- The partnership can continue to use the scheme until its total turnover (including VAT, but excluding sales of capital assets) for the previous year exceeds £230,000.
- If the partnership had used the flat rate scheme throughout the year ended 5 April 2012 then it would have paid VAT calculated as follows:

  VAT inclusive taxable turnover = (£142,200 + £28,440) = £170,640

  VAT payable = (£170,640 × 14%) = £23,890
- This is a saving of £4,230 (£28,120 part (d)(ii) – £23,890) for the year.

Tutorial notes

To calculate the VAT payable under the flat rate scheme, the flat rate is simply applied to the VAT inclusive taxable turnover for the year, with no deduction for input VAT.

In the first 12 months of VAT registration, if the business joins the flat rate scheme, HMRC allow a 1% reduction in the appropiate percentage for that trade group.

However, knowledge of this is not required in the exam. Therefore, the examiner will give you the rate that should apply in the first 12 months and you do not need to deduct 1%, just use the percentage given.

Examiner's report

This question was well answered, especially parts (b) and (c).

In part (a) several candidates simply repeated the information contained within the question rather than explaining the 183 day rule and the substantial visits rule.

There were generally no problems with part (b) although a number of candidates did not appreciate that they had to deduct the salary and interest on capital before allocating the balance of profits.

Most candidates scored maximum marks for part (c).

In part (d) the tax point was explained reasonably well, although some candidates wasted time by also giving details for the supply of goods.

Some students struggled with the VAT calculation, assuming this to be much more complicated than it actually was. For 2 marks, all that was required was to select the output VAT of £28,440 and input VAT of £140 and £180 from the text, and then calculate the amount payable of £28,120. It was not necessary to calculate any VAT figures.

The main problem as regards the VAT calculation using the flat rate scheme was that candidates incorrectly deducted input VAT.

ACCA marking scheme

		Marks
(a)	Auy Man	1.0
	Bim Men	1.0
		2.0
(b)	**Trading profit**	
	Depreciation	0.5
	Input VAT	0.5
	Motor expenses	1.0
	Entertaining employees	0.5
	Appropriation of profit	0.5
	Excessive salary	0.5
	Deduction of capital allowances	0.5
	Capital allowances – Main pool	2.0
	– Motor car (1)	1.5
	– Motor car (2)	2.0
	– Special rate pool	1.5
	– FYA	1.5
	Trading income assessments	
	Salary	0.5
	Interest on capital	1.0
	Balance of profits	1.0
		15.0
(c)	Auy Man	2.0
	Bim Men	1.0
		3.0

			Marks
(d)	(i)	**Tax point**	
		Basic tax point	1.0
		Payment received or invoice issued	1.0
		Issue of invoice within 14 days	1.0
			3.0
	(ii)	**VAT paid**	
		Output VAT and input VAT	1.0
		Calculation	1.0
			2.0
	(iii)	**Flat rate scheme**	
		Joining the scheme	1.0
		Continuing to use the scheme	1.5
		VAT payable	2.0
		VAT saving	0.5
			5.0
Total			30.0

PENSIONS AND NIC

24 DUKE AND EARL UPPER-CRUST (ADAPTED)

Key answer tips

Part (a) involves a couple of income tax computations:

- one for an additional rate taxpayer with reduced personal allowances requiring the extension of the basic rate band for pension relief;
- the other is a basic rate taxpayer requiring no entries in the income tax computation in respect of pensions.

Parts (b) and (c) are wholly written, covering the rules on additional pension contributions and the significance of the annual allowance.

(a) **Duke Upper-Crust**

Income tax computation – 2011/12

	£
Employment income (£115,000 + £40,000)	155,000
Less: Adjusted PA (W1)	(2,475)
Taxable income	152,525

Income tax

£	£
80,000 at 20% (W2)	16,000
72,525 at 40%	29,010
152,525	
Income tax liability	45,010

Net amount paid to pension company

All of Duke's pension contribution of £45,000 qualifies for tax relief as it is less than 100% of his earnings (£155,000).

He will therefore have paid £36,000 (£45,000 less 20%) to his personal pension company.

Workings

(W1) **Adjusted personal allowance**

	£		£
Personal allowance			7,475
Employment income = Total income			
= Net income	155,000		
Less: Gross PPC	(45,000)		
	110,000		
Less: Limit	(100,000)		
	10,000	× 50%	(5,000)
Adjusted PA			2,475

(W2) **Extension of basic rate and additional rate band**

	£	£
Basic rate band threshold	35,000	150,000
Plus: Gross PPC	45,000	45,000
Extended basic rate band	80,000	195,000

As taxable income is £152,525, is all employment income, and falls below £195,000, all of the income in excess of £80,000 will be taxed at 40%.

Earl Upper-Crust

Income tax computation – 2011/12

	£
Trading profit	34,000
Less: PA	(7,475)
Taxable income	26,525
Income tax liability (£26,525 at 20%)	5,305

Tutorial note

As Earl is a basic rate taxpayer there is no need to extend his basic rate band for the pension contribution. Relief for allowable contributions is given at source.

Net amount paid to pension company

Only £34,000 of Earl's pension contribution of £40,000 qualifies for tax relief, since relief is only available up to 100% of his earnings.

The amount of tax relief is therefore £6,800 (£34,000 at 20%), which is given at source, and so Earl will have paid £33,200 (£40,000 – £6,800) to his personal pension company.

(b) **Effect of annual allowance**

- Although tax relief is available on pension contributions up to the amount of earnings for a particular tax year, there is no limit as to the amount of earnings that can qualify for tax relief. However, the annual allowance limit of £50,000 acts as an effective annual limit.
- Any tax relieved contributions paid in excess of the annual allowance are subjected to an additional tax charge for the tax year in which the contributions are paid. The tax charge is calculated at the taxpayer's marginal rate of tax.
- The annual allowance limit (£50,000) is increased by any unused annual allowance from the previous three tax years.
- Although the rules changed and the limit reduced to £50,000 in 2011/12, unused annual allowance is available from the previous three years based on an assumed annual allowance limit of £50,000 for all three years.

(c) **Maximum additional contributions**

- There is no restriction regarding the amounts that Duke and Earl could have contributed into a personal pension scheme for 2011/12.
- However, tax relief is available on the lower of:
  - (i) Gross contributions paid
  - (ii) Higher of:
    - £3,600
    - 100% of relevant earnings

Duke

- Duke could therefore receive tax relief on additional contributions of up to £110,000 (£155,000 relevant earnings – £45,000 gross contributions paid).
- However, if his gross contributions exceed £65,000 (£50,000 plus unused AA limit of £5,000 (£50,000 – £45,000) in each of the last three years) an annual allowance charge will arise.

Earl

- Earl has already made a pension contribution in excess of his earnings for 2011/12, and so any additional pension contribution would not have qualified for any tax relief.

Due date

- Pension contributions for 2011/12 would have had to have been paid between 6 April 2011 and 5 April 2012, as it is not possible to carry back contributions.

Key answer tips

Remember to state the due date of payment; an easy mark to gain, but easily lost if you are not efficient in making sure you address all parts of a question or run out of time.

This could have been answered early in the answer before getting involved with the computations, to make sure you gain the easy marks as quickly as possible.

25 VANESSA AND SERENE (ADAPTED) *Walk in the footsteps of a top tutor*

Key answer tips

This question is really like two separate questions.

Part (a) is fairly straightforward, and asks for income tax and national insurance computations for a sole trader and an employee, with advice regarding payments under self assessment.

Part (b) is all about VAT and the flat rate scheme.

The highlighted words in the written sections are key phrases that markers are looking for.

Tutor's top tips

You should be able to score highly on part (a)(i), although there were a few tricky points.

Where a sole trader has just purchased a single asset, there is no need to do a full capital allowances computation, as long as you show your workings. Remember that only the business proportion of the allowances can be claimed.

The car provided to Serene has CO_2 emissions below 120 g/km and therefore a special rate applies. Note also that the question specifically says that the company did not provide Serene with any fuel for private journeys, so don't waste time calculating a fuel benefit! (See examiner's comments).

Watch out for the pension contributions:

- *the contribution to the personal pension is paid net, and extra relief is given by extending the basic rate band by the gross amount*
- *the occupational pension is paid gross, and is simply deducted from employment income.*

Try not to get these confused.

Remember that you will score full marks for the calculation of tax if you use the correct rates, even if your taxable income figure is wrong.

(a) (i) **Vanessa Serve**

Income tax computation – 2011/12

	Total	*Other income*	*Savings income*
	£	£	£
Trading income	52,400		
Less: Capital allowances (W1)	(1,456)		
	50,944	50,944	
Interest received (Note)	1,100		1,100
Total income	52,044	50,944	1,100
Less: PA	(7,475)	(7,475)	
Taxable income	44,569	43,469	1,100
Income tax:			
On Other income (W2)	41,400	@ 20%	8,280
On Other income	2,069	@ 40%	828
	43,469		
On Savings income	1,100	@ 40%	440
	44,569		
Income tax payable			9,548

Tutorial note

Interest from investment accounts at the National Savings & Investments Bank is taxable and is received gross.

Workings

(W1) **Capital allowances**

The car is an expensive car brought forward.

The WDA is the lower of £3,000 or 20% of the TWDV brought forward.

In this case the WDA is not restricted to £3,000 as the 20% WDA is lower.

Only the business proportion of the allowance can be claimed.

WDA = (£10,400 × 20%) × 14,000/20,000 = £1,456

(W2) **Extension of basic rate band**

	£
Basic rate band threshold	35,000
Plus: Personal pension contribution (gross)	6,400
Extended basic rate band	41,400

Serene Volley

Income tax computation – 2011/12

	£
Salary	26,400
Less: Pension contributions (£26,400 × 5%)	(1,320)
	25,080
Car benefit (W)	3,458
Employment income	28,538
Interest from savings certificate (exempt)	Nil
Total income	28,538
Less: Personal allowance	(7,475)
Taxable income	21,063
Income tax liability (£21,063 at 20%)	4,213
Less: Tax suffered at source – PAYE	(3,985)
Income tax payable	228

Working: Car benefit

CO_2 emissions = 87 g/km, available all year

As the CO_2 emissions are between 76 – 120 g/km, the basic percentage of 10% is used.

However, as it is a diesel car, the appropriate percentage is 13%.

Car benefit (£26,600 x 13%)	£3,458

There is no fuel benefit as private petrol is not provided by the company.

(ii) **National Insurance**

Tutor's top tips

Remember that sole traders pay Class 2 and 4 national insurance, whereas employees pay Class 1 primary contributions.

As long as you calculate Vanessa's Class 4 contributions correctly based on your adjusted trading income figure from part (a)(i), you will be awarded full marks.

Vanessa Serve

Class 2 NICs	£
(£2.50 for 52 weeks)	130

Class 4 NICs	£
(£42,475 – £7,225) × 9%	3,172
(£50,944 – £42,475) × 2%	169
	3,341

Serene Volley

Class 1 NICs	
(£26,400 – £7,225) × 12%	2,301

Tutorial note

Class 1 NICs are based on cash earnings, without any allowable deductions. Therefore, pension contributions are ignored, and benefits are not subject to employee Class 1 NIC.

Benefits are assessed to Class 1A NICs which are payable by the employer only, not the employee. However, the requirement is to calculate the NICs payable by the employee only, not the employer.

(iii) **Payment of tax**

Tutor's top tips

You must learn the rules and key dates for payment of tax under self assessment, as these are very often examined, and the examiner is repeatedly disappointed when students do not seem to learn these important rules. See examiner's comments to this question, and others.

Don't forget that Vanessa's balancing payment due under self assessment covers both income tax and Class 4 NICs.

As long as this payment and the instalments for 2012/13 are calculated correctly based on your figures, you will be given full marks.

Vanessa Serve

Balancing payment for 2011/12 – due on 31 January 2013

	£
Income tax liability	9,548
Class 4 NIC	3,341
	12,889
Less: Paid on account	(8,705)
	4,184

Payments on account for 2012/13

		£
Due 31 January 2013	(£12,889 × 50%)	6,445
Due 31 July 2013	(£12,889 × 50%)	6,444

Serene Volley

No payments on account have been made, so the balancing payment for 2011/12 due on 31 January 2013 is £228.

Payments on account for 2012/13 are not required because Serene's income tax payable for 2011/12 was less than £1,000.

Also, more than 80% of her income tax liability (£4,213 × 80% = £3,370) was met by deduction at source.

(b) (i) **VAT Return – Quarter ended 30 June 2012**

Tutor's top tips

Part (b) is a stand alone part about VAT which could have been attempted before part (a) if you are confident with your VAT knowledge.

A standard VAT return is required, but be careful to read the question carefully to see whether the figures in the question include or exclude VAT.

In this case, the appropriate rate is as follows:

- *If the figure excludes VAT, the VAT is 20%*
- *If the figure includes VAT, the VAT is 20/120 or 1/6.*

The requirement is to 'calculate' and therefore the explanatory notes are not required as part of the answer.

	£	£
Output VAT		
Sales (£18,000 × 20%)		3,600
Input VAT		
Telephone (£600 × 60% × 20%) (Note 1)	72	
Motor car (Note 2)	Nil	
Motor repairs (£882 × 20/120) (Note 3)	147	
Equipment (£1,760 × 20%) (Note 4)	352	
Other expenses (£2,200 – £400) × 20% (Note 5)	360	
		(931)
VAT payable		2,669

Tutorial note

1. *An apportionment is made where a service such as the use of a telephone is partly for business purposes and partly for private purposes.*

2. *Input VAT cannot be recovered in respect of the motor car as this was not exclusively for business purposes.*
3. *No apportionment is necessary for motor expenses provided there is some business use.*
4. *Vanessa can recover the input VAT in respect of the equipment in the quarter ended 30 June 2012 because the actual tax point was the date that the equipment was paid for.*
5. *Input tax on business entertaining cannot be recovered unless it relates to entertaining staff or overseas customers.*

(ii) **Flat rate scheme**

Tutor's top tips

You need to learn the key rules and features of the VAT schemes, but then you must make sure that you apply them to the specific question.

There was an easy mark available for calculating the VAT saving compared to your VAT payable from part (b)(i).

Conditions

- Vanessa can use the flat rate scheme if her expected taxable turnover for the next 12 months does not exceed £150,000.

Advantages

- The main advantage of the scheme is the simplified VAT administration. Vanessa's customers are not VAT registered, so there will be no need to issue VAT invoices.
- If Vanessa had used the flat rate scheme for the quarter ended 30 June 2012 then she would have paid VAT of £1,836 ((£18,000 + £3,600) × 8.5%).
- This is a saving of £833 (£2,669 – £1,836) for the quarter.

Tutorial note

The flat rate % is applied to the VAT inclusive taxable supplies for the quarter.

In the first 12 months of VAT registration, if the business joins the flat rate scheme, HMRC allow a 1% reduction in the appropiate percentage for that trade group. However, it is not applicable here as Vanessa has been registered for some time and knowledge of this 1% reduction is not required in the exam.

Therefore, the examiner will always give you the rate that you should apply.

Examiner's comments

This question was generally very well answered.

In part (a) many candidates did not appreciate that it was not necessary to gross up the interest received from an investment account at the National Savings & Investment Bank, or that interest from savings certificates is exempt from tax.

The contribution to the occupational pension scheme was often used to extend the basic rate tax band rather than being deducted in calculating employment income.

Many candidates wasted time in calculating a fuel benefit despite the question clearly stating that no fuel was provided for private journeys.

The one aspect of the question that consistently caused problems was the calculation of the balancing payments and the payments on account, and this section was often not answered at all. It was disappointing that many candidates were not aware of the relevant due dates.

The VAT aspects in part (b) were well answered, although far too many candidates incorrectly deducted input VAT when calculating the amount of VAT payable using the flat rate scheme.

ACCA marking scheme

			Marks
(a)	(i)	**Vanessa Serve**	
		Trading profit	0.5
		Capital allowances	1.5
		Interest from NSI Bank	1.0
		Personal allowance	0.5
		Extension of basic rate band	1.0
		Income tax	1.0
		Serene Volley	
		Salary	0.5
		Pension contributions	1.0
		Car benefit	1.5
		Interest from savings certificate	0.5
		Personal allowance	0.5
		Income tax	1.0
		Tax suffered at source – PAYE	0.5
			11.0
	(ii)	**Vanessa Serve**	
		Class 2 NIC	1.0
		Class 4 NIC	1.5
		Serene Volley	
		Class 1 NIC	1.5
			4.0
	(iii)	**Vanessa Serve**	
		Balancing payment	1.5
		Payments on account	1.5
		Serene Volley	
		Balancing payment	1.0
		Payments on account not required	1.0
			5.0

			Marks
(b)	(i)	Sales	0.5
		Telephone	1.0
		Motor car	0.5
		Motor repairs	1.0
		Equipment	1.0
		Other expenses	1.0
			5.0
	(ii)	Limit	1.0
		Simplified administration	2.0
		VAT saving	2.0
			5.0
Total			30.0

26 ANN, BASIL & CHLOE (ADAPTED) ***Walk in the footsteps of a top tutor***

Key answer tips

A question covering the pension relief available to three different individuals. This should be a straightforward question provided the rules had been learnt.

Relief for pension contributions is a key area of the syllabus that is tested regularly.

Note that this question has been adapted in light of the new syllabus and part (b) is a new addition to the question to test new rules introduced in the pension legislation.

Tutor's top tips

This question is classic in style with individuals in different situations contributing to a personal pension scheme.

The key is to:

- *Remember the definition of "relevant earnings"*
- *Compare the gross contributions paid with the "relevant earnings" (or £3,600 if this is higher) to decide the maximum tax allowable amount*
- *Consider the annual allowance limit charge.*

Note that the maximum contribution allowable for a person without any relevant earnings in the tax year (£3,600) is given in the exam.

(a) (i) **Anne Peach**

Amount of pension contributions qualifying for relief

Anne can obtain relief for the lower of:

(1) Gross contributions of £52,000

(2) Higher of:

(i) £3,600

(ii) Relevant earnings of £48,000

Therefore, £48,000 will qualify for tax relief and her basic rate is extended to £83,000 (W).

Her taxable income falls into the extended basic rate band and is therefore taxed at 20%.

Income tax liability

	£
Trading profit	48,000
Less: PA	(7,475)
Taxable income	40,525
Income tax liability (£40,525 x 20%) (W)	8,105

Working: Extension of basic rate band

	£
Basic rate band	35,000
Plus: Gross allowable pension contributions	48,000
Extended basic rate band	83,000

(ii) **Basil Plum**

Amount of pension contributions qualifying for relief

Basil can obtain relief for the lower of:

(1) Gross contributions of £50,000

(2) Higher of:

(i) £3,600

(ii) Relevant earnings of £120,000

Therefore, £50,000 will qualify for tax relief and his basic rate band is extended to £85,000 (W2).

Tutorial note

Note that this scenario differs from the treatment for Anne (above) as Anne had contributed more than 100% of her relevant earnings into a scheme, whereas Basil has contributed less than 100% of his relevant earnings into the scheme.

Income tax liability

		£
Employment income		120,000
Less: PA (W1)		(7,475)
Taxable income		112,525
Income tax:		
£		
85,000	x 20% (W2)	17,000
27,525	x 40%	11,010
112,525		
Income tax liability		28,010

Workings

(W1) **Personal allowance**

Although Basil's income is in excess of £100,000, there is no restriction of his personal allowance and he will be entitled to the full personal allowance as his adjusted net income (ANI) is £70,000.

His ANI is calculated as follows:

	£
Employment income = Total income = Net income	120,000
Less: Gross PPC	(50,000)
ANI	70,000

(W2) **Extension of basic rate band**

	£
Basic rate band	35,000
Plus: Gross PPC	50,000
Extended basic rate band	85,000

(iii) **Chloe Pear**

Amount of pension contributions qualifying for relief

Property income does not qualify as relevant earnings.

Therefore, as Chloe has no relevant earnings, she will only receive tax relief on £3,600 of her pension contributions.

Her taxable income falls below the basic rate band even before extension due to pension contributions; therefore her income is taxed at 20%.

Income tax liability

	£
Property income	23,900
Less: PA	(7,475)
Taxable income	16,425
Income tax (£16,425 x 20%) (W)	3,285

(b) **Consequences of Banana Bank plc contributing into Basil's pension fund**

There is no limit on the amount that can be put into a personal pension fund by an individual and his employer.

However, there is a maximum amount of tax relief

- that the individual can obtain on their contributions into the scheme (i.e. the maximum contribution each year), and
- on the total contributions paid into a scheme by the individual and others on their behalf (i.e. the annual allowance).

If Basil's employer contributes into his personal pension scheme, the employer contributions are:

- a tax free benefit
- a tax allowable deduction in Banana Bank's corporation tax computation
- combined with Basil's contributions and compared to the annual allowance of £50,000.

Where the annual allowance is exceeded (as is the case if Banana Bank pay £100,000 into the scheme):

- a tax charge is levied on the individual.

Unused allowances from the previous three tax years can be carried forward.

In Basil's case the maximum contributions that can be made in 2011/12 without incurring the annual allowance charge is £80,000 (£50,000 + (£50,000 – £40,000) x 3).

Basil will therefore pay the annual allowance charge in 2011/12 on contributions of £70,000 (£50,000 + £100,000 – £80,000).

The tax charge is calculated at the taxpayer's marginal rate of tax. In Basil's case this is 40%, as the higher rate band is extended by his gross contribution in 2011/12 to £200,000 (£150,000 + £50,000).

Examiner's report

This question was reasonably well answered, although there were few first-rate answers.

For the first taxpayer the most common mistake was to extend the basic rate tax band by the amount of contributions rather than earnings.

For the second taxpayer the basic rate band was often extended by the amount of annual allowance rather than the contributions.

Very few candidates stated that the third taxpayer would have received tax relief up to £3,600 of her contributions.

Note that this question has been adapted in light of the new syllabus and part (b) is a new addition to the question.

ACCA marking scheme

		Marks
(a)	**Ann Peach**	
	Taxable income	0.5
	Extension of basic rate band	1.0
	Income tax	0.5
	Amount qualifying for tax relief	1.0
		3.0

		Marks
	Basil Plum	
	Taxable income	0.5
	Personal allowance	1.0
	Extension of basic rate band	1.5
	Income tax	1.0
	Amount qualifying for tax relief	1.0
		5.0
	Chloe Pear	
	Taxable income	0.5
	Income tax	0.5
	Amount qualifying for tax relief	1.0
		2.0
(b)	Employer contributions	
	No limit to contributions	0.5
	Limit to relief for individual	0.5
	Tax free benefit	0.5
	Tax allowable deduction for corporation tax	0.5
	Exceeding annual allowance	0.5
	Unused annual allowance for previous 3 years bfwd	0.5
	Basil's maximum contributions	1.0
	Charged at marginal rate	0.5
	Charged at 40% for Basil	0.5
		5.0
		15.0
Total		

SELF ASSESSMENT

27 PI CASSO

Key answer tips

The first part of this question involves detailed calculations to work out the income tax, Class 4 NICs and CGT payable under self-assessment and when the payments are due.

The remaining three parts require wholly written answers on three common self-assessment topics.

These are marks which are easy to gain if you have done your work, but easy to lose if you do not invest the time in learning the self-assessment rules.

(a) **Due dates of payment of tax under self-assessment**

Due date	*Tax year*	*Payment*	£
31 July 2011	2010/11	Second payment on account (W1)	2,240
31 January 2012	2010/11	Balancing payment (W2)	5,980
31 January 2012	2011/12	First payment on account (W3)	1,860
31 July 2012	2011/12	Second payment on account (W3)	1,860
31 January 2013	2011/12	Balancing payment (W4)	Nil
31 January 2013	2012/13	First payment on account (W5)	1,860

Workings

(W1) Second payment on account – 2010/11

The second payment on account for 2010/11 is based on Pi's income tax and Class 4 NIC liability for 2009/10 as follows:

	£
Income tax	3,240
Class 4 NICs	1,240
	4,480
Payments on account (50%)	2,240

(W2) Balancing payment – 2010/11

	£
Income tax	4,100
Class 4 NICs	1,480
Capital gains tax (see Tutorial Note)	4,880
	10,460
Less: POAs (£2,240 x 2)	(4,480)
Balancing payment	5,980

(W3) Payments on account – 2011/12

Pi will make a claim to reduce her total payments on account for 2011/12 as follows:

	£
Income tax	2,730
Class 4 NICs	990
	3,720
Payments on account (50%)	1,860

(W4) Balancing payment – 2011/12

	£
Income tax and Class 4 NICs	3,720
Capital gains tax	Nil
	3,720
Less: POAs (£1,860 x 2)	(3,720)
Balancing payment	Nil

(W5) **First payments on account – 2012/13**

The first payment on account for 2012/13 is based on Pi's income tax and Class 4 NIC liability for 2011/12.

	£
Income tax	2,730
Class 4 NICs	990
	3,720
Payments on account (50%)	1,860

Tutorial note

Class 2 NICs are payable collected twice a year on 31 January in the tax year and 31 July after the end of the tax year. Payments can be made in a number of ways, including six monthly direct debits or following payment requests by HMRC. Note that they are not paid via the self-assessment system.

Capital gains tax is collected via self-assessment and is payable all in one payment on 31 January following the end of the tax year along with the balancing payment for income tax and Class 4 NICs.

Payments on account are not required for CGT.

(b) **Reduction of payments on account to £Nil**

- If Pi's payments on account for 2011/12 were reduced to £Nil, then she would be charged late payment interest on the payments due of £1,860 from the relevant due date to the date of payment.
- A penalty will be charged if the claim to reduce the payments on account to £Nil was made fraudulently or negligently.

(c) **Latest submission date**

- Unless the return is issued late, the latest date that Pi can submit a paper based self-assessment tax return for 2011/12 is 31 October 2012.
- If Pi completes a paper based tax return by 31 October 2012 then HMRC will prepare a self-assessment tax computation on her behalf.
- Alternatively, Pi has until 31 January 2013 to file her self-assessment tax return for 2011/12 online.
- A self-assessment tax computation is then automatically provided as part of the filing process.

(d) **HMRC enquiry**

- If HMRC intend to enquire into Pi's 2011/12 tax return they will have to notify her within twelve months of the date that they receive the return.
- HMRC has the right to enquire into the completeness and accuracy of any return and such an enquiry may be made on a completely random basis.
- However, enquiries are generally made because of a suspicion that income has been undeclared or because deductions have been incorrectly claimed.

Examiner's report

This question was generally not well answered, and the impression given was that candidates had struggled with time management and had a lack of time remaining for this question.

Part (a) caused the most problems, with the vast majority of candidates not being able to demonstrate how payments are calculated and paid under the self-assessment system.

Class 2 national insurance contributions were often incorrectly included, whilst few candidates appreciated that a claim to reduce payments on account was possible.

In part (b) most candidates appreciated that interest would be due, but very few mentioned the potential penalty that could be charged.

It was disappointing that the self-assessment tax return submission dates were often not know in part (c), despite these being covered in the Finance Act article.

The same comment applies to part (d). Candidates often gave a long list of reasons why HMRC could enquire into a return, but failed to mention that an enquiry might be on a completely random basis.

ACCA marking scheme

		Marks
(a)	Second payment on account for 2010/11	1.5
	Balancing payment for 2010/11	2.0
	Claim to reduce payments on account	1.0
	Payments on account for 2011/12	1.0
	Balancing payment for 2011/12	0.5
	First payment on account for 2012/13	1.0
		7.0
(b)	Interest	1.0
	Penalty	1.0
		2.0
(c)	Paper based return	2.0
	Return filed online	1.0
		3.0
(d)	Notification date	1.0
	Random basis	1.0
	Income/Deductions	1.0
		3.0
Total		15.0

28 ERNEST VADER *Walk in the footsteps of a top tutor*

Key answer tips

This is an unusual and tricky question requiring substantial written explanations and statements about ethical issues and self assessment.

Detailed knowledge is required to score highly on this question; however the application of some basic common sense would also gain quite a few marks.

No calculations are required except for part (e) (i) which accounts for 2 of the 15 marks.

The highlighted words are key words or phrases that markers are looking for.

Tutor's top tips

Remember to read the requirement carefully and allocate the time spent on each section.

Part (a) covers the classic topic of tax evasion and tax avoidance, but care must be taken to apply your knowledge to Ernest's particular problem.

Parts (b) and (c) require the application of common sense if the specific guidelines have not been learnt.

Parts (d) and (e) are straightforward if the self assessment rules have been learnt, difficult if not learnt.

(a) **Tax evasion and tax avoidance**

- Tax evasion is illegal and involves the reduction of tax liabilities by not providing information to which HMRC is entitled, or providing HMRC with deliberately false information.
- In contrast, tax avoidance involves the minimisation of tax liabilities by the use of any lawful means. However, certain tax avoidance schemes must be disclosed to HMRC.
- If Ernest makes no disclosure of the capital gain then this will be viewed as tax evasion as his tax liability for 2011/12 will be understated by £18,000.

(b) **Failure to disclose information to HMRC**

- How to deal with the failure to disclose is a matter of professional judgement, and a trainee Chartered Certified Accountant would be expected to act honestly and with integrity.
- Ernest should therefore be advised to disclose details of the capital gain to HMRC.
- If such disclosure is not made by Ernest, you would be obliged to report under the money laundering regulations, and you should also consider ceasing to act for Ernest.

  In these circumstances you would be advised to notify HMRC that you no longer act for him although you would not need to provide any reason for this.

(c) **Action by HMRC to obtain information**

- HMRC can request information from Ernest by issuing a written information notice.

(d) **HMRC entitlement to raise an assessment**

- A discovery assessment can be raised because Ernest's self-assessment tax return did not contain sufficient information to make HMRC aware of the capital gain.
- The normal time limit for making a discovery assessment is four years after the end of the tax year, but this is extended to 20 years where tax is lost due to deliberate behaviour.

(e) **Interest and penalties**

(i) **Interest payable**

- Late payment interest will run from the due date of 31 January 2013 to the payment date of 31 July 2013.
- The interest charge will therefore be £270 (£18,000 × 3% × 6/12).

(ii) **Penalties**

- The amount of penalty is based on the tax due but unpaid as a result of the failure to notify. The maximum penalty is therefore the CGT liability of £18,000.
- However, the actual penalty payable will be linked to Ernest's behaviour.
- Since Ernest would appear to have deliberately failed to notify HMRC of his capital gain, the actual penalty is likely to be 70% of the tax unpaid which is £12,600 (£18,000 × 70%). This assumes that there is no attempt at concealment.
- The penalty would have been substantially reduced if Ernest had disclosed the capital gain, especially if the disclosure had been unprompted by HMRC prior to discovery. The maximum reduction would be to 20% of the tax unpaid.

Examiner's report

This question was not well answered, with many candidates attempting it as their final question or omitting it altogether. This was disappointing given that several sections covered recent tax management changes which have been covered in my Finance Act articles.

In part (a) most candidates knew the difference between tax evasion and tax avoidance, but many failed to score an easy mark by not stating that the taxpayer's actions would be viewed as tax evasion.

Part (b) caused problems for most candidates but a common sense approach would have gained most of the available marks. Unfortunately, far too many candidates instead just incorrectly explained that it would be necessary to inform HMRC themselves.

In part (c) far too many candidates wrote at length about an enquiry rather than just stating that HMRC would issue a written information notice.

The time limits in part (d) were often not known, and most candidates were unaware of the use of a discovery assessment despite being given help in the wording of the requirement.

There was little excuse for getting the interest calculation wrong in part (e) as candidates were given the tax liability, the due date, the payment date and the rate of interest.

There was little awareness of the new penalty regime.

ACCA marking scheme

			Marks
(a)	Tax evasion		1.0
	Tax avoidance		1.0
	Non-disclosure of disposal		1.0
			3.0
(b)	Professional judgement		1.0
	Advise disclosure		1.0
	Obligation to report		1.0
			3.0
(c)	Written information notice		1.0
(d)	Lack of sufficient information		1.0
	Time limits		1.0
			2.0
(e)	(i)	Interest period	1.0
		Calculation	1.0
			2.0
	(ii)	Maximum penalty	1.0
		Link to behaviour	1.0
		Actual penalty	1.0
		Disclosure	1.0
			4.0
			15.0

CHARGEABLE GAINS

INDIVIDUALS – CAPITAL GAINS TAX

29 ALICE LIM (ADAPTED)

Key answer tips

This question tests reliefs available for the individual on the disposal of business assets. There are some common exam traps to watch out for.

In part (a), not all the proceeds of sale of the warehouse are reinvested, so not all of the gain can be rolled over.

In part (b), Alice receives some cash on the incorporation of her business, so she cannot roll over all the gains on incorporation.

In part (c), even though Alice buys the shares from her mother, you still use the market value as the proceeds as they are connected persons.

In part (d) it is important not to give letting relief because that relief is only available for the letting of your principal private residence.

This question was originally a 20 mark question, but it was set when the rules for CGT were considerably more complicated. Under the current syllabus and rules, this question would now be worth 15 marks.

(a) **Freehold office building**

	£	£
Disposal proceeds		152,000
Less: Cost	134,000	
Rolled over gain (W)	(41,000)	
		(93,000)
Chargeable gain		59,000

Working: Rollover relief

The sale proceeds of the warehouse disposed of in April 2010 were not fully reinvested.

Accordingly, a capital gain of £15,000 (£149,000 – £134,000) would have been chargeable at the time.

The amount of gain rolled over must therefore have been £41,000 (£56,000 – £15,000).

Tutorial note

The question says ignore Entrepreneurs' relief.

However, for tutorial purposes, Entrepreneurs' relief is not available anyway as the disposal of the office building is not a qualifying disposal of the whole or part of a business.

There is no relief for the disposal of individual assets out of a business.

(b) **Incorporation of the business**

	£
Total gains before reliefs	120,000
Less: Incorporation relief	
(£120,000 × (£200,000 / £300,000))	(80,000)
Chargeable gain (Note)	40,000

Tutorial note

Per the question, Entrepreneurs' relief is to be ignored.

However, for tutorial purposes, Entrepreneurs' relief is available on incorporation as it is the disposal of a qualifying business provided it has been owned for more than one year.

In this case, the availability of Entrepreneurs' relief would mean that the remaining gain of £40,000 would be taxed at 10%.

Note that Alice could elect to disapply the incorporation relief to increase the gain eligible for Entrepreneurs' relief now if she wants to.

The base cost of the 200,000 £1 shares received will be:

	£
MV of shares	200,000
Less: Incorporation relief	(80,000)
Base cost	120,000

Disposal of 150,000 shares in Alilim Ltd

	£
Disposal proceeds	275,000
Less: Base cost (£120,000 × 150,000/200,000)	(90,000)
Chargeable gain (see advice below)	185,000

Advice to Alice

Alice will not be entitled to Entrepreneurs' relief on the £185,000 gain on the disposal of her shares in Alilim Ltd as she has not held the shares for at least one year.

Therefore she should disclaim the incorporation relief on the transfer of her business to the company and claim Entrepreneurs' relief on the whole of the gain arising in incorporation instead.

As a result, all of the £120,000 gain arising would be taxed at 10% and the base cost of the shares would be £200,000.

This would therefore reduce the later gain chargeable on the shares which would be taxed at 28%.

Tax is therefore saved at 18% (28% – 10%).

Alternatively she could delay the sale of the shares until she has held them for 12 months and then she will qualify for Entrepreneurs' relief on their disposal.

Tutorial note

Calculations were not required in this advice part of the question.

However, for tutorial purposes, if incorporation relief is disapplied the following would arise:

Gains on incorporation of the business = £120,000

Disposal of 150,000 shares in Alilim Ltd (see working below) = £125,000

Her total CGT would be £47,000 ((£120,000 x 10%) + (£125,000 x 28%))

Her original tax charge would have been £55,800 ((£40,000 x 10%) + (£185,000 x 28%))

Therefore the tax saving would be £8,800 (£55,800 – £47,000).

Working for tutorial note:

Incorporation of the business – Disapplying incorporation relief

	£
Total gains taxed at 10%	120,000

The base cost of her shares will be £200,000

Disposal of 150,000 shares in Alilim Ltd

The gain on the disposal of the shares would be:

	£
Disposal proceeds	275,000
Less: Base cost (£200,000 × 150,000/200,000)	(150,000)
Chargeable gain	125,000

(c) **Family Ltd**

	£	£
Disposal proceeds (Note)		230,000
Less: Cost	168,000	
Held over gain (W)	(40,000)	
		(128,000)
Chargeable gain		102,000

Tutorial note

Alice and her mother are connected persons, and therefore the market value would have been used when the shares were sold on 21 May 2011.

Working: Gift relief

The consideration paid for the shares did not exceed the allowable cost therefore full gift relief is available at the time of the gift.

The total gain of £40,000 (£168,000 – £128,000) was therefore held over.

Tutorial note

Per the question, Entrepreneurs' relief is to be ignored. However, it is not available on this gift anyway as Alice does not work for Family Ltd and has not held the shares for 12 months.

(d) **Property**

	£
Disposal proceeds	180,000
Less: Deemed acquisition cost (Note)	(50,000)
Chargeable gain	130,000

Tutorial note

Alice's husband is deemed to have transferred the asset at its acquisition cost (i.e. £50,000), such that no gain or loss arises on the transfer

Alice's deemed acquisition cost is the same as her husband's deemed proceeds (i.e. £50,000).

As the property has never been occupied as the principal private residence the property does not qualify for either principal private residence relief or letting relief.

30 CHANDRA KHAN (ADAPTED)

Key answer tips

This question focuses on the capital gains reliefs available to individuals.

One unusual feature is the factory in part (b) which has been used partly for non business purposes. The rest of the question covers common situations and should not cause problems.

Note however that the requirement asks for the chargeable gains, not the capital gains tax liability. Therefore you should ignore the annual exempt amount and Entrepreneurs' relief.

This question was originally a 20 mark question, and under the current syllabus and rules, this question would still be worth 20 marks.

No attempt has been made to reduce the question as it is still representative of the type of question you will see in the examination and provides good practice for your revision. However, under the new syllabus the question on capital gains will only be 15 marks and therefore will probably have fewer disposals to deal with in the time available than this question has.

(a) **Universal Ltd shares – Sale at undervaluation**

	£
Deemed proceeds (Note)	110,000
Less: Cost	(38,000)
	72,000
Less: Gift relief (Balancing figure)	(35,000)
Chargeable gain after gift relief (W)	37,000

Tutorial note:

Chandra and her daughter are connected persons, and therefore the market value of the shares sold is used as consideration. The actual sale proceeds received are ignored.

Working: Chargeable gain after gift relief

Where there is a sale at undervaluation, a chargeable gain will arise if the actual consideration received exceeds the allowable cost:

	£
Actual proceeds	75,000
Less: Cost	(38,000)
Chargeable gain after gift relief	37,000

Gift relief will be the remaining gain of £35,000 (£72,000 – £37,000)

Tutorial note:

The question only requires the calculation of the chargeable gain, therefore Entrepreneurs' relief is not considered.

The relief is not however available anyway as Chandra is not employed by Universal Ltd.

(b) **Freehold factory**

	£
Disposal proceeds	146,000
Less: Cost	(72,000)
	74,000
Less: Rollover relief (W)	(55,500)
Chargeable gain	18,500

Working: Rollover relief

The proportion of the gain relating to non-business use is £18,500 (£74,000 × 25%), and this amount does not qualify for rollover relief.

The remaining gain of £55,500 (£74,000 – £18,500) can be rolled over provided:

- the business proportion of the sale proceeds is fully reinvested
- within the relevant time period between 8.11.2010 to 7.11.2014.

The business portion of sale proceeds = (£146,000 × 75%) = £109,500

Amount reinvested in qualifying business assets = £156,000

Reinvested on 10.11.11

Therefore, rollover relief is available for all of the remaining gain of £55,500.

Tutorial note:

Per the question, only the chargeable gain is required, therefore Entrepreneurs' relief need not be considered.

However, Entrepreneurs' relief is not available on this disposal anyway as the disposal of a factory is not a qualifying disposal.

The whole or substantial part of a business must be disposed of. There is no relief for the disposal of individual assets out of a business.

(c) **Goodwill**

	£
Proceeds	100,000
Less: Cost	(Nil)
	100,000
Less: Incorporation relief (W)	(80,000)
Chargeable gain (See Tutorial note)	20,000

Working: Incorporation relief

Where a business is incorporated and cash consideration is received, the proportion of the gain relating to the cash consideration cannot be deferred.

Therefore, the gain relating to the cash consideration is immediately chargeable.

Total consideration = (£200,000 + £50,000) = £250,000

Proportion of the gain relating to the cash consideration

= (£100,000 × £50,000/£250,000) = £20,000

Incorporation relief is the remaining gain relating to the share consideration

= (£100,000 – £20,000) = £80,000

or can be calculated as

= (£100,000 × £200,000/£250,000) = £80,000

Tutorial note:

Per the question, only the chargeable gain is required. Therefore, consideration of Entrepreneurs' relief is not required.

However, for tutorial purposes, note that provided the business has been owned for at least one year, Entrepreneurs' relief will be available on the incorporation of a business. This is because there is a disposal of a qualifying business.

Entrepreneurs' relief:

- *is applied to the remaining gain left in charge to tax, and*
- *the remaining gain (£20,000) would then be taxed at 10%*

Chandra could elect to disapply the incorporation relief to increase the gain eligible for Entrepreneurs' relief now if she wants to.

This would be beneficial if Chandra was not employed by the new company or if she planned to sell her shares within 12 months, as in both of these cases her subsequent disposal of the shares would not qualify for Entrepreneurs' relief.

(d) **Private residence**

	£
Disposal proceeds	350,000
Less: Cost	(75,000)
	275,000
Less: Principal private residence (PPR) exemption (W1)	(240,625)
	34,375
Less: Letting relief (W2)	(34,375)
Chargeable gain	Nil

Workings

(W1) **PPR relief**

Chargeable and exempt periods of ownership

		Total months	*Exempt months*	*Chargeable months*
1.4.04 – 31.3.08	(actual occupation)	48	48	
1.4.08 – 31.3.09	(absent – let out)	12		12
1.4.09 – 1.4.12	(final 36 months)	36	36	
		96	84	12

PPR relief = (£275,000 × 84/96) = £240,625

Tutorial note:

After Chandra left her residence to live with a friend she never returned. Consequently the exemption for absence for any reason up to 3 years is not available as there is no actual occupation both before and after the period of absence.

In contrast the exemption for the final 36 months of ownership has no such restriction and is therefore still available.

Make sure that you include a brief explanation for the periods you allow as exempt due to the deemed occupation rules – as the examiner has said that such explanations are required to obtain maximum marks in these questions.

(W2) **Letting relief**

Letting relief = lowest of:

(1) £40,000

(2) PPR = £240,625

(3) Gain on letting = (£275,000 × 12/96) = £34,375

31 MICHAEL CHIN (ADAPTED) *Online question assistance*

Key answer tips

A typical exam question on capital gains tax with a series of disposals covering a variety of topics. All the disposals are gifts and so you must use the market value as the proceeds in the computation of the gains.

Be careful to distinguish disposals (1) and (2), which do qualify for gift relief, from the remaining disposals which do not.

This question was originally a 20 mark question, but it was set when the rules for CGT were considerably more complicated. Under the current syllabus and rules, this question would now be worth 15 marks.

Capital gains tax liability – 2011/12

Disposal of business (Note 1)

	£	£
Goodwill		
Deemed proceeds = MV	60,000	
Less: Cost	Nil	
	60,000	
Less: Gift relief	(60,000)	
		Nil
Freehold property		
Deemed proceeds = MV	150,000	
Less: Cost	(86,000)	
	64,000	
Less: Gift relief (W1)	(48,000)	
		16,000
Net current assets		Nil
Total chargeable gains on the disposal of the business		16,000
Ordinary shares in Minnow Ltd (Note 2)		
Deemed proceeds = MV	180,000	
Less: Cost	(87,500)	
	92,500	
Less: Gift relief (W2)	(74,000)	
		18,500
Ordinary shares in Whale plc (Note 3)		
Deemed proceeds (18,000 × £6·40) (W3)	115,200	
Less: Cost (W4)	(59,600)	
		55,600
Chargeable gains c/f		90,100

	£	£
Chargeable gains c/f		90,100
Painting (Notes 4 and 5)		
Deemed proceeds = MV	7,500	
Less: Cost	(4,000)	
Gain	3,500	
Chargeable gain restricted to maximum of:		
5/3 × (£7,500 – £6,000)	2,500	2,500
Land (Notes 4 and 6)		
Deemed proceeds = MV	50,000	
Less: Cost (£50,000 / (£50,000 + £600,000)) × £500,000	(38,462)	
		11,538
Necklace (Note 5)		
Non-wasting chattel bought and sold for < £6,000 = exempt		Nil
Total chargeable gains		104,138
Less: Capital loss brought forward (W5)		(15,600)
Net chargeable gains		88,538
Less: AE		(10,600)
Taxable gain		77,938
Capital gains tax (£77,938 x 28%)		21,823

Tutorial note

1. *Disposal of the business*

   The disposal of a business is treated as separate disposals of each chargeable asset in the business. A gain must be calculated on each chargeable asset.

   However, the net current assets are not chargeable assets for capital gains tax purposes.

   Gift relief is available on any gain relating to qualify business assets disposed of, but not on the portion of the building that had never been used for his business.

   Per the question, Entrepreneurs' relief is to be ignored.

   However, for tutorial purposes, where the full gain is not covered by gift relief, Entrepreneurs' relief may be available. It will be available on the gift of a qualifying business provided the business has been owned for at least 12 months. If this is the case, the remaining gain would be taxed at 10%.

2. *Minnow Ltd shares*

   Gift relief is available as ordinary shares in an unquoted trading company are qualifying assets for gift relief purposes. However full relief is not available as the company holds investments.

Per the question, Entrepreneurs' relief is to be ignored. However, for tutorial purposes, where the full gain is not covered by gift relief, Entrepreneurs' relief may be available.

It will be available on the gift of shares in a personal trading company (i.e. donor owns at least 5% interest), provided the donor works for for the company and has owned the shares for at least one year. If this is the case, the remaining gain would be taxed at 10%.

3. *Whale plc shares*

   Gift relief is only available on shares in a quoted company if the donor owns at least 5% of the shares in the company and the company is a trading company. As Michael owns less than 1% in Whale plc, gift relief is not available.

   For the same reason, Entrepreneurs' relief would not be available.

4. *Painting and Investment land*

   A painting and investment land are not qualifying assets for gift relief purposes.

5. *Chattels*

   It is important to be able to recognise when an asset is a chattel (i.e. tangible and moveable) and therefore that the disposal is subject to special rules. The painting and antique necklace are both chattels.

6. *Part disposal*

   On a part disposal the cost of the part disposed of is calculated using A/(A+B) where A is the value of the part disposed of and B is the value of the part retained.

Workings

(W1) **Freehold property**

The proportion of the freehold property gain relating to non-business use is £16,000 (£64,000 × 25%), and this amount does not qualify for gift relief.

The remaining gain of £48,000 (£64,000 – £16,000) can be held over (i.e. deferred) with a gift relief claim.

(W2) **Minnow Ltd**

The gift relief in respect of the ordinary shares in Minnow Ltd is restricted because the company has investment assets.

The proportion of gain eligible for gift relief is the proportion of chargeable business assets to chargeable assets, calculated as follows:

Gift relief = (£92,500 × £200,000/£250,000) = £74,000

(W3) **Valuation of the Whale plc shares**

Quarter up method = (£6.36 + $^1/_4$ × (£6.52 – £6.36)) = £6.40 per share

(W4) **Share pool – Whale plc shares**

		Number of shares	*Cost £*
December 2010	Purchase	15,000	63,000
August 2011	Purchase	12,000	26,400
		27,000	89,400
February 2012	Disposal (£89,400 x 18,000/27,000)	(18,000)	(59,600)
Balance c/f		9,000	29,800

(W5) **Capital loss brought forward**

	£
Capital gain – 2010/11	11,800
Less: Capital loss b/f from 2009/10 – Used (Note)	(1,200)
Net chargeable gains	10,600
Less: AE	(10,600)
Taxable gain	Nil

Tutorial note

The capital loss brought forward is used in 2010/11 but the offset is restricted to preserve the annual exemption.

Loss left to c/f to 2011/12

	£
Capital loss	16,800
Less: Used in 2010/11 (above)	(1,200)
Loss c/f to 2011/12	15,600

32 PAUL OPUS (ADAPTED)

Key answer tips

This is a capital gains computation for an individual covering the commonly tested areas of shares, chattels, principal private residence exemption, part disposals and a husband and wife transfer.

Be careful with the share valuation rules for the Concerto shares. Also remember that for part disposals, you split the cost in proportion to the values of the part disposed of and the part kept, and not their sizes.

Even if you do not manage to calculate all the gains, make sure you get the easy marks for calculating the capital gains tax liability (based on your figures) and stating the due date of payment.

Entrepreneurs' relief is an important business relief tested in parts (b) and (c).

This question was originally a 20 mark question, but it was set when the rules for CGT were considerably more complicated. Under the current syllabus and rules, this question would now be worth 15 marks.

(a) **Capital gains tax liability – 2011/12**

	£	£
Ordinary shares in Symphony Ltd (Note 1)		
Disposal proceeds	23,600	
Less: Cost (£110,400 × 5,000/40,000)	(13,800)	
		9,800
Ordinary shares Concerto plc (Note 2)		
Deemed proceeds (10,000 × £5.11) (W1)	51,100	
Less: Cost	(14,000)	
		37,100
Car (exempt) (Note 3)		Nil
Antique vase (W2)		4,000
House		
Disposal proceeds	220,000	
Less: Cost	(114,700)	
	105,300	
Less: Principal private residence exemption (W3)	(97,500)	
		7,800
Land		
Disposal proceeds	285,000	
Less: Cost of part disposal (W4)	(167,200)	
		117,800
Holiday cottage		
Disposal proceeds	125,000	
Less: Cost (Note 4)	(101,600)	
		23,400
Total chargeable gains		199,900
Less: AE		(10,600)
Taxable gain		189,300
Capital gains tax (£189,300 × 28%)		53,004
Due date		31 January 2013

Tutorial note

1. *There is no Entrepreneurs' relief on the Symphony shares as Paul does not work for the company.*
2. *There is no gift relief available on the quoted shares in Concerto plc as it is not Paul's personal trading company (i.e. Paul owns less a 5% interest in the company). For the same reason, Entrepreneurs' relief is not available.*
3. *Motor cars are exempt from CGT.*
4. *The transfer of the holiday cottage between Paul and his wife is a nil gain / nil loss transfer. This means that the asset is transferred to Paul at the original cost, which is then used in his computation on the subsequent disposal of the shares.*

Workings

(W1) **Value of Concerto plc shares**

The shares in Concerto plc are valued at the lower of:

(i) Quarter up method = (£5.10 + 1/4 × (£5.18 – £5.10)) = £5.12

(ii) Average of marked bargains = (£5.00 + £5.22) × 1/2 = £5.11

Therefore valued at £5.11 per share

(W2) **Antique vase**

	£
Proceeds	8,400
Less: Cost	(4,150)
Gain	4,250
Chargeable gain cannot exceed:	
5/3 × (£8,400 – £6,000)	4,000

Tutorial note

The antique vase is a non-wasting chattel.

It is important to be able to recognise when an asset is a chattel (i.e. tangible and moveable) and therefore that the disposal is subject to special rules.

In this case the chattel cost less than £6,000 but was sold for more than £6,000 and so the 5/3 rds rule applies.

(W3) **Principal private residence relief**

The total period of ownership of the house is 81 months, of which a total of 75 months qualify for exemption (i.e. 39 months period of actual occupation from 1 April 2005 to 30 June 2008, plus final 36 months).

PPR exemption = (£105,300 × 75/81) = £97,500

(W4) **Cost of part disposal**

The cost of the three acres of land sold:

(£285,000 / (£285,000 + £90,000)) × £220,000 = £167,200

Tutorial note

On a part disposal the cost of the part disposed of is calculated using A/(A + B) where:

A = the value of the part disposed of, and

B = the value of the part retained.

(b) **Conditions for obtaining Entrepreneurs' relief on shares**

- Shares must have been owned for 1 year prior to the year of disposal
- The shares must be in a trading company
- The individual disposing of the shares must be:
  - an employee of the company, and
  - own at least 5% of the ordinary share capital and voting rights of the company.

(c) **Tax reduction if Entrepreneurs' relief on shares in Symphony Ltd**

Entrepreneurs' relief reduces the tax on the gain to 10%.

The capital gains tax reduction would therefore be £1,764 (£9,800 × (28% – 10%)).

Tutorial note

Entrepreneurs' relief reduces the capital gains tax payable on certain qualifying business disposals.

If applicable, the first £10 million of gains on qualifying business disposals will be taxed at 10%, as opposed to 18% or 28% (depending on the level of the taxpayer's taxable income).

ACCA marking scheme

			Marks
(a)	Symphony Ltd		1.0
	Concerto plc	– Proceeds	1.0
		– Cost	0.5
	Motor car		0.5
	Antique vase		1.5
	House	– Proceeds	0.5
		– Cost	0.5
		– Exemption	1.5
	Land	– Proceeds	0.5
		– Cost	1.0
	Holiday cottage		1.0
	Annual exemption		0.5
	Capital gains tax		0.5
	Due date		0.5
			11.0
(b)	1 mark per condition		3.0
(c)	Calculation		1.0
Total			15.0

33 DAVID AND ANGELA BROOK (ADAPTED) *Walk in the footsteps of a top tutor*

Key answer tips

A classic question involving the calculation of capital gains tax liabilities of both a husband and his wife, with joint assets and assets held personally.

This question was originally a 20 mark question, and under the current syllabus and rules, this question would still be worth 20 marks.

No attempt has been made to reduce the question as it is still representative of the type of question you will see in the examination and provides good practice for your revision. However, under the new syllabus the question on capital gains will only be 15 marks and therefore will probably have fewer disposals to deal with in the time available than this question has.

Tutor's top tips

Be careful to spot the exempt assets. You don't need to do any calculations for these – just say that they are exempt!

Predictably a husband and wife nil gain/nil loss transfer is included, with the subsequent disposal by the recipient spouse.

Remember also to consider Entrepreneurs' relief on the disposal of shares and gift relief if they have been gifted.

David Brook
Capital gains tax liability – 2011/12

	£
Motor car (exempt)	Nil
House (W1)	20,343
Antique table (W3)	Nil
Shares in Bend Ltd (W4)	Nil
Shares in Galactico plc (W5)	14,850
Total chargeable gains	35,193
Less: AE	(10,600)
Taxable gain	24,593
Capital gains tax (£24,593 at 18%)	4,427

Tutorial note

David has no taxable income. All of his gains therefore fall into his basic rate band and are taxed at 18%. Entrepreneurs' relief is not available on any of his gains.

Angela Brook

Capital gains tax liability – 2011/12

	£
House (W1)	20,343
Antique clock (W8)	2,000
Ordinary shares in Bend Ltd (W9)	26,400
Chargeable gains	48,743
Less: AE	(10,600)
Taxable gain	38,143

£		
700	x 18% (W10)	126
37,443	x 28%	10,484
38,143		
Capital gains tax liability		10,610

Tutorial note:

Angela has taxable income that uses some of, but not all of, her basic rate band. Therefore part of her taxable gain is taxed at 18% and the majority is taxed at 28%.

There is no Entrepreneurs' relief available on any of her gains therefore the 10% rate does not apply.

Workings

(W1) **House**

Tutor's top tips

If an asset is jointly owned by husband and wife, all you need to do is to calculate the gain as usual and then split it 50:50.

Make sure you show your working for the calculation of principal private residence relief. Even if you can't count months, you will still be given marks for applying the correct principles!

	£
Disposal proceeds	381,900
Less: Cost	(86,000)
	295,900
Less: Principal private residence exemption (W2)	(255,214)
Chargeable gain	40,686

David and Angela will each be assessed on 50% of the chargeable gain:

Chargeable gain each = (£40,686 × 50%) = £20,343

(W2) **Occupation of the house**

The total period of ownership of the house is 240 months (207 + 33), of which 207 months qualify for exemption as follows:

		Total months	*Exempt months*	*Chargeable months*
1.10.91 to 31.3.95	(occupied)	42	42	
1.4.95 to 31.12.98	(working in UK)	45	45	
1.1.99 to 31.12.05	(occupied)	84	84	
1.1.06 to 30.9.08	(unoccupied)	33		33
1.10.08 to 30.9.11	(final 36 months)	36	36	
		240	207	33

PPR relief = (207/240 × £295,900) = £255,214

Tutor's top tips

Make sure that you include a brief explanation for the periods you allow as exempt due to the deemed occupation rules – as the examiner has said that such explanations are required to obtain maximum marks in these questions.

(W3) **Antique table**

Tutor's top tips

As soon as you see the word 'antique', think about the special chattels rules.

This is a chattel bought and sold for no more than £6,000 and hence is exempt.

(W4) **Shares in Bend Ltd – gift by David**

Tutor's top tips

Remember that the market value at the time of the inter-spouse gift is a red herring and irrelevant. The transfer will be at nil gain/nil loss.

Transfers between husband and wife are no gain-no loss transfers.

David makes no gain and Angela takes over David's cost of £48,000.

(W5) **Shares in Galactico plc**

	£
Proceeds (Market value for a gift) (15,000 × £2.95) (W6)	44,250
Less: Cost (W7)	(29,400)
Chargeable gain	14,850

Tutorial note

There is no gift relief available on these shares as Galatico plc is a quoted company and David has a less than 5% interest.

For the same reason, and because David does not work for the company, Entrepreneurs' relief is not available.

(W6) **Value of Shares in Galactico plc shares**

Quarter up method = £2.90 + ¼ x (£3.10 – £2.90) = £2.95

(W7) **Share pool – Galactico plc**

		Number of shares	Cost £
15.6.10	Purchase	8,000	17,600
24.8.10	Purchase	12,000	21,600
		20,000	39,200
14.2.12	Gift (£39,200 × 15,000/20,000)	(15,000)	(29,400)
Balance c/f		5,000	9,800

(W8) **Antique clock**

	£
Disposal proceeds	7,200
Less: Cost	(3,700)
Gain	3,500

Chargeable gain cannot exceed: 5/3 × (£7,200 – £6,000) = £2,000

Tutorial note

The clock is a chattel sold at a marginal gain, therefore in the answer the gain is compared with the 5/3rds rule.

In fact, HMRC accept that antique clocks are a form of machinery, and are therefore wasting chattels, which will be exempt (if not used in a business). However, the examiner did not expect you to know this.

(W9) **Shares in Bend Ltd – Sale by Angela**

	£
Disposal proceeds	62,400
Less: Cost (£48,000 × 15,000/20,000)	(36,000)
Chargeable gain	26,400

Tutorial note

It is not clear what percentage interest Angela has in Bend Ltd and whether it is her personal trading company (i.e. she holds 5% interest or more). However, even if she does hold at least 5%, Entrepreneurs' relief is not available as Angela does not work for the company.

(W10) **Remaining basic rate band**

	£
Basic rate band	35,000
Less: Taxable income	(34,300)
Remaining basic rate band	700

Examiner's report

Although there were some very good answers to this question from well prepared candidates, it caused problems for many and was often the reason that they failed to achieve a pass mark.

One particular problem was that a lot of time was often spent performing unnecessary calculations for the exempt assets, and then not having sufficient time to deal with the chargeable assets.

Many candidates therefore did a lot of work for this question but scored few marks.

The jointly owned property caused particular difficulty. Only a few candidates correctly calculated the principal private residence exemption.

Some candidates did not allocate the resulting chargeable gain between the couple but instead deducted an annual exemption and calculated a separate tax liability.

ACCA marking scheme

	Marks
Jointly owned property – Motor car	0.5
– House – Proceeds	0.5
– Cost	0.5
– Period of exemption	2.5
– Exemption	1.0
– Division of gain	1.0
David Brook – Antique table	1.0
– Bend Ltd	0.5
– Galatico plc – Deemed proceeds	1.0
– Cost	2.0
– No gift relief	1.0
– No Entrepreneurs' relief	1.0
– Annual exempt amount	0.5
– Capital gains tax	1.0
Angela Brook – Antique clock	2.0
– Bend Ltd – Proceeds	0.5
– Cost	1.0
– No Entrepreneurs' relief	1.0
– Annual exempt amount	0.5
– Capital gains tax	1.0
Total	20.0

34 WILSON BIAZMA (ADAPTED)

Key answer tips

In part (a) easy marks were available for defining two key terms, namely residence and ordinary residence. However, don't forget to read all the requirements and state the consequences of the residence on the liability of an individual to capital gains tax.

Part (b) involved a series of disposals testing the various reliefs available, part disposals and incorporation. This style of question is a regular feature in the Paper F6 exam.

This was, however, the first time the compensation rules for damaged assets were tested.

This question was originally a 20 mark question, and under the current syllabus and rules, this question would still be worth 20 marks.

No attempt has been made to reduce the question as it is still representative of the type of question you will see in the examination and provides good practice for your revision. However, under the new syllabus the question on capital gains will only be 15 marks and therefore will probably have fewer disposals to deal with in the time available than this question has.

(a) **Residence**

- A person will be resident in the UK during a tax year if they are present in the UK for 183 days or more.
- A person will also be treated as resident if they visit the UK regularly, with visits averaging 91 days or more a tax year over a period of four or more consecutive tax years.

Ordinary residence

- Ordinary residence is not precisely defined, but a person will normally be ordinarily resident in the UK if this is where they habitually reside.

Liability to capital gains tax

- A person is liable to capital gains tax (CGT) on the disposal of assets during any tax year in which they are either resident or ordinarily resident in the UK.

(b) **Chargeable gains – 2011/12**

	£	£
Gains not qualifying for Entrepreneurs' relief:		
Office building (W1)	110,000	
Ordinary shares in Gandua Ltd (W4)	8,000	
Antique vase (W6)	Nil	
Land (W7)	17,000	
Gains qualifying for Entrepreneurs' relief:		
Goodwill (W3)		120,000
Total chargeable gains	135,000	120,000
Less: AE	(10,600)	
Taxable gains	124,400	120,000

Capital gains tax:		£
Qualifying gains	(£120,000 × 10%)	12,000
Not qualifying gains	(£124,400 × 28%)	34,832
CGT payable		46,832

Tutorial note:

Wilson is a higher rate taxpayer. Therefore he will pay capital gains tax at 28% on his gains that do not qualify for Entrepreneurs' relief.

Those gains that qualify for Entrepreneurs' relief will be taxed at 10% regardless of whether they fall into the basic rate or higher rate band. If applicable, these qualifying gains are deemed to utilise any remaining basic rate band first before the gains not qualifying for the relief.

Workings

(W1) **Office building**

	£
Disposal proceeds	246,000
Less: Cost	(104,000)
Capital gain before reliefs	142,000
Less: Rollover relief (W2)	(32,000)
Chargeable gain	110,000

Tutorial note

Entrepreneurs' relief is not available as this is the disposal of a single asset, not the whole or part of a business.

(W2) **Rollover relief**

Rollover relief is not available in full because not all the proceeds are reinvested.

The gain remaining chargeable is the lower of:

(i) Total gain of £142,000, or

(ii) Proceeds not reinvested (£246,000 – £136,000) = £110,000

Rollover relief is therefore £32,000 (£142,000 – £110,000).

(W3) **Goodwill**

	£
Disposal proceeds	120,000
Less: Cost	Nil
	120,000

Tutorial note

Entrepreneurs' relief is available as Wilson has disposed of a complete business which he has owned for at least one year.

Wilson has chosen to disapply incorporation relief, therefore the mixed consideration received is irrelevant.

*However, had Wilson **not** elected to disapply the incorporation relief, there would be a gain arising now due to the mixed consideration received.*

Incorporation relief would only apply to the proportion of the gain relating to the share consideration leaving a gain relating to the cash consideration as follows:

Total consideration = £200,000

Proportion of the gain relating to the cash consideration

= (£120,000 × £60,000/£200,000) = £36,000

Incorporation relief is therefore the remaining gain relating to the share consideration

= (£120,000 – £36,000) = £84,000

or can be calculated as = (£120,000 × £140,000/£200,000) = £84,000.

The chargeable gain arising on incorporation of £36,000 would then be taxed at the Entrepreneurs' relief rate of 10%. The £84,000 gain relating to the share consideration would not crystallise until the shares are sold in the future.

(W4) **Ordinary shares in Gandua Ltd**

	£
Deemed proceeds (Market value)	160,000
Less: Cost	(112,000)
	48,000
Less: Gift relief (W5)	(40,000)
Chargeable gain	8,000

Tutorial note

Although Gandua Ltd qualifies as Wilson's personal company, Entrepreneurs' relief is not available unless he also works for the company.

(W5) **Gift relief on shares in Gandua Ltd**

Gift relief is available on these shares as Wilson owns 100% of the shares (and there is no requirement for him to work for the company for the purposes of gift relief).

However, the gift relief in respect of the ordinary shares in Gandau Ltd is restricted because the company has investment assets.

The proportion of gain eligible for gift relief is the proportion of chargeable business assets to chargeable assets, calculated as follows:

Gift relief = (£48,000 × £150,000/£180,000) = £40,000

(W6) **Antique vase**

The insurance proceeds of £68,000 received by Wilson have been fully reinvested in a replacement antique vase.

The disposal is therefore on a no gain / no loss basis.

The capital gain of £19,000 (insurance proceeds of £68,000 less original cost of £49,000) is set against the cost of the replacement antique vase.

(W7) **Land – part disposal**

	£
Disposal proceeds	85,000
Less: Deemed cost (see below)	(68,000)
Chargeable gain	17,000

Cost of part disposed of = £120,000 × £85,000 / (£85,000 + £65,000) = £68,000.

Tutorial note

The cost relating to the ten acres of land sold is calculated as A / (A + B) where:

A = Market value of part disposed of

B = Market value of the remainder

Examiner's report

Part (a) was reasonably well answered, although only a few candidates appreciated that ordinary residence is a matter of where a person habitually resides.

Many candidates missed an easy mark by not stating that people who are resident or ordinarily resident will be liable to capital gains tax.

Part (b) was also reasonably well answered. The disposal that caused the most problems was the incorporation of the business, with many candidates not appreciating that the gain was simply based on the value of the goodwill transferred.

ACCA marking scheme

		Marks
(a)	183 day rule	1.0
	91 day rule	1.0
	Ordinary residence	1.0
	Liability to CGT	1.0
		4.0

		Marks
(b)	**Office building**	
	Gain	1.0
	Rollover relief	1.5
	No Entrepreneurs' relief	1.0
	Goodwill	
	Gain	1.0
	No incorporation relief	0.5
	Entrepreneurs' relief – need to keep gain separate	0.5
	Ordinary shares in Gandua Ltd	
	Gain	1.0
	Gift relief	1.5
	No Entrepreneurs' relief	1.0
	Antique vase	
	Proceeds fully reinvested	1.0
	No gain no loss	1.0
	Gain reduces base cost	0.5
	Land	
	Proceeds	0.5
	Cost	2.0
	Calculation of CGT payable	
	Annual exemption	0.5
	Entrepreneurs' relief rate	1.0
	Rate for remainder of gains	0.5
		16.0
Total		20.0

35 NIM AND MAE LOM (ADAPTED) *Walk in the footsteps of a top tutor*

Key answer tips

A typical capital gains tax question, requiring the calculation of capital gains tax liabilities for a husband and wife.

Although there is only one requirement, the question can be broken down between the two individuals and then into the different assets sold by each.

This question was originally a 20 mark question, and under the current syllabus and rules, this question would still be worth 20 marks.

No attempt has been made to reduce the question as it is still representative of the type of question you will see in the examination and provides good practice for your revision. However, under the new syllabus the question on capital gains will only be 15 marks and therefore will probably have fewer disposals to deal with in the time available than this question has.

Tutor's top tips

Nim's assets are mostly straightforward. As with any capital gains question, be careful to spot the exempt assets (gilts). You don't need to do any calculations for these – simply state that they are exempt.

There is a classic husband to wife transfer, which from Nim's perspective is simply a nil gain/nil loss disposal.

When dealing with shares, make sure you consider the matching rules first. There is a purchase within 30 days of the disposal, so this will need to be matched before the shares bought earlier, and these shares will NOT go into the share pool.

Nim Lom

Capital gains tax liability – 2011/12

	£
Ordinary shares in Kapook plc (W1)	13,600
Ordinary shares in Jooba Ltd (Note 1)	Nil
Antique table (W4)	3,500
UK Government securities (Note 2)	Nil
Total chargeable gains	17,100
Less: Capital loss brought forward (see below)	(6,500)
Net chargeable gains	10,600
Less: AE	(10,600)
Taxable gain	Nil
Capital gains tax	Nil

Capital losses carried forward

The set off of the brought forward capital losses is restricted to £6,500 so that chargeable gains are reduced to the amount of the annual exemption.

Nim therefore has capital losses carried forward of £10,200 (£16,700 – £6,500).

Workings

(W1) **Ordinary shares in Kapook plc**

The disposal is first matched against the purchase on 24 July 2011 of 2,000 shares (this is within the following 30 days), and then against the shares in the share pool.

	£	£
Matched with purchases in next 30 days:		
Deemed proceeds (2,000 x £3.70) (W2)	7,400	
Less: Cost	(5,800)	
		1,600
Matched with share pool:		
Deemed proceeds (8,000 × £3.70) (W2)	29,600	
Less: Cost (W3)	(17,600)	
		12,000
		13,600

(W2) **Valuation of ordinary shares in Kapook plc**

The shares in Kapook plc are valued at the lower of:

(i) Quarter up method = £3·70 + ¼ x (£3·90 – £3·70) = £3.75

(ii) Average of highest and lowest marked bargains = (£3·60 + £3·80)/2 = £3.70

(W3) **Share pool – Kapook plc**

The cost of the shares in the share pool is calculated as:

		Number of shares	*Cost £*
Purchase	19 February 2003	8,000	16,200
Purchase	6 June 2008	6,000	14,600
		14,000	30,800
Disposal	20 July 2011 (£30,800 x 8,000/14,000)	(8,000)	(17,600)
Balance carried forward		6,000	13,200

(W4) **Antique table**

The antique table is a non-wasting chattel (Note 3).

	£
Sale proceeds	8,700
Less: Cost	(5,200)
Chargeable gain	3,500
Chargeable gain is not restricted as the maximum gain is: 5/3 × (£8,700 – £6,000)	4,500

Tutorial note

1. *The transfer of the 5,000 £1 ordinary shares in Jooba Ltd to Mae does not give rise to any gain or loss, because it is a transfer between spouses.*
2. *The disposal of UK Government securities is exempt from CGT.*
3. *Whenever you see the word 'antique' in a question, you should immediately be thinking about the chattel rules.*
4. *It is important to be familiar with the rules for the use of capital losses, which are very regularly tested. Brought forward losses are restricted to utilise the annual exemption, but current year losses must be used in full.*

Mae Lom
Capital gains tax liability – 2011/12

Tutor's top tips

Mae has disposed of the shares that she received from her husband. Remember this was a nil gain nil loss transfer, and in order for Nim to have a gain of nil, he is deemed to have transferred the asset to Mae at original cost.

The house has been Nim and Mae's main residence throughout the period of ownership, so there is no need to consider the absence rules here, however as one room was used exclusively for business purposes, principle private residence relief cannot be given in respect of that part of the gain.

When dealing with business assets make sure you consider their eligibility for Entrepreneurs' relief.

The hardest asset to deal with is the copyright, as this kind of disposal has not been seen in exam questions before. The asset is wasting (it has a useful life of less than 50 years), however it is not a chattel so the £6,000 rules do not apply. Instead the cost must be reduced on a straight line basis for the period of time that the asset has been held by Mae.

	£	£	£
Gains not qualifying for Entrepreneurs' relief:			
Ordinary shares in Jooba Ltd			
Disposal proceeds	30,400		
Less: Cost (£16,000 x 2,000/5,000) (Note 1)	(6,400)		
		24,000	
Principal private residence			
Disposal proceeds	186,000		
Less: Cost	(122,000)		
	64,000		
Less: PPR relief (W)	(56,000)		
		8,000	
Investment property (Note 2)		34,000	
Copyright			
Disposal proceeds	9,600		
Less: Cost (£10,000 x 15/20) (Note 3)	(7,500)		
		2,100	
Gains qualifying for Entrepreneurs' relief:			
Business			
Goodwill	80,000		
Freehold office building	136,000		
			216,000
Total chargeable gains (Note 4)		68,100	216,000
Less: Capital loss brought forward		(8,500)	
Less: AE		(10,600)	
Taxable gains		49,000	216,000

		£
Capital gains tax (Note 5)		
Qualifying gains	(£216,000 × 10%)	21,600
Non-qualifying gains	(£49,000 × 28%)	13,720
CGT payable		35,320

Capital losses carried forward

There is no capital loss remaining to carry forward as it is all utilised in 2011/12.

Tutorial note:

1. *Nim's original cost is used in calculating the gain on the disposal of the shares in Jooba Ltd.*
2. *The investment property does not qualify for Entrepreneurs' relief because it was never used for business purposes.*
3. *The copyright is a wasting asset. The cost of £10,000 must therefore be depreciated based on an unexpired life of 20 years at the date of acquisition and an unexpired life of 15 years at the date of disposal.*
4. *The annual allowance and capital losses brought forward can be deducted in the most advantageous way. Therefore they are deducted from the gains not eligible for Entrepreneurs' relief, leaving the whole £216,000 to be taxed at 10%.*
5. *Although Mae has taxable income of only £30,000 and £5,000 of the basic rate band remains, gains qualifying for Entrepreneurs' relief are deemed to utilise the remaining basic rate band before non-qualifying gains. Therefore all of the non-qualifying gains are taxed at 28%.*

Working: Principal private residence relief

One of the eight rooms in Mae's house was always used exclusively for business purposes, so the principal private residence exemption is restricted to £56,000 (£64,000 x 7/8).

Examiner's report

This question was generally well answered.

For the husband, quite a few candidates surprisingly had problems with the valuation rules for quoted shares.

It was also not always appreciated that the transfer between spouses and the sale of the UK Government securities were respectively at no gain, no loss, and exempt. Candidates thus wasted time performing unnecessary calculations.

Many candidates had difficulty with the cost of the quoted shares disposed of, and they incorrectly included the purchase within the following 30 days as part of the share pool.

The restriction of the brought forward capital losses so that chargeable gains were reduced to the amount of the annual exemption was often missed.

For the wife, many candidates treated the private portion of the principal private residence as taxable rather than the business portion.

The investment property included within the disposal of the business was sometimes treated as exempt, and sometimes Entrepreneurs' relief was claimed in respect of it.

Only a minority of candidates correctly calculate the cost of the wasting asset.

ACCA marking scheme			Marks
	Nim Lom		
	Kapook plc	– Deemed proceeds	2.0
		– Cost	1.0
		– Share pool	2.0
	Jooba Ltd		1.0
	Antique table		1.5
	UK Government securities		0.5
	Capital losses brought forward		1.0
	Annual exemption		0.5
	Capital losses carried forward		0.5
	Mae Lom		
	Jooba Ltd	– Proceeds	0.5
		– Cost	1.0
	House	– Proceeds	0.5
		– Cost	0.5
		– Exemption	1.0
	Business	– Goodwill	0.5
		– Office building	0.5
		– Investment property	1.0
	Copyright	– Proceeds	0.5
		– Cost	1.0
	Capital losses brought forward		0.5
	Annual exemption		0.5
	Capital gains tax		2.0
Total			20.0

36 AMANDA, BO AND CHARLES *Walk in the footsteps of a top tutor*

Key answer tips

A capital gains tax question requiring the calculation of chargeable gains for three different individuals.

Each scenario covers a different capital gains tax relief: incorporation relief, gift relief and principal private residence relief, and requires the consideration of an alternative assumption in the second part.

The requirement specifically asked for the chargeable gain, not the capital gains tax liability. Therefore, Entrepreneurs' relief is not relevant, but to make sure the examiner clearly indicated in the notes to the question that you should ignore Entrepreneurs' relief.

This question was originally a 20 mark question, and under the current syllabus and rules, this question would still be worth 20 marks.

No attempt has been made to reduce the question as it is still representative of the type of question you will see in the examination and provides good practice for your revision. However, under the new syllabus the question on capital gains will only be 15 marks and therefore will probably have fewer disposals to deal with in the time available than this question has.

Tutor's top tips

Part (a) involves the incorporation if a business.

Remember that when an individual disposes of a business they are not treated as disposing of an asset (i.e. the business). They are treated as disposing of each of the individual chargeable assets within the business separately.

Therefore potentially several computations are required, but there is no need to do a computation for an asset which is not chargeable for capital gains tax purposes (i.e. the net current assets).

Incorporation relief is then given against the net chargeable gains in respect of all of the disposals.

(a) (i) **Amanda Moon**

Chargeable gains – 2011/12

- Amanda has total chargeable gains calculated as follows:

	£
Goodwill (MV £90,000 – Cost of Nil)	90,000
Freehold shop (MV £165,000 – Cost £120,000)	45,000
Net current assets (not chargeable assets)	Nil
Total chargeable gains	135,000

- The consideration from Ammoon Ltd is entirely in the form of shares, so all of Amanda's chargeable gains can be rolled over (i.e. deferred) against the base cost of the shares acquired, under the incorporation relief rules.
- The base cost of the 300,000 £1 ordinary shares will be:

	£
MV of business = MV of shares acquired	300,000
Less: Incorporation relief	
(i.e. total chargeable gains deferred)	(135,000)
Base cost of shares	165,000

(ii) **Mixed consideration received**

- The proportion of the gain relating to the consideration taken in the form of shares can be rolled over (i.e. deferred); however any gain relating to the cash consideration is chargeable at the time of the incorporation.
- Therefore £45,000 (£135,000 × £100,000/£300,000) of the gain would be chargeable to CGT during 2011/12.
- The remaining gain of £90,000 (£135,000 – £45,000) is rolled over against the base cost of the shares acquired.
- The cost of the 200,000 £1 ordinary shares in Ammoon Ltd is £200,000 (£300,000 – £100,000), so the base cost will be £110,000 (£200,000 – £90,000).

(b) (i) **Bo Neptune**

Chargeable gain – 2011/12

Tutor's top tips

Part (b) involves the gift of shares in an unquoted trading company. You should be aware that these shares qualify for gift relief. However even if you couldn't remember the definition of a qualifying asset for gift relief purposes, the question clearly states that an election has been made to holdover (i.e. defer) the gain arising.

Remember that full relief is available for outright gifts of qualifying assets, but there may only be partial gift relief for sales at an undervaluation (i.e. where the actual sale proceeds received are less than the market value of the asset at the time of the gift).

Full relief is not available where the actual sale proceeds received exceed the original cost of the asset. This is because, despite selling the asset for less than it is worth now, an actual capital profit has still been made by the owner on the disposal.

- This is a gift, and therefore the market value of the shares sold is used. Bo therefore has a chargeable gain of £116,000 (MV £210,000 – Cost of £94,000).
- Since no consideration has been paid for the shares, all of Bo's chargeable gain can be held over (i.e. deferred) with a gift relief claim.
- The base cost of the son's 50,000 £1 ordinary shares in Botune Ltd will be:

	£
MV of shares acquired	210,000
Less: Gift relief	(116,000)
Base cost of shares	94,000

(ii) **Sale at undervaluation**

- The consideration paid for the shares is less than the market value, but will exceed the allowable cost by £66,000 (£160,000 – £94,000). This amount will be immediately chargeable to capital gains tax.
- The remaining gain of £50,000 (£116,000 – £66,000) can be deferred with a gift relief claim.
- The base cost of the son's 50,000 £1 ordinary shares in Botune Ltd will be:

	£
MV of shares acquired	210,000
Less: Gift relief	(50,000)
Base cost of shares	160,000

Tutorial note

With a sale at undervaluation, the chargeable gain will still be calculated using the full market value of the asset, as before.

However, any actual capital profit made by the owner at the time of the sale will be immediately chargeable.

(c) (i) **Charles Orion**

Chargeable gain – 2011/12

Tutor's top tips

Part (c) involves the disposal of Charles' house. It tests the application of the deemed occupation rules and in the second part, letting relief.

This is a classic PPR question which is fairly straightforward but be careful with the dates and identifying the impact of the last 36 months rule.

Charles' chargeable gain on the house is calculated as follows:

	£
Disposal proceeds	282,000
Less: Cost	(110,000)
	172,000
Less: PPR relief (W)	(107,500)
Chargeable gain	64,500

Working: PPR relief

		Total months	*Exempt months*		*Chargeable months*
1.10.99 to 31.3.01	(occupied)	18	18		
1.4.01 to 30.9.08	(unoccupied)	90	36	(Note 1)	54
1.10.08 to 31.12.09	(unoccupied)	15	15	(Note 2)	
1.1.10 to 30.9.11	(occupied)	21	21	(Note 2)	
		144	90		54

PPR exemption = (£172,000 × 90/144) = £107,500

Tutor's top tips

Make sure that you include a brief explanation for the periods you allow as exempt due to the deemed occupation rules – as the examiner has said that such explanations are required to obtain maximum marks in these questions.

Tutorial note

1. *The first 36 months of the "unoccupied" period is a period of "deemed occupation" because 36 months are allowed for no reason provided:*
   - *the property is actually occupied at some time before and at some time after the period of absence, and*
   - *there was no other PPR at that time.*
2. *The last 36 months are always allowable provided the property was the taxpayer's PPR at some time.*

   Note that the last 36 months covers the last 21 months of actual occupation and the last 15 months of the "unoccupied" period.

(ii) **If the property is rented**

- The letting relief exemption will be available if the property is let during periods that are not covered by the PPR exemption.
- The letting relief exemption is the lowest of:
  - (i) PPR exemption = £107,500
  - (ii) the amount of the gain not covered by PPR that is attributable to the period of letting = £64,500 (Note)
  - (iii) Maximum = £40,000.
- Charles' chargeable gain will therefore be:

	£
Gain after PPR relief	64,500
Less: Letting relief	(40,000)
Chargeable gain	24,500

Tutorial note

In this part the house is let for the whole period of Charles' absence.

Therefore, the "amount of the gain not covered by PPR that is attributable to the period of letting" will be the whole of the remaining gain after PPR, as it is let throughout the whole period.

If the property had only been let for a portion of that chargeable period, letting relief would be restricted accordingly.

Examiner's report

This question was not as well answered as would have been expected given that it was effectively three short separate questions on reasonably straightforward areas of capital gains tax.

On an overall note, the question clearly stated that Entrepreneurs' relief was to be ignored, yet some candidates still showed this relief as being claimed.

Base costs were often not shown despite these being required in parts (a) and (b).

In part (a) far too many candidates treated this as one disposal rather than dealing with each asset separately. In the second section only a few candidates appreciated that incorporation relief was restricted according to the proportion of cash consideration to total consideration.

Part (b) was reasonably well answered, although few candidates could correctly calculate the revised base cost following the restriction of holdover relief in the second section.

Although there were some very good answers to part (c), far too many candidates had problems calculating the principal private residence exemption, and often lost marks by not showing detailed workings.

Even when the correct exemption was calculated this was often shown as the amount chargeable rather than the exempt amount. In the second section it was not always appreciated that letting relief was available.

ACCA marking scheme				
				Marks
(a)	(i)	Goodwill		1.0
		Freehold shop		1.0
		Gains rolled over		1.0
		Base cost of shares		1.0
				4.0
	(ii)	Gain chargeable	– Explanation	1.0
			– Calculation	1.0
		Base cost of shares		1.0
				3.0
(b)	(i)	Chargeable gain		1.0
		Gain held over		1.0
		Base cost of shares		1.0
				3.0
	(ii)	Gain chargeable		1.0
		Base cost of shares		1.0
				2.0
(c)	(i)	Proceeds		0.5
		Cost		0.5
		Period of exemption		3.0
		Principal private residence relief		1.0
				5.0
	(ii)	Letting relief		2.0
		Revised chargeable gain		1.0
				3.0
Total				20.0

COMPANIES – CHARGEABLE GAINS

37 FORWARD LTD (ADAPTED)

Key answer tips

This question requires the corporation tax liability of a company, however before that can be calculated several chargeable gains need to be calculated.

Remember that disposals by a company are entitled to an indexation allowance and rollover relief for replacement of business assets is a key relief available for companies. No other reliefs are available. Note that the effect of reinvesting in a depreciating asset as in part (b) must be understood as this is an area that is often tested.

This question was originally a 20 mark question, but it was set when the rules for capital gains were considerably more complicated. Under the current syllabus and rules, this question would now be worth 15 marks.

(a) **Corporation tax liability – year ended 31 March 2012**

	£
Trading profit	78,000
Net chargeable gains	
(£30,000 (W1) + £35,982 (W3) + £9,837 (W5))	75,819
Taxable total profits	153,819
Corporation tax liability	
FY 2011 (£153,819 × 20%)	30,764
Due date	1 January 2013

Workings

(W1) **Freehold office building**

	£
Disposal proceeds	290,000
Less: Cost	(148,000)
Unindexed gain	142,000
Less: Indexation allowance	
(234.8 – 138.8)/138.8 = 0.692 × £148,000	(102,416)
Chargeable gain before reliefs	39,584
Less: Roll over relief (W2)	(9,584)
Chargeable gain	30,000

(W2) **Rollover relief**

The sale proceeds of the office building are not fully reinvested.

The chargeable gain cannot be rolled over:

	£
Disposal proceeds	290,000
Less: Reinvested in qualifying business asset	(260,000)
Sale proceeds not reinvested = chargeable now	30,000

The remaining gain of £9,584 (£39,584 – £30,000) can be deferred with a rollover relief claim.

(W3) **Ordinary Shares in Backward plc**

	£
Disposal proceeds	62,500
Less: Cost (W4)	(12,895)
Unindexed gain	49,605
Less: Indexation allowance (£26,518 – £12,895) (W4)	(13,623)
Chargeable gain	35,982

Tutorial note

The gain cannot be rolled over into the acquisition of the shares in Sideways plc as shares are not qualifying assets for the purpose of rollover relief.

(W4) **Share pool – Backward plc**

		Number	*Cost*	*Indexed cost*
			£	£
April 1986	Purchase	9,000	18,000	18,000
Indexation to November 2011 £18,000 × (238.2 – 97.7)/97.7 (do not round indexation factor)				25,885
				43,885
November 2011	Purchase	500	6,500	6,500
		9,500	24,500	50,385
November 2011 Cost × (5,000 / 9,500)	Disposal	(5,000)	(12,895)	(26,518)
Balance c/f		4,500	11,605	23,867

(W5) **Painting**

	£
Deemed proceeds	22,000
Less: Deemed cost (see Tutorial Note)	
£15,000 x (£22,000 / (£22,000 + £20,000))	(7,857)
Unindexed gain	14,143
Less : Indexation to February 2012	
(242.9 – 156.9)/156.9 = 0.548 x £7,857	(4,306)
Chargeable gain	9,837

Tutorial note

Where an asset is damaged, compensation is received and the proceeds are not used to restore the asset, there is a part disposal of the asset for capital gains purposes.

The deemed cost is calculated using A/(A+B) where:

A = Insurance proceeds received

B = Value of asset after damage

The date of disposal is the date that the compensation is received not the date that the asset is damaged.

(b) **Reinvestment in leasehold office building**

- The freehold office building's sale proceeds of £290,000 will be fully reinvested, and so the whole of the gain of £39,584 is eligible for rollover relief.
- The leasehold office building is a depreciating asset, so its base cost will not be adjusted.
- The base cost of the 15 year lease will therefore be its actual cost of £300,000.
- The gain will be deferred until the earliest of:
  – ten years from the date of acquisition of the leasehold building,
  – the date that it is disposed of, or
  – the date that it ceases to be used for trading purposes.

38 HAWK LTD *Walk in the footsteps of a top tutor*

Key answer tips

This question requires the computation of a corporation tax liability for a company, however several chargeable gains need to be calculated before the corporation tax liability computation can be performed.

You need to remember that disposals made by a company will usually have some element of indexation allowance, so you need to be aware of the rules regarding the rounding of the indexation factor.

The only capital gains relief available to companies is rollover relief and therefore it is not surprising to see it here in this question and it is often tested in corporation tax questions.

This question was originally a 20 mark question, and under the current syllabus and rules, this question would still be worth 20 marks.

No attempt has been made to reduce the question as it is still representative of the type of question you will see in the examination and provides good practice for your revision. However, under the new syllabus the question on capital gains will only be 15 marks and therefore will probably have fewer disposals to deal with in the time available than this question has.

Tutor's top tips

Part (a) consisted of a number of reasonably straightforward disposals made by a company. As long as the gains are calculated individually, a good mark can be achieved in this question.

It is important not to get bogged down with any particular computation. If you cannot remember how to deal with a disposal, move on! You will pick up far more marks by moving forward, and if you have time you can revisit the problem area again later.

Part (b) covers rollover relief and requires you to apply your knowledge of the relief.

(a) Hawk Ltd

Corporation tax computation – year ended 31 March 2012

	£
Trading profit	125,000
Net chargeable gains (W)	83,551
Taxable total profits	208,551
Corporation tax liability	
FY 2011 (£208,551 × 20%)	41,710

Tutorial note

Hawk Ltd has no associated companies; therefore the taxable total profits of £208,551, which fall entirely in FY 2011, are taxed at 20% as profits fall below the lower limit of £300,000.

Workings: Chargeable gains

	£	£
Office Building		
Proceeds (April 2011)	260,000	
Less: Costs of disposal	(3,840)	
Net disposal proceeds	256,160	
Less: Cost and legal fees (July 1991) (£81,000 + £3,200)	(84,200)	
Enhancement (May 2003)	(43,000)	
Unindexed gain	128,960	
Less: Indexation allowance		
On cost (July 1991 to April 2011) (233.9 – 133.8)/133.8 = 0.748 x £84,200	(62,982)	
On enhancement (May 2003 to April 2011) (233.9 – 181.5)/181.5 = 0.289 x £43,000	(12,427)	
		53,551
Shares in Albatross plc (5,000 shares)		
Proceeds (August 2011)	42,500	
Less: Cost (below) (Note 1)	(17,500)	
		25,000

Share pool – Albatross plc	*Number*	*Cost*
		£
1 August 2011 Purchase	6,000	18,600
17 August 2011 Purchase	2,000	9,400
	8,000	28,000
29 August 2011 Disposal	(5,000)	
(£28,000 x 5,000/8,000)		(17,500)
	3,000	10,500

	£	£
Shares in Cuckoo (10,000 preference shares)		
Proceeds (October 2011)	32,000	
Less: Cost (below)	(15,000)	
		17,000
Consideration received at time of takeover:		
Ordinary shares (5,000 x 3 x £4.50)	67,500	
Preference shares (5,000 x 2 x £2.25)	22,500	
	90,000	
Therefore cost of shares disposed of in October 2011: £60,000 x (£22,500/£90,000)	15,000	
Chargeable gains c/f		95,551

	£	£
Chargeable gains b/f		95,551
Land		
Proceeds (March 2012)	120,000	
Less: Cost of part disposed of (Note 2)		
£203,500 x (£120,000 / (£120,000 + £65,000))	(132,000)	
Allowable loss		(12,000)
Net chargeable gains		83,551

Tutorial note

1. *There is no indexation allowance available on either of the share disposals, as the purchase and sale occur in the same month.*
2. *There is no indexation allowance available on the disposal of the land, as indexation cannot create or increase a loss.*

   The disposal of the land is a part disposal and therefore the allowable cost is calculated by apportioning the original cost to the part disposed of as follows:

   Original cost x A / (A + B) where: A = MV of the element disposed of
   B = MV of the element retained

(b) **Rollover relief**

(i) **Minimum amount of reinvestment**

- The only disposal that qualifies for rollover relief is the sale of the freehold office building.
- The office building was sold for £256,160 (net of disposal expenses) and this is therefore the amount that Hawk Ltd will have to reinvest in order to claim the maximum possible amount of rollover relief.

Tutorial note

HMRC allow full rollover relief provided the net sale proceeds are reinvested in qualifying assets within the qualifying time period.

It is not necessary to reinvest the gross sale proceeds. However, the examiner gave credit if the gross sale proceeds were used in this part.

(ii) **Period of reinvestment**

- The reinvestment will have to take place between 1 May 2010 and 30 April 2014 (i.e. one year before and three years after the date of sale).

(iii) **Amount of corporation tax deferred**

- Corporation tax of £10,710 (£53,551 at 20%) will be deferred if the maximum possible amount of rollover relief is claimed.

Examiner's report

Part (a) was reasonably well answered.

As regards the freehold office building, many candidates did not appreciate that indexation would also be available for the incidental costs of acquisition.

For the quoted shares many candidates based their answers on the rules applicable to individuals rather than the pooling rules. The allocation of cost following the reorganization also caused problems.

Part (b) was also reasonably well answered, with a number of candidates providing perfect answers.

ACCA marking scheme

		Marks
(a)	**Office building**	
	Disposal proceeds	0.5
	Costs of disposal	0.5
	Cost	0.5
	Costs of acquisition	0.5
	Enhancement expenditure	0.5
	Indexation – Cost	1.0
	– Enhancement	1.0
	Albatross plc	
	Proceeds	0.5
	Cost	2.0
	Cuckoo Ltd	
	Proceeds	0.5
	Value of shares – Ordinary shares	1.0
	– Preference shares	1.0
	Cost	1.5
	Land	
	Proceeds	0.5
	Cost	2.0
	Corporation tax liability	
	Net chargeable gains	1.0
	Calculation	1.5
		16.0
(b)	Qualifying disposal	1.0
	Amount of reinvestment	1.0
	Period of reinvestment	1.0
	Corporation tax saving	1.0
		4.0
Total		20.0

39 PROBLEMATIC LTD *Walk in the footsteps of a top tutor*

Key answer tips

This is a standard chargeable gains question, based on a company making four disposals.

Part (a) requires the taxable total profits of the company, but as there is only one other source of income, it really requires the calculation of the total net chargeable gains and one number adding to it!

Part (b) is unusual in that it requires advice about the base costs to carry forward in respect of those assets still owned by the company after the disposals.

The two parts are inter-linked and consideration of the remaining base costs is best calculated as each disposal is considered. It is therefore more time efficient to answer both parts (a) and (b) together as you consider each disposal. Make sure that you highlight your answer to part (b) clearly in your answer though.

This question was originally a 20 mark question, and under the current syllabus and rules, this question would still be worth 20 marks.

No attempt has been made to reduce the question as it is still representative of the type of question you will see in the examination and provides good practice for your revision. However, under the new syllabus the question on capital gains will only be 15 marks and therefore will probably have fewer disposals to deal with in the time available than this question has.

Tutor's top tips

There are four disposals to deal with here, some more complicated than others. There is no need for you to calculate the gains in order if you prefer to do the easier computations first – as long as you clearly label each disposal as you attempt it.

(a) **Problematic Ltd**
Taxable total profits – y/e 31 March 2012

	£
Trading profit	108,056
Net chargeable gains (£27,661 + £16,200 + £45,550) (see below)	89,411
Taxable total profits	197,467

Chargeable gain computations:

Easy plc shares

Tutor's top tips

The disposal of shares by a company requires the construction of a share pool and the calculation of the indexation allowance before recording each operative event.

The calculation of the gain is then straightforward.

	£
Disposal proceeds	54,400
Less: Cost (below)	(18,880)
	35,520
Less: Indexation (£26,739 – £18,880) (below)	(7,859)
Chargeable gain	27,661

Share pool – Easy plc	*Number*	*Cost*	*Indexed cost*
		£	£
Purchase – June 1994	15,000	12,600	12,600
Indexation to September 2006			
£12,600 × (200·1 – 144·7)/144·7			4,824
Rights issue – September 2006			
15,000 × 1/3 = 5,000 × £2·20	5,000	11,000	11,000
	20,000	23,600	28,424
Indexation to June 2011			
£28,424 × (235.3 – 200·1)/200·1			5,000
			33,424
Disposal – June 2011			
Cost × 16,000/20,000	(16,000)	(18,880)	(26,739)
Balance c/f	4,000	4,720	6,685

Tutorial note

1. *The movement in the RPI in the share pool of a company is not rounded to three decimal places.*
2. *The "balance carried forward" figures in the share pool are the information required to answer part (b) of this question.*

Office building

Tutor's top tips

This part of the question may have thrown a number of students, who are perhaps less familiar with the rules regarding damage or destruction of an asset.

However, the examiner has given a hint in the question, in saying that Problematic Ltd has made a claim to defer the gain, and this information could be used to make a sensible assumption about the treatment of the insurance proceeds.

If you are ever unsure of how to deal with part of a question it is important to make a sensible guess and move on, rather than wasting time, or potentially missing easy marks by not attempting to answer the part.

- The insurance proceeds of £36,000 received by Problematic Ltd have been fully applied in restoring the office building.
- Therefore, provided an election is made, there is no chargeable gain arising on the receipt of the insurance proceeds.

Tutorial note

Where an asset is damaged, insurance proceeds are received and the proceeds are fully reinvested in restoring the asset, if an election is made to defer the gain; no chargeable gain arises at that time.

Instead, the base cost of the asset is adjusted for the receipt of the insurance proceeds (i.e. the proceeds are deducted from the base cost) and the cost of the restoration is treated as enhancement expenditure and is added.

Freehold factory

Tutor's top tips

A gain on the disposal of the factory needs to be calculated and then rollover relief needs to be considered.

You need to check that the necessary conditions are satisfied to make a claim. Then you need to recognise that the replacement asset is a depreciating asset and know the consequences as a result.

	£
Disposal proceeds	171,000
Less: Indexed cost	(127,000)
Chargeable gain before reliefs	44,000
Less: Rollover relief (£44,000 – £16,200) (Note 1)	(27,800)
Chargeable gain	16,200

Tutorial note

1. *Rollover relief is available as Problematic has:*

   Disposed of a qualifying business asset (Freehold factory), and
   Replaced with another qualifying business asset (Leasehold factory),
   Within the qualifying reinvestment period of 28 January 2011 to 27 January 2015

   (i.e. 12 months before and 36 months after the date of disposal).

2. *The sale proceeds are not fully reinvested, and so £16,200 (£171,000 – £154,800) of the gain cannot be held over.*

   The rollover relief is therefore £27,800 (£44,000 – £16,200).

3. *The replacement asset is a depreciating asset (i.e. has a life of less than 60 years).*

   As a result, the rollover relief is deferred, but the gain is not deducted from the base cost of the replacement asset.

   Instead, the gain is "frozen" and becomes chargeable on the earliest of.

   - *The disposal of the replacement asset.*
   - *The date the replacement asset is no longer used in the business.*
   - *Ten years after the acquisition of the replacement asset (i.e. in this case, 10 December 2021).*

Land

Tutor's top tips

Part disposals are regularly examined, and it is important to learn the formula for calculating the cost and to know how to apply it. You should not be misled by the size of the parts bought and sold; it is the values which are used in the calculation.

	£
Disposal proceeds	130,000
Less: Incidental costs of disposal	(3,200)
	126,800
Less: Indexed cost	
(£130,000/(£130,000 + £350,000)) × £300,000	(81,250)
Chargeable gain	45,550

Tutorial note

This standard part disposal computation requires the appropriate proportion of the indexed cost to be calculated using the A / (A + B) formula.

Note however that all of the incidental disposal costs are deducted as they relate entirely to this disposal.

(b) **Indexed base costs carried forward for capital gains tax purposes**

Tutor's top tips

All of the thought processes required to answer this part will have been considered when calculating the gains arising on the individual disposals.

A summary is therefore now required in this part to highlight the remaining base costs for the asset s not disposed of.

Easy plc shares

- The 4,000 £1 ordinary shares in Easy plc have an indexed base cost of £6,685 (see part (a) share pool working).

Office building

- The indexed base cost of the office building is:

	£
Original indexed cost	169,000
Less: Insurance proceeds received	(36,000)
Plus: Restoration costs	41,000
Indexed base cost	174,000

(See tutorial note in part (a) for explanation).

Leasehold factory

- The leasehold factory is a depreciating asset, and so there is no adjustment to the base cost of £154,800.

  (See tutorial note in part (a) for explanation).

Remaining three acres

- The indexed base cost of the remaining three acres of land is £218,750 (£300,000 – £81,250 used in the part disposal computation).

Examiner's report

It was pleasing to see that this question was well answered.

On an overall note, it does not create a very good impression when candidates deduct the annual exemption when dealing with a company.

The only aspect that consistently caused problems in part (a) was the restoration of the asset. Despite the question telling candidates that a claim to defer the gain had been made, many insisted that such a claim was not possible and instead calculated a capital loss.

Many candidates did not even attempt part (b) despite the fact that this section generally just required them to provide figures already calculated in part (a).

ACCA marking scheme

		Marks
(a)	**Easy plc**	
	Share pool – Purchase	0.5
	– Rights issue	1.5
	– Indexation	2.0
	– Disposal	1.0
	Chargeable gain	1.5
	Office building	
	Proceeds fully reinvested	1.0
	No chargeable gain arising	1.0
	Freehold factory	
	Disposal proceeds	0.5
	Indexed cost	0.5
	Rollover relief	2.0
	Land	
	Proceeds	0.5
	Incidental costs of disposal	1.0
	Cost	2.0
	Taxable total profits	
	Chargeable gains	0.5
	Calculation	0.5
		16.0
(b)	Ordinary shares in Easy plc	0.5
	Office building	1.5
	Leasehold factory	1.0
	Land	1.0
		4.0
Total		20.0

INHERITANCE TAX

40 BRUCE VINCENT

Key answer tips

A classic inheritance tax question involving two lifetime gifts, one CLT and one PET, requiring both lifetime and death tax calculations and a death estate computation.

Be careful to calculate the cumulation of gifts correctly when calculating the available nil rate band.

Note that there is no set way to present an IHT computation, however the columnar approach avoids repetition of narrative headings and aids the correct allocation of annual exemptions and calculating cumulation totals.

Lifetime tax on lifetime gifts

	CLT – Gift into trust Jan 2007		*PET – Gift to nephew May 2008*	
		£		£
Transfer of value		350,000		100,000
Less: Annual exemption				
Current year	2006/07	(3,000)	2008/09	(3,000)
Previous year	2005/06 b/f	(3,000)	2007/08 b/f	(3,000)
Chargeable amount	Net	344,000		94,000
NRB @ date of gift	£			
2006/07	285,000			
Less: GCTs < 7 years before gift (Jan 2000 – Jan 2007)	(Nil)			
NRB available		(285,000)		
Taxable amount		59,000		Nil
IHT payable (Notes 1 and 2)	@ 25%	14,750		Nil
Paid by		Bruce		
Due date of payment		31.7.2007		
Gross chargeable amount c/f (£344,000 + £14,750)		358,750		94,000

Tutorial notes:

1. *The question states that Bruce paid the IHT the tax is calculated at 25% and it is necessary to gross up the net gift as the value of the transfer (i.e. the loss to Bruce's estate) is the value of the gift and the related tax.*
2. *The gift to the nephew is a PET; therefore no lifetime IHT is payable.*

   The information in the question about the nil rate band in 2008/09 is not relevant. Only the nil rate band at the date of death is required to calculate the tax on death.

Death tax on lifetime gifts

Date of death: August 2011
7 years before: August 2004

	CLT – Gift into trust Jan 2007		*PET – Gift to nephew May 2008*	
	£	£	£	£
Gross chargeable amount b/f		358,750		94,000
NRB @ date of death – 2011/12	325,000		325,000	
Less: GCTs < 7 years before gift				
(Jan 2000 – Jan 2007)	(Nil)			
(May 2001 – May 2008)			(358,750)	
NRB available		(325,000)		(Nil)
Taxable amount		33,750		94,000
IHT payable @ 40%		13,500		37,600
Less: Taper relief				
(Jan 2007 – Aug 2011) (4 – 5 yrs)	(40%)	(5,400)		
(May 2008 – Aug 2011) (3 – 4 yrs)			(20%)	(7,520)
Less: IHT paid in lifetime		(14,750)		(Nil)
IHT payable on death		Nil		30,080
	No refund possible			
Paid by				Nephew
Due date of payment				28.2.12

Tax on death estate

	£	£
Gross chargeable estate (W)		797,500
Nil rate band at death	325,000	
Less: GCTs in 7 years pre death		
(August 2004 – August 2011) (£358,750 + £94,000)	(452,750)	
Nil rate band available		(Nil)
Taxable amount		797,500
IHT (£797,500 × 40%)		319,000
Due date		28 February 2012
Paid by		Executors

Working: Estate at death – August 2011

	£
House	450,000
Less: Mortgage (interest only)	(100,000)
	350,000
Holiday cottage	280,000
Quoted shares	145,000
Bank and cash	10,000
Personal chattels	50,000
	835,000
Liabilities:	
Credit card debts	(12,000)
Outstanding income tax	(8,000)
Funeral expenses	(7,500)
	807,500
Exempt legacy to wife	(10,000)
Chargeable estate	797,500

41 PETER DAY

Key answer tips

A classic inheritance tax question involving three lifetime gifts, two PETs and one CLT, requiring both lifetime and death tax calculations and a death estate computation.

Be careful to calculate the cumulation of gifts correctly when calculating the available nil rate band:

- Always cumulate CLTs
- For lifetime calculations; ignore PETs as they have not become chargeable
- For death calculations;

  cumulate PETs if they have become chargeable on death, but not if they have become completely exempt.

Note that there is no set way to present an IHT computation, however the columnar approach avoids repetition of narrative headings and aids the correct allocation of annual exemptions and calculating cumulation totals.

Lifetime tax on lifetime gifts

		PET 1.5.2007		*PET 1.6.2008*			*CLT 1.7.2008*
		£		£			£
Transfer of value		500		7,500			337,000
Less: Marriage exemption				(1,000)			
Less: Annual exemption							
Current year	2007/08	(500)	2008/09	(3,000)	2008/09		(Nil)
Previous year	2006/07 b/f	(Nil)	2007/08 b/f	(2,500)	2007/08 b/f		(Nil)
Chargeable amount		Nil		1,000	Net		337,000
NRB @ date of gift						£	
2008/09						312,000	
Less: GCTs < 7 years before gift (1.7.2001 – 1.7.2008) (ignore PETs)						Nil	
NRB available							(312,000)
Taxable amount		Nil		Nil			25,000
IHT payable		Nil		Nil	@ 25%		6,250
Paid by							Peter
Due date of payment							30 April 2009
Gross chargeable amount		Nil		1,000	(£337,000 + £6,250)		343,250

Tutorial notes

1. *Gifts up to £250 per person in any one tax year are exempt. As the gift to the granddaughter exceeds £250 the small gifts exemption cannot be used. The gift, even though it is a PET uses the annual exemption. The current year annual exemption is used first.*
2. *The gift to the nephew is on consideration of marriage and will be a PET which qualifies for a wedding gift exemption of £1,000.*
3. *Peter agreed to pay any tax due on the gift into the trust, therefore it is a net gift and the appropriate rate of lifetime tax is 25%. Don't forget to add the tax onto the net chargeable amount to carry forward the gross chargeable amount for subsequent computations.*
4. *The lifetime tax on a CLT is due the later of 30 April following the tax year of the gift and 6 months from the end of the month of the gift.*

IHT payable on death

Date of death: 3 November 2011

7 years before: 3 November 2004

PET – 1.5.2007

The PET becomes chargeable as it was made within 7 years of death. However the gross chargeable transfer is £Nil and therefore there is no tax to pay on death.

	PET *1.6.2008*		*CLT* *1.7.2008*	
	£	£	£	£
Gross chargeable amount b/f		1,000		343,250
NRB @ date of death – 2011/12	325,000		325,000	
Less: GCTs < 7 years before gift				
(1.6.2001 – 1.6.2008)				
(include PET but £Nil value)	(Nil)			
(1.7.2001 – 1.7.2008)				
(include PETs as chargeable)			(1,000)	
NRB available		(325,000)		(324,000)
Taxable amount		Nil		19,250
IHT payable @ 40%		Nil		7,700
Less: Taper relief				
(1.7.2008 – 3.11.11) (3 – 4 yrs)			(20%)	(1,540)
Less: IHT paid in lifetime		(Nil)		(6,250)
IHT payable on death		Nil		Nil
	No refund possible			

Tax on death estate

	£	£
Gross chargeable estate (W)		117,000
Nil rate band at death	325,000	
Less: GCTs in 7 years pre death		
(3.11.04 – 3.11.11) (£343,250 + £1,000)	(344,250)	
Nil rate band available		(Nil)
Taxable amount		117,000
IHT (£117,000 × 40%)		46,800
Due date		31 May 2012
Paid by		Executors

Working: Estate at death – 3 November 2011

	£	£
House	210,000	
Less: Mortgage	(40,000)	
		170,000
Ordinary shares in Beach plc		50,000
Cash ISA accounts		45,000
Car	10,000	
Less: Car loan	(2,000)	
		8,000
		273,000
Less: Funeral expenses		(6,000)
		267,000
Less: Exempt legacy to spouse		(150,000)
Gross chargeable estate		117,000

Tutor's top tips

Note that the estate computation is usually the easiest part of an IHT question as it basically requires you to:

– *copy out the question*
– *present the information is a standard way, and*
– *add it up!*

This part could therefore be calculated first to get the easy marks as soon as possible.

However, note that you cannot calculate the tax on the estate value until the lifetime gifts have been dealt with.

42 PAUL MASTERS

(a) **IHT liabilities if Paul dies on 31 December 2011**

Lifetime tax on lifetime gifts

Gift 1.7.2009 – The gift to the niece is exempt as a small gift under £250.

	CLT – Gift into trust 1.11.2003		*PET – Gift to son 1.10.2008*	
		£		£
Transfer of value		203,000		150,000
Less: Marriage exemption				(5,000)
Less: Annual exemption				
Current year	2003/04	(3,000)	2008/09	(3,000)
Previous year	2002/03 b/f	(3,000)	2007/08 b/f	(3,000)
Chargeable amount	Gross	197,000		139,000
NRB @ date of gift	£			
2003/04	255,000			
Less: GCTs < 7 years before gift (1.11.1996 – 1.11.2003)	(Nil)			
NRB available		(255,000)		
Taxable amount		Nil		Nil
IHT payable		Nil	(Note)	Nil
Gross chargeable amount c/f		197,000		139,000

Tutorial note

Note that as the gift on 1.10.2008 is a PET, no lifetime IHT is payable, therefore the information in the question about the nil rate band in 2008/09 is not relevant.

Only the nil rate band at the date of death is required to calculate the tax on death.

Death tax on lifetime gifts

Date of death: 31.12.2011

7 years before: 31.12.2004

1 November 2003 – CLT

The gift is more than seven years before the date of Paul's death, and therefore there is no tax due on Paul's death.

It is, however, within seven years of the other lifetime transfer, and will reduce the nil rate band available by £197,000.

		PET – Gift to son 1.10.2008	
	£	£
Gross chargeable amount b/f (as above)		139,000
NRB @ date of death – 2011/12	325,000	
Less: GCTs < 7 years before gift (1.10.2001 – 1.10.2008)	(197,000)	
NRB available		(128,000)
Taxable amount		11,000
IHT payable @ 40%		4,400
Less: Taper relief (1.10.2008 – 31.12.2011) (3 – 4 yrs)	(@ 20%)	(880)
Less: IHT paid in lifetime		(Nil)
IHT payable on death		3,520
Due date of payment		30.6.2012

Tax on death estate

	£	£
Gross chargeable estate		580,000
Nil rate band at death	325,000	
Less: GCTs in 7 years pre death (31.12.04 – 31.12.11) (first gift is too old, but include PET as it became chargeable))	(139,000)	
Nil rate band available		(186,000)
Taxable amount		394,000
IHT (£117,000 × 40%)		157,600
Due date		30 June 2012
Paid by		Executors

(b) (i) **Main advantages in lifetime giving for IHT purposes**

Possible advantages of lifetime giving include:

– Making use of lifetime IHT exemptions (e.g. marriage exemption, small gifts and annual exemption) in reducing a taxpayer's chargeable estate at death. In particular, gifts between individuals will not become liable to IHT unless the donor dies within seven years of making the gift.

- If the donor dies prematurely there may still be an IHT advantage in lifetime giving because usually:
  - The value of the asset for calculating any additional IHT arising upon death is fixed at the time the gift is made.
  - The availability of tapering relief (providing the donor survives at least three years) may help reduce the effective IHT rate.

(ii) **Main factors to consider in choosing assets to gift**

The main factors to consider include:

- Whether an asset is appreciating in value.

  Because any additional IHT arising as a result of death will be based on the (lower) value of the asset at the date of gift it may be advantageous to select assets that are likely to significantly appreciate in value.
- Whether the donor can afford to make the gift.

  Whilst lifetime gifting can result in significant IHT savings this should not be at the expense of the taxpayer's ability to live comfortably, particularly in old age.
- Whether or not a significant CGT liability will arise upon making the gift.

  Lifetime gifting may give rise to a capital gains tax liability unless gift relief is available (on qualifying business assets) and/or the annual exemption is available.

  However, no capital gains tax liability arises upon death.

  Therefore the availability of gift relief and CGT annual exemption is relevant in selecting assets to gift during lifetime.

Tutorial note

The answer to part (b) is included for completeness sake, however this level of detail would not be required to obtain the full 5 marks for this part.

43 HENRY HIGGINS *Walk in the footsteps of a top tutor*

Key answer tips

This question deals with the calculation of lifetime and death tax on two chargeable lifetime transfers, and the calculation of IHT due on an estate at death.

The computations are straightforward and should not present any particular problems.

However, be careful to note the dates of the events and in particular note that the first gift is more than seven years before Henry's death.

The second part required some standard basic tax planning advice concerning the transfer of the nil rate band.

Tutor's top tips:

In the calculations remember to approach the answer in strict date order:

Step 1: Calculate the lifetime tax on the lifetime gifts

Step 2: Calculate the death tax on lifetime gifts

Step 3: Calculate the value of the estate on death

Step 4: Calculate the IHT due on the estate.

Be careful to use the correct nil rate band and to calculate the cumulation period of seven years accurately.

Remember to write down the dates so that the marker can give method marks even if you do not get the numbers right:

For lifetime IHT calculations

- *NRB = at **date of the gift***
- *Cumulation = 7 years **before the gift***
- *include **CLTs only***

For death calculations on lifetime gifts

- *NRB = at **date of death***
- *Cumulation = 7 years **before the gift***
- *include **CLTs and PETs which have become chargeable** (if any)*

For death estate computation

- *NRB = at **date of death***
- *Cumulation = 7 years **before death***
- *Include **all CLTs and PETs** in the 7 year period*

(a) **Inheritance tax liabilities**

Tutorial note

1. *The annual exemptions are allocated to the first gift in each tax year. The current year annual exemption must be deducted before the previous year's unused amount.*
2. *Henry agreed to pay any tax due on the gifts into the trusts, therefore they are net gifts and the appropriate rate of lifetime tax is 25%. Don't forget to add the tax onto the net chargeable amount to carry forward the gross chargeable amount for subsequent computations.*

(i) Lifetime tax on lifetime gifts

	CLT – Gift into trust 1.1.2004		*CLT – Gift into trust 1.1.2007*	
		£		£
Transfer of value		181,000		164,000
Annual exemption				
Current year	2003/04	(3,000)	2006/07	(3,000)
Previous year	2002/03 b/f	(3,000)	2005/06 b/f	(3,000)
Chargeable amount	Net	175,000	Net	158,000
NRB @ date of gift	£			
2003/04	255,000			
2006/07			285,000	
Less: GCTs < 7 years before gift				
(1.1.1997 – 1.1.2004)	(Nil)			
(1.1.2000 – 1.1.2007)			(175,000)	
NRB available		(255,000)		(110,000)
Taxable amount		Nil		48,000
IHT payable		Nil	(25%) (Note 2)	12,000
Gross chargeable amount c/f		175,000	(£158,000 + £12,000)	170,000

(ii) Death tax on lifetime gifts

Date of death: 5 October 2011

Seven years before: 5 October 2004

1 January 2004 – CLT

This gift is more than seven years before death; therefore there is no IHT payable on death.

	CLT 1.1.2007	
	£	£
Gross chargeable amount b/f		170,000
NRB @ date of death – 2011/12	325,000	
Less: GCTs < 7 years before gift (1.1.2000 – 1.1.2007)	(175,000)	
NRB available		(150,000)
Taxable amount		20,000
IHT payable @ 40%		8,000
Less: Taper relief (1.1.2007 – 5.10.11) (4 – 5 yrs)	(40%)	(3,200)
Less: IHT paid in lifetime		(12,000)
IHT payable on death		Nil
	No refund possible	

Tutorial note

1. *Tax is only due on lifetime gifts within seven years of death. Therefore, any gifts before 5 October 2004 are too old and there will be no tax to pay on those gifts.*

   Be careful though: any CLTs are still taken into account in the cumulation for the calculation of tax on later gifts.
2. *Taper relief is available as more than 3 years has elapsed since the gift.*
3. *Lifetime tax can be deducted in the death calculation; however there will never be a repayment of lifetime IHT paid.*

Tax on death estate

	£	£
Gross chargeable estate(W)		40,921
Nil rate band at death		
Less: GCTs in 7 years pre death		
(5.10.04 – 5.10.11) (first gift is too		
Nil rate band available		000)
Taxable amount		Nil
IHT payable		Nil

Advantages of lifetime gifts,
Main factors to consider in choosing assets to gift.

Working: Estate at death – 5 October 2011

Tutor's top tips

Note that the estate computation is usually the easiest part of an IHT question as it basically requires you to:

– *copy out the question*
– *present the information is a standard way, and*
– *add it up!*

This part could therefore be calculated first to get the easy marks as soon as possible.

However, note that you cannot calculate the tax on the estate value until the lifetime gifts have been dealt with.

	£
Shares – Petal plc (100,000 × 202p)	202,000
Government stock	20,100
Cash (£25,000 + £18,000)	43,000
Income tax refund due	821
Home	450,000
	715,921
Less: Exempt legacy to spouse	(675,000)
Gross chargeable estate	40,921

(b) **Tax implications of transferring unused nil rate band**

Tutor's top tips

In terms of this syllabus there are very limited areas of tax planning that the examiner can ask.

The main areas are:

- *the transfer of unused nil rate band (covered in this question)*
- *making use of lifetime exemptions*
- *gifting appreciating assets as lifetime gifts are frozen in value at the time of the gift.*

It is important that you make sure that you apply the standard advice to the particular circumstances of the question.

Transfer of unused nil rate band

The terms of Henry's will resulted in the majority of the estate being covered by an exempt transfer to his wife. This has left £114,079 (£155,000 – £40,921) of his nil band unused.

Therefore the percentage of unused nil rate band (rounded up to the nearest whole percentage) is as follows:

(£114,079 / £325,000) × 100% = 36%.

This unused proportion can be transferred to Sally and utilised against her death estate, in addition to her own available nil rate band (i.e. she will be entitled to 136% of the nil rate band available at the date of her death).

The executors of Sally's estate must claim the transferable nil rate band on submission of Sally's IHT return within 2 years of her death.

44 HELGA EVANS *Walk in the footsteps of a top tutor*

Key answer tips

This question deals with a classic scenario:

Should Helga give assets away now or die owning them?

Calculations of the two options are required and a conclusion of what she should do and how much tax will be saved as a result of the advice.

The calculations are straightforward, but you must read the question carefully to sort out which assets are to be gifted now and which will remain in the estate – and their values at the different points in time.

Tutor's top tips:

Dealing with the retention of assets first – a straightforward estate computation is required.

Remember to bear in mind that:

- *there has already been a lifetime gift within seven years, and*
- *part of the estate is left to the spouse and is therefore exempt.*

(i) Helga retains assets until death

IHT implications

Cash gift – September 2010

The cash gift made to Louise in September 2010 is a PET.

No IHT would have been payable at the time, however the PET will become chargeable if Helga dies within seven years of making the gift.

If Helga therefore dies in four years time (i.e. June 2016) this gift will be within seven years of death and IHT will become payable on the PET in September 2010 as follows:

	£	£
Gross chargeable transfer		360,000
(after exemptions per question)		
Nil rate band **at date of death**	325,000	
Less: GCTs in 7 years pre-gift		
(September 2003 – September 2010)	(Nil)	
		(325,000)
Taxable amount		35,000
IHT (£35,000 × 40%)		14,000
Less: Taper relief (September 2010 – June 2016)		
(5 – 6 years) (60%)		(8,400)
Less: Lifetime tax paid		(Nil)
IHT payable		5,600

Tutorial note

Note that as the gift is a PET, no lifetime IHT is payable, therefore the information in the question about the nil rate band in 2010/11 is not relevant.

Only the nil rate band at the date of death is required to calculate the tax on death.

There are no other lifetime gifts made in this scenario.

Estate at death – 30 June 2016

	£
Residence	600,000
Starling plc shares	200,000
Wren loan stock	25,000
Antique plates	10,000
Cash deposits	170,000
Other chattels	20,000
	1,025,000
Less: Exempt legacy to spouse (£600,000 + £20,000)	(620,000)
Gross chargeable estate	405,000

	£	£
Gross chargeable estate		405,000
Nil rate band at death	325,000	
Less: GCTs in 7 years pre death (30.6.09 – 30.6.16) (include PET as chargeable on death)	(360,000)	
		(Nil)
Taxable amount		405,000
IHT due on death (£405,000 × 40%)		162,000

(ii) **Helga gifts selected assets to Louise now**

Tutor's top tips

Assuming another lifetime gift is made, the death tax on two PETs is required but no estate tax as the remaining estate is to be left to the husband and will be exempt.

Remember to deal with each gift in date order – and as the PETs become chargeable on death, they are included in cumulation for later computations.

IHT implications

Cash gift – September 2010

The implications for the PET made in September 2010 are as above with £5,600 of IHT becoming payable as a result of Helga's expected death in four years time.

Gifts to Louise now

Assume the gift is made on 6 July 2012.

The gifts of assets to Louise will be further PETs.

So, no lifetime tax payable, but they are likely to become chargeable on Helga's death, with further IHT arising as follows:

	£	£
Starling plc shares (10,000 × £14.62)		146,200
Wren plc loan stock		25,750
Cash deposits		151,333
		323,283
Less: Annual exemption – 2012/13		(3,000)
– 2011/12 b/f		(3,000)
Gross chargeable amount		317,283
Nil rate band at date of death	325,000	
Less: GCTs in 7 years pre-death (30.6.09 – 30.6.16) (include PET as chargeable on death)	(360,000)	
		(Nil)
Taxable amount		317,283

	£
IHT (£317,283 × 40%)	126,913
Less: Taper relief (6.7.12 – 30.6.16) (3 – 4 years) (20%)	(25,383)
	101,530
Less: Lifetime tax paid	(Nil)
IHT payable	101,530

Estate on death

When Helga dies the transfers of the house and personal chattels to Gordon will be exempt under the inter-spouse provisions.

Therefore there is no IHT payable on the estate at death.

Conclusion

The tax payable under both options is as follows:

	£
Retention of assets (£5,600 + £162,000)	167,600
Gifting of assets now (£5,600 + £101,530)	107,130

It would therefore appear that, providing the key assumptions hold (i.e. asset values in four years, Helga survives four years), it is preferable to make the gifts to Louise now giving a tax saving of £60,470 (£167,600 – £107,130).

CORPORATION TAX

CORPORATION TAX BASICS AND ADMINISTRATION

45 ARABLE LTD (ADAPTED)

Key answer tips

This question deals with the calculation of corporation tax for a short accounting period. You should remember that the length of the period affects the calculation of the maximum AIA and the WDA for capital allowances, and the limits for determining the rate of corporation tax to apply.

Other things to watch out for in this question are the effect of the short period on the lease premium deduction, the fact that the company has associated companies, which affects the small company limits for calculating corporation tax and that the accounting period falls into two financial years.

Make sure you attempt the administration points in part (b) which should be easy marks to obtain.

(a) **Corporation tax computation – 9 months ended 31 October 2011**

	£	£
Trading profit		301,189
Capital allowances – Plant and machinery (W2)	77,875	
Deduction for lease premium (W1)	2,700	
		(80,575)
		220,614
Property business income (W3)		31,700
Interest income – Loan interest (£6,000 + £3,000)		9,000
Chargeable gain (W4)		25,861
Taxable total profits		287,175
Plus: Franked investment income (£18,000 × 100/90)		20,000
Augmented profits		307,175
Corporation tax (W5)		
FY2010		
£287,175 x 28% x 2/9	17,869	
Less: Marginal relief		
7/400 x (£375,000 – £307,175) x £287,175/£307,175 x 2/9	(247)	
		17,622
FY2011		
£287,175 x 26% x 7/9	58,073	
Less: Marginal relief		
3/200 x (£375,000 – £307,175) x £287,175/£307,175 x 7/9	(740)	
		57,333
Corporation tax liability		74,955

Workings

(W1) **Deduction for lease premium**

The first office building has been used for business purposes, and so a proportion of the lease premium assessed on the landlord can be deducted.

Assessment on landlord:

	£
Premium received	75,000
Less: 2% x £75,000 x (15 – 1)	(21,000)
Assessment on landlord (Note)	54,000
Allowable deduction for 9 month period (£54,000 ÷ 15 x 9/12)	2,700

Tutorial note

Alternative calculation of the assessment on the landlord:

£75,000 x (51 – 15)/50 = £54,000

(W2) **Plant and machinery**

		Pool	*Special rate pool*	*Allowances*
	£	£	£	£
Additions (no AIA or FYA) (Note 1)				
Car (CO_2 between 111 – 160 g/km)		11,200		
Car (CO_2 > 160 g/km)			14,600	
Additions (with AIA) (Note 2)				
Machinery	31,000			
Alterations	3,700			
Lorry	22,000			
Computer	5,400			
	62,100			
Less: AIA (Max £75,000) (Note 3)	(62,100)			62,100
		Nil		
WDA (20% × 9/12) (Note 4)		(1,680)		1,680
WDA (10% × 9/12) (Note 4)			(1,095)	1,095
Additions (with FYA) (Note 1)				
Car (CO_2 < 111 g/km)	13,000			
Less: FYA (100%)	(13,000)			13,000
		Nil		
TWDV c/f		9,520	13,505	
Total allowances				77,875

Tutorial notes:

1. *Capital allowances on new car purchases are now calculated based on the CO_2 emissions of the car as follows:*

   CO_2 emissions of < 111 g/km:
   eligible for a FYA of 100%.

   CO_2 emissions of between 111 – 160 g/km:
   put in main pool, eligible for a WDA at 20%.

   CO_2 emissions of > 160 g/km:
   put in special rate pool, eligible for a WDA at 10%.

   The appropriate rates are given in the tax rates and allowances.

2. *The machinery purchased on 5 January 2011 and the related building alterations are incurred pre-trading, but are eligible for capital allowances and are treated as if incurred on 1 February 2011. They are therefore brought into the first capital allowances computation.*

3. *The maximum AIA and WDAs are time apportioned because Arable Ltd's accounting period is nine months long. The maximum AIA is £75,000 (£100,000 × 9/12).*

(W3) **Property business income**

	£
Premium received for sub-lease	50,000
Less: 2% x £50,000 x (5 – 1)	(4,000)
Assessment on premium received (Note)	46,000
Less: Relief for premium paid for head lease (Note) (£54,000 × 5 /15)	(18,000)
	28,000
Plus: Rent receivable (£14,800 × 3/12)	3,700
Property business income	31,700

Tutorial note

Alternative calculation of the assessment on the sub lease:

£50,000 x (51 – 5)/50 = £46,000

Relief for premium paid on head lease:

= Assessment on landlord x (duration of sub-lease)/(duration of head lease)

Assessment on landlord = same as for the other leasehold building = £54,000 (see W2)

(W4) **Chargeable gain**

Share Pool – Ranch plc	*Number*	*Cost*	*Indexed cost*
		£	£
Purchase (May 2011)	15,000	12,000	12,000
Indexation to August 2011 £12,000 × (235.8 – 234.8)/234.8			51
			12,051
Purchase (August 2011)	5,000	11,250	11,250
	20,000	23,250	23,301
Indexation to October 2011 £23,301 × (237.1 – 235.8)/235.8			128
			23,429
Disposal (October 2011) Cost × 10,000/20,000	(10,000)	(11,625)	(11,715)
Balance carried forward	10,000	11,625	11,714

Tutorial note

The indexation allowance in the share pool is not rounded to three decimal places.

	£
Disposal proceeds	37,576
Less: Cost (see pool working)	(11,625)
Unindexed gain	25,951
Less: Indexation (£11,715 – £11,625) (see pool working)	(90)
Chargeable gain	25,861

(W5) **Corporation tax rates**

		£
Upper limit	(£1,500,000 x 1/3 x 9/12)	375,000
Lower limit	(£300,000 x 1/3 x 9/12)	75,000
Augmented profits		307,175
		Marginal relief applies

The limits are reduced for a nine month period and there are three associated companies in the group.

The accounting period falls partly within FY2010 (2 months) and partly within FY2011 (7 months).

The limits are the same for both financial years but the tax rates are different so the corporation tax liability must be calculated separately for each financial year.

(b) **Self assessment corporation tax return**

- Arable Ltd's self-assessment corporation tax return for the period ended 31 October 2011 must be submitted by 31 October 2012.
- It will be possible for Arable Ltd to amend its return at any time before 31 October 2013, being 12 months after the filing date.
- If an error or mistake in a return is subsequently discovered, which results in an overpayment of tax then Arable Ltd can make a claim for overpayment relief before 31 October 2015, being four years from the end of the chargeable accounting period.

46 ZOOM PLC (ADAPTED) *Online question assistance*

Key answer tips

This question has many of the usual features of corporation tax questions with marks for computing capital allowances and corporation tax.

One unusual aspect however is part (a)(ii) where the examiner gives you the figure of taxable total profits and asks for a reconciliation between that and the profit before tax.

Do not waste time trying to make your reconciliation agree if it doesn't on your first attempt. Since you are given the taxable total profits you can use that figure in part (c) to calculate corporation tax even if your reconciliation does not quite balance.

Knowledge of the quarterly instalment rules is often tested and should give some easy marks if you know the rules.

(a) (i) **Capital allowances for plant and machinery**

y/e 31 March 2012		*Pool*	*Motor car*	*Special rate pool*	*Allow -ances*
	£	£	£	£	£
TWDV b/f		19,600	20,200		
Additions (no AIA or FYA) (Note 1)					
Car (CO_2 > 160 g/km)				16,600	
Car (CO_2 between 111 – 160 g/km)		11,850			
Additions (with AIA)					
Equipment	54,600				
Computer (Note 2)	12,300				
	66,900				
Less: AIA	(66,900)				66,900
		Nil			
Disposal proceeds			(23,200)		
(£9,800 + £1,000)		(10,800)			
		20,650	(3,000)		
Balancing charge			3,000		(3,000)
WDA (20%)		(4,130)			4,130
WDA (10%)				(1,660)	1,660
Addition (with 100% FYA)					
Car (CO_2 < 111 g/km)	14,200				
Less: FYA (100%)	(14,200)				14,200
		Nil			
TWDV c/f		16,520		14,940	
Total allowances					83,890

Tutorial note

1. *Capital allowances on new car purchases are now calculated based on the CO_2 emissions of the car as follows:*

   CO_2 emissions of < 111 g/km:
   eligible for a FYA of 100%.

CO_2 emissions of between 111 – 160 g/km:
put in main pool, eligible for a WDA at 20%.

CO_2 emissions of > 160 g/km:
put in special rate pool, eligible for a WDA at 10%.

The appropriate rates are given in the tax rates and allowances.

There is only one AIA of £100,000 for a group of companies which can be allocated to any of the group companies in whatever proportions the group requires.

However, this aspect of capital allowances is not examinable, so you should assume that the maximum AIA is claimed by Zoom plc.

2. *It is assumed that the election to treat the computer as a short life asset has not been made.*

   If it had been made, a separate column would be set up, but the allowances in this year would be identical whether or not the election is made.

3. *The sale proceeds for the expensive motor car, lorry and the equipment are deducted from the main pool as they are less than the original cost.*

(ii) **Reconciliation of profits – year ended 31 March 2012**

Key answer tips

In the adjustment to profits part of the reconciliation it is important to list all the major items indicated in the question requirement, showing a zero (0) for expenditure that is allowable. This is because credit will be given for showing no adjustment where none is needed. List the adjustments in the order they appear in the question.

If required, also add notes to show why you have not adjusted for an item, or why you have added it back. However, lengthy explanations are not required where the requirement is just to 'calculate' the adjusted profits, rather than to explain them.

Always show your workings if the figure you are adjusting for is not clear from the question.

	£	£
Profit before taxation	910,000	
Depreciation	59,160	
Capital allowances (part (a)(i))		83,890
Patent royalties (Note 1)	0	
Income from investments		127,100
Interest payable (Note 2)	0	
	969,160	210,990
	(210,990)	
Trading profit	758,170	
Interest income – Bank interest	10,420	
– Loan interest	22,500	
Property business profit (W)	29,750	
Taxable total profits	820,840	

> ***Tutorial note***
>
> *1. The patent royalties received are included as part of the trading profit, so no adjustment is required.*
>
> *2. The interest on a loan used for trading purposes is deductible in calculating the trading profit and has already been deducted, so no adjustment is required.*

Working – Property business profit

	£	£
Rent receivable – Office 1 (£3,200 × 10 months)		32,000
– Office 2 (£26,400 × 8/12)		17,600
		49,600
Irrecoverable rent (£3,200 × 2)	6,400	
Advertising	4,800	
Decorating	5,200	
Insurance ((£3,360 × 9/12) + (£3,720 × 3/12))	3,450	
		(19,850)
Property business profit		29,750

(b) **Quarterly instalment payments – y/e 31 March 2012**

- Large companies have to make quarterly instalment payments in respect of their corporation tax liability. A large company is one paying corporation tax at the main rate.
- Zoom plc has three associated companies, so the upper limit is reduced to £375,000 (£1,500,000 × 1/4). Corporation tax will therefore be at the main rate for the year ended 31 March 2012.
- The exceptions for quarterly instalments do not apply because Zoom plc was also a large company for the year ended 31 March 2011.

(c) **Corporation tax liability – y/e 31 March 2012**

- Zoom plc's corporation tax liability for the year ended 31 March 2012 is £213,418 (£820,840 at 26%).
- The company will have paid this in four quarterly instalments of £53,354.50 (£213,418 x 1/4) as follows:

	£
14.10.2011	53,355
14.01.2012	53,354
14.04.2012	53,355
14.07.2012	53,354
	213,418

(d) **If Zoom plc had no associated companies**

- Zoom plc's 'augmented profits' for corporation tax purposes for the year ended 31 March 2012 is:

	£
Taxable total profits	820,840
Plus: FII (£49,500 x 100/90)	55,000
Augmented profits	875,840

- Zoom plc is no longer a large company since its profits are below the upper limit of £1,500,000.
- The corporation tax liability will therefore be due in one amount on 1 January 2013 (i.e. nine months and one day after the end of the chargeable accounting period).
- The corporation tax liability will be:

	£
Corporation tax (£820,840 at 26%)	213,418
Less: Marginal relief	
3/200 × (£1,500,000 – £875,840) × £820,840/£875,840	(8,774)
Corporation tax liability	204,644

47 BALLPOINT LTD (ADAPTED) *Walk in the footsteps of a top tutor*

Key answer tips

This is a wide ranging corporation tax question involving adjustment of profits, capital allowances and a chargeable gain to calculate.

The highlighted words in the written sections are key phrases that markers are looking for.

Tutor's top tips

It is important when answering questions as long as this, that you have a good technique for dealing with all the information.

You should read the question carefully and highlight key pieces of information as you go through.

Part (a) should have been a very quick and easy way to earn 3 marks, as long as you broke your answer down into 3 separately identifiable points.

(a) **Residency status**

- Companies that are incorporated overseas are only treated as being resident in the UK if their central management and control is exercised in the UK.
- Since the directors are UK based and hold their board meetings in the UK, this would indicate that Ballpoint Ltd is managed and controlled from the UK, and therefore it is resident in the UK.
- If the directors were to be based overseas and to hold their board meetings overseas, the company would probably be treated as resident overseas since the central management and control would then be exercised outside the UK.

(b) **Trading profit – year ended 31 March 2012**

	£	£
Profit before taxation	520,000	
Depreciation	71,488	
Gifts to customers – pens (Note 1)	0	
Gifts to customers – food hampers (Note 1)	770	
Gifts to employees (Note 2)	0	
Gift aid donation (Note 3)	600	
Donation to local charity (Note 4)	0	
Donation to political party (Note 4)	300	
Replacement roof (Note 8)	0	
Initial repairs to office building (Note 9)	13,900	
Accountancy and audit (Note 5)	0	
Legal fees:		
• issue of share capital (Note 6)	3,100	
• issue of a loan note (Note 6)	0	
• defence of internet domain name (Note 7)	0	
Car lease costs (Note 10)	0	
Entertaining overseas customers (Note 11)	3,700	
Entertaining employees (Note 11)	0	
Counseling services for employees (Note 12)	0	
Fine	2,600	
Dividends		45,000
Disposal of factory		60,000
Interest payable (Note 13)	0	
Capital allowances – plant and machinery (W)		79,898
	616,458	184,898
	(184,898)	
Trading profit	431,560	

Tutor's top tips

In the adjustment to profits calculation it is important to list all the major items indicated in the question requirement, showing a zero (0) for expenditure that is allowable. This is because credit will be given for showing no adjustment where none is needed.

List the adjustments in the order they appear in the question.

If required, also add notes to show why you have not adjusted for an item, or why you have added it back. However, lengthy explanations are not required where the requirement is just to 'calculate' the adjusted profits, rather than to explain them.

Always show your workings if the figure you are adjusting for is not clear from the question.

Tutorial note

1. *Gifts to customers are an allowable deduction if they cost less than £50 per recipient per year, are not of food, drink, tobacco, or vouchers for exchangeable goods, and carry a conspicuous advertisement for the company making the gift.*
2. *Gifts to employees are allowable, although the gift might result in a taxable benefit as regards the employee.*
3. *The Gift Aid donation is allowable but is deducted from total profits in the TTP computation; it is not an allowable deduction in the adjustment of profits and therefore needs to be added back.*
4. *Small donations to a local charity are allowable but political donations are not.*
5. *Accountancy and audit fees are allowable as incurred wholly and exclusively for the purposes of the trade.*
6. *Legal fees in connection with the issue of share capital are not allowable, being capital in nature.*

   However, under the loan relationship rules all costs associated with loans related to the trade (i.e. loan notes) are deductible in calculating trading profits. The costs of obtaining loan finance (even if abortive) are therefore allowable.
7. *The costs of defending the right to an asset (the internet domain name) are also an allowable trading deduction.*
8. *The replacement of the roof is allowable since the whole structure is not being replaced.*
9. *The repairs to the office building are not allowable, being capital in nature, as the building was not in a usable state when purchased and this was reflected in the purchase price.*
10. *All of the car leasing costs are allowable as the car has CO_2 emissions of less than 160 g/km. If the CO_2 emissions had exceeded 160 g/km, 15% of the lease costs would be disallowable.*
11. *The only exception to the non-deductibility of entertainment expenditure is when it is in respect of employees.*
12. *The costs of counselling services for redundant employees are allowable, whilst fines are generally not allowable.*
13. *Interest on a loan used for trading purposes is deductible in calculating the trading profit on an accruals basis.*

Working: Plant and machinery

		Pool	*Expensive car*	*Special rate pool*	*Allowances*
	£	£	£	£	£
TWDV b/f		8,200	9,800		
Additions (no AIA):					
Car (CO_2 > 160 g/km)				18,200	
Car (CO_2 between 111 – 160 g/km)		11,400			
Additions (with AIA):					
Equipment (Note 2)	61,260				
Equipment (Note 2)	4,300				
	65,560				
Less: AIA					
(Max £100,000)	(65,560)				65,560
		Nil			
Disposal proceeds					
– Equipment		(2,700)			
– Car (2)		(10,110)			
		6,790	9,800	18,200	
WDA (20%)		(1,358)			1,358
WDA (20%)			(1,960)		1,960
WDA (10%)				(1,820)	1,820
Addition with FYA:					
Car (CO_2 < 111 g/km)	9,200				
Less: FYA (100%)	(9,200)				9,200
		Nil			
TWDV c/f		5,432	7,840	16,380	
Total allowances					79,898

Tutor's top tips

It is important to look carefully at the CO_2 emissions for the cars. There are three categories, all treated differently. Remember that the appropriate rates of allowances are given to you in the tax rates and allowances in the examination.

Tutorial note

1. *Capital allowances on new car purchases are now calculated based on the CO_2 emissions of the car as follows:*

   CO_2 emissions of < 111 g/km:
   eligible for a FYA of 100%.

CO_2 emissions of between 111 – 160 g/km:
put in main pool, eligible for a WDA at 20%.

CO_2 emissions of > 160 g/km:
put in special rate pool, eligible for a WDA at 10%.

The appropriate rates are given in the tax rates and allowances.

2. *There is only one AIA of £100,000 for Ballpoint Ltd and its 100% subsidiary, and this AIA can be shared between the two companies in any way they choose. However, this aspect of capital allowances is not examinable, so you should assume that the maximum AIA is claimed by Ballpoint Ltd.*

(c) **Corporation tax computation – year ended 31 March 2012**

Tutor's top tips

Don't worry if you made some mistakes in part (b) as you can still score full marks here for calculating the tax correctly based on your figures.

You must make sure you set out your workings clearly so that the marker can see what you have done.

	£
Trading profit	431,560
Chargeable gain (W1)	24,960
	456,520
Less: Gift Aid donation	(600)
	455,920
Less: Group relief (Note 1)	(42,000)
Taxable total profits	413,920
Plus: FII (£27,000 × 100/90) (Note 2)	30,000
Augmented profits	443,920
Corporation tax (W2) (£413,920 at 26%)	107,619
Less: Marginal relief	
3/200 × (£750,000 – £443,920) × £413,920/£443,920	(4,281)
Corporation tax liability	103,338

Tutorial note

1. *Remember that group relief is set off after Gift Aid, whereas if a company claims relief for its own loss, the loss is set off before Gift Aid.*
2. *Group dividends are not included as franked investment income.*

Workings

(W1) **Chargeable gain**

	£
Disposal proceeds	300,000
Less: Cost	(240,000)
Unindexed gain	60,000
Less: Indexation allowance	(35,040)
Chargeable gain	24,960

(W2) **Corporation tax rates**

		£
Upper limit	(£1,500,000 x ½)	750,000
Lower limit	(£300,000 x ½)	150,000
Augmented profits		443,920

Therefore marginal relief applies.

48 DO-NOT-PANIC LTD (ADAPTED)

Key answer tips

Originally this was a short question containing just part (a) for 10 marks involving a long period of account which requires knowledge of the rules of how to split income and gains between two chargeable accounting periods.

When the question was set, the capital allowance rules were different and more was involved in the calculation than under the current rules.

This question has been extended to become a 15 mark question in line with the new syllabus style of question.

(a) **Corporation tax liabilities – fifteen-month period ended 31 March 2012**

	y/e 31.12.2011	p/e 31.3.2012
	£	£
Trading profit (12/15 : 3/15) (Note 1)	252,000	63,000
Less: Capital allowances (W1)	(24,000)	(Nil)
	228,000	63,000
Net chargeable gains (£42,000 – £4,250) (Note 2)	Nil	37,750
Taxable total profits	228,000	100,750
Plus: Franked investment income	Nil	25,000
Augmented profits	228,000	125,750

	y/e 31.12.2011	p/e 31.3.2012
	£	£
Corporation tax (W2)		
FY2010: (£228,000 × 21% x 3/12)	11,970	
FY2011: (£228,000 × 20% x 9/12)	34,200	
FY2011: (£100,750 × 26%)		26,195
Less: Marginal relief		
3/200 × (£375,000 – £125,750) × £100,750/£125,750		(2,995)
Corporation tax liability	46,170	23,200
Due dates	1 Oct 2012	1 Jan 2013
Total liability	£69,370	

Tutorial note

1. *Trading profits are allocated on a time basis: 12/15 to the year ended 31 December 2011 and 3/15 to the period ended 31 March 2012.*
2. *The capital loss £4,250 for the year ended 31 December 2011 is carried forward and set against the first available future gains in 3 months ended 31 March 2012.*

Workings

(W1) **Capital allowances**

		Pool	*Allowances*
Year ended 31 December 2011	£	£	£
Additions (with AIA)			
Equipment	24,000		
Less: AIA (100%)	(24,000)		24,000
		Nil	
TWDV c/f		Nil	
Period ended 31 March 2012			
WDA		Nil	Nil
TWDV c/f		Nil	

(W2) **Corporation tax rate**

		y/e 31.12.11	*p/e 31.3.12*
		£	£
Upper limit	(Full / 3/12)	1,500,000	375,000
Lower limit	(Full / 3/12)	300,000	75,000
Augmented profits		228,000	125,750
		Small profit	*Marginal relief applies*

The accounting period ended 31 December 2011 falls partly into FY2010 (3 months) and partly into FY2011 (9 months).

As the tax rates are different in these financial years the liability must be calculated separately for each year.

Examiner's report

This is the examiner's report for part (a) which was the entire original question.

Depending on whether candidates appreciated that the period of account needed to be split into a twelve-month period and a three-month period, this question was either answered very well or quite badly.

Invariably many of the less well prepared candidates calculated corporation tax based on a fifteen-month period.

Even when the correct approach was taken, many candidates did not appreciate that the first twelve month period spanned two financial years.

The due dates were often omitted or incorrect.

(b) **Corporation tax liabilities – two sets of account prepared**

	p/e 31.3.2011	y/e 31.3.2012
	£	£
Trading profit (3/15 : 12/15) (Note 1)	63,000	252,000
Less: Capital allowances (Note 2)	(24,000)	(Nil)
	39,000	252,000
Net chargeable gains (£42,000 – £4,250) (Note 3)	Nil	37,750
Taxable total profits	39,000	289,750
Plus: Franked investment income	Nil	25,000
Augmented profits	39,000	314,750
Corporation tax (W2)		
FY2010: (£39,000 × 21%)	8,190	
FY2011: (£289,750 × 26%)		75,335
Less: Marginal relief		
3/200 × (£1,500,000 – £314,750) × £289,750/£314,750		(16,367)
Corporation tax liability	8,190	58,968
Due dates	1 Jan 2012	1 Jan 2013
Total liability	£67,158	

Tutorial note

1. *Trading profits are assumed to accrue evenly over the fifteen month period.*
2. *The capital allowances are the same as in part (a).*

Remember that the AIA is time apportioned in a short accounting period, however, the first period is 3 months in length and the maximum AIA is therefore £25,000. As the actual expenditure is £24,000, the maximum AIA is not a restricting factor.

3. *The capital loss and the capital gain both fall in the year ended 31 March 2012.*

Working: Corporation tax rate

		p/e 31.3.11	*y/e 31.3.12*
		£	£
Upper limit	(3/12 / Full)	375,000	1,500,000
Lower limit	(3/12 / Full)	75,000	300,000
Augmented profits		39,000	314,750
		Small profits	*Marginal relief applies*

The accounting period ended 31 March 2011 falls entirely in FY2010 and the accounting period ended 31 March 2012 falls entirely in FY2011.

(c) **Total tax**

The lower total tax liability is £67,158 which is obtained if two separate accounts are prepared, rather than a long period of account which gives a total liability of £69,370.

ACCA marking scheme

		Marks
(a)	Trading profit	1.0
	Capital allowances	
	– Year ended 31 December 2011	1.0
	– Period ended 31 March 2012	1.0
	Capital gains	1.0
	Franked investment income	1.0
	Corporation tax	
	– Year ended 31 December 2011	2.0
	– Period ended 31 March 2012	2.0
	Due dates	1.0
		10.0
(b)	Trading profit	1.0
	Capital allowances	
	– Period ended 31 March 2011	1.0
	– Year ended 31 March 2012	1.0
	Capital gains	1.0
	Franked investment income	1.0
	Corporation tax	
	– Period ended 31 March 2011	1.0
	– Year ended 31 March 2012	2.0
	Due dates	1.0
		9.0
(c)	Lower total tax liability	1.0
Total		20.0

49 GASTRON LTD *Walk in the footsteps of a top tutor*

Key answer tips

This was a classic corporation tax computational question, requiring an adjustment of profits and capital allowances computation, corporation tax computation, and some self assessment.

All these areas are highly likely to be tested and should be well practiced.

Parts (d) and (e) involve capital gains groups, which may be seen as tricky, but most of the marks can be won by simply stating the rules, rather than needing application to the question.

Tutor's top tips

This question has clear mark allocations, which should be used to allocate the time spent on each section. You need to adopt a logical approach, using the requirements to break down the information and plan your answer.

It is possible to score very well on this sort of question, which is not technically difficult, as long as you do not panic over the quantity of information.

Part (a) gives you clear guidance on the approach that is needed, and you should follow this – starting with the profit before tax and then making the necessary adjustments.

Work through the notes in order, and ensure you have dealt with every single item, as credit is given for showing an adjustment of nil where one is not necessary, as stated in the requirement.

If you are not sure of how to deal with an item, make a sensible assumption and move on, but do not ignore it, or waste unnecessary time.

Note that as the question has asked you to 'calculate' the adjusted profits you do not need to explain each adjustment that you make, but you should show any workings.

Make sure you do a separate capital allowances working, which is clearly referenced, as there are a number of purchases and disposals in the period, and a full working is required.

(a) Trading profit – year ended 31 March 2012

	£	£
Profit before taxation	640,000	
Depreciation	85,660	
Amortisation of leasehold property (Note 1)	6,000	
Deduction for lease premium (W2)		4,920
Gifts of pens to customers (Note 2)	1,200	
Gifts of hampers to customers (Note 2)	1,100	
Donation (Note 3)	0	
Legal fees re renewal of lease (Note 4)	0	
Legal fees re issue of a loan note (Note 4)	0	
Entertaining suppliers (Note 5)	1,300	
Entertaining employees (Note 5)	0	
Income from investments		87,000
Profit on disposal of shares		80,700
Interest payable (Note 6)	0	
Capital allowances (W1)		62,640
	735,260	235,260
Allowable deductions	(235,260)	
Tax adjusted trading profit	500,000	

Tutorial note

1. *The amortisation of a lease is disallowable (just like depreciation), but there is relief for the 'revenue' element of the premium. See working 2 for the calculation of the allowable deduction.*

   The annual allowable deduction is calculated as the assessment on the landlord spread over the length of the lease.

2. *Gifts to customers are only an allowable deduction if they cost less than £50 per recipient per year, are not of food, drink, tobacco, or vouchers for exchangeable goods, and carry a conspicuous advertisement for the company making the gift.*

   The pens cost £60 and the hampers contain food, therefore neither are allowable.

3. *Small donations to a local charity are allowable.*

4. *The costs of renewing a short-lease (less than 50 years) and of obtaining loan finance are specifically allowable.*

5. *The only exception to the non-deductibility of entertainment expenditure is when it is in respect of employees.*

6. *Interest on a loan used for trading purposes is deductible in calculating the trading loss on an accruals basis.*

Workings

(W1) **Plant and machinery – year ended 31 March 2012**

		Pool	*Expensive car*	*Allowances*
	£	£	£	£
TWDV b/f		16,700	18,400	
Additions (no AIA or FYA):				
Car (CO_2 between 111 – 160 g/km)		9,800		
Additions (with AIA):				
Equipment	21,600			
Lorry	17,200			
	38,800			
Less: AIA (100%)	(38,800)			38,800
		Nil		
Disposal proceeds – equipment		(3,300)		
		23,200	18,400	
WDA (20%)		(4,640)		4,640
WDA (Restricted) (Note 1)			(3,000)	3,000
Addition qualifying for FYA				
Car (CO_2 < 111 g/km)	16,200			
Less: FYA (100%)	(16,200)			16,200
		Nil		
TWDV c/f		18,560	15,400	
Total allowances				62,640

Tutorial note

1. *Brought forward 'expensive' cars are dealt with under the old rules. A WDA of 20% is available regardless of the car's CO_2 emissions; however, the total WDA for a 12 month period is restricted to a maximum of £3,000.*

2. *Capital allowances on new car purchases are now calculated based on the CO_2 emissions of the car as follows:*

   CO_2 emissions of < 111 g/km:
   eligible for a FYA of 100%.

   CO_2 emissions of between 111 – 160 g/km:
   put in main pool, eligible for a WDA at 20%.

   CO_2 emissions of > 160 g/km:
   put in special rate pool, eligible for a WDA at 10%.

   The appropriate rates are given in the tax rates and allowances.

(W2) **Deduction for lease premium**

Tutor's top tips

Many students find dealing with lease premiums tricky; however, it is simply a case of learning the formula and applying it to the figures in the question.

There is no other way to attempt to deal with this question if you haven't learnt the formula!

The office building has been used for business purposes, and so the proportion of the lease premium assessed on the landlord can be deducted.

The allowable deduction is the amount assessed on the landlord, spread over the life of the lease.

Assessment on landlord:

	£
Premium received	60,000
Less: 2% x £60,000 x (10 – 1)	(10,800)
Assessment on landlord (Note)	49,200
Allowable deduction (£49,200 ÷ 10)	4,920

Tutorial note

Alternative calculation of the assessment on the landlord:

£60,000 x (51 – 10)/50 = £49,200

(b) **Corporation tax computation – year ended 31 March 2012**

Tutor's top tips

Part (b) requires a corporation tax computation, which will incorporate the figure calculated in part (a).

As long as you use the adjusted trading profit figure you have calculated correctly you can score full marks here, even if you have made errors earlier in the question.

The year-end falls entirely in FY2011 and therefore the corporation tax liability can be calculated in one computation.

	£
Trading profit	500,000
Property business profit (W1)	12,800
Bank interest	12,400
Chargeable gain	74,800
Taxable total profits	600,000
Plus: FII (£36,000 x 100/90) (Note)	40,000
'Augmented profits'	640,000
Corporation tax	
FY2011: (£600,000 at 26%) (W2)	156,000
Less: Marginal relief	
3/200 x (£750,000 – £640,000) x £600,000/£640,000	(1,547)
Corporation tax liability	154,453

Tutorial note:

Group dividends are not included as franked investment income. Therefore only the dividends received from Tasteless plc, the unconnected company will be grossed up and added to the taxable total profits to calculate augmented profits.

Workings:

(W1) **Property business profit**

		£	£
Rent receivable	– First tenant (£1,800 x 9)		16,200
	– Second tenant (£1,950 x 2)		3,900
			20,100
Irrecoverable rents (£1,800 x 2) (Note)		3,600	
Decorating costs		3,700	
			(7,300)
Property business profit			12,800

Tutorial note

The rent is taxable on an accruals basis, and therefore all 9 months of rent for the first tenant are included. However, as the tenant left owing two months' rent, the irrecoverable rent is an allowable deduction.

(W2) **Corporation tax rate**

Gastron Ltd has one associated company, so the upper limit is reduced to £750,000 (£1,500,000 x ½) and the lower limit £150,000 (£300,000 x ½).

Augmented profits fall in between the limits, therefore marginal relief applies.

(c) **Corporation tax due dates and interest**

Tutor's top tips

Part (c) requires the due date for payments of corporation tax and the interest that will be charged if the tax is paid late.

It is important to actually calculate the interest here, rather than simply stating the way it will be calculated. All calculations should be to the nearest month unless the question says otherwise.

Note that the rates of late payment interest and repayment interest are given in the tax tables.

- Gastron Ltd's corporation tax liability for the year ended 31 March 2012 must be paid by 1 January 2013.
- If the company does not pay its corporation tax until 31 August 2013, then interest of £3,089 (£154,453 at 3% = £4,634 x 8/12) will be charged by HM Revenue and Customs for the period 1 January 2013 to 31 August 2013.

(d) **Definition of a capital gains group**

Tutor's top tips

This part requires only a definition of a capital gains group for 2 marks.

It is useful to learn this definition, as this is a common requirement in a question involving groups.

- Companies form a capital gains group if at each level in the group structure there is a 75% shareholding.
- However, the parent company must also have an effective interest of over 50% in each group company.

(e) **Gains group election**

Tutor's top tips

Knowledge of time limits and deadlines is very useful for obtaining easy marks.

The most common deadline for claims and elections for corporation tax is two years from the end of the accounting period, and if you don't know the deadline, this can be a good guess to make!

However, it is important to state the actual date, not just the general rule, so you must apply the rule to the dates in the question.

- Gastron Ltd and Culinary Ltd must make the election by 31 March 2014 (i.e. within two years of the end of the accounting period in which the disposal outside of the group occurred).

- Culinary Ltd's otherwise unused capital loss of £66,000 can be set against Gastron Ltd's chargeable gain of £74,800.
- It is beneficial for the balance of the chargeable gain of £8,800 (£74,800 – £66,000) to arise in Culinary Ltd as it will only be taxed at the rate of 20%, instead of at the marginal rate (27.5%) in Gastron Ltd.

Tutorial note

It is not necessary to do a further corporation tax computation in order to calculate the most beneficial way of making this election.

The question states that Culinary is paying tax at 20%, and in part (b) you have calculated that Gastron Ltd is paying tax at 26% less marginal relief. This means that profits falling into the marginal band suffer tax at an effective rate of tax of 27.5%.

It can be useful to learn the effective rate of tax in the margin, as this will help you to quickly calculate the benefit of any tax or loss relief.

Examiner's report

This question was very well answered, with only part (e) consistently causing problems.

In part (a) candidates were instructed to list all of the items referred to in the notes, and to indicate by the use of zero any items that did not require adjustment. This method should be quicker for candidates than writing separate explanatory notes, and shows that they have considered any non-taxable and non-deductible items, rather than simply forgetting about them.

Candidates are advised that this will be a standard approach in future and they should ensure they follow this instruction to be able to score full marks.

Despite the instruction some candidates did not list those items not requiring any adjustment.

Parts (a) and (b) were kept separate for a very good reason – namely to help candidates. Therefore those candidates who attempted to combine both parts into one calculation not surprisingly often had problems.

Given the new capital allowances rules, it was pleasing to see many candidates correctly calculate the correct figure for capital allowances. Although I can applaud candidate's attempts to save paper, it is not good examination technique to try and squeeze a capital allowances computation of this size into 5 or 6 lines at the end of a page.

In part (c) a disappointing number of candidates gave 31 January as the payment date.

Only a few candidates appreciated that interest would be due, and fewer still correctly calculated the actual amount payable.

In part (d) most candidates appreciated that a 75% shareholding was necessary, but were then often unsure where the 50% limit fitted in. The holding company must have an effective interest of 50%.

In part (e) many candidates simply stated that losses could be set against profits, without making any attempt to use the information given in the question.

ACCA marking scheme			
			Marks
(a)	Profit before taxation		0.5
	Depreciation		0.5
	Amortisation of leasehold property		0.5
	Lease premium – assessable amount		1.5
	Lease premium – deduction		1.0
	Gifts of pens to customers		0.5
	Gifts of hampers to customers		0.5
	Donation		0.5
	Legal fees re renewal of lease		0.5
	Legal fees re issue of loan note		0.5
	Entertaining suppliers		0.5
	Entertaining employees		0.5
	Income from investments		1.0
	Disposal of shares		0.5
	Interest payable		0.5
	Plant and machinery	– Main pool	2.0
		– AIA	1.5
		– Expensive car	1.0
		– FYA	1.0
			15.0
(b)	Trading profit		0.5
	Property business profit		2.0
	Bank interest		0.5
	Chargeable gain		0.5
	Franked investment income		1.0
	Group dividends		0.5
	Corporation tax		2.0
			7.0
(c)	Due date		1.0
	Interest		2.0
			3.0
(d)	75% shareholding		1.0
	50% effective interest		1.0
			2.0
(e)	Time limit		1.0
	Set off of capital losses		1.0
	Tax rate		1.0
			3.0
Total			30.0

50 QUAGMIRE LTD *Walk in the footsteps of a top tutor*

Key answer tips

This question covers the quarterly instalment system of payment for large companies. It is not difficult provided the self assessment rules for companies have been learnt.

In particular you need to know the conditions for determining whether or not a company is large for this purpose, and the key due dates of payment.

Tutor's top tips

Part (a) requires an explanation of why the company does have to pay by instalments. The clue that the company is large is therefore in the requirement.

The question itself gives taxable total profits and FII which should trigger alarm bells that the level of 'augmented profits' is an important consideration.

The fact that both this year and last year information is given should also be a clue that they are both important to determine the status of the company.

(a) **Quarterly instalment payments**

- Large companies have to make quarterly instalment payments in respect of their corporation tax liability. A large company is one paying corporation tax at the main rate.
- Quagmire plc has one associated company, so the upper limit is reduced to £750,000 (£1,500,000 × 1/2). Corporation tax will therefore be at the main rate for the year ended 31 January 2012.
- There is an exception for the first year that a company is large, provided profits do not exceed £10 million (divided by the number of associated companies).

  However, no exception applies in this case because Quagmire plc was also a large company for the year ended 31 January 2011.

Tutorial note

The instalment payment system is not applied if:

1. *The corporation tax liability is less than £10,000, or*
2. *The company is 'large' for the first time and the profits do not exceed £10 million (divided by number of associates if applicable)*

(b) **Corporation tax liability and due dates for payment**

	£
Corporation tax – year ended 31 January 2012	
FY2010 (£1,200,000 x 28% x 2/12)	56,000
FY2011 (£1,200,000 x 26% x 10/12)	260,000
Corporation tax liability	316,000

The accounting period falls partly within FY2010 (2 months) and partly within FY2011 (10 months).

The tax rates are different in each financial year so the corporation tax liability must be calculated separately for each financial year.

- Quagmire plc's corporation tax liability for the year ended 31 January 2012 is £316,000.
- The company will have paid this in four quarterly instalments of £79,000 (£316,000/4).
- The instalments will have been due on the 14th of August 2011, November 2011, February 2012 and May 2012.

Tutorial note

Remember that the corporation tax liability is calculated on taxable total profits, not 'augmented profits'.

The instalments are due on the 14th day of the 7th, 10th, 13th and 16th month after the start of the chargeable accounting period.

(c) **Revised position assuming Quagmire did not have an associated company**

Tutor's top tips

The requirement asks for an explanation of the effect if there is no associate – so make sure that you explain in words and do not just do a calculation.

The revised calculation is worth only 1.5 of the 4 marks available.

- Quagmire plc's augmented profits for the year ended 31 January 2012 is £1,400,000 (£1,200,000 plus franked investment income of £200,000).
- Quagmire plc is no longer a large company since its profits are below the upper limit of £1,500,000. The corporation tax liability will therefore be due in one amount on 1 November 2012.

- The corporation tax liability will be:

	£
Corporation tax	
FY2010	
(£1,200,000 at 28% x 2/12)	56,000
Less: Marginal relief	
7/400 × (£1,500,000 – £1,400,000) × £1,200,000/£1,400,000 x 2/12	(250)
FY2011	
(£1,200,000 at 26% x 10/12)	260,000
Less: Marginal relief	
3/200 × (£1,500,000 – £1,400,000) × £1,200,000/£1,400,000 x 10/12	(1,071)
	314,679

Tutorial note

The normal due date for corporation tax is 9 months and 1 day after the end of the chargeable accounting period.

Examiner's report

This question was reasonably well answered.

In part (a) very few candidates appreciated that there was a possible exception and that the exception did not apply. This was the reason why figures were given for the previous year, and less well prepared candidates created a lot of problems for themselves by trying to use these figures as part of their calculations.

Candidates had little difficulty in calculating the corporation tax liability in part (b), but they often struggled with the quarterly due dates.

There was a similar problem in part (c) where many candidates failed to score an easy mark by omitting the due date.

ACCA marking scheme

		Marks
(a)	Large companies	1.0
	Associated company	1.0
	No exception	1.0
		3.0
(b)	Corporation tax liability	1.0
	Instalments	1.0
	Due dates	1.0
		3.0
(c)	Profit	1.0
	No longer a large company	0.5
	Due date	1.0
	Corporation tax	1.5
		4.0
Total		10.0

WITH OVERSEAS ASPECTS

51 ALBERT LTD (ADAPTED)

Key answer tips

This is a question with two distinct parts that can be answered independently.

The first part of this question is a standard computation of corporation tax. This should not cause you any particular difficulty but watch out for the trade losses brought forward.

The second part is a more testing requirement to calculate corporation tax if either a foreign branch or a subsidiary is set up. However, with recent changes to the treatment of overseas dividends, this part is now much simpler than the original question.

It is advisable to deal with the branch and the subsidiary separately rather than try to do side by side computations.

(a) **Albert Ltd**

Corporation tax liability – year ended 31 March 2012

	£
Trading profit (W1)	902,689
Less: Trading losses b/f	(25,000)
	877,689
Interest income	12,000
Chargeable gain	120,000
	1,009,689
Less: Gift Aid	(15,500)
Taxable total profits	994,189
Plus: FII	Nil
Augmented profits	994,189
Corporation tax (£994,189 x 26%) (W3)	258,489
Less: Marginal relief	
3/200 x (£1,500,000 – £994,189)	(7,587)
Corporation tax liability	250,902

Workings

(W1) **Trading profit**

Key answer tips

In the adjustment to profits calculation it is important to list all the major items indicated in the question requirement, showing a zero (0) for expenditure that is allowable.

> This is because credit will be given for showing no adjustment where none is needed. List the adjustments in the order they appear in the question.
>
> If required, also add notes to show why you have not adjusted for an item, or why you have added it back. However, lengthy explanations are not required where the requirement is just to 'calculate' the adjusted profits, rather than to explain them.
>
> Always show your workings if the figure you are adjusting for is not clear from the question.

	£	£
Operating profit	873,429	
Depreciation	82,000	
Gift Aid	15,500	
Political donation	48,000	
Legal fees for the collection of trade debts	0	
Capital allowances (W2)		116,240
	1,018,929	116,240
	(116,240)	
Tax adjusted trading profit	902,689	

(W2) **Plant and machinery – capital allowances computation**

		Main pool	*Expensive car*	*SR pool*	*Allowances*
	£	£	£	£	£
TWDV b/f		45,200	22,400	150,000	
Additions (with AIA)					
Machine	63,000				
Less: AIA	(63,000)				63,000
		Nil			
Disposal proceeds			(18,200)		
		45,200	4,200		
Balancing allowance			(4,200)		4,200
WDA (20%)		(9,040)			9,040
WDA (10%)				(15,000)	15,000
Addition: Car					
(CO_2 < 111 g/km)	25,000				
Less: FYAs (100%)	(25,000)				25,000
		Nil			
TWDV c/f		36,160		178,200	
Total allowances					116,240

Tutorial note

1. *Private use of the expensive motor car by the finance director is irrelevant for companies, full allowances are available. The director will be assessed to income tax on the private use of the car as an employment benefit.*
2. *A car purchased with CO_2 emissions below 111 g/km is eligible for a FYA of 100%.*

(W3) **Corporation tax rates**

Albert Ltd has no associated companies and therefore its augmented profits of £994,189 are compared to the full limits.

As augmented profits fall between £300,000 and £1,500,000; marginal relief applies.

The accounting period falls entirely in FY2011.

(b) **Corporation tax liabilities with an overseas operation in 2013**

(i) **Overseas branch**

Albert Ltd – Corporation tax liability – year ending 31 March 2013

	£
Trading profit – UK	1,200,000
Trading profit – Branch (Note 1)	180,000
Taxable total profits	1,380,000
Corporation tax (£1,380,000 x 26%) (W1) (Note 3)	358,800
Less: Marginal relief	
3/200 × (£1,500,000 – £1,380,000)	(1,800)
	357,000
Less: Double tax relief (W2)	(45,000)
Corporation tax liability	312,000

(ii) **Overseas subsidiary**

Albert Ltd – Corporation tax liability – year ending 31 March 2013

	£
Trading profit – UK	1,200,000
Overseas dividend income (Note 2)	Nil
Taxable total profits	1,200,000
Corporation tax (£1,200,000 x 26%) (W1) (Note 3)	312,000
Less: Double tax relief (Note)	(Nil)
Corporation tax liability	312,000

Tutorial note

1. *With a branch, the UK company is taxable on the whole of the profits and DTR is available for withholding tax.*
2. *With a foreign subsidiary the UK company is no longer taxed on the profits as dividends received from the subsidiary are exempt from UK corporation tax. DTR is therefore no longer a consideration as overseas dividends are not taxed twice.*
3. *Remember that the subsidiary will count as an associated company, but a branch operation will not. Therefore, an overseas subsidiary (but not a branch) will affect the UK company's corporation tax rate as the limits are divided by the number of associated companies.*

   Albert Ltd's 'augmented profits' are compared to the appropriate limits to determine the rate of tax, but remember that the overseas dividends of a subsidiary are not treated as Franked Investment Income in the calculation of 'augmented profits'.

Workings:

(W1) **Corporation tax rate**

		Branch	Subsidiary
		£	£
Upper limit	(Full / x 1/2)	1,500,000	750,000
Lower limit	(Full / x 1/2)	300,000	150,000
Augmented profits		1,380,000	1,200,000
		Marginal relief applies	*Main rate applies*

An overseas subsidiary is an associated company and therefore the limits are divided by two.

(W2) **Double taxation relief – Branch income**

DTR = lower of:

(i)	Overseas tax suffered on branch income	£45,000
(ii)	UK tax on overseas income (£357,000/£1,380,000) × £180,000	£46,565

Therefore DTR is £45,000.

52 CRASH BASH LTD (ADAPTED) *Walk in the footsteps of a top tutor*

Key answer tips

A standard corporation tax question requiring a capital allowances computation for plant and machinery followed by a corporation tax computation. This part of the question carries the majority of the marks available in part (a).

These areas are often tested and should not have caused many difficulties.

The overseas aspects of residency status and transfer pricing are more esoteric, however the level of detail required in the answer is not great and relatively easy marks were available if you had learnt the rules.

The separate VAT section for 10 marks at the end is also a classic requirement – easy to score highly on, provided the rules have been learnt!

Tutor's top tips

Be sure to read the requirement carefully and pay attention to the mark allocation.

Part (a)(i) only requires two bullet points to be made, but remember to relate your answer to the specific information given in the question.

Part (a)(ii) is where the time should be spent, however, there is no reason why you could not attempt part (a)(iii) first and get it out of the way! It is a standalone part requiring the detailing of four facts about transfer pricing.

If you have learnt the rules you should be able to write them down quickly and then return to the meaty part of the question.

Even if you can only write down a couple of points, get them down early and leave some space in case you think of something to add later – but make sure you write something and don't run out of time in attempting this part because you spend too long on the computations required in part (a)(ii).

(a) (i) **Residence status**

- Companies that are incorporated overseas are only treated as being resident in the UK if their central management and control is exercised in the UK.
- Since the directors are UK based and hold their board meetings in the UK, this would indicate that Crash-Bash Ltd is managed and controlled from the UK, and therefore it is resident in the UK.

(ii) **Corporation tax liability – period ended 31 March 2012**

Tutor's top tips

Remember to use your time effectively for this part.

Computations for capital allowances are required in workings before the corporation tax computation can be drawn up. Remember to reference your workings clearly to your main answer to the question.

Note that this question is now simpler than the original question set as there are no longer any DTR implications on the receipt of the overseas dividends; however the capital allowances computation is a little more complicated than before.

The mark allocation in this answer has been adjusted accordingly.

	£	£
Trading profit per question		442,400
Advertising expenditure (Note 1)	12,840	
Capital allowances – Plant and machinery (W2)	91,050	
		(103,890)
Tax adjusted trading profit		338,510
Overseas income (Note 2)		Nil
Taxable total profits		338,510
Plus: FII (Note 3)		40,000
Augmented profits		378,510
Corporation tax (W1) (£338,510 at 26%)		88,013
Less: Marginal relief		
3/200 × (£562,500 – £378,510) × £338,510/£378,510		(2,468)
Corporation tax liability		85,545

Tutorial note

1. *The advertising expenditure incurred during June 2011 is pre-trading revenue expenditure. Accordingly it is treated as incurred on the first day of trading (i.e. 1 July 2011) and is therefore an allowable deduction for corporation tax purposes.*

   As no adjustment has been made for this expenditure yet, an adjustment is required.

2. *Overseas dividends received by a company are exempt from UK corporation tax. The income is therefore not included in the corporation tax computation and DTR is no longer a consideration as overseas dividends are not taxed twice. See Note 3 for the impact on FII.*

3. *If the dividends are received from a non-associated company (UK or overseas), they must be grossed up at 100/90 and included in FII. However, dividends from an associated company (UK or overseas) are excluded from the definition of FII. Safety Inc is a 100% overseas subsidiary and therefore it is an associated company, but any dividends received are not FII.*

Workings

(W1) **Corporation tax rate**

- The accounting period is nine months long and falls entirely in FY2011. Crash-Bash Ltd has one associated company.
- The upper and lower limits for corporation tax purposes are:

Upper limit	(£1,500,000 × 9/12 × ½)	£562,500
Lower limit	(£300,000 × 9/12 × ½)	£112,500

- The augmented profits of £378,510 fall in between the limits and therefore Crash-Bash Ltd is a marginal relief company

(W2) **Plant and machinery**

		Pool	Allowances
	£	£	£
Additions (No AIA or FYA):			
Car (Note 1)			
(CO_2 between 111 – 160 g/km)		14,000	
Additions (with AIA):			
Machinery	90,000		
Less: AIA (Maximum) (Note 2)	(75,000)		75,000
	———	15,000	
Disposal (restricted to cost)		(10,000)	
		———	
		19,000	
Less: WDA (Note 2)			
(£19,000 × 20% × 9/12)		(2,850)	2,850
Additions (with FYA):			
Car (CO_2 ≤ 110 g/km)	13,200		
Less: FYA (100%)	(13,200)		13,200
	———	Nil	
		———	
TWDV c/f		16,150	
		———	———
Total allowances			91,050
			———

Tutorial note

1. Capital allowances on new car purchases are now calculated based on the CO_2 emissions of the car as follows:

   CO_2 emissions of ≤ 110 g/km:
   eligible for a FYA of 100%
   CO_2 emissions of between 111 – 160 g/km:
   put in main pool and eligible for a WDA at 20%.

2. The maximum Annual Investment Allowance is £75,000 (£100,000 × 9/12) because Crash-Bash Ltd's accounting period is nine months long.

   The writing down allowance is similarly restricted to 9/12, however first year allowances are never restricted according to the length of the accounting period.

(iii) **Transfer pricing**

- Invoicing for the exported crash helmets at less than the market price will reduce UK trading profits and hence UK corporation tax.
- A true market price will therefore have to be substituted for the transfer price.
- The true market price is the 'arms length' price that would be charged if the parties to the transaction were independent of each other.
- Crash-Bash Ltd will be required to make the adjustment in its corporation tax self-assessment tax return.

Tutorial note

The question clearly states that Crash-Bash Ltd is a large company for the purposes of the transfer pricing legislation.

This means that because Crash-Bash Ltd is not a small or medium sized enterprise, there is no possibility of claiming an exemption from the transfer pricing rules.

(b) (i) **Compulsory registration**

Tutor's top tips

Part (b) of this question is an independent part and could be answered before part (a) if you want to get it out of the way and have learnt the relevant VAT rules!

Remember that VAT will always feature in the exam for between 10 – 15 marks and the requirements are usually straightforward and easy to score highly on provided you put in the time to learn the rules.

However, even if you are a bit vague on some of the areas, you need to attempt each part and write something – try not to spend too long on part (a) so that you run out of time to do part (b) justice.

Part (b)(i) should have been straightforward as it required the application of the compulsory registration rules.

Part (b)(ii) was a little more tricky in computing the recoverability of the pre-registration input VAT, but there are some straightforward points to make and numbers to calculate.

For part (b)(iii) you have either learnt the rules, or you haven't. You would struggle on this part if you haven't.

- Traders must register for VAT if at any time they expect their taxable supplies for the following 30-day period to exceed £73,000.
- Crash-Bash Ltd realised that its taxable supplies for September 2011 were going to be at least £100,000. The company was therefore liable to register from 1 September 2011, being the start of the 30-day period.
- Crash-Bash Ltd had to notify HMRC by 30 September 2011, being the end of the 30-day period.

(ii) **Recovery of pre-registration input VAT**

- Input VAT of £21,720 (£108,600 × 20%) can be recovered on the stock of goods at 1 September 2011.
- The stock was not acquired more than four years prior to registration, nor was it sold or consumed prior to registration.
- Input VAT of £11,000 ((£22,300 + £32,700) × 20%) can be recovered on the services incurred from 1 July to 31 August 2011.
- This is because the services were not supplied more than six months prior to registration.
- The total input VAT recovery is therefore £32,720 (£21,720 + £11,000).

(iii) **Voluntary disclosure of errors in a VAT return**

- If the net errors totalled less than the higher of £10,000 or 1% of the turnover for the VAT period, then they could have been voluntarily disclosed by simply entering them on the VAT return for the quarter ended 28 February 2012.
- If the net errors exceeded the limit, they could have been voluntarily disclosed but disclosure would have been made separately to HMRC.
- Default interest is only charged where the limit is exceeded and it is therefore necessary to make separate disclosure to HMRC.

Examiner's report

Although the numerical aspects of this question were well answered, most candidates achieved lower marks for this question than for question one, despite this question being five marks longer.

In the first section of part (a) most candidates were not aware that the essential point regarding residence is where a company's central management and control is exercised.

Most candidates had little difficulty with the corporation tax computation, and there were many perfect answers to this part of the question. However, the overseas income was often treated as franked investment income or simply ignored. The double taxation relief was sometimes used to reduce the overseas income rather than the corporation tax liability.

As for transfer pricing, very few candidates gave detailed enough answers to score more than one or two marks. It was surprising that very few candidates even appreciated that the pricing policy would result in the company's UK corporation tax liability being reduced.

In part (b) the VAT aspects of the question were not so well answered.

Many candidates incorrectly stated that VAT registration was necessary because the company had exceeded the registration limit over the previous 12 months; they even gave the wrong date of registration despite this being given in the question.

A number of candidates prepared the company's VAT return showing output VAT and input VAT, rather than calculating the amount of pre-registration input VAT.

Very few candidates were aware of when default interest is charged.

ACCA marking scheme

				Marks
(a)	(i)	Central management and control		1.0
		Board meetings held in the UK		1.0
				2.0
	(ii)	Trading profit		0.5
		Advertising expenditure		1.0
		P & M	– AIA	1.5
			– Pool	1.5
			– Disposal restricted to cost	1.0
			– WDA	1.5
			– FYA (100%)	1.5
		Treatment of overseas dividend	– exempt income	0.5
			– not included in FII	1.0
			– no DTR implications	1.0
		Franked investment income		1.0
		Corporation tax calculation		2.0
				14.0

			Marks
	(iii)	Reduction in UK corporation tax	1.0
		Use of market price	1.0
		Definition of market price	1.0
		Adjustment under self assessment	1.0
			4.0
(b)	(i)	Registration limit	1.0
		Taxable supplies for September 2011	1.0
		Notification	1.0
			3.0
	(ii)	Stock of goods – Calculation	0.5
		– Explanation	1.0
		Services – Calculation	1.0
		– Explanation	1.0
		Total input VAT recovery	0.5
			4.0
	(iii)	Net errors less than the limit	1.0
		Net errors exceeding the limit	1.0
		Default interest	1.0
			3.0
Total			30.0

WITH VAT ASPECTS

53 STRETCHED LTD (ADAPTED)

Key answer tips

This question deals with the rules for a 15 month period of account which must be split into two accounting periods of 12 months and 3 months.

For ease, use a columnar layout to do the corporation tax computations side by side. Don't forget to pick up the easy marks for stating the due dates of payment.

At least 10 marks of VAT will be included in the examination and it is most likely to appear as part of question 1 or 2. In this case it appears as an independent part (b) to the question.

It is important not to neglect VAT. The points tested in this question are all commonly examined.

(1) (a) **Corporation tax computations**

	y/e 31.12.11	p/e 31.3.12
	£	£
Trading profit (12/15 : 3/15) (Note 1)	264,000	66,000
Less: Capital allowances (W1)	Nil	(25,100)
	264,000	40,900
Less: Loss relief b/f	(23,000)	–
	241,000	40,900
Property business profit (12/15 : 3/15) (Note 1)	36,000	9,000
Chargeable gains (£44,000 – £3,000) (Note 2)	41,000	Nil
	318,000	49,900
Less: Gift Aid donation	–	(5,000)
Taxable total profits	318,000	44,900
Plus: Franked investment income	30,000	–
Augmented profits	348,000	44,900
Corporation tax (W2)		
FY2010		
(£318,000 x 28% x 3/12)	22,260	
Less: Marginal relief		
7/400 x (£1,500,000 – £348,000) x £318,000/£348,000 x 3/12	(4,606)	
FY2011		
(£318,000 x 26% x 9/12)	62,010	
Less: Marginal relief		
3/200 x (£1,500,000 – £348,000) x £318,000/£348,000 x 9/12	(11,843)	
FY2011: (£44,900 x 20%)		8,980
	67,821	8,980
Due dates	1 Oct 2012	1 Jan 2013

Tutorial note

1. *Trading profits and property business profits are allocated on a time basis: 12/15 to the year ended 31 December 2011 and 3/15 to the period ended 31 March 2012.*
2. *The capital loss of £6,700 for the period ended 31 March 2012 is carried forward, it cannot be carried back and set off against previous gains.*

Workings

(W1) **Capital allowances**

		Pool	Allowances
	£	£	£
3 months ended 31 March 2012			
Additions (with AIA)			
Office equipment	27,000		
Less: AIA (Max £100,000 x 3/12)	(25,000)		25,000
		2,000	
Less: WDA (20%) x 3/12		(100)	100
TWDV c/f		1,900	
Total allowances			25,100

Tutorial note

The AIA and WDA must be time apportioned as the chargeable accounting period is only three months in length.

(W2) **Corporation tax rates**

		y/e 31.12.11	*p/e 31.3.12*
		£	£
Upper limit	(Full / x 3/12)	1,500,000	375,000
Lower limit	(Full / x 3/12)	300,000	75,000
Augmented profits		348,000	44,900
		Marginal relief	*Small profits*

The accounting period ended 31 December 2011 falls partly into FY2010 (3 months) and partly into FY2011 (9 months).

As there has been a change in rate of tax the corporation tax liability must be calculated separately for each financial year.

(b) **Advantages of 31 March year end**

- Being aligned with the financial year will make it easier for a company to calculate its corporation tax liability, since the same rates, reliefs and legislation will apply throughout the accounting period.
- For owner-managed companies, alignment with the income tax year (the odd five days can be ignored) will make it easier as regards calculating the most tax efficient method of extracting profits from the company.

(2) (a) VAT return for quarter to 30 June 2012

Tutorial note

The appropriate rate of VAT for the quarter to 30 June 2012 is as follows:

- *If the figure excludes VAT, the VAT is 20%*
- *If the figure includes VAT, the VAT is 20/120 or 1/6.*

(i) **Goods**

The basic tax point for sale of the goods is the date of despatch (i.e. 20 June 2012).

Deposit received

Where payment is received before the basic tax point this becomes the actual tax point.

Output VAT of £833 (£5,000 × 1/6) should therefore be accounted for in respect of the deposit in the quarter to 30 June 2012.

Balance of invoice

Where an invoice is issued within 14 days of the basic tax point, the invoice date will become the actual tax point.

The actual tax point in respect of the invoice for the balance due of £25,000 is therefore 1 July 2012.

Output VAT will therefore not be due in respect of the invoice until the quarter ended 30 September 2012.

(ii) **Sales director's cars**

Purchase and sale of cars

As the sale director's new car is to be used partly for private purposes, input VAT is not recoverable in respect of the purchase of this car.

VAT would not have been reclaimed on the purchase of the sales director's old car, as this was also used for private purposes.

No output VAT is therefore charged on the sale of this car.

Fuel costs

The company can reclaim input VAT on the full cost of the fuel.

Input VAT of £100 (£600 × 1/6) should be reclaimed in the quarter to 30 June 2012.

As there is some private use of the cars output VAT, in respect of the private fuel, based on a prescribed scale charge, is payable in the quarter to 30 June 2012.

(iii) **Entertaining costs**

Input VAT of £167 (£1,000 × 1/6) is recoverable in respect of staff entertaining.

Input VAT of £83 (£500 × 1/6) in respect of entertaining UK customers is not recoverable.

(b) Implications of submitting and paying VAT late

The late submission of the VAT return for the quarter ended 30 September 2011 will have resulted in HM Revenue & Customs issuing a surcharge liability notice specifying a surcharge period running to 30 September 2012.

The late payment of VAT for the quarter ended 30 June 2012 will be the first default in the surcharge period.

A surcharge of 2% of the VAT due will be charged.

In addition, the surcharge period will be extended to 30 June 2013.

54 SCUBA LTD (ADAPTED) *Walk in the footsteps of a top tutor*

Key answer tips

This is a classic question testing your knowledge of corporation tax. There is a great deal of information to deal with and it is essential you have a methodical approach.

First draw up the proforma for the adjusted profit computation and insert the profit figure. Include in your computation both the items that need adjustment, with the relevant figure, **and** the items that do not need adjustment with a zero (0).

Before you can complete the adjusted profit computation you need to do workings to calculate capital allowances.

Then you can complete the calculation of taxable total profits and the corporation tax liability. Note carefully the information about associated companies.

Part (b) contains 11 marks for VAT and requires detailed knowledge of the default surcharge and the treatment of errors on a VAT return.

Remember that VAT is an important area in the syllabus and will always appear in the examination for about 10 marks and can be as high as 15 marks of the paper.

Tutor's top tips

It is important when answering questions as long as this, that you have a good technique for dealing with all the information.

You should read the question carefully and highlight key pieces of information as you go through.

Part (a) (i) is a standard adjustment of profits computation.

Remember that in the adjustment to profits calculation it is important to list all the major items indicated in the question requirement, showing a zero (0) for expenditure that is allowable. This is because credit will be given for showing no adjustment where none is needed. List the adjustments in the order they appear in the question.

If required, also add notes to show why you have not adjusted for an item, or why you have added it back. However, lengthy explanations are not required where the requirement is just to 'calculate' the adjusted profits, rather than to explain them.

Always show your workings if the figure you are adjusting for is not clear from the question.

(a) (i) **Trading profit – year ended 31 March 2012**

	£	£
Operating profit	198,400	
Depreciation and amortisation of lease	45,200	
Entertaining customers (Note 1)	7,050	
Entertaining employees (Note 1)	0	
Gifts to customers – diaries (Note 2)	0	
Gifts to customers – food hampers (Note 2)	1,600	
Deduction for lease premium (W1)		1,860
Capital allowances (W2)		64,780
	252,250	66,640
	(66,640)	
Trading profit	185,610	

Tutorial note

1. *The only exception to the non-deductibility of entertainment expenditure is when it is in respect of employees.*
2. *Gifts to customers are an allowable deduction if they cost less than £50 per recipient per year, are not of food, drink, tobacco, or vouchers for exchangeable goods, and carry a conspicuous advertisement for the company making the gift.*

   The gift of diaries is therefore allowable but the gift of hampers is not allowable.

Workings

(W1) **Deduction for lease premium**

The office building is used for business purposes, and so a proportion of the lease premium assessed on the landlord can be deducted.

Assessment on landlord:

	£
Premium received	80,000
Less: 2% x £80,000 x (20 – 1)	(30,400)
Assessment on landlord (Note)	49,600

This is deductible over the life of the lease, starting from 1 July 2011, so the deduction for the year ended 31 March 2012:

(£49,600 ÷ 20) × 9/12 = £1,860.

Tutorial note

Alternative calculation of the assessment on the landlord:

£80,000 x (51 – 20)/50 = £49,600

(W2) **Plant and machinery**

		Main pool	*Special rate pool*	*Motor car*	*Allow -ances*
	£	£	£	£	£
TWDV b/f		47,200		22,400	
Addition (no AIA) (Notes 1, 2 and 3):					
Car (CO_2 between 111 – 160 g/km)		10,400			
Car (CO_2 > 160 g/km)			15,400		
Additions (with AIA):					
Machinery	22,800				
Computer	1,100				
Machinery	7,300				
	31,200				
Less: AIA (Note 3)	(31,200)				31,200
		Nil			
Less: Disposal proceeds – Lorry		(12,400)			
		45,200			
Less: WDA (20%)		(9,040)			9,040
Less: WDA (10%)			(1,540)		1,540
Less: WDA (Restricted)				(3,000)	3,000
Additions qualifying for FYA:					
Car (CO_2 > 110 g/km)	20,000				
Less: FYA (100%)	(20,000)				20,000
		Nil			
TWDV c/f		36,160	13,860	19,400	
Total allowances					64,780

Tutorial note

1. *Brought forward 'expensive' cars are dealt with under the old rules. A WDA of 20% is available regardless of the car's CO_2 emissions; however, the total WDA for a 12 month period is restricted to £3,000.*
2. *New car purchases where the CO_2 emissions are between 111 – 160 g/km are put in the main pool, and are eligible for a WDA at 20%.*
3. *The private use of the motor car by the factory manager is irrelevant, full allowances are available. The manager will be assessed to income tax on the private use of the car as an employment benefit.*

(ii) **Corporation tax computation – year ended 31 March 2012**

> ***Tutor's top tips:***
>
> *A straightforward corporation tax computation is required in part (a) (ii) but first a property income computation must be calculated.*
>
> *These should have been easy marks to gain and full credit would be given for this part even if your trading profit computation in part (a) (i) is incorrect.*

	£
Trading profit (part (a) (i))	185,610
Property business profit (W1)	11,570
Interest	430
Taxable total profits	197,610
Corporation tax liability (W2) (£197,610 × 20%)	39,522

Workings

(W1) **Property business profit**

	£
Rent receivable	
(£7,200 x 1/3) = £2,400 per month × 8 months	19,200
Less: Decorating	(6,200)
Advertisements	(1,430)
Property business profit	11,570

(W2) **Corporation tax rates**

Scuba Ltd has no franked investment income, therefore the taxable total profits = Augmented profits.

Scuba Ltd has no associated companies and therefore augmented profits are compared to the full upper and lower limits of £1,500,000 and £300,000.

As augmented profits are £197,610, the company is a small profits company and therefore the rate of corporation tax is 20%.

(b) (i) **Default surcharge**

> ***Tutor's top tips***
>
> *This part of the question is an independent part on VAT which could have been answered first, before part (a).*
>
> *Popular topics were tested, namely the default surcharge rules and errors on a VAT return.*

There are easy marks to be gained here if you have learnt the rules, but difficult to score highly on if you have neglected VAT in your studies.

Remember that you will always have 10 to 15 marks on VAT in the exam.

- The late submission of the VAT return for the quarter ended 30 June 2009 will have resulted in HM Revenue & Customs issuing a surcharge liability notice specifying a surcharge period running to 30 June 2010.
- The late payment of VAT for the quarter ended 30 September 2009 will have resulted in a surcharge of £644 (£32,200 × 2%).
- The late payment of VAT for the quarter ended 31 March 2010 will have resulted in a surcharge of £170 (£3,400 × 5%), but this will not have been collected as it was less than £400.
- Although the VAT return for the quarter ended 30 June 2010 was submitted late, this will not have resulted in a surcharge as Scuba Ltd was due a refund for this period.
- The continued late submission of VAT returns will have resulted in the surcharge period being extended to 30 September 2010, then to 31 March 2011, and finally to 30 June 2011.
- Scuba Ltd then submitted the four consecutive VAT returns during the surcharge period running to 30 June 2011 on time, and so will have reverted to a clean default surcharge record.
- The late submission of the VAT return for the quarter ended 30 September 2011 will therefore result in a surcharge liability notice specifying a surcharge period running to 30 September 2012.

(ii) **Errors on VAT return**

- If the net errors total less than the higher of £10,000 or 1% of turnover (max £50,000), then they can be voluntarily disclosed by simply entering them on the VAT return for the quarter ended 31 March 2012.
- If the net errors total more than this limit, then they can be voluntarily disclosed, but disclosure must be made separately to HM Revenue & Customs.
- Default interest will be charged if the net errors total more than the limit.

Tutorial note

In either case a penalty for submitting an incorrect return can be charged.

However, it is unlikely that a penalty will be charged for an error due to a mistake, rather than a deliberate error, where the mistake is small enough to be disclosed on the next VAT return.

ACCA marking scheme			
			Marks
(a)	(i)	Trading profit	
		Operating profit	0.5
		Depreciation and amortisation	0.5
		Entertaining (Staff 0.5 Customers 0.5)	1.0
		Gifts to customers (Diaries 0.5 Food hampers 0.5)	1.0
		Lease premium – Assessable amount	1.5
		– Deduction	1.5
		P & M – Pool	2.0
		– Motor car	1.0
		– Special rate pool	2.0
		– AIA	2.0
		– Low emission car	2.0
			15.0
	(ii)	Corporation tax computation	
		Trading profit	0.5
		Property business profit	
		– Rent receivable	1.0
		– Expenses	1.0
		Interest	1.0
		Corporation tax	0.5
			4.0
(b)	(i)	Default surcharge	
		Quarter ended 30 June 2009	1.0
		Quarter ended 30 September 2009	1.0
		Quarter ended 31 March 2010	2.0
		Quarter ended 30 June 2010	1.0
		Extension of surcharge period	1.0
		Four consecutive VAT returns on time	1.0
		Quarter ended 30 September 2011	1.0
			8.0
	(ii)	Errors on VAT return	
		Net errors below limit	1.0
		Net errors above limit	1.0
		Default interest	1.0
			3.0
Total			30.0

55 WIRELESS LTD (ADAPTED) *Walk in the footsteps of a top tutor*

Key answer tips

This question has two independent parts.

Part (a) involved a classic corporation tax computation with the standard need to compute capital allowances. There was a small amount of overseas income to deal with in the computation but otherwise it is straightforward.

Part (b) covers various aspects of VAT, and is mainly written.

The highlighted words in the written sections are key phrases that markers are looking for.

Tutor's top tips

Part (a) (i) should be an easy 2 marks, although you must make sure that you have two separately identifiable points in your answer.

Note that the requirement is only for the definition of when an accounting period starts, not when it ends. Try not to waste time giving information which is not mark earning.

Part (b) on VAT could have been answered next to obtain some more relatively easy marks very quickly.

(a) (i) **Start of an accounting period for corporation tax purposes**

- An accounting period will normally start immediately after the end of the preceding accounting period.
- An accounting period will also start when a company commences to trade or when its profits otherwise become liable to corporation tax.

(ii) **Wireless Ltd**

Tutor's top tips

Most important in this part was the need to read the question carefully and only produce the taxable total profits for the company.

There is no requirement to calculate the tax liability and you should not waste time producing unnecessary computations that will waste time and earn no marks.

There were a few tricky bits, notably the director's remuneration: remember that the employer's NIC is deductible too.

Taxable total profits – period ended 31 March 2012

	£
Trading profit	95,626
Less: Director's remuneration (W1)	(25,198)
Capital allowances – Plant and machinery (W2)	(54,090)
	16,338
Loan interest	1,110
Overseas income (W3)	7,500
	24,948
Less: Gift Aid donation	(1,800)
Taxable total profits	23,148

Workings

(W1) **Director's remuneration**

The director's remuneration can be deducted as it was paid within nine months of the end of the period of account.

The employer's Class 1 NIC will be:

(£23,000 – £7,072) x 13·8% = £2,198

Total allowable deduction for employing director

(£23,000 salary + £2,198 employer's NIC) = £25,198

(W2) **Capital allowances – plant and machinery**

		Pool	*Allowances*
	£	£	£
Additions (no AIA or FYA) (Note 1):			
Car (CO_2 between 111 – 160 g/km)		10,600	
Additions (with AIA):			
Office equipment	10,400		
Machinery	10,200		
Van (Note 2)	15,000		
Computer and software (Note 3)	40,000		
Alterations	4,700		
	80,300		
Less: AIA (Note 4)	(50,000)		50,000
		30,300	
		40,900	
Less: WDA (20% × 6/12) (Note 4)		(4,090)	4,090
TWDV c/f		36,810	
Total allowances			54,090

Tutorial note

1. *Cars purchased with CO_2 emissions of between 111 – 160 g/km are put in main pool, and are eligible for WDA of 20%.*
2. *The CO_2 emissions are only relevant in relation to cars acquired after April 2009. A van is always a general pool addition.*
3. *Software is specifically deemed to be plant and machinery for capital allowances.*
4. *The maximum AIA must be time apportioned for a six month period, the maximum AIA is therefore £50,000 (£100,000 x 6/12).*
   WDAs are also restricted to 6/12 because of Wireless Ltd's short accounting period.
5. *The private use of the car is irrelevant, full allowances are available. The director will be assessed to income tax on the private use of the car as an employment benefit.*
6. *The office equipment purchased on 20 September 2011 is pre-trading and is treated as incurred on 1 October 2011.*

(W3) **Overseas income**

Overseas dividends

Overseas dividends are exempt from UK corporation tax.

As the dividends are received from an overseas subsidiary, they are group income and are not treated as Franked Investment Income.

Overseas branch profits

Overseas branch profits are taxable and DTR is available for withholding tax.

The gross amount of the branch profits must included in the taxable total profits calculation and is calculated as follows:

	£
Net branch profits	6,750
Plus: Withholding tax (£6,750 × 10/90)	750
Gross branch profits	7,500

Tutor's top tips

There is no need to calculate the Double Taxation Relief on branch profits as the corporation tax liability has not been asked for – only 'total taxable profits' is required.

(b) **VAT issues**

Tutor's top tips

The examiner was disappointed with the candidates' lack of VAT knowledge.

The VAT rules are not hard, they are however extensive but they will be examined. Emphasis in your revision must therefore be put into learning the VAT rules as there is a guaranteed 10% of the exam on VAT each sitting.

It is useful to use bullet points for this type of written answer. Try to at least match the number of bullet points with the number of marks available.

(i) **Compulsory registration**

- Wireless Ltd would have been liable to compulsory VAT registration when its taxable supplies during any 12-month period exceeded £73,000.
- This happened on 28 February 2012 when taxable supplies amounted to £87,100 (£9,700 + £18,200 + £21,100 + £14,800 + £23,300).
- Wireless Ltd would have had to notify HMRC by 30 March 2012, being 30 days after the end of the period.
- The company will have been registered from 1 April 2012 or from an agreed earlier date.

(ii) **Input VAT on goods purchased prior to registration**

- The goods must have been acquired for business purposes and not be sold or consumed prior to registration.
- The goods were acquired in the four years prior to VAT registration.

Input VAT on services supplied prior to registration

- The services must have been supplied for business purposes.
- The services were supplied in the six months prior to VAT registration.

(iii) **Advantage of voluntary registration**

- Wireless Ltd's sales are all to VAT registered businesses, so output VAT can be passed on to customers.
- The company's revenue would therefore not have altered if it had registered for VAT on 1 October 2011.
- However, registering for VAT on 1 October 2011 would have allowed all input VAT incurred from that date to be recovered.

(iv) **Additional information for a valid VAT invoice**

The following information is required:

(1) An identifying number (invoice number).

(2) Wireless Ltd's VAT registration number.

(3) The name and address of the customer.

(4) The type of supply.

(5) The rate of VAT for each supply.

(6) The quantity and a description of the goods supplied.

Examiner's report

Although fairly well answered, most candidates scored less marks on this question than on question one, despite it being potentially worth five marks more.

The first section of part (a) caused no problems for well prepared candidates.

The second section was also well answered, although many candidates were unsure as to what adjustment was necessary for the director's remuneration, and the related national insurance contributions, that had not been taken into account when preparing the draft accounts.

However, the VAT aspects in part (b) were not so well answered.

Few candidates appreciated when VAT registration would have been necessary, with many candidates basing their answer on the future test rather than the historical test.

As regards voluntary VAT registration, few candidates appreciated that the company's revenue would not have altered given that all its customers were VAT businesses.

Very few candidates could provide more than two or three of the six pieces of additional information that the company needed to show on its sales invoices in order for them to be valid for VAT purposes.

ACCA marking scheme			
			Marks
(a)	(i)	End of preceding accounting period	1.0
		Commencement of trading	1.0
			2.0
	(ii)	Trading profit	0.5
		Director's remuneration	1.0
		Employer's Class 1 NIC	1.5
		P & M – Car treated correctly	1.0
		– No Private use adjustment	0.5
		– Office equipment included	0.5
		– Van treated correctly	1.0
		– Software treated as P&M	1.0
		– Alterations treated as P&M	1.0
		– AIA restricted	1.0
		– WDA on bal of additions	0.5
		– WDA	1.0
		Loan interest	0.5
		Overseas income	2.0
		Gift Aid donation	1.0
			14.0
(b)	(i)	Registration limit	1.0
		February 2011	1.0
		Notification	1.0
		Date of registration	1.0
			4.0
	(ii)	Goods	
		Business purposes/Not sold or consumed	1.5
		Three year limit	1.0
		Services	
		Business purposes	0.5
		Six month limit	1.0
			4.0
	(iii)	Output VAT	1.0
		Revenue	1.0
		Input VAT	1.0
			3.0
	(iv)	An identifying number	0.5
		Wireless Ltd's VAT registration number	0.5
		The name and address of the customer	0.5
		The type of supply	0.5
		The rate of VAT for each supply	0.5
		Quantity and description	0.5
			3.0
Total			30.0

RELIEF FOR TRADING LOSSES

56 HALF-LIFE LTD (ADAPTED)

Key answer tips

A loss question which is largely computational but it involves the use of a normal ongoing trading loss, and a terminal loss.

There are two consecutive losses, the first arising from a short three month period. The second is the terminal loss of the last twelve months trading.

Make sure you give get the easy marks and give the dates required in part (b).

For ease, use a columnar format to present the loss offset in part (a) and remember to show your record of the losses and their usage.

(a) **Taxable total profits**

	y/e 31.3.09	y/e 31.3.10	y/e 31.3.11	p/e 30 .6.11	y/e 30.6.12
	£	£	£	£	£
Trading profit	224,000	67,400	38,200	Nil	Nil
Property income	8,200	12,200	6,500	4,400	–
Chargeable gains	–	–	5,600	–	23,700
	232,200	79,600	50,300	4,400	23,700
Less: Loss relief					
– p/e 30.6.11 loss			(50,300)	(4,400)	
– y/e 30.6.12 loss (W)	(174,150)	(79,600)			(23,700)
	58,050	Nil	Nil	Nil	Nil
Less: Gift Aid	(1,200)	wasted	–	–	wasted
Taxable total profits	56,850	Nil	Nil	Nil	Nil

Loss Memorandum

Loss for the period ended 30 June 2011	61,700	
Loss for the year ended 30 June 2012		308,800
Losses utilised:		
Current period claim		
– Period ended 30 June 2011	(4,400)	
12 month carry back claim		
– y/e 31 March 2011	(50,300)	
Current year claim		
– y/e 30 June 2012		(23,700)
36 month terminal loss carry back claim		
– y/e 31 March 2010		(79,600)
– y/e 31 March 2009 (W)		(174,150)
Losses unrelieved	7,000	31,350

Working: Terminal loss – set off in y/e 31.3.09

For the year ended 31 March 2009, loss relief is restricted to £174,150 (£232,200 × 9/12) as only 9 months of the year falls into the 36 months carry back period from the start of the final loss making accounting period.

Tutorial note

The trading loss for the period ended 30 June 2011 can be relieved against total profits of the current period and the previous 12 months.

The trading loss for the year ended 30 June 2012 can be relieved against total profits of the current year and the previous 36 months because it is a terminal loss.

Unrelieved Gift Aid Donations

Gift Aid of £1,000 and £700 for respectively the year ended 31 March 2010 and the year ended 30 June 2012 are unrelieved.

(b) **Due date for loss relief claims**

- The loss relief claims against total profits in respect of the loss for the period ended 30 June 2011 must be made by 30 June 2013.
- The loss relief claims against total profits in respect of the loss for the year ended 30 June 2012 must be made by 30 June 2014.

(c) **Corporation tax repayments**

Year ended 31 March 2009

- Corporation tax of £36,571 (£174,150 at 21%) will be repaid in respect of the year ended 31 March 2009, since the relevant tax rate both before and after the loss relief claim is 21%.

Year ended 31 March 2010

- Taxable total profits for the year ended 31 March 2010 were originally £78,600 (£79,600 – £1,000 Gift Aid)
- Taxable total profits after loss relief is £Nil
- Corporation tax of £16,506 (£78,600 at 21%) will be repaid.

Year ended 31 March 2011

- Taxable total profits for the year ended 31 March 2011 were originally £50,300
- Taxable total profits after loss relief is £Nil
- Corporation tax of £10,563 (£50,300 at 21%) will be repaid.

57 LOSER LTD (ADAPTED)

Key answer tips

A tricky question on corporation tax loss reliefs. There are two trading losses to deal with and it is important to deal with the earlier loss first. It is also important to lay out your answer using a standard proforma.

(a) **Factors influencing the choice of loss reliefs**

- The rate of corporation tax at which relief will be obtained, with preference being given to profits charged at the marginal rate of 27.5% in FY2011 (29.75% in earlier years) and the main rate of 26% in FY2011 (28% in earlier years).
- The timing of the relief obtained, with a claim against total profits in the current year and previous 12 months resulting in earlier relief than a claim to carry forward the loss against future trading profits.
- The extent to which relief for Gift Aid payments will be lost, since these cannot be carried forward.

(b) **Loser Ltd – Taxable total profits**

	y/e 30 June 2009	*p/e 31 March 2010*	*y/e 31 March 2011*	*y/e 31 March 2012*
	£	£	£	£
Trading profit	86,600	Nil	27,300	Nil
Property profit	–	4,500	8,100	5,600
Total profits	86,600	4,500	35,400	5,600
Less: Loss relief				
– Current period		(4,500)		(5,600)
– 12 months c/b	(21,200)		(35,400)	
	65,400	Nil	Nil	Nil
Less: Gift Aid	(1,400)	wasted	wasted	wasted
Taxable total profits	64,000	Nil	Nil	Nil

Loss working

Trading loss	25,700	78,300
Loss against total profits		
– Current period (p/e 31.3.10)	(4,500)	
– 12 month carry back (y/e 30.6.09)	(21,200)	
– Current period (y/e 31.3.12)		(5,600)
– 12 month carry back (y/e 31.3.11)		(35,400)
Loss carried forward	Nil	37,300

(c) **If Loser Ltd ceased to trade on 31 March 2012**

- The whole of the trading loss for the final twelve months of trading can be relieved against total profits for the previous 36 months under the terminal loss relief rules.
- Therefore the unrelieved losses of £37,300 could have been carried back and fully set off in the year ended 30 June 2009.

ACCA marking scheme		
		Marks
(a)	Rate of corporation tax	1.0
	Timing of relief	1.0
	Gift Aid	1.0
		3.0
(b)	Trading profit	0.5
	Property business profit	0.5
	Loss relief – current and carry back 12 months	2.0
	Gift Aid	1.0
	Unrelieved trading loss	1.0
		5.0
(c)	Terminal loss relief – carry back 36 months	
	Year ended 30 June 2009	2.0
		2.0
Total		10.0

58 SOFA LTD (ADAPTED) *Online question assistance*

Key answer tips

The first part of this question involves a standard adjustment of profit computation where the company is loss making. A detailed capital allowances computation is required and care should be taken as there are many places where this computation could go wrong.

The second part is more difficult and requires detailed group relief knowledge and the calculation of the maximum surrender possible to three subsidiaries including one with a non-coterminous year end and another which only joined the group part way through the year.

The part is independent and could be answered first, before part (a), as the question tells you to assume a loss of £200,000.

(a) **Trading loss – year ended 31 March 2012**

Tutorial note:

An adjustment to profits calculation is required and the fact that the company is making a loss should not change your approach in any way.

Just start with a negative figure for the loss, then make the same adjustments as you would make if it were a profit and lay out your answer in the same way.

Remember that it is important to list all the major items indicated in the question requirement, showing a zero (0) for expenditure that is allowable. This is because credit will be given for showing no adjustment where none is needed.

List the adjustments in the order they appear in the question.

If required, also add notes to show why you have not adjusted for an item, or why you have added it back. However, lengthy explanations are not required where the requirement is just to 'calculate' the adjusted profits, rather than to explain them.

Always show your workings if the figure you are adjusting for is not clear from the question.

	£	£
Loss before taxation	(240,000)	
Depreciation	150,820	
Audit and accountancy (Note 1)	0	
Legal fees – issue of share capital (Note 2)	7,800	
Legal fees – renewal of 10 year lease (Note 3)	0	
Legal fees – issue of loan note (Note 2)	0	
Construction of new wall (Note 4)	9,700	
Repairing wall (Note 4)	0	
Entertaining suppliers (Note 5)	1,360	
Entertaining employees (Note 5)	0	
Counselling employees (Note 6)	0	
Health and safety fine	420	
Profit on disposal of shares		4,300
Bank interest received		8,400
Interest payable (Note 7)	0	
Capital allowances – Plant and machinery (W1)		118,100
	(69,900)	130,800
	(130,800)	
Trading loss	(200,700)	

Tutorial note

1. *Audit and accountancy is allowable, as incurred wholly and exclusively for the purposes of the trade.*
2. *Legal fees in connection with the issue of share capital are not allowable, being capital in nature. However, the cost of obtaining loan finance is allowable as a trading expense under the loan relationship rules as the loan was used for trading purposes.*
3. *The cost of renewing a short-lease (less than 50 years) is specifically allowable as a trading expense.*
4. *The new wall is not allowable, being capital in nature. However, repairing a wall is allowable.*
5. *The only exception to the non-deductibility of entertainment expenditure is when it is in respect of employees.*
6. *The costs of counselling services for redundant employees are specifically allowable.*
7. *Interest on a loan used for trading purposes is deductible in calculating the trading loss on an accruals basis.*

Workings

(W1) **Plant and machinery – Capital allowances computation**

Tutorial note

1. *Capital allowances on new car purchases are now calculated based on the CO_2 emissions of the car as follows:*

   CO_2 emissions of < 111 g/km:
   eligible for a FYA of 100%.

   CO_2 emissions of between 111 – 160 g/km:
   put in main pool, eligible for a WDA at 20%.

   CO_2 emissions of > 160 g/km:
   put in special rate pool, eligible for a WDA at 10%.

   The appropriate rates are given in the tax rates and allowances.

2. *Remember to include the expenditure on the fixtures and fittings in the second hand building as they are eligible for plant and machinery allowances.*

		Pool	*Expensive Car*	*Special rate pool*	*Allow-ances*
	£	£	£	£	£
TWDV b/f		16,700	16,400		
Additions (No AIA or FYA) (Note 1):					
Car (CO_2 > 160 g/km)				22,200	
Car (CO_2 between 111 – 160 g/km)		10,900			
Additions (with AIA):					
Equipment	61,400				
Fixtures (Note 2)	44,800				
	106,200				
Less :AIA (Max)	(100,000)				100,000
		6,200			
Disposal proceeds: Expensive Car			(17,800)		
Car (2)		(8,800)			
Lorry		(7,600)			
		17,400	(1,400)	22,200	
Balancing charge			1,400		(1,400)
WDA (20%)		(3,480)			3,480
WDA (10%)				(2,220)	2,220
Additions with FYA					
Car (CO_2 < 111 g/km)	13,800				
Less: FYA (100%)	(13,800)				13,800
		Nil			
TWDV c/f		13,920		19,980	
Total allowances					118,100

(b) **Maximum group relief**

Settee Ltd

The accounting periods of Settee Ltd and Sofa Ltd are not coterminous. Therefore, Settee Ltd's taxable total profits and Sofa Ltd's trading loss must be apportioned on a time basis.

Year ended 31 March 2012 and year ended 30 June 2011

The corresponding accounting period is 1 April 2011 to 30 June 2011 (3 months)

Year ended 31 March 2012 and year ended 30 June 2012

The corresponding accounting period is 1 July 2011 to 31 March 2012 (9 months)

Settee Ltd can therefore claim the following group relief:

CAP to 30 June 2011

Sofa Ltd can surrender (3/12 × £200,000)	£50,000
Settee Ltd can accept (3/12 × £240,000)	£60,000

Therefore maximum loss claim is £50,000.

CAP to 30 June 2012

Sofa Ltd can surrender (9/12 × £200,000)	£150,000
Settee Ltd can claim (9/12 × £90,000)	£67,500

Therefore maximum loss claim is £67,500.

Couch Ltd

Couch Ltd is not a 75% subsidiary of Sofa Ltd, so no group relief claim is possible.

Futon Ltd

Futon Ltd did not commence trading until 1 January 2012, so the corresponding accounting period is the 3 months from 1 January 2012 to 31 March 2012.

Sofa Ltd can surrender (3/12 × £200,000)	£50,000
Futon Ltd can claim	£60,000

Therefore maximum loss claim is £50,000.

Examiner's report

Part (a) of this question was very well answered.

A certain amount of bad examination technique was evident as regards the adjustments in computing the trading loss.

Some candidates went into far too much detail explaining the adjustments made, thus wasting time, whilst others produced figures without any workings at all. This was fine for correct answers, but not so for incorrect ones.

Where no adjustment was necessary, such as for the interest payable, then this fact should have been clearly shown or stated.

Most candidates did not answer part (b) very well.

Many candidates wasted a lot time by performing detailed calculations showing the amount of group relief that should have been claimed rather than the amount that actually could be claimed.

ACCA marking scheme			
			Marks
(a)	Loss before taxation		0.5
	Depreciation		0.5
	Professional fees		2.5
	Repairs and renewals		1.0
	Other expenses		2.5
	Profit on disposal of shares		0.5
	Bank interest received		0.5
	Interest payable		1.0
	P & M	– Purchases	1.5
		– Expensive motor car sold	1.5
		– Special rate motor car acquired	1.0
		– Fixtures	1.0
		– AIA and WDA	3.0
		– Balancing charge	1.0
		– Pool items sold	1.0
		– Low emission car	1.0
			20.0
(b)	Settee Ltd		2.5
	Couch Ltd		1.0
	Futon Ltd		1.5
			5.0
Total			25.0

59 JOGGER LTD (ADAPTED) *Walk in the footsteps of a top tutor*

Key answer tips

This question was difficult in that it included several topics that students are traditionally uncomfortable with, namely: losses; lease premiums; and associated companies.

However, the question still contained some straight forward marks which should have been obtained.

Tutor's top tips

As with many F6 questions, at first sight the question may seem daunting. However, if you approach it with care, you should be able to score well. It is easy to see a question such as this and panic. However, there is no need. A good layout and calm approach is necessary.

Part (i) is straight forward, once you see past the loss.

Part (ii) requires a little manipulation to account for the lease premium and the associated companies. Once these areas are dealt with the computational side of the question is not difficult.

Part (iii) deals with the implications of missing filing deadlines, and is a straightforward test of knowledge retention.

(a) (i) **Jogger Ltd – Trading loss for the year ended 31 March 2012**

	£	£
Operating loss (Note)	(56,400)	
Depreciation	12,340	
Capital allowances – Plant and machinery (W1)		110,060
	(44,060)	110,060
	(110,060)	
Tax adjusted trading loss	(154,120)	

Tutorial note

As requested in the question, the model answer starts with the operating loss and therefore only depreciation and capital allowances need to be adjusted for.

However, the original question did not specify which figure to start with.

The normal start point is the profit before tax. The examiner could have asked you to start the computation with the profit before tax of £268,000. You would then have needed to deduct all of the sources of income from investments of £222,060 and the profit on the disposal of shares of £102,340 to give a loss of £56,400.

In this instance, starting with the operating loss of £56,400 is therefore an acceptable short cut which saves time in the exam.

However, since setting this question, the examiner has stated in an article that he will in future always give the starting point. He will also ask you to list all of the items referred to in the question which may impact on the adjustment of profits computation, and to indicate with the use of a zero (0) any items that do not require adjustment.

(W1) **Capital Allowances**

	£	*Main pool* £	*Exp car* £	*SR pool* £	*Allow-ances* £
TWDV b/f		21,600	8,800		
Additions (no AIA or FYA) (Note 1):					
Car (CO_2 between 111 – 160 g/km)		11,800			
Additions (with AIA):					
Air-conditioning (Note 2)	120,000				
Less: AIA (Note 3)	(100,000)				100,000
				20,000	
Furniture	30,000				
Less: AIA	(Nil)				
		30,000			
Disposal proceeds (Note 4)		(8,600)	(11,700)		
		54,800	(2,900)		
Balancing charge			2,900		(2,900)
Less: WDA (20%)/(10%)		(10,960)		(2,000)	12,960
TWDV c/f		43,840		18,000	
Total allowances					110,060

Tutorial note

1. *A car purchased with CO_2 emissions of between 111 – 160 g/km is put into the general pool and is eligible for a WDA of 20%. Cars are not eligible for the AIA.*
2. *The air-conditioning has an expected life of 25 years and is therefore a long-life asset. The company has spent more than £100,000 on such assets in the year and the air-conditioning unit is therefore included in the special rate pool.*
3. *The AIA is allocated to the special rate pool additions in priority to the general pool additions. The maximum AIA of £100,000 is therefore all allocated to the air-conditioning unit.*
4. *The proceeds of both disposals were less than the original cost of the asset; therefore the disposal proceeds are deducted.*

(ii) **Corporation tax computation – year ended 31 March 2012**

	£
Trading profits	Nil
Property income (W1)	126,000
Bank interest	8,460
Loan interest (£16,400 + £8,200)	24,600
Chargeable gain	98,300
Total profits	257,360
Less: Loss relief – Current year claim	(154,120)
Taxable total profits	103,240
Plus: FII (£45,000 × 100/90)	50,000
Augmented profits	153,240
Corporation tax (£103,240 × 26%) (W2)	26,842
Less: Marginal relief	
3/200 x (£500,000 – £153,240) × £103,240/£153,240	(3,504)
Corporation tax liability	23,338

Workings

(W1) **Property income**

	£
Premium received	100,000
Less: 2% x £100,000 x (10 – 1)	(18,000)
Assessment on premium	82,000
Rent receivable	44,000
Property income	126,000

Tutorial note

Alternative calculation of the assessment on the premium:

£100,000 x (51 – 10)/50 = £82,000

(W2) **Corporation tax rates**

Jogger Ltd has two associated companies, therefore the lower and upper limits are:

Lower limit = £100,000 (£300,000 x 1/3)

Upper limit = £500,000 (£1,500,000 x 1/3)

As augmented profits are £153,240, marginal relief applies.

(iii) **Implications of late filing and payment**

- Jogger Ltd's self-assessment tax return for the year ended 31 March 2012 must be submitted by 31 March 2013.
- If the company submits its self-assessment tax return eight months late, then there will be an automatic fixed penalty of £200, since the return is more than three months late.
- There will also be an additional corporation tax related penalty of £2,334 being 10% of the tax unpaid, since the self-assessment tax return is more than six months late.

Tutorial note

The tax geared penalty starts when 18 months or more have passed after the end of the return period (i.e. this is the same as saying 6 months or more after the filing date).

(b) **VAT**

Tutor's top tips

Part (b) was quite difficult, as it required students to recall a large amount of knowledge regarding various different VAT issues which is not difficult if learnt, but extremely difficult if neglected in revision.

VAT is an important area and students should take care to ensure that all areas of the syllabus are covered as the 11 marks available for this particular part of the question were challenging.

When answering written elements in the exam; keep your comments short and to the point.

One mark will be available for a well explained point. Don't take the opportunity to write everything you know about VAT. Keep your comments relevant to the question.

(i) **Implications of late filing and payment of VAT returns**

- The late submission of the return for the quarter ended 30 September 2010 will have resulted in HMRC issuing a surcharge liability notice specifying a surcharge period running to 30 September 2011.
- The late payment of VAT for the quarter ended 31 March 2011 will have resulted in a surcharge of £778 (£38,900 × 2%).
- The surcharge period will also have been extended to 31 March 2012.
- Although Jogger Ltd then submitted three consecutive VAT returns during this surcharge period on time, this was insufficient to revert to a clean default surcharge record.
- The late payment of VAT for the quarter ended 31 March 2012 will therefore have resulted in a surcharge of £4,455 (£89,100 × 5%).
- The surcharge period will also have been extended to 31 March 2013.

(ii) **Benefits and conditions of using the Annual Accounting Scheme**

- The reduced administration from only having to submit one VAT return each year should mean that default surcharges are avoided in respect of the late submission of VAT returns.
- In addition, making payments on account based on the previous year's VAT liability will improve both budgeting and possibly cash flow where a business is expanding.
- Jogger Ltd can apply to use the annual accounting scheme if its expected taxable turnover for the next 12 months does not exceed £1,350,000 exclusive of VAT.
- In addition, the company must be up to date with its VAT returns.

Examiner's report

This question was generally well answered, and it was pleasing to see many very good answers for the VAT aspects in part (b).

When calculating the trading loss a number of candidates made this far more complicated than necessary by commencing with the profit before taxation figure rather than the operating loss figure.

Those candidates who attempted to combine the first two aspects of part (a) into one computation generally had difficulty, and can only be advised to deal with each requirement separately.

Those few candidates who treated the dividend income as part of the taxable total profits cannot expect to pass this examination.

In part (b) surprisingly few candidates knew the turnover limit applicable to the annual accounting scheme.

ACCA marking scheme

			Marks
(a)	(i)	Operating loss	0.5
		Depreciation	0.5
		P&M – Pool	2.0
		P&M – Expensive car	1.5
		P&M – Long life asset	1.0
		P& M – Furniture	0.5
		P&M – Allocation of AIA	1.0
			7.0

			Marks
	(ii)	Property income	2.0
		Bank interest	0.5
		Loan interest	1.0
		Chargeable gain	0.5
		Loss relief	1.0
		Franked investment income	1.0
		Corporation tax	2.0
			8.0
	(iii)	Due date	1.0
		Fixed penalty	1.5
		Corporation tax related penalty	1.5
			4.0
(b)	(i)	Q/e 30.09.10	2.0
		Q/e 31.03.11	2.0
		Q/e 31.03.12	2.0
			6.0
	(ii)	One VAT return	1.5
		Payments on account	1.5
		Limit	1.0
		VAT returns	1.0
			5.0
Total			30.0

60 VOLATILE LTD (ADAPTED) *Walk in the footsteps of a top tutor*

Key answer tips

A familiar style corporation tax losses question requiring relief to be claimed as soon as possible and a calculation of the loss left to carry forward.

Tutor's top tips

Part (a) requires a purely written answer highlighting the key factors that influence the choice of loss relief.

Only 3 marks are available, suggesting that 3 bullet points will suffice to answer this part.

This requirement is a common request in losses questions and you should learn the factors so that you can jot them down quickly in the exam.

(a) **Factors influencing the choice of loss reliefs**

- Rate of relief

  The rate of corporation tax at which relief will be obtained is an important factor. Preference should be given to profits charged at the marginal rate of 27.5% (29.75% prior to FY2011) first, then profits charged at the main rate of 26% (28% prior to FY2011) and lastly profits charged at the small profits rate of 20% (21% prior to FY2011).

- Cash flow

  The timing of the relief obtained is a key factor. A claim against total profits in the loss making period, then carry back will result in earlier relief than a claim against future trading profits.

- Wastage of Gift Aid donations

  The extent to which relief for Gift Aid donations will be lost is another factor, since these cannot be carried forward.

Tutorial note

Remember that for companies, a carry back election cannot be made until the current year total profits have been relieved first.

(b) **Taxable total profits**

	y/e 31 Dec 2009	*9 m/e 30 Sept 2010*	*y/e 30 Sept 2011*
	£	£	£
Trading profit	15,200	78,700	Nil
Property business profit	6,500	–	–
Chargeable gains	–	–	9,700
Total profits	21,700	78,700	9,700
Less: Loss relief (W)			
Current year			(9,700)
Carry back – 12 months	(5,425)	(78,700)	
	16,275	Nil	Nil
Less: Gift Aid	(1,200)	wasted	wasted
Taxable total profits	15,075	Nil	Nil

Loss working

	£
Trading loss	101,800
Current year relief (Note)	(9,700)
Carry back relief (previous 12 months)	
– 9 m/e 30 September 2010	(78,700)
	13,400
– y/e 30 September 2009 (£21,700 x 3/12)	(5,425)
Unrelieved loss as at 30 September 2011	7,975

Tutorial note

For the year ended 31 December 2009 loss relief is restricted to lower of:

(i) *proportion of the profits of that period of account that falls into the 12 months carry back period preceding 1 October 2010 (i.e. 3 months)*

= (£21,700 × 3/12) = £5,425

(ii) *Remainder of the loss = £13,400*

Examiner's report

This question was not particularly well answered.

In part (a) far too many candidates explained the loss reliefs available rather than the factors influencing the choice of claims.

In part (b) many candidates approached this on a year by year basis, rather than one computation with a column for each of the periods. This not only wasted time in having to write out several computations, but also made it very difficult to calculate the correct loss relief claims.

Other common mistakes included treating the chargeable gains separately (rather than as part of the taxable total profits), and deducting gift aid donations from trading profits rather than total income after loss relief.

ACCA marking scheme

		Marks
(a)	Rate of corporation tax	1.0
	Timing of relief	1.0
	Impact on Gift Aid donations	1.0
		3.0
(b)	Trading profits	0.5
	Property business profits	0.5
	Chargeable gains	0.5
	Loss relief – Year ended 30 September 2011	1.0
	– Period ended 30 September 2010	1.0
	– Year ended 31 December 2009	2.0
	Gift Aid donations	1.0
	Unrelieved trading losses	0.5
		7.0
Total		10.0

WITH GROUP ASPECTS

61 STRAIGHT PLC (ADAPTED)

Key answer tips

This question starts with a diagram of a group but most of the marks in the question can be obtained without having to think about the group aspects at all. However, be careful to answer the question set, so that in part (a) you are asked simply to calculate the trading profit.

When writing an explanation of why the companies form a gains group, it is important to give enough detail in your answer and to apply your knowledge to the facts of the question. A calculation of the effective interest of Straight plc in each of the companies is necessary to illustrate your answer.

(a) **Tax adjusted trading profit – year ended 31 March 2012**

	£	£
Operating profit	173,915	
Depreciation	21,200	
Car lease costs (15% x £8,500) (Note 1)	1,275	
Entertaining customers (Note 2)	10,000	
Entertaining staff (Note 2)	0	
Fine (Note 3)	1,250	
Capital allowances (W)		22,640
	207,640	22,640
	(22,640)	
Tax adjusted trading profit	185,000	

Tutorial note

1. *A flat rate disallowance of 15% of the leasing costs applies to cars with CO_2 emissions exceeding 160 g/km. Note that there is no disallowance for cars with CO_2 emissions 160 g/km or less.*
2. *The only exception to the non-deductibility of entertainment expenditure is when it is in respect of employees.*

   The £150 limit per head for staff entertaining is only relevant in determining whether the party represents a taxable benefit on the employees, all of the cost is an allowable deduction for the company.
3. *Fines for breach of regulations are disallowable.*

Working: Plant and machinery capital allowances

		Main pool	Expensive car	Allowances
	£	£	£	£
TWDV b/f		35,200	18,400	
Addition (with AIA)	12,400			
Less: AIA	(12,400)			12,400
		Nil		
Disposal proceeds			(15,200)	
		35,200	3,200	
Balancing allowance			(3,200)	3,200
Less: WDA (20%)		(7,040)		7,040
TWDV c/f		28,160		
Total allowances				22,640

(b) (i) **Capital gains group**

- Companies form a capital gains group if at each level in the group structure there is a 75% shareholding.
- The parent company must have an effective interest of over 50% in each group company.
- Arc Ltd, Bend Ltd and Curve Ltd are all 75% subsidiaries, and Straight plc has an effective interest of 100% in Arc Ltd, 80% in Bend Ltd and 60% (80% × 75%) in Curve Ltd.
- If Straight plc's holding in Arc Ltd were 80%, it would have an effective interest of less than 50% in Curve Ltd (80% × 80% × 75% = 48%).

(ii) **Corporation tax computation – year ended 31 March 2012**

	£
Trading profit (part (a))	185,000
Less: Loss relief b/f	(15,000)
	170,000
Net chargeable gains (W1)	70,000
Taxable total profits	240,000
Plus: FII (£9,000 x 100/90) (Note)	10,000
Augmented profits	250,000
Corporation tax (W2) (£240,000 at 26%)	62,400
Less: Marginal relief	
3/200 × (£375,000 – £250,000) × £240,000/£250,000	(1,800)
Corporation tax payable	60,600

Tutorial note

Group dividends are not included as franked investment income. Therefore only the dividend from Triangle plc is included in the calculation of augmented profits.

Workings

(W1) **Net chargeable gain**

	£
Chargeable gain	140,000
Less: Rollover relief (see below)	(60,000)
Chargeable gains after rollover relief	80,000
Less: Capital loss b/f	(10,000)
Net chargeable gain	70,000

The sale proceeds of £80,000 (£350,000 – £270,000) is not reinvested in qualifying business assets.

Therefore £80,000 of the £140,000 gain will be chargeable in the year ended 31 March 2012.

A rollover relief claim can be made to defer the balance of the gain of £60,000 (£140,000 – 80,000). The gain is rolled over against the base cost of the replacement asset.

(W2) **Corporation tax rates**

		£
Upper limit	(£1,500,000 x 1/4)	375,000
Lower limit	(£300,000 x 1/4)	75,000
Augmented profits		250,000
		Marginal relief applies

There are four associated companies in the group

(iii) **Joint election for capital gains**

- Straight plc and Arc Ltd must make the election by 31 March 2014 (i.e. within two years of the end of the accounting period of the company making the disposal outside of the group).
- Arc Ltd's unused capital loss of £40,000 can be set against Straight plc's gain of £70,000, leaving £30,000 net chargeable gain.
- This is beneficial as relief for the capital loss is obtained at the highest marginal rate of corporation tax in FY2011 of 27.5%, and would otherwise be unused and carried forward.

62 ANIMAL LTD (ADAPTED)

Key answer tips

A familiar style of group loss relief question requiring group losses to be allocated to group members in the most beneficial manner.

The group relief calculations are quite tricky, involving companies joining and leaving the group and recognising the different rates of tax paid by the group members. The examiner has however made the question slightly easier by telling you how many associated companies to use when calculating the small profits limits.

Note also that 40% of the marks for this question do not relate to the group relief calculations – so do not get bogged down in these and make sure you pick up the marks for the written sections which were easy marks if the relevant definitions had been learnt.

There were easy marks available for explaining the definition of a group for group loss relief purposes. Note that for 3 marks you would expect to make three separate points.

Similarly there were three easy marks for explaining when companies are associated. The examiner has kindly given you additional guidance by stating how many associates there are in the Animal Ltd group. Again for three marks you would be expected to make three separate points.

(a) **Group relief group**

- One company must be a 75% subsidiary of the other, or both companies must be 75% subsidiaries of a third company.
- The holding company must have an effective interest of at least 75% of the subsidiary's ordinary share capital.
- The holding company must have the right to receive at least 75% of the subsidiary's distributable profits and net assets on a winding up.

(b) **Associated companies**

- Bat Ltd, Cat Ltd, Dog Ltd, Fox Ltd and Gnu Ltd are all under the common control (shareholding of over 50%) of Animal Ltd, and are therefore associated companies.
- Where a company such as Elk Ltd has been dormant throughout the accounting period, it does not count as an associated company.
- Companies that are only associated for part of the accounting period, such as Cat Ltd and Dog Ltd, count as associated companies for the whole of the period.

(c) **Taxable total profits – year ended 31 March 2012**

	Animal Ltd	*Bat Ltd*	*Cat Ltd*	*Dog Ltd*	*Fox Ltd*
	£	£	£	£	£
Trading profit	450,000	65,000	85,000	100,000	60,000
Property income	5,000	15,000			
	455,000	80,000	85,000	100,000	60,000
Less: Group relief (W)	(95,000)	(30,000)	(35,000)	(25,000)	(15,000)
Taxable total profits	360,000	50,000	50,000	75,000	45,000

Reasons for group relief strategy

- The primary aim for the group is to save as much tax as possible when utilising the loss.
- Gnu Ltd's trading loss is most effectively relieved so as to bring the augmented profits of as many group companies as possible down to the small profits rate limit (see working below).
- The relevant lower and upper limits for corporation tax purposes are £50,000 (£300,000 ÷ 6) and £250,000 (£1,500,000 ÷ 6) respectively.

Tutorial note

It has been assumed that neither Cat Ltd nor Dog Ltd have any further associated companies arising from the periods when they were not part of the Animal Ltd group of companies.

- Given the level of TTP and FII, Gnu Ltd should bring the augmented profits of Bat Ltd, Cat Ltd, Dog Ltd and Fox Ltd down to £50,000.

  This saves corporation tax at the highest marginal rate of 27.5%.
- As Dog Ltd has only been part of the group for three months of the year, group relief is restricted to a maximum of £25,000, being 3/12ths of its TTP (£100,000 x 3/12).
- Cat Ltd left the group part way through the year, however loss relief given to Cat Ltd is not restricted as the maximum group relief is the lower of the available loss of Gnu Ltd (£200,000) and the available profits of Cat Ltd of £63,750 (£85,000 x 9/12). Only £35,000 loss is required to bring its augmented profits down to £60,000.
- The balance of Gnu Ltd's trading loss of £95,000 (£200,000 – £30,000 – £35,000 – £25,000 – £15,000) is surrendered to Animal Ltd.

  This saves corporation tax at the main rate of 26%.

Working: Augmented profits

	Animal Ltd	*Bat Ltd*	*Cat Ltd*	*Dog Ltd*	*Fox Ltd*
	£	£	£	£	£
TTP before group relief	455,000	80,000	85,000	100,000	60,000
Plus: FII	20,000				5,000
Augmented profits	475,000	80,000	85,000	100,000	65,000
Lower limit	50,000	50,000	50,000	50,000	50,000
Group relief required to bring to lower limit	425,000	30,000	35,000	75,000	15,000
Rate of tax saving	26%	27.5%	27.5%	27.5%	27.5%

ACCA marking scheme

		Marks
(a)	75% subsidiary	1.0
	Ordinary share capital	1.0
	Distributable profits/Net assets	1.0
		3.0
(b)	Identification of companies	1.0
	Dormant companies	1.0
	Associated for part of accounting period	1.0
		3.0
(c)	Trading profits	1.0
	Property business income	0.5
	Group relief – Relevant limits	1.0
	Group relief – Tax rates	1.0
	Group relief – Animal Ltd	1.0
	Group relief – Bat Ltd	0.5
	Group relief – Cat Ltd	1.0
	Group relief – Dog Ltd	1.0
	Group relief – Fox Ltd	1.0
	FII	1.0
		9.0
Total		15.0

63 TOCK-TICK LTD (ADAPTED)

Key answer tips

A long question requiring a computation of corporation tax with some group aspects included as a separate requirement.

It is important to have a methodical way of working through the question so you do not miss any important information. Use the standard proformas for adjustment of profit and for capital allowances.

When considering the group aspects in part (c), don't forget that a subsidiary is counted as an associate, so reducing the small profits limits for calculating corporation tax.

(a) **Tax adjusted trading profit – year ended 31 March 2012**

Key answer tips

In the adjustment to profits calculation it is important to list all the major items indicated in the question requirement, showing a zero (0) for expenditure that is allowable.

This is because credit will be given for showing no adjustment where none is needed. List the adjustments in the order they appear in the question.

If required, also add notes to show why you have not adjusted for an item, or why you have added it back. However, lengthy explanations are not required where the requirement is just to 'calculate' the adjusted profits, rather than to explain them.

Always show your workings if the figure you are adjusting for is not clear from the question.

Tutorial note

1. *Impaired debts charged in accordance with financial accounting guidelines by a company are allowable for tax purposes, as they will be specific in nature.*
2. *Gifts to customers are an allowable deduction if they cost less than £50 per recipient per year, are not of food, drink, tobacco, or vouchers exchangeable for goods, and carry a conspicuous advertisement for the company making the gift.*

   Therefore the gift of the pens is allowable, but the gift of hampers of food is not allowable.
3. *The long service award is deductible in calculating the trading profit.*
4. *The Gift Aid donation is allowable as a deduction from total profits in the company's taxable total profits computation. It is not also allowable in the adjustment of profits computation, therefore it must be added back in this computation.*

   Small gifts to local charities, where the company receives some benefit (e.g. advertising) are an allowable deduction from the adjustment of profits.
5. *Audit and accountancy fees, costs of registering a trademark and debt collection fees are all allowable as incurred wholly and exclusively for the purposes of the trade.*
6. *Legal fees in connection with the issue of share capital are not allowable, being capital in nature. However, legal fees in connection with the* ***re****newal of a* ***short*** *lease (i.e. life of 50 years or less) are specifically allowable.*
7. *The replacement of the roof is allowable since the whole structure is not being replaced. The office extension is not allowable, being capital in nature.*
8. *The only exception to the non-deductibility of entertainment expenditure is when it is in respect of employees.*
9. *The costs of counselling services for redundant employees and of seconding an employee to charity are allowable.*
10. *Interest on a loan used for trading purposes is deductible in calculating the trading profit* on an accruals basis.

	£	£
Profit before taxation	186,960	
Impaired debts (Note 1)	0	
Depreciation	99,890	
Gifts to customers – pens (Note 2)	0	
Gifts to customers – food hampers (Note 2)	720	
Donation to political party	6,450	
Long service awards (Note 3)	0	
Gift Aid donation (Note 4)	600	
Donation to local charity (Note 4)	0	
Audit and accountancy (Note 5)	0	
Legal fees – issue of share capital (Note 6)	2,900	
Costs of registering a trademark (Note 5)	0	
Legal fees – renewal of a short lease (Note 6)	0	
Legal fees – debt collection (Note 5)	0	
Legal fees – court action	900	
Replacing roof (Note 7)	0	
Office extension (Note 7)	53,300	
Entertaining suppliers (Note 8)	2,160	
Counselling services for staff (Note 9)	0	
Secondment of staff to a charity (Note 9)	0	
Disposal of office building		78,100
Loan interest received		12,330
Capital allowances (W)		13,380
Interest payable (Note 10)	0	
	353,880	103,810
	(103,810)	
Tax adjusted trading profit	250,070	

Working – Plant and machinery

	£	*Pool* £	*Expensive car* £	*Short-life asset* £	*Allowances* £
TWDV b/f		12,200	21,600	2,300	
Additions (with AIA)					
Equipment	6,700				
Less: AIA	(6,700)				6,700
		Nil			
Less: Disposal proceeds (Note)			(33,600)	(460)	
		12,200	(12,000)	1,840	
Balancing charge			12,000		(12,000)
Balancing allowance				(1,840)	1,840
Less: WDA (20%)		(2,440)			2,440
Additions (with FYA)					
Car (CO_2 < 111 g/km)	14,400				
Less: FYA (100%)	(14,400)				14,400
		Nil			
TWDV c/f		9,760	Nil	Nil	
Total allowances					13,380

Tutorial note

The sale proceeds for the expensive motor car sold are restricted to original cost.

(b) **Taxable total profits – y/e 31 March 2012**

	£
Trading profit	250,070
Interest income – Loan interest	12,330
Chargeable gain (W)	11,660
	274,060
Less: Gift Aid	(600)
Taxable total profits	273,460

Working: Chargeable gain

	£
Sale proceeds	300,000
Less: Cost	(197,900)
	102,100
Less: Indexation allowance (given)	(90,440)
Chargeable gain	11,660

(c) **Effect on taxable total profits**

(i) **Group relief**

- Tock-Tick Ltd owns more than 75% of the share capital of Clock Ltd. They therefore form a group for group relief purposes.
- The accounting periods are not coterminous, so the claim for group relief would be restricted to the lower of:
  (i) Available loss of Clock Ltd
  (1 April 2011 – 31 December 2011) = (£62,400 x 9/12) = £46,800
  (ii) Available profits of Tock-Tick Ltd
  (1 April 2011 – 31 December 2011) = (£273,460 x 9/12) = £205,095
- Tock-Tick Ltd's taxable total profits would therefore have been reduced by £46,800.

Group rollover relief

- Tock-Tick Ltd owns more than 75% of the share capital of Clock Ltd. They therefore form a gains group. In a gains group, gains realised by one group company can be rolled over into assets acquired by another group company.
- The sale proceeds from the disposal of the office building are not fully reinvested, and so £6,000 (£300,000 – £294,000) of the capital gain cannot be rolled over.
- Tock-Tick Ltd's taxable total profits would therefore have been reduced by £5,660 (£11,660 – £6,000).

(ii) **Corporation tax liability – year ended 31 March 2012**

	£
Original taxable total profits	273,460
Less: Group relief	(46,800)
Gain rolled over	(5,660)
Revised taxable total profits	221,000
Corporation tax (£221,000 at 26%) (W)	57,460
Less: Marginal relief	
3/200 × (£750,000 – £221,000)	(7,935)
Corporation tax liability	49,525

Working: Corporation tax rates

Tock-Tick Ltd has one associated company.

The small profit rate limits are therefore £750,000 (£1,500,000 x 1/2) and £150,000 (£300,000 x 1/2).

The company is therefore a marginal relief company.

64 MUSIC PLC (ADAPTED)

Key answer tips

In this question there are 9 marks for written explanations of the gains group and associated company rules. It is important to state the basic rule and then apply to the facts of the question. Be careful with the overseas company, which is included but unable to enjoy the benefits of gains group status.

When calculating property business profit, always watch out for furnished lettings which will need a calculation of wear and tear allowance. Property 3 has lease premiums paid and received which is a tricky area but is examined fairly regularly and so you should learn the proforma calculation.

(a) **Capital gains group**

- Companies form a capital gains group if at each level in the group structure there is a 75% shareholding, provided the parent company has an effective interest of at least 50%.
- Alto Ltd, Bass Ltd, Cello Ltd, Echo Inc and Flute Ltd are all 75% subsidiaries, and Music plc has an effective interest of 60% (80% × 75%) in Flute Ltd. All of these companies therefore form a capital gains group.
- However, Bass Ltd and Cello Ltd will only be included in respect of assets acquired or disposed of whilst they were members of the group.
- Drum Ltd and Gong Ltd are not included since Drum Ltd is not a 75% subsidiary, and Music plc's effective interest in Gong Ltd is only 48% (80% × 75% × 80%).
- Although Echo Inc is included in the definition of the capital gains group, companies that are resident overseas are not able to take advantage of the provisions applicable to a capital gains group.

(b) **Associated companies**

- Alto Ltd, Bass Ltd, Cello Ltd, Echo Inc, Flute Ltd and Gong Ltd are all under the common control of Music plc, and are therefore associated companies.
- For associated company purposes, it does not matter where a company is resident. Echo Inc is therefore included despite being resident overseas.
- Companies that are only associated for part of the accounting period, such as Bass Ltd and Cello Ltd, count as associated companies for the whole of the period.
- Drum Ltd is not included as an associated company since Music plc's effective interest in this company is only 45%.

(c) **Property business income – year ended 31 March 2012**

	£	£
Rent – Property 1 (£2,500 × 4 × 7/12)		5,833
– Property 2 (£650 × 9) + £700 (Note)		6,550
– Property 3 (£2,000 × 9/12)		1,500
– Property 4 (£500 × 9)		4,500
		18,383
Lease premium – Property 3 (W1)		28,500
		46,883
Allowable deductions:		
Irrecoverable debt – Property 2	650	
Decoration – Property 1	2,500	
Advertising/fees (£1,500 + £250)	1,750	
Council tax/water rates (£1,200 + £600)	1,800	
Repairs – Property 2	500	
Wear and tear allowance – Property 1 (£5,833 – £1,800) × 10% (Note)	403	
		(7,603)
Property business income		39,280

Key answer tips

The company is assessed on the net profits from all properties.

It is therefore not necessary to compute profits / losses for each property separately and one combined computation is all that is needed.

Tutorial note:

Property 1

The replacement dishwasher is disallowed as it is an item of capital as Music plc claims the wear and tear allowance. The wear and tear allowance is calculated on rent received less council tax and water rates paid by the landlord.

Property 2

Property business income is calculated on the accruals basis. The date that rent is received is irrelevant.

Relief is available for irrecoverable debts.

Similarly the invoice received in April for work carried out in March 2012 should be accrued for in the accounts to 31 March 2012.

Property 3

The premium paid for the head lease is deductible over the duration of the sublease divided by the duration of the head lease (see W2).

Property 4

Expenditure incurred on making the property inhabitable is capital and is therefore not deductible.

Workings

(W1) **Property business income**

	£
Premium received for sub-lease	45,000
Les: 2% x £45,000 x (10 – 1)	(8,100)
Assessment on premium received (Note)	36,900
Less: Relief for premium paid for head lease (W2) (£25,200 × 10/30)	(8,400)
Property business income	28,500

Tutorial note

Alternative calculation of the assessment on the sub lease:

£45,000 x (51 – 10)/50 = £36,900

Relief for premium paid on head lease:

= Assessment on landlord x (duration of sub-lease)/(duration of head lease)

Assessment on landlord = (see W2)

(W2) **Assessment on head lease**

	£
Premium received	60,000
Les: 2% x £60,000 x (30 – 1)	(34,800)
Assessment on landlord (Note)	25,200

Tutorial note

Alternative calculation of the assessment on the sub lease:

£60,000 x (51 – 30)/50 = £25,200

(d) Corporation tax liability – year ended 31 March 2012

	£
Trading profit	92,000
Interest income	12,000
Property business income (part (c))	39,280
Net chargeable gains (W1)	23,000
Taxable total profits	166,280
Plus: Franked investment income	15,000
Augmented profits	181,280
Corporation tax (£166,280 × 26%) (W2)	43,233
Less: Marginal relief	
3/200 × (£214,286 – £181,280) × £166,280/£181,280	(454)
Corporation tax liability	42,779

Tutorial note

1. *The capital gain of £120,000 is included in Music plc's taxable total profits since an appropriate election has been made with Alto Ltd. Capital losses may be set against this gain.*
2. *Group dividends are not included as franked investment income.*

Workings

(W1) **Net chargeable gain**

	£
Net chargeable gain in the year (by election)	120,000
Less: Capital losses in the year	(65,000)
	55,000
Less: Capital losses b/f	(32,000)
Net chargeable gain	23,000

(W2) **Corporation tax rates**

		£
Upper limit	(£1,500,000 x 1/7)	214,286
Lower limit	(£300,000 x 1/7)	42,857
Augmented profits		181,280
		Marginal relief applies

There are seven associated companies in the group.

(e) **Bank loan**

All costs incurred in connection with the loan will be taxed in accordance with the loan relationship rules. Therefore the tax treatment of the loan interest and the arrangement fee will be the same.

Under the loan relationship rules costs incurred in relation to loans used for the purposes of the trade are deductible as trading expenses. If the loan was therefore used to acquire plant and machinery, the interest and arrangement fee would be deducted from the company's trading profit.

Costs incurred in relation to loans used for non-trade purposes are deductible from interest income. If the loan was used to acquire a property which was to be rented out, the interest and fees would therefore be deducted not from trading income, and not from property business income (as for individuals), but from the company's interest income.

65 MICE LTD *Walk in the footsteps of a top tutor*

Key answer tips

This corporation tax question is lengthy and time pressured with a lot of information to assimilate quickly and efficiently.

Part (a) starts with some detailed property income calculations and then the application of the corporation tax loss rules. With the recent change in rules for losses, this part is now simpler than when the question was originally set.

Parts (b) and (c) have a less familiar style in that they require advice and explanations (without revising previous calculations) in respect of the maximum possible surrender of losses within a group for 3 marks, and the maximum capital allowances that can be claimed.

The answers show that what the examiner expected was not difficult and only applied mainstream knowledge, however in an unfamiliar style. They also involved concentrating on specific aspects of the calculations, which may have caused some problems if unprepared.

Part (d) was also unusual in that students would not have come across this style of question before. It required advice about the increased tax cost to both the company and the individual should they increase the remuneration of a higher paid employee.

Again, the calculations are not difficult but it is necessary to be able to understand the impact of transactions on tax and "think in the margin". All that was required is the additional tax chargeable, not the total tax cost.

Tutor's top tips

This question can appear daunting on first reading; however it is possible to score very well on this sort of question as long as you do not panic over the quantity of information.

Remember to read the requirements carefully.

The requirements to this question lead you through how to tackle the question in the correct logical order, and it has clear mark allocations, which should be used to allocate the time spent on each section.

The first part requires a calculation of the property business profit before you consider the impact of the losses.

(a) (i) **Property business profit – year ended 31 March 2012**

Tutor's top tips

Where a company (or individual) has several rental properties, the profits and losses are pooled / aggregated to calculate the net profit or loss (i.e. current period losses are automatically set off against current period profits).

There is no need to do separate calculations of the profit and loss for each property, only one computation is required.

Set up your answer with sub-headings "Income" and "Allowable expenses" and leave space underneath to insert the relevant information as you go through each property in the question.

	£	£
Rent accrued – Property 1 (£3,200 × 4)		12,800
– Property 2		6,000
– Property 3		Nil
		18,800
Premium received for sub-lease (Property 2)	18,000	
Less: £18,000 × 2% × (8 – 1)	(2,520)	
		15,480
		34,280
Business rates	2,200	
Repairs	1,060	
Rent paid	7,800	
Advertising	680	
Insurance (£460 + £310 + (£480 × 3/12))	890	
Loan interest	Nil	
		(12,630)
Property business profit		21,650

Tutorial note

1. *The enlargement of the car park is capital expenditure which cannot be deducted when calculating the property business profit.*
2. *For Property 2, the rental paid by Mice Ltd for the original lease is an allowable deduction from the income received from the sub-lease.*

   There is no further relief for premiums paid on the original head lease as Mice Ltd did not pay a premium for acquiring the original lease.

3. *For Property 3, rents accrued up to 31 March are assessed in the year ended 31 March 2012. As the property is not let until 1 April 2012, there is no assessable income. The rent received in advance before 1 April 2012 is not relevant to this question and will be assessed next year.*
4. *Interest paid in respect of a loan used to purchase property by a company is not an allowable deduction against property income, but is an allowable deduction against interest income under the loan relationship rules.*

(ii) **Taxable total profits**

Tutor's top tips

Note that the question asks for the taxable total profits of the current year, which is clearly loss making, and the previous years as the loss will be carried back if reliefs are to be claimed as soon as possible.

The examiner's answer did this in two sets of computations; however one set of computations including all of the years would gain equal credit and may save time.

Remember to highlight the "total profits" subtotal against which the loss is deducted (i.e. total profits before Gift Aid).

	p/e 31.3.09	*y/e 31.3.10*	*y/e 31.3.11*	*y/e 31.3.12*
	£	£	£	£
Trading profit	83,200	24,700	51,200	Nil
Property business profit	2,800	7,100	12,200	
part (a)(ii)				21,650
Interest income (Note 1)				
(£6,400 + £3,200 – £1,800)				7,800
Overseas income (Note 2)				Nil
Chargeable gain				10,550
Total profits	86,000	31,800	63,400	40,000
Less: Loss relief (Note 3)				
Current year				(40,000)
Carry back 12 months			(63,400)	
	86,000	31,800	Nil	Nil
Less: Gift Aid	(1,000)	(1,500)	–	–
Taxable total profits	85,000	30,300	Nil	Nil

Loss working

	£
Trading loss	180,000
Current year relief – y/e 31 March 2012	(40,000)
Carry back relief (12 months) – y/e 31 March 2011	(63,400)
Unrelieved loss as at 31 March 2012	76,600

Tutorial note

1. *Interest income includes all interest received and receivable (i.e. accrued) to 31 March 2012 and interest paid and payable in respect of the loan to purchase Property 3 is deducted.*
2. *The overseas dividend is exempt and therefore all of the information about the rate of withholding tax deducted at source is irrelevant.*

   Note however, that the dividend received grossed up by 100/90 is treated as franked investment income when calculating the applicable rate of corporation tax, but this is not part of the requirement of this question.
3. *Remember that, for companies, a carry back election for losses cannot be made unless the current year total profits have been relieved first.*
4. *There is no restriction to the amount of loss relief that can be claimed for carry back to the previous 12 months (i.e. year ended 31 March 2011).*

(b) **Maximum amount of group relief – year ended 31 March 2012**

Tutor's top tips

Web-Cam Ltd has been a subsidiary throughout the whole of Mice Ltd's year ended 31 March 2012, however it has a June year end, not March.

As a result, time apportionment of the profits and losses is required to calculate the maximum group relief in each corresponding accounting period.

It was not necessary to consider the optimum use of the loss here, as the requirement asked only for the ***maximum*** *amount of group relief which could be claimed.*

Any time spent considering how the loss should be used would be wasted, and would not score any marks.

- For the three-month period ended 30 June 2011, the maximum group relief is:

  The lower of

  (i) Available profits of Web-Cam Ltd = £28,000
  (ii) Available loss of Mice Ltd for the corresponding period
  = (£180,000 × 3/12) = £45,000

- For the year ended 30 June 2012, the maximum group relief is calculated for the corresponding period of 9 months from 1 July 2011 to 31 March 2012 as:

  The lower of

  (i) Available profits of Web-Cam Ltd = (£224,000 × 9/12) = £168,000
  (ii) Available loss of Mice Ltd = (£180,000 × 9/12) = £135,000

- The total maximum group relief that Mice Ltd can surrender to Web-Cam Ltd in respect of its £180,000 loss in the year ended 31 March 2012 is therefore:

  (£28,000 + £135,000) = £163,000

(c) **Maximum amount of capital allowances claim**

Tutor's top tips

Two alternative purchases are to be considered here and 4 marks are available in total. Make sure an equal amount is spent on each part and try not to overrun on this part.

Remember that the requirement is to explain and not to just calculate a number.

Equipment

- The first £100,000 of expenditure will qualify for the annual investment allowance (AIA) at the rate of 100%, whilst the balance of expenditure will qualify for the writing down allowance (WDA) at the rate of 20%.
- The maximum capital allowances claim will therefore be:
  (£100,000 + (£25,000 at 20%)) = £105,000

Ventilation system

- The AIA will be available in the same way as for the equipment. However, the ventilation system will be integral to the factory and is therefore classified as 'special rate pool' expenditure. The balance of expenditure will therefore only qualify for a writing down allowance (WDA) of 10%.
- The maximum capital allowances claim will therefore be:
  (£100,000 + (£25,000 at 10%)) = £102,500

(d) **Additional amount of income tax and National Insurance**

Tutor's top tips

The managing director is clearly a higher rate taxpayer already and will remain so after the bonus payment. Therefore tax will be paid at the marginal rate of 40%.

Calculations can therefore be performed 'in the margin'; i.e. calculating the additional tax due at the marginal rate, rather than working the full income tax computation.

- The managing director's additional income tax liability for 2011/12 will be:
  (£40,000 at 40%) = £16,000
- The additional employee's Class 1 NIC will be:
  (£40,000 at 2%) = £800
- The additional employer's Class 1 NIC will be:
  (£40,000 at 13·8%) = £5,520

Tutorial note

As the managing director is clearly higher paid with taxable income in excess of £35,000, any additional income will be taxed to income tax at 40%.

Additional Class 1 Primary NICs payable by the managing director will be payable at 2% as the upper limit for NIC of £42,475 is also clearly exceeded.

Employers pay 13.8% Class 1 Secondary NICs on all of an employee's cash earnings in excess of £7,072, with no upper limit.

It is assumed that the MD has no other income in 2011/12 such that his total taxable income will not exceed £100,000 and there will be no restriction of the personal allowance.

Examiner's report

This question was generally very well answered, especially the calculation of the property business profit in part (a) where most candidates scored virtually maximum marks.

In part (b) several candidates explained whether or not group relief would be available rather than calculating the amount of relief.

In part (c) most candidates were aware of what capital allowances were available.

Many candidates complicated part (d) by performing long calculations, making this much more time consuming than necessary for 3 marks. However, they should have appreciated that this was additional remuneration so the calculations were simply £40,000 x 40%, £40,000 x 2% and £40,000 x 13.8% for the 3 marks.

ACCA marking scheme

			Marks
(a)	(i)	Lease premium received	1.5
		Rent receivable – Property 1	1.0
		– Property 2 and 3 (0.5 marks each)	1.0
		Business rates	0.5
		Repairs	1.0
		Rent paid	0.5
		Advertising	0.5
		Insurance	1.5
		Loan interest	0.5
			8.0
	(ii)	Year ended 31 March 2012 – Property business profit	0.5
		Loan interest	1.5
		Overseas income	0.5
		Chargeable gain	0.5
		Loss relief	0.5
		Other periods – Trading profit	0.5
		Property business profit	0.5
		Loss relief	2.0
		Gift aid donation	0.5
			7.0
(b)	Period ended 30 June 2011		1.5
	Year ended 30 June 2012		1.5
			3.0
(c)	Equipment		2.0
	Ventilation system		2.0
			4.0
(d)	Income tax		1.0
	Employee's NIC		1.0
	Employer's NIC		1.0
			3.0
Total			25.0

VALUE ADDED TAX

66 CONFUSED LTD

Key answer tips

A more difficult question than usual testing less mainstream topics in VAT.

The first part requires clear explanation of the differences between standard rated, zero rated and exempt supplies. Do not worry if you missed the point that traders making wholly zero rated supplies need not register.

The last part has some tricky points on sale of a business and the difference between selling assets individually or as a complete business.

(a) **Standard rated supplies**

- Confused Ltd will be required to register for VAT as it is making taxable supplies in excess of the registration limit of £73,000.
- Output VAT of £15,000 (£75,000 × 20%) per month will be due, and input VAT of £1,667 (£10,000 × 20/120) per month will be recoverable.

Zero-rated supplies

- Confused Ltd will be required to register for VAT as it is making taxable supplies in excess of the registration limit of £73,000.
- However, as it is making zero-rated supplies, when it is required to register it can apply for an exemption from registration if it wishes.
- Output VAT will not be due, but input VAT of £1,667 per month will be recoverable if it registers for VAT.

Exempt supplies

- Confused Ltd will not be required or permitted to register for VAT as it will not be making taxable supplies.
- Output VAT will not be due and no input VAT will be recoverable.

(b) **Disclosure of errors**

- If the net errors total less than the greater of £10,000 or 1% of turnover (max £50,000), then they can be voluntarily disclosed by simply entering them on the next VAT return.
- If the net errors total more than this limit then they can be voluntarily disclosed, but disclosure must be made separately to HM Revenue & Customs (HMRC).
- Default interest will be charged if the net errors total more than the limit.

(c) **Sale of assets on a piecemeal basis**

- Perplexed Ltd will cease to make taxable supplies so its VAT registration will be cancelled on 31 December 2012 or an agreed later date.
- The company will have to notify HMRC by 30 January 2013, being 30 days after the date of cessation.
- Output VAT will be due in respect of fixed assets on which VAT has been claimed (although output VAT is not due if it totals less than £1,000).

Sale of business as a going concern

- If the purchaser is already registered for VAT then Perplexed Ltd's VAT registration will be cancelled as above.
- If the purchaser is not registered for VAT then it can take over Perplexed Ltd's VAT registration.
- A sale of a business as a going concern is outside the scope of VAT, and therefore output VAT is not due.

67 ASTUTE LTD (ADAPTED)

Key answer tips

A straight forward question on the three special accounting schemes available to small businesses.

Make sure you illustrate your answer by referring to the numbers in the question and do not just write about the schemes in general.

(a) **Annual accounting scheme**

- Astute Ltd can apply to use the annual accounting scheme if its expected taxable turnover for the next 12 months does not exceed £1,350,000 exclusive of VAT.
- In addition the company must be up to date with its VAT returns.
- The reduced administration from only having to submit one VAT return each year should mean that default surcharges are avoided in respect of the late submission of VAT returns.
- In addition, making payments on account based on the previous year's VAT liability will improve both budgeting and possibly cash flow where a business is expanding.

(b) **Flat rate scheme**

- Bright Ltd can use the flat rate scheme if its expected taxable turnover for the next 12 months does not exceed £150,000.
- The main advantage of the scheme is the simplified VAT administration. Bright Ltd's customers are not VAT registered, so there will be no need to issue VAT invoices.
- Using the normal basis of calculating the VAT liability, Bright Ltd will have to pay annual VAT of £10,833 (£75,000 – £10,000 = £65,000 × 20/120).
- If Bright Ltd uses the flat rate scheme then it will pay VAT of £8,250 (£75,000 × 11%), which is an annual saving of £2,583 (£10,833 – £8,250).

Tutorial note

In the first 12 months of VAT registration, HMRC allow a 1% reduction in the appropriate percentage for that trade group. However, knowledge of this is not required in the exam.

Therefore, the examiner will give you the rate that should apply in the first 12 months and you do not need to deduct 1%, just use the rate given.

(c) **Cash accounting scheme**

- Clever Ltd can use the cash accounting scheme if its expected taxable turnover for the next 12 months does not exceed £1,350,000 exclusive of VAT.
- In addition, the company must be up to date with its VAT returns and VAT payments.
- Output VAT will be accounted for three months later than at present since the scheme will result in the tax point becoming the date that payment is received from customers.
- The recovery of input VAT on expenses will not be affected as these are paid in cash.
- The scheme will also provide automatic bad debt relief should a customer default on the payment of a debt.

(d) Group VAT registration

- Companies under common control may apply for group VAT registration.

  For these purposes control only needs to be via a 'person' which can include individuals as well as companies in traditional parent/subsidiary relationships.
- As Robert controls both Talented Limited and Gifted Limited, it is possible for these two companies to be group VAT registered.
- The effect of a group registration would be that the two companies are effectively treated as a single entity for VAT purposes.
- One of the companies will be nominated as the representative member and will submit only one VAT return for the group. This can save in administration costs.
- As the two companies trade with each other, output VAT would not be charged on inter-group supplies and therefore the purchasing company would not need to reclaim input VAT. This provides a cash flow advantage.

68 VICTOR STYLE *Online question assistance*

Key answer tips

This is a question covering the common issues of registration and the flat rate scheme and also asks for the effect of registration on profit. This is unusual because traders usually pass on the cost of VAT to their customers, but in this case the question clearly states that it was not possible to raise prices as a consequence of becoming registered.

Provided you work carefully through the numbers, this should be a straight forward question.

(a) **Compulsory registration**

- A trader must register for VAT when taxable supplies during any 12-month period exceed £73,000.
- This will have happened on 30 November 2011 when taxable supplies amounted to £73,620 ((£5,600 x 10) + (£8,810 x 2)) for the previous 12 months.

- Victor therefore had to notify HM Revenue & Customs by 30 December 2011, being 30 days after the end of the 12-month period.
- Victor was liable to register from 1 January 2012, being the end of the month following the month in which the limit was exceeded.

(b) **VAT payable – y/e 31 December 2012**

- Output VAT will be £17,620 (£8,810 × 12 = £105,720 × 20/120) since Victor must absorb this himself rather than pass it on to his customers.
- Input VAT will be £800 (£400 × 12 = £4,800 × 20/120).
- The total VAT payable by Victor during the year ended 31 December 2012 is therefore £16,820 (£17,620 – £800).

(c) **Flat rate scheme**

- The main advantage of the flat rate scheme is the simplified VAT administration. Victor's customers are not registered for VAT, so there will be no need to issue VAT invoices.
- If Victor had used the flat rate scheme from 1 January 2012, then he would have paid VAT of £13,744 (£105,720 × 13%) during the year ended 31 December 2012.
- This is a saving of £3,076 (£16,820 – £13,744) for the year.

Tutorial note

In the first 12 months of VAT registration, HMRC allow a 1% reduction in the appropriate percentage for that trade group. However, knowledge of this is not required in the exam.

Therefore, the examiner will give you the rate that should apply in the first 12 months and you do not need to deduct 1%, just use the rate given.

(d) **Reduction in net profit**

- If Victor had not increased his prices, his net profit for the year ended 31 December 2012 based on the information given would have been £62,400 (£5,600 – £400 = £5,200 × 12).
- As a result of increasing his prices, Victor's net profit will be as follows:

	£
Sales (£105,720 – £17,620)	88,100
Less: Expenses (£4,800 – £800)	(4,000)
Net profit	84,100

- This is an increase in net profit of £21,700 (£84,100 – £62,400).
- If the flat rate scheme had been used from 1 January 2012 there would have been an increase in net profit of £24,776 (£21,700 + £3,076).

69 VECTOR LTD (ADAPTED)

Key answer tips

A typical mixed bag of VAT topics. The first part requires a calculation of VAT for a quarter including overseas transactions within and outside the EU. Remember to check carefully to see if figures are given inclusive of VAT or exclusive of VAT.

The tricky points are the scale charge for private fuel, the treatment of impaired debts and the overseas aspects.

There are some easy marks in part (b) for stating the conditions for and effects of cash accounting, and part (c) should be straightforward provided the topic has been revised!

(a) **VAT Return – Quarter ended 31 March 2012**

	£
Output VAT	
Sales in UK (£128,000 × 97.5% × 20%)	24,960
Advance payment (£4,500 × 20/120)	750
Motor car scale charge (£488 × 20/120)	81
Sales outside EU (zero rated)	Nil
Sales within EU (VAT registered companies) (zero rated)	Nil
Sales within EU (non VAT registered companies) (standard rated) (£14,250 × 20%)	2,850
	28,641
Input VAT	
Expenses (£74,800 – £4,200) × 20%	(14,120)
Bad debt relief (£4,000 + £4,000) × 20%	(1,600)
VAT payable to HMRC	12,921

Notes

(1) The calculation of output VAT on UK sales must take into account the discount for prompt payment, even if customers do not take it. VAT is therefore calculated on 97.5% (100% – 2.5%) of the sales value.

(2) Input VAT on business entertainment is not recoverable.

(3) Relief for an impaired debt is not given until six months from the time that payment is due. Therefore relief can only be claimed in respect of the invoices due for payment on 15 August and 15 September 2011.

(4) Input VAT cannot be recovered in respect of the motor car as it is not used exclusively for business purposes.

Tutorial note:

Although the examiner uses a VAT fraction of 20/120 you may find it easier and equally valid to use a VAT fraction of 1/6.

(b) **Cash accounting scheme**

- Vector Ltd can use the cash accounting scheme if its expected taxable turnover for the next 12 months does not exceed £1,350,000.
- In addition, the company must be up to date with its VAT returns and VAT payments.
- The scheme will result in the tax point becoming the date that payment is received from customers.
- This will provide for automatic impaired debt relief should a customer not pay.
- However, the recovery of input VAT on expenses will be delayed until payment is made.

(c) **Group VAT registration**

Advantages

- VAT does not have to be accounted for on and intra-group sales as supplies by one group company to another are outside the scope of VAT.
- A representative member for the group is responsible for accounting for all output and input VAT on behalf of the group and only one VAT return is required for all members of the VAT group.
- Membership of the VAT group is optional and flexible. Vector Ltd can choose whether or not to be a member of the VAT group – it is not compulsory for all group companies to join the VAT group.

Disadvantages

- All members of a VAT group are jointly and severally liable for the VAT for the group as a whole.
- Increased administration may arise in collecting and collating the information for the one joint return.
- The input VAT recovery of Vector Ltd may be reduced if a company making wholly or mainly exempt supplies is included in the VAT group.

Tutorial note:

Companies under common control can elect for group VAT registration, provided they are UK resident or are trading in the UK via a permanent establishment in the UK.

70 RAM-ROM LTD

Key answer tips

This question required some detailed knowledge about pre registration VAT and the information required on VAT invoices. The last part required application of the rules about cash accounting to the particular circumstances of the company.

This is a tricky question to score highly on, but there are easy marks to be gained and these should be obtained as quickly as possible rather than getting bogged down with detail.

(a) **Input VAT recovered on registration**

- Input VAT of £18,400 (£92,000 × 20%) can be recovered on the stock of goods held at 1 January 2012.

  The stock was not acquired more than four years prior to registration, nor was it sold or consumed prior to registration.

- The same principle applies to fixed assets, so input VAT of £21,720 (£42,000 + £66,600 = £108,600 × 20%) can be recovered on the fixed assets that have not been sold.

- Input VAT of £9,720 (£7,400 + £6,300 + £8,500 + £9,000 + £9,200 + £8,200 = £48,600 × 20%) can be recovered on the services incurred from 1 July 2011 to 31 December 2011.

  This is because these services were not supplied more than six months prior to registration.

(b) **VAT invoices**

The following additional information is required on the invoices:

(1) A sequential and unique identifying number (invoice number).

(2) Ram-Rom Ltd's VAT registration number.

(3) The rate of VAT for each supply.

(4) The VAT-exclusive amount for each supply.

(5) The total VAT-exclusive amount.

(6) The amount of VAT payable.

(c) **Discounts**

- Where a discount is offered for prompt payment then output VAT is calculated on the selling price less the amount of discount offered.

- There is no amendment to the amount of output VAT charged if the customer does not take the discount but instead pays the full selling price.

(d) **Cash accounting scheme**

Conditions of the scheme

- Ram-Rom Ltd can use the cash accounting scheme if its expected taxable turnover for the next 12 months does not exceed £1,350,000 exclusive of VAT.

- In addition, the company must be up to date with its VAT returns and VAT payments.

Advantages of the scheme

- Output VAT will be accounted up to four months later than at present since the scheme will result in the tax point becoming the date that payment is received from customers.

- The recovery of input VAT will only be delayed by one month.

- The scheme will also provide automatic relief for impaired debts should a customer default on the payment of a debt.

71 LITHOGRAPH LTD (ADAPTED)

Key answer tips

Monthly payments on account under the annual accounting scheme are based on the VAT payable for the previous year.

This first part of the question was only worth three marks and therefore it should be clear that detailed computations are not required and that the reason for the previous year information in the question is for the purposes of this part.

Calculations based on the current year position were not required until the next part of the question, which required a VAT return and should be an expected standard requirement.

(a) **Monthly payments on account of VAT**

- Each payment on account of VAT will be £1,020 (£10,200 × 10%), being 10% of the VAT payable for the previous year.
- Lithograph Ltd will have made nine payments on account, and these will have been paid for the months of April to December 2012, being months 4 to 12 of the annual VAT return period.

(b) (i) **VAT payable – year ended 31 December 2012**

	£	£
Output VAT		
Sales (£160,000 × 20%)		32,000
Motor car scale charge (£2,020 × 20/120)		337
Office equipment (£8,000 × 20%)		1,600
		33,937
Input VAT		
Purchases (£38,000 × 20%)	7,600	
Expenses (Note 1) (£28,000 × 20%)	5,600	
Machinery (£24,000 × 20%)	4,800	
Impaired debt (Note 3) (£4,800 × 20%)	960	
		(18,960)
VAT payable		14,977

Tutorial note

1. *Input VAT on business entertainment is not recoverable unless it relates to overseas customers.*
2. *Input VAT cannot be recovered in respect of the motor car as this is not exclusively for business purposes.*

3. *Relief for the impaired debt is available because the claim is made more than six months from the time that payment was due, and the debt has been written off in the company's books.*

4. *The tax is calculated as 20/120 for transactions quoted gross, however the use of 1/6 is also acceptable.*

(ii) **Annual VAT return**

- Lithograph Ltd made payments on account totalling £9,180 (£1,020 × 9), so a balancing payment of £5,797 (£14,977 – £9,180) would have been due with the annual VAT return.
- The annual VAT return, along with the balancing payment, would have been due by 28 February 2013, being two months after the end of the annual VAT period.

72 DENZIL DYER

Key answer tips

A question ranging over a number of VAT issues. Make sure you consider each part and write enough for each part.

Remember also to relate your answer to the specific circumstances of the business.

Numbered points or bullet points are the best way to make your answer 'marker friendly'.

(a) **Identification of the type of supply**

- The type of supply, whether standard rated or zero-rated, has no effect on the recovery of input VAT for Denzil.
- However, output VAT is only due in respect of standard rated supplies. Incorrectly classifying a supply as zero-rated would not remove Denzil's liability to pay the output VAT which is calculated on the actual price charged. This would then be an additional cost to the business.

(b) **Accounting for output VAT**

- Output VAT must be accounted for according to the VAT period in which the supply is treated as being made. This is determined by the tax point.
- The printing contracts are supplies of services, so the basic tax point for each contract will be the date that it is completed.
- Where payment is received before the basic tax point, then this date becomes the actual tax point. The tax point for each 10% deposit is therefore the date that it is received.
- If an invoice is issued within 14 days of the basic tax point, the invoice date will usually replace the basic tax point date and becomes the actual tax point. This will apply to the balance of the contract price since Denzil issues invoices within three to five days of completion.

(c) **VAT implications of discounts**

- Where a discount of 5% is given for an order of more than £500 then output VAT is simply calculated on the revised, discounted, selling price.
- As regards the 2.5% discount offered for prompt payment, output VAT is calculated on the selling price less the amount of discount offered.
- There is no amendment to the amount of output VAT charged if the customer does not take the discount but instead pays the full selling price.

(d) **Conditions for the recovery of input VAT**

- The supply must be made to Denzil since he is the taxable person making the claim.
- The supply must be supported by evidence, and this will normally take the form of a VAT invoice. Denzil will therefore not be able to recover any input VAT in respect of the purchases of office supplies for cash, where there is no invoice.
- Denzil must use the goods or services supplied for business purposes, although an apportionment can be made where supplies are acquired partly for business purposes and partly for private purposes.

(e) **Circumstances for issuing VAT invoices**

- Denzil must issue a VAT invoice when he makes a standard rated supply to one of his VAT registered customers.
- A VAT invoice is not required if the supply is zero-rated or if the supply is to a non-VAT registered customer.
- A VAT invoice should be issued within 30 days of the date that the supply of services is treated as being made.

73 ANNE ATTIRE *Walk in the footsteps of a top tutor*

Key answer tips

Standalone VAT questions are not as common as seeing VAT as part of a longer income tax or corporation tax question, but either way VAT will be tested (a guaranteed 10%) and there are easy marks to be had if you have learnt the rules, as they are very straightforward to apply.

It is an important area of the syllabus and you should take care to ensure you have covered all areas.

The question has three independent parts, which have clear requirements and mark allocations. If you do not have the required knowledge to deal with part (b) do not allow this to put you off attempting the other parts.

Tutor's top tips

Part (a) is a standard VAT return, which does not have any particularly difficult items.

Cash and credit sales are both dealt with in the same way, except that the discount is only applicable to the credit sales.

Be careful to ensure you deal with the discounts correctly, in respect of both the credit sales and the impaired debts.

(a) **VAT return – Quarter ended 31 May 2012**

	£	£
Output VAT		
Cash sales (£28,000 x 20%)		5,600
Credit sales (Note 2) (£12,000 x 95% x 20%)		2,280
		7,880
Input VAT		
Purchases and expenses (£11,200 x 20%)	2,240	
Impairment loss (Note 3) (£800 x 95% x 20%)	152	
		(2,392)
VAT payable		5,488

The VAT return for the quarter ended 31 May 2012 should have been submitted by 30 June 2012, being one month after the end of the VAT period.

Tutorial note

1. *The calculation of output VAT on the credit sales takes into account the discount for prompt payment, even for those 10% of customers that did not take it.*
2. *Relief for an impairment loss is not given until six months from the time that payment is due. Therefore relief can only be claimed in respect of the invoice due for payment on 10 November 2011. Relief is based on the amount of output VAT that would originally have been paid taking into account the discount for prompt payment.*

(b) **Cash accounting**

Tutor's top tips

Part (b) requires students to recall a reasonable amount of knowledge regarding the cash accounting scheme, which is not difficult if learnt, but extremely difficult if neglected in revision. These are not rules that you will be able to make up in the exam, so do take the time to learn them!

When answering written elements in the exam, keep your comments short and to the point. Bullet points or a numbered answer (one mark per well explained point), are useful both in structuring your answer and for the marker reading it. Don't take the opportunity to write everything you know about VAT. Keep your comments relevant to the question.

- Anne can use the cash accounting scheme if her expected taxable turnover for the next 12 months does not exceed £1,350,000.
- In addition, Anne must be up-to-date with her VAT returns and VAT payments.
- Output VAT on most credit sales will be accounted for up to one month later than at present since the scheme will result in the tax point becoming the date that payment is received from customers.
- However, the recovery of input VAT will be delayed by two months.
- The scheme will provide automatic relief for impaired losses should a credit sale customer default on the payment of a debt.

(c) (i) **Sale of assets on a piecemeal basis**

Tutor's top tips

Part (c) concerns the disposal of a VAT registered business.

Again, it is important to make short, clear points, matched to the number of marks available. Therefore two points are required for each part of the answer, although here the same point can be made twice!

If you do not know all the rules, you could still potentially pick up a mark or two, with some sensible comments, such as the need to deregister when you cease trading.

- Upon the cessation of trading Anne will cease to make taxable supplies, so her VAT registration will be cancelled on the date of cessation or an agreed later date.
- Output VAT will be due in respect of the value of the fixed assets at the date of deregistration on which VAT has been claimed (although output VAT is not due if it totals less than £1,000).

(ii) **Sale of business as a going concern**

- Since the purchaser is already registered for VAT, Anne's VAT registration will be cancelled as above.
- A sale of a business as a going concern is outside the scope of VAT, and therefore output VAT will not be due.

Tutorial note

If the purchaser was not already registered for VAT, Anne could consider transferring her VAT registration. However, that point would not be relevant to this scenario.

Always make your comments relevant to the circumstances in the question.

Examiner's report

This was the first time that VAT has been examined as a separate question, and it was therefore pleasing to see many very good answers.

In part (a) candidates often did not appreciate that output VAT on credit sales had to take account of the discount for prompt payment even if it was not taken by customers.

In part (b) the answers of many candidates lacked sufficient depth to gain full marks. For example, the turnover limit of £1,350,000 was usually known, but only a minority of candidates correctly stated that it applied for the following 12-month period.

The same comment applies to part (c). For example, candidates generally appreciated that the taxpayer's VAT registration would be cancelled, but few stated that the reason for the cancellation was the cessation of making taxable supplies.

Many candidates stated that on a sale of the business as a going concern the VAT registration could be taken over by the purchaser despite the question clearly stating that the purchaser was already registered for VAT.

ACCA marking scheme

		Marks
(a)	Output VAT – Cash sales	1.0
	– Credit sales	1.5
	Input VAT – Purchases and expenses	1.0
	– Impairment loss	1.5
	Due date	1.0
		6.0
(b)	Limit	1.0
	VAT returns and VAT payments	1.0
	Output VAT	1.0
	Input VAT	1.0
	Relief for impairment loss	1.0
		5.0
(c) (i)	**Sale of assets on a piecemeal basis**	
	Cancellation of VAT registration	1.0
	Output VAT	1.0
		2.0
(ii)	**Sale of business as a going concern**	
	Cancellation of VAT registration	1.0
	Output VAT not due	1.0
		2.0
Total		15.0